General Maurice Sarrail
1856-1929

General Maurice Sarrail
courtesy of Monique Rittenberg-Sarrail

General Maurice Sarrail
1856-1929

The French Army and Left-Wing Politics

by Jan Karl Tanenbaum

The University of North Carolina Press
Chapel Hill

Manufactured in the United States of America
Library of Congress Catalog Card Number 73-17109
ISBN 0-8078-1222-6

Library of Congress Cataloging in Publication Data
Tanenbaum, Jan Karl, 1936-
  General Maurice Sarrail, 1856-1929

  Bibliography: p.
  1. Sarrail, Maurice Paul Emmanuel, 1856-1929.
  2. France—Politics and government—1914-1940.
  DC373.S3T36   1974   320.9′44′081 B   73-17109
  ISBN 0-8078-1222-6

To My Mother and Father

Contents

Maps

Prepared by Robert H. Chamberlain

Preface

General Maurice Paul Emmanuel Sarrail was commander of the French Third Army at the Battle of the Marne, commander of the Allied Balkan forces during World War I, and French high commissioner to Syria and Lebanon in 1925. Although his military capabilities have been widely disputed, most of the controversy surrounding General Sarrail stems from his involvement with French left-wing politics.

This book attempts to shed light on the political and military aspects of Sarrail's public life. An analysis of Sarrail's career offers an opportunity to examine several important though neglected aspects of modern French history: the relationship between the French political Left and the army; France's World War I military-civilian relationship; the tensions between a radical republican general and the conservative military establishment; the exploits of a skilled field commander; the Allies' World War I Balkan military policies; the repercussions within the Entente resulting from Sarrail's wartime role in Greek and Albanian domestic politics; France and Britain's wartime Greek policies; the inadequacies of French liberalism's postwar colonial policy; and last, the relationship between Sarrail's tenure as high commissioner to Syria and Lebanon and French domestic politics.

In the course of this study I have benefited from the assistance of several institutions: the United States National Archives; in France, the Bibliothèque Nationale, Archives Nationales, Bibliothèque de l'Institut de France, Service des Archives de l'Assemblée Nationale, Archives du Sénat, Archives du Ministère des Affaires Etrangères, Archives Centrales du Ministère de la Marine, Archives du Ministère de la Guerre; and in England, the Beaverbrook Library, British Museum, Centre for Military Archives at King's College, the Public Record Office, the Bodleian Library at Oxford, and the University Library and Churchill College Library at Cambridge.

This book is the extensive revision of a thesis submitted to the University of California at Berkeley. I would like to express my gratitude to Professor Robert O. Paxton of Columbia University for his advice and generosity in directing the dissertation.

I am particularly indebted to the late Madame la Générale Sarrail, who graciously permitted me to consult the general's personal papers. I want to thank the general's daughter, Monique Rittenberg-Sarrail, for her generous assistance and support. Above all, I owe a special debt to General Louis Pirot and his family for their warm hospitality, aid, and advice. This work could not have been undertaken without General Pirot's unstinting efforts on my behalf.

Finally, I owe an immense debt of gratitude to my wife Joanne and my family for their help and encouragement over many years.

General Maurice Sarrail
1856-1929

I. The Protagonist

I was . . . to become a military man, but never a militarist.
                        —SARRAIL, *"Souvenirs"*

Despite the shattering defeat of 1870, the French professional officer corps maintained its position for the next thirty years as a nearly autonomous body within the state, unfettered by direct civilian control. The ability of the French military establishment to maintain its prerogatives after the collapse of the Second Empire was the result of contemporary political realities. Although the republicans, Bonapartists, and monarchists could not agree on a wide range of religious and political issues, they did have, however, one area of fervent agreement—the reorganization and strengthening of the military establishment.

But enthusiasm for the army by both monarchists and republicans was of recent vintage. Royalists were dubious, even frightened, of the army immediately after 1815 because it was identified with the revolutionary upheavals of the previous twenty-five years; it had been the vehicle of revolutionary ideas while overturning traditional European political, social, and economic institutions. During the Restoration, the conservative middle class was also critical of the army, considering it an economic waste, a drain on the national resources, and thus a hindrance to economic development. But as the century progressed, conservatives were to have a greater appreciation of the army: during the July Monarchy it crushed the politically and socially inspired insurrections; it was the army that snuffed out the June, 1848, uprising. And in 1871 the army was seen not as the inept and decrepit machine that had been ignominiously routed at Sedan, but as the courageous victor over revolutionary Paris and the Commune.[1]

The 1871 civil war, while it demonstrated once again that the army was the savior of the established social and economic order, did suc-

[3]

ceed in greatly reshaping the conservatives' traditional attitudes toward the army's institutional arrangements. From the Restoration to the Commune conservatives had wholeheartedly supported the country's basic institutional means of national defense: a professional army that, for all intents and purposes, excluded the middle class, since the lower economic classes could not afford to buy a substitute or pay the state 2,500 francs and thus escape long-term military service. But once the Commune had been crushed, the monarchist-dominated National Assembly adopted in 1872 a traditionally republican military concept—universal military training. Yet, for the conservatives, five years of compulsory military service was much less a military program than a social and political prescription; military service was to be an antidote for France's internecine strife, social and political. Conservatives envisaged the army as an instrument of national regeneration. It was hoped that by infusing the young recruits with the military values of discipline, obedience, respect for hierarchical order, and patriotism, all subversive political ideas would be extirpated, and, consequently, domestic harmony would prevail.[2]

The Franco-Prussian War had also radically changed republican military attitudes. During the Second Empire, republicans, looking forward to a world of international cooperation, general disarmament, and universal peace, advocated the abolition of the professional standing army. The permanent army, considered a support for the authoritarian regime, was a threat to a nation's domestic liberties and drained the national finances and corrupted the country's youth. The republicans wanted short-term universal military training for all citizens; the Swiss militia system was the paradigm of republican military theory.[3] But following the declaration of war against Prussia, republicans, rekindling the Jacobin tradition of the revolutionary wars when patriotism, liberty, and equality were fused into one great passion, formed the Government of National Defense and were prepared to wage war to the bitter end.

For the next two decades the radical republicans exalted the army. Léon Gambetta exemplified this new republican patriotism. In 1867 he demanded the suppression of permanent standing armies. In the aftermath of the crushing defeat in 1870, however, he supported the 1872 recruitment law. He believed the reconstruction of France's military power to be the country's major priority. Gambetta not only considered the permanent army a necessity, but he considered military service the basic attribute of citizenship. He reminded his contemporaries that henceforth all Frenchmen should know how to handle weapons and be prepared for the rigors of military life, for "when a French citizen is born, he is born a soldier."[4]

The moderate republicans, or Opportunists, also wanted a strong standing army. Assuming power in the late 1870s, the moderate republicans believed that national security obviated any large-scale personnel changes within the army. The foremost concern of republican leaders such as Charles de Freycinet was to escape diplomatic isolation and German domination. The army was to be the vehicle by which France would once again be a great power; a strong, modernized army was a prerequisite for a successful foreign policy, for a powerful army would inspire confidence in potential allies. Unfortunately, in their desire to create a strong army, the moderates failed to consider the spirit and political attitudes of the higher echelons of the army; technical competence was considered more important than political allegiance.[5]

During the first decades of the Third Republic the French officer corps' political attitudes were characterized by an admiration of strong governments and an antipathy to parliamentary institutions. General François Du Barail, who served the July Monarchy, the Second Empire, and the Third Republic—the Third Republic as war minister—reflected the basic attitudes of the French officer. Du Barail evinced little interest in politics; only when a republican form of government was in question was he stirred to strong political comments. He would have welcomed any type of government—except a republic. Republican and military ideals were for him contradictory and irreconcilable. The military ethic of obedience, respect, and submission were undermined by the republican ideal of liberty and equality.[6]

These conservative attitudes were reinforced by the influx of aristocracy entering Saint-Cyr, the elite military college, during the first years of the Third Republic. The depression of the 1870s and the 1880s forced many of the sons of the traditional nobility to seek a career other than on the land. Also, as the judicial, administrative, and political positions of the state were arrogated by the republicans, the army—the only public institution not republicanized—remained a source of employment and power for the nobility.[7]

Two additional factors gave the officer corps a deep conservative hue. As a result of the Falloux Law of 1850, a high proportion of men entering Saint-Cyr were graduates of Catholic secondary schools. From 1865 to 1886 approximately 25 to 35 percent of each year's class entered from Catholic schools.[8] This Catholic and conservative tendency was accentuated and reinforced by the method of promotion, which was determined by co-optation. One-half of the majors were selected by seniority, the other half by choice; above the rank of major all promotions were governed by choice. Classification commissions, composed of divisional generals and corps commanders, drew up the annual lists of those officers to be promoted by choice. These commissions were autonomous organs, free from civilian control; the war minister, usually a general, simply approved the choices made by the commissions. Under such a method of selection, social, religious, and political affinities played a preponderant role in advancement.[9]

The army, despite its antirepublican sentiments, was, for the most part, a disciplined bureaucracy, prepared to obey the mandates of the war minister; nonintervention in political affairs satisfied the traditional military dictates of obedience to the then established political regime. Political neutrality was carried to such an extreme that as late as 1892 General Théodore Iung noted somewhat ironically that the officer corps, which considered itself the servant of France and not of the Republic, chastised those officers who displayed enthusiasm for the republican regime.[10] While it is true that the army did not initiate the major political crises of the first twenty-five years of the Third Republic, it was involved, if only tangentially, in the two critical conflicts of the young Republic. During the constitutional crisis of May 16, 1877, several generals, including General Charles Ducrot and the premier, General Gaëtan de Rochebouët, were preparing to use the army to dissolve the recently elected republican Chamber.[11] However, Marshal Patrice de Mac-Mahon, president of the Republic, refused to employ the troops; he would not overstep the constitutional boundaries. Several years later, in January, 1889, when General Georges Boulanger won the Paris constituency by an overwhelming majority and was urged to lead the frenzied mob to the Elysée Palace, the General Staff, hostile to Boulanger, refused to initiate any action against the Republic. However, the army might very well not have prevented the overthrow of the Republic had Boulanger marched on the Elysée.[12]

It was during the Dreyfus case, turned into a nightmarish *affaire* by the army, that the salient characteristics of the army were clearly elucidated. By mid-1898 the evidence of Dreyfus's innocence appeared irrefutable; Esterhazy's espionage and Henry's forgeries had been revealed. Yet the General Staff refused to reconsider the case. War ministers resigned rather than undertake revision. Military honor was at

stake; to admit the possibility of Dreyfus's innocence after his con-
viction by a military court would damage the army's prestige and its
aura of infallibility. As the Dreyfusards increased their criticism of the
army's concept of justice and questioned its values, judicial pro-
cedures, and political motives, the officer corps became infuriated.
The officer corps, which prided itself as a hierarchical structure within
the state yet apart from the national community, bitterly resented
civilian interference in matters that solely concerned the army.[13]

Despite the willingness of one thousand French officers to contribute to Edouard Drumont's subscription for Madame Henry's legal
action "against the Jew, Reinach" and the proliferation of incidents
whereby French officers publicly calumniated the Dreyfusards, the
nationalists found it difficult to find a military leader who would play
the role of Napoleon. In February, 1899, General Gabriel de Pellieux
considered taking part in a coup with Paul Déroulède, leader of the
League of Patriots. The coup was to take place during the funeral procession of former president of the Republic Félix Faure; at the last
moment, however, Pellieux, who was to have led a detachment of
troops in the funeral procession, lost his nerve and withdrew his
support.[14]

When René Waldeck-Rousseau became premier in June, 1899,
France was in a state of frenzied excitement. Dreyfusards, Protestants,
and Jews were denigrated by the nationalist and much of the Catholic
press; anti-Semitic rioting erupted in France and in the colonies. The
new premier's main concern was to end the affair by having Dreyfus
declared innocent and to restore discipline within the officer corps.
For the delicate position of war minister he appointed the shrewd,
colorful, and highly knowledgeable General Gaston de Galliffet.
Galliffet's military prestige within the army and conservative society
was beyond question. He had served Napoleon III and had taken an
active role in crushing the Commune. In the early years of the Republic he had been won over to the Republic, for he realized that the
republicans had the same interests as the military: an efficient fighting
force and the eventual reconquest of Alsace-Lorraine.[15]

Galliffet's observations during the critical summer months of 1899
offer a fine insight into the army's political inclinations at a time when
civil war was no chimera. Military discipline was disintegrating.
General François de Négrier, a member of the Superior War Council,
instructed his subordinates that if the government continued to tolerate any further attacks against the army, "the High Command will
bring about the necessary measures in order to stop them."[16] In a letter

to Waldeck-Rousseau, Galliffet commented on Négrier's actions:

The act committed by him is of *the most serious gravity.*
Négrier is setting himself up to be a Boulanger. . . . Instead of
pacifying the army he is preparing it for rebellion. . . . No
war minister can tolerate such provocations. They are an act
of disobedience of the highest degree and constitute a danger. . . .
If necessary I will make it clear to the President [Loubet] that
if the organizer of a coup d'état is not broken, the war minister, being defenseless, will resign.[17]

In August, 1899, a coup planned by Déroulède and Jules Guérin, a
pronounced anti-Semite, was easily thwarted, but Guérin and a
handful of his followers succeeded in reaching a well-fortified house
on the rue Chabrol; a long forty-day siege ensued. While Waldeck-
Rousseau pondered how to break the siege, Galliffet counseled the
premier that only the police be used for any action taken against
Guérin's headquarters. The army would not be dependable because its
spirit "has been worked to the point that anything 'out of the ordinary'
which is asked of it will seem suspicious. The army is at present anti-
Semitic—and Guérin has proclaimed himself the pontiff of this
doctrine."[18] The premier refused to use the army or the police against
Guérin. Receiving public support from only *La Libre Parole* and
Cardinal Richard, the rue Chabrol insurgents finally surrendered on
September 20.[19]

On September 9, 1899, a second court-martial, this time held at
Rennes, again found Dreyfus guilty of treason, but with "extenuating
circumstances." Waldeck-Rousseau immediately sought a method to
negate the absurd verdict. He could turn to the Court of Appeals,
which would probably set aside the verdict and refer the case to a military court. Dreyfus, however, would have very little chance to win a
favorable verdict if he were judged by another military court. Furthermore, a protracted legal process would keep the affair aflame with its
accusations and political agitation.

Even before the Rennes verdict had been announced on September
9, Galliffet believed that Dreyfus would again be convicted. He urged
Waldeck-Rousseau to accept the Rennes verdict. With a good deal of
anxiety Galliffet warned the premier that military unrest was increasing; the army would only accept a pardon, for any further
legal action "would stir up storms more dangerous than the ones we
want to quell."[20] The army would possibly desert the government if
the legal battle were protracted. Galliffet reminded Waldeck-Rousseau

not to forget that "in France the great majority is anti-Semitic. We shall therefore be in the following position: on one side, the whole army, the majority of Frenchmen . . . , and all the agitators; and on the other side, the ministry, the Dreyfusards, and foreign countries."[21] The premier drew the necessary conclusion from the war minister's sagacious observations. On September 19, 1899, President Loubet offered Dreyfus a pardon. He accepted it.

The granting of a pardon to Dreyfus did not end the Dreyfus affair. Indeed the Dreyfus affair was far from being closed, for it had dramatically demonstrated how disparate the army's political and religious philosophy was from that of the civilian institutions. The army demonstrated that it was a potential threat to the country's established political institutions. Military reform was imperative; thus, with Galliffet's resignation in 1900, Premier Waldeck-Rousseau, supported by a newly formed coalition of Socialists and radical republicans, appointed as war minister the relatively obscure Louis André, one of the few generals known to believe in the dominant democratic ideals of republican France.[22] André brought with him to the War Ministry those officers whom he knew would be supporters of the Republic. This launched a remarkable career for one of those officers— Maurice Paul Emmanuel Sarrail.

Although General Sarrail was shrouded in political and military controversy, both critics and admirers agreed that he was perhaps the most captivating French officer of his era. Tall and broad, the general's whole being conveyed an air of agile elegance. His strikingly handsome virile face radiated with natural majesty. The white hair, brushed back, revealed a high broad forehead, and the flowing white mustache concealed a delicate mouth. He looked out from a pair of astonishingly expressive, clear blue eyes. The general was a man endowed with vigorous health and uncommon energy.[23]

His family background was as solid as was his bearing. His mother was a Teisseire, one of the socially prominent and politically potent families of nineteenth-century Carcassonne. The family had begun its economic ascent in the seventeenth century as textile producers, and, as befitted many ambitious and wealthy bourgeois families of the eighteenth century, one of its members, by purchasing a seat in the local *sénéchaussée* court, became a member of the *noblesse de robe*. But it was in the nineteenth century that the Teisseire family reached the pinnacle of its prestige when René-Joseph Teisseire married the daughter of General François Dejean. General Dejean had fought for the revolutionary armies and then served Napoleon Bonaparte in the

War Ministry. René-Joseph Teisseire added further luster to the family name when during the July Monarchy he served as mayor of Carcassonne and then represented the Aude as a deputy in the Chamber. To the great disappointment of the family, however, one of René-Joseph's daughters, Mélanie, married a certain Antoine Louis Edouard Sarrail, a young, ambitious, hardworking civil servant in the tax bureau. Although Antoine Sarrail was the son of a landowning, middle-class family of Carcassonne, his family was not in the same economic and social stratum as the Teisseires. Father René-Joseph boycotted the wedding and refused to give the customary dowry. As a result, the Sarrail family supplied much of the economic security for the newly-weds.[24]

From this marriage was born in Carcassonne on April 6, 1856, Maurice Paul Emmanuel Sarrail, the second of three sons. Although reared in economically secure surroundings, young Maurice received neither warmth nor emotional consideration from his father. Rather, the elder Sarrail devoted his energies to climbing up the administrative ladder. Each promotion, coming in rapid succession, meant a new town for the family: Castlenaudary, Nîmes, Dijon, Toulouse, and Chambéry. Although he wanted Maurice to do well in his studies, he showed little interest in his son's work. His mother was very often ill and unable to give him all the attention he needed. As a result of this lack of attention and of his father's stern, even gruff behavior, Maurice learned early to rely upon himself.[25]

In his youth Maurice already displayed those traits that were later to characterize him. He was quietly confident, but occasionally he flashed a searing temper. Industrious, loyal, highly ambitious, possessed of a wry sense of humor, he was gifted with an extraordinary memory and a fiercely independent, though not original, mind. He had a strong bent toward the practical. Seemingly imperturbable, he often conveyed the impression of severity and imperiousness. In his relations with others he was direct and candid, sometimes brusque; he loathed pretentiousness. Most significant of all, Sarrail was strong-willed, at times inflexible, as he quickly demonstrated by rejecting both the family religion and its occupational plans for him.

While Maurice's father was a skeptic, his mother and most of his relatives were devout Catholics. When the question of young Maurice's education arose, a family dispute erupted; the solution was to hire a tutor who had taught at an Assumptionist college—but one who had been dismissed. In this way the religious sensibilities of the Teisseires were not unduly disturbed and attention was paid to

Antoine Sarrail's secular outlook. A few years later, the elder Sarrail decided that Maurice, age ten, would attend a lycée rather than a Catholic *collège*.

Maurice was steeped in the faith of his pious Catholic family. Yet despite his religious training, he first questioned, then eventually rebelled against the validity, indeed the sincerity, of church dogma and ritual. When not yet ten years old, he viewed the religious processions in which children dressed as saints and angels as a travesty if not a sacrilege. Later he was shocked at the idea of having a rehearsal for so sacred a ceremony as the First Communion, and when at the actual ceremony he experienced no emotion beyond that felt at the rehearsal, he was sadly disappointed. As he grew older, and despite attempts by the more devout family members, Sarrail refused to submit to Catholic dogma, which he quickly regarded as an endeavor to control the mind.

The Sarrail family quickly discovered that Maurice's rejection of Catholicism was more enduring than simply an outburst of adolescent perversity; Sarrail, in fact, would remain a lifelong nonbeliever, tolerant of all religious beliefs. As a young lieutenant in North Africa, he moved easily within Jewish social circles. Upon returning to France, he married a young widow of Protestant nobility, Eugénie Adrienne Alice Garrison d'Estilhac. Because of the wishes of his devout in-laws, the ceremony took place in a Protestant church on October 14, 1887. Sarrail's father and younger brother, Maurice Marie Xavier,[26] were the only members of the family to attend the wedding; illness prevented his mother from attending, but his older brother, François, and the rest of the family refused to attend. One of the Teisseires even disinherited him for marrying a non-Catholic. And in military circles the marriage added further fuel to the already smoldering political and religious rancors against Sarrail, rancors that were later to spread into flames of hatred.

Although his religious independence offended the more devout members of the family, Sarrail nevertheless felt a genuine affection for his family. He was extremely close to his immediate family, especially to his mother and his younger brother. He eventually persuaded his younger brother to enter Saint-Cyr and the professional officer corps. In the frequent letters to his parents, while always showing a lively interest in family matters, he discreetly avoided raising religious or political questions.[27]

Young Maurice was only a mediocre student in his first years at the lycée, but he was a highly motivated and assiduous worker and in the last years he always ranked among the first ten in his class. He pursued his studies alone, for he had learned early never to ask for help. His teachers recognized his ability and pushed him to greater efforts. He showed a flair for mathematics and the elder Sarrail wanted his son to attend the Polytechnic after receiving the baccalaureate and then enter the state administration, preferably, like himself, in the financial branch. Unlike his older brother François, who entered the world of finance and eventually had a highly successful career with the Bank of France, Maurice rejected his father's plans. Instead, he took the entrance examinations for Saint-Cyr in 1875 and to the amazement of his professors, who felt a special post-lycée preparation indispensable for success, was accepted. Although his father was very pleased with his son's excellent scores—Sarrail ranked 79 out of 350—he looked on his choice of profession without enthusiasm. Even though Maurice had several distant relatives in the officer corps, including one general, and this may have had some bearing on Sarrail's choice of profession, Sarrail insisted that in 1875 he knew very little about the military profession:

I wanted to lead a somewhat independent life as soon as possible and no longer be a dependent of my parents.
To become an officer in order to be "free" may seem strange, if not ridiculous; to wear the *épaulette* in order to be able to live without asking one's parents for anything may also seem equally paradoxical! These were, however, the essential reasons why I entered Saint-Cyr, for I knew absolutely nothing about the military profession.[28]

Sarrail was graduated from Saint-Cyr in 1877, ranking third in a class of 345.[29] The class produced very few first-rate generals; only Sarrail, and to a much lesser extent, Louis Maud'huy, Augustin Gérard, Paul Leblois, and Marie-Antoine de Mitry had exceptional careers during World War I. Jean Bermond d'Auriac, Louis Puineuf, Edgard de Montjou, and Emile Driant, on the other hand, only had lackluster military careers, yet each achieved some degree of prominence as a nationalist deputy. Driant, married to Boulanger's daughter, had become by 1911 the leading nationalist deputy in the Chamber. Other members of the class were General Claude Lejaille, a republican, and later to be a member of the André ministry; Major Nettinger, commander of the presidential escort at Lyons in 1894, the day President Sadi Carnot was assassinated by a deranged anarchist; and General Marie-Alexandre Gallet, a member of the historic seven-man military court that unanimously convicted Dreyfus of treason in 1894. A few years later, in 1898, realizing that he had erred, Gallet publicly announced that Dreyfus was innocent; he joined André's ministry in 1900.

For the next twenty-three years, from 1877 to 1900, Sarrail had a highly successful and satisfying career. He selected the infantry, and served it with distinction in Algeria and Tunisia. He was accepted for two years of further study at the elite Staff College and in 1885 was graduated twenty-sixth out of sixty-six.[30] He then served on various divisional and corps' general staffs: Montauban, Perpignan, Toulouse, Cherbourg. His superiors considered his work to be outstanding. When Sarrail finished his two-year probationary period with the General Staff of the 33rd Division at Montauban, his report read: "Great distinction, a very fine intellect, subtle and alert mind, easy worker, a loyal, serious, and pleasant nature, very fine officer, a loyal aide-de-camp. Destined for a great future."[31]

Extremely ambitious and one who scrutinized the promotion lists as closely as anyone else, he worked diligently and unobtrusively and with a thoroughness that amazed his superiors.[32] His only diversion was the theater. Although he had the ability to be on good terms with his comrades, he had no close friends. He kept his thoughts to himself just as he had when he was younger.[33]

Sarrail was a republican, a stout defender of the Revolution en bloc. Since politics was seldom discussed in the conservative Sarrail home and never at the lycée, it is impossible to ascertain who influenced his political views. As a student and later as a junior officer, he was not interested in pursuing the machinations of politics; school work and career plans consumed all his time. But he was deeply shocked by the antirepublican remarks and actions of some of his fellow officers at the July 14 celebration in 1880, and by the early 1880s he had already become a steady subscriber to *La Dépêche de Toulouse*, the country's outstanding radical republican newspaper. In 1883 he wrote his parents that he was prepared to resign his commission if the royalists took power.[34] But it was not until the early 1890s, while serving on the General Staff of the XVII Corps at Toulouse, that his political and religious attitudes became more overt: "As soon as I arrived, it was easy to see that I did not go to mass, that my wife was Protestant. . . . Besides, I handled all requests in the same way; that was already one of the directives which governed my behavior; but for some people, not to reserve all information and all favors exclusively for clericals or antirepublicans seemed a real iniquity."[35] In 1894 Captain Sarrail applied for a position on the General Staff of the army. His request was refused. According to Sarrail, he was informed that he would never be allowed to enter the General Staff because of his unorthodox views.[36]

A few years later, when the Dreyfus affair reached a feverish climax, Sarrail, unlike the majority of the officer corps, maintained a discreet silence: "I continued to observe but said nothing; when pushed to the wall, my answer was always the same: in order to have an opinion, it would be necessary to be able to substantiate it with positive facts. . . . Before long this sort of silence was judged, and certain people were able to make inquiries and state that I had never howled with the wolves."[37] Many years later, four months after the outbreak of World War I, Major Alfred Dreyfus, then a staff officer at Montmorency, wrote General Sarrail, requesting to be a member of his staff and telling Sarrail that he would be "happy to serve so eminent a chief as you."[38]

Sarrail's reticence during the affair had marked him. Although his political ideas had come to the attention of his conservative superiors, they had also attracted the notice of one Captain Bernard, with whom he had served at Toulouse. Bernard was the nephew of General André. In 1899 Captain Bernard asked Sarrail what personnel changes should be made in the higher echelons of the army. "My answer had shown him [André] that I shared his views completely." A few months later, on May 30, 1900, Major Sarrail received word that he had been selected to serve in the newly formed War Ministry of Louis André. "With the firm resolution . . . to collaborate in restoring order and legality to the disorder and arbitrariness in which the army was floundering," Major Sarrail left for Paris.[39]

II. In the Political Arena

From the moment I entered André's Cabinet, I have been constantly attacked—and I am proud of it.

—SARRAIL, *"Souvenirs"*

Riding the train to Paris in the late spring of 1900, General André recalled the fate of those few republican officers in the French army. They were the pariahs of the army. André had seen many of them, "downtrodden, discouraged, despairing, rejected, deprived of advancement, pushed aside, forced to conceal their ideas behind a stony façade. Was this because they admitted to being republicans? No, simply because they manifested no hostility to the regime."[1]

At their first meeting newly appointed War Minister André and Premier Waldeck-Rousseau agreed that the Dreyfus affair had clearly revealed that the army would have to be republicanized, that is, the basic ideals and attitudes of the officer corps would have to be changed. Furthermore, the two decided on the means André would employ in his attempt to transform the army into an institution that would correspond to the democratic ideals of the regime. Faced with the choice of either large-scale peremptory dismissals, a method the republicans had effectively employed two decades earlier in order to remove monarchist-appointed judges and prefects, or a methodical weeding-out process, Waldeck-Rousseau chose the latter. Though supported by Socialists and Radicals, the Waldeck-Rousseau government nevertheless needed moderate republican support, and the premier feared that a purge of reactionaries in the army would alienate those few moderates who supported the government.[2] By opting for a method that relied on retirements, promotions, and reassignments as a means to republicanize the army, it meant that it would be several years, perhaps even decades, before there would be a fundamental change in the basic political attitudes of the professional officer corps.

[15]

It was only a matter of weeks before André faced his initial crisis. The problem centered on the question of whether power in military matters rested with the war minister, who was responsible to the elected representatives, or the traditionally autonomous military bodies such as the General Staff, the Superior War Council, and the classification commissions. In an attempt, albeit moderate, to reaffirm the supremacy of the civilian government, André replaced three officers of the eighty-five member General Staff. Although successful, he immediately encountered open resistance from General Alfred Delanne, chief of staff, who refused both to accredit André's new appointees and to recognize the removal of the three former staff officers. In a further move designed to force André to retreat in his attempt to name officers to the General Staff, the vice-president of the Superior War Council and commander in chief in time of war, General Edouard Jamont, resigned. André explained why his apparently mild steps provoked a crisis within the military's upper echelons: "The cause is that a representative of civilian power had dared touch the holy arch; the cause is that the isolation, independence, and the autonomy of the military congregation found itself questioned and consequently endangered."[3]

In the immediate aftermath of the Dreyfus affair, when society was critical of the army and when the chance for war was considered minimal, the traditional function of the officer appeared anachronistic. In order to justify the officer's existence and thus repel the increasing attacks against the army, André introduced a concept that had been formulated a decade earlier by Lieutenant Louis-Hubert Lyautey. The officer, assuming a new function, was to teach civic and moral virtues to his recruits. The officer was to lecture on the benefits of cooperatives, the means of improving agriculture, and the dangers of social diseases and excessive liquor; in addition, the recruit was to be supplied with libraries and recreation facilities so that he could spend his spare time profitably. Moreover, social and economic topics would not only aid the recruit, but they would also involve the professional officer with other than military concerns; hopefully, this would help to break the isolation of the officer corps, which traditionally disdained civil society and its concerns.[4]

Yet for any meaningful attempt to republicanize the army André realized that he would have to possess absolute control over the promotion lists. Thus in 1901 he abolished the classification commissions; henceforth, the war minister, not the field commanders, would be the exclusive agency in establishing the promotion tables. André quickly realized that his major problem was to ferret out those officers who were not only militarily competent but who were also republicans. And because the conservative divisional and corps commanders offered him no assistance, he thus relied on local government officials, republican politicians, and the nationally organized Freemasons in order to ascertain the political and religious sentiments of thousands of officers. In order to be promoted, officers were to demonstrate "proof not only of professional capacity and virtues, but also of that virtue—also professional—of devotion to the Republic, its institutions, and its laws."[5]

André readily admitted that his sanguine expectations fell far short of realization. He faced innumerable problems in his modest attempt to reform a labyrinthian bureaucracy of 25,000 officers. He found that there were not enough republican officers who also possessed the necessary technical knowledge; as a result, several reactionary officers were promoted to the army's highest echelons. Moreover, André often followed the field commander's personnel recommendations; not to do so would have lowered morale. But perhaps the most important reason for the minor impact of André's reforms was his excessive moderation in carrying out his overall program; a moderate reform program was, however, not unexpected from a professional officer whose background included forty years of military service. André's advice to future republican war ministers called for the energy that he himself failed to demonstrate. At the end of his five years as war minister, André urged his successors to recognize "that the battle against the counterrevolution is endless and without respite, and that in resorting to procrastination, half-measures, and precautions, one risks making a dupe out of the Republic."[6]

However tepid the reforms of André appeared, he earned the enmity of the Right. The Right in the nineteenth century had often been accused of being antinationalistic. In 1871 it was the monarchists and not the radical republicans who wanted a peace treaty with Prussia. The Right had even been accused of subordinating French national interests to those of Rome. But beginning with Boulanger and particularly during the Dreyfus affair, the Right emerged as the supporters of a virulent form of nationalism. The authoritarians, royalists, nationalists, anti-Semites, and anti-Dreyfusards despised the laic, anticlerical, egalitarian, antimilitaristic, and legalistic Republic. It was this Republic that had rallied to the cause of a single Jewish officer and in the process had sullied the honor of the army.[7]

The Right considered the very life of France threatened from within by the Dreyfusards and from without by England and Germany. The army, embodying all the sentiments cherished by the Right, was considered not only the guarantee of France's existence, but it was also to be the instrument of reactionary political change. Whereas the Left believed that the Republic and army could only exist as mutual partners if the army were radically changed, the Right maintained that the army and the Republic could not co-exist unless the regime were changed. The Right looked to the army for the eventual overthrow of the Republic. Thus, each reform implemented by André that minimized the conservative attributes of the army, be it institutional, educational, or personnel brought a shrill and pained outcry from the Right.[8]

Major Sarrail joined André at the War Ministry on the rue Saint-Dominique in May, 1900. Sarrail and the other leading members of André's staff, Colonel Alexandre Percin, Major Claude Lejaille, and Captains Antoine Louis Targe and Jules Mollin, were all devoted republicans who wanted to transform the spirit of the army. Sarrail believed that far too many officers had been trained in Jesuit schools and that almost all of the generals were antirepublicans who "openly and in no uncertain terms worked against the legal government of France."[9] He concurred with Captain Targe's assessment of the work that had to be accomplished: "We must clean out the stables whose keys we now possess."[10] However, in his nine months as a member of André's Cabinet, Sarrail was in no position to alter the structure of the army. He handled routine paper work dealing with the technical aspects of the infantry and found that, for the most part, his job was not satisfying. Occasionally, however, he was assigned a delicate task. When General Jamont resigned, for example, André selected Sarrail to obtain Jamont's original letter of command. Sarrail also had the task of personally informing the prominent anti-Dreyfusard, Colonel du Paty de Clam, that he had been placed on the inactive list.[11]

Waldeck-Rousseau had emphasized to André that the military schools should play an important role in democratizing the army, for it was in the schools where the future officers would learn "to serve our institutions and not to fight them."[12] In March, 1901, André appointed Sarrail commandant of the Infantry School at Saint-Maixent, the officers' training school for those men coming up through the ranks. Sarrail warmly welcomed the appointment; it not only meant a promotion, but for the first time he would have complete freedom of action. Displaying his characteristic zeal and energy, Sarrail set out for the dreary western garrison town to reform the school.

Saint-Maixent, founded in the aftermath of the 1870 defeat, offered a one-year program to prospective officers chosen among the noncommissioned officers. The program, which emphasized rifle drills, reviews, physical exercise, and rote memorization of field regulations, was simply a continuation of the corporal's daily routine. Sarrail did make some minor changes in the military program of the school: lectures on the usefulness of artillery were introduced, the seventy-five millimeter cannon was used in field maneuvers, and night maneuvers were regularly scheduled. But Sarrail's purpose at Saint-Maixent was to change the basic attitudes of the prospective officer; he wanted to break the parochialism of the professional soldier. Thus, he immediately established a course of instruction that attempted to broaden the political and social outlook of the future officer. He introduced courses that emphasized contemporary religious, economic, and political questions. Qualified military instructors or local civilian authorities presented courses on topics such as the following: economic history, since Sarrail believed that war is often the result of economic competition; the political role of the French army from 1875 to 1900, which according to Sarrail offered graphic examples of improper behavior; the history of socialism, since socialism was an emerging political force; and the history of conflicts between church and state since 1789, an important question, since the clash between the church and state was reaching the boiling point. In addition, famed Pacifist Lucien Le Foyer delivered a series of lectures in which the possibilities of universal peace and international disarmament were favorably presented to the future officers. Sarrail also emphasized the officers' new social functions; he brought in qualified civilians to discuss new agricultural methods and effective ways of establishing and managing cooperatives.[13]

In political matters Sarrail preached one basic tenet: the officers must be loyal to the Republic:

> Moreover, they [the cadets] must be convinced that the time when the army could live apart, when the officer corps could exist outside the life of the Nation, . . . is fortunately over.
> We are now educating our officers to be faithful to the motto . . . inscribed on the first tricolors, on the flags of the Convention: "Discipline and submission to the laws."[14]

A freethinker, but no sectarian and certainly not a Freemason, Sarrail issued an order of the day in January, 1904, that enjoined all students from forming or joining any Catholic clubs, irrespective of whether these clubs were led by a clergyman or a layman. While he considered Catholic clubs as potential "hotbeds of sedition," his decree closed with the reaffirmation that all cadets had "complete liberty to fulfill their religious duties."[15]

Sarrail's unilateral action, taken without a formal order from the war minister, brought much comment from the political press. For the first time, the name of Commandant Sarrail was widely introduced to the French public. The radical republican newspaper, *La Lanterne*, wrote that "republican chiefs are unfortunately still so rare in the army that when we have the good fortune to meet one of them, it is quite natural that we extend to him our congratulations and our encouragement."[16] The Right also focused on Sarrail. Edouard Drumont, author of the best seller, *La France juive*, and journalist Léon Daudet, splenetic as ever, considered Sarrail the puppet of Combes, Jaurès, and Clemenceau; Sarrail, "cringing and licking Masonic feet," was attempting to attract public attention by his "anticlerical onslaught."[17]

Shifting for a moment from the realm of politics to that of evaluating Sarrail's actual accomplishments at Saint-Maixent, it must be recognized that although his overall program raised the quality of Saint-Maixent to a level comparable to Saint-Cyr,[18] his aspirations for the school were never fulfilled. Sarrail and André had wanted Saint-Maixent to provide the opportunity by which a noncommissioned officer of modest family background could enter the officer corps. It had been hoped that the Saint-Maixent graduates, intensely devoted to the Republic, would counter the traditionally aristocratic and antirepublican graduates of Saint-Cyr.[19]

During the 1890s the graduates of Saint-Cyr made up about 60 percent of the annual promotion list for second lieutenants entering the infantry; the Saint-Maixentais composed the other 40 percent. In the 1903 promotion list 48 percent of the second lieutenants in the infantry were graduates of Saint-Maixent; in 1904, 55 percent of the second lieutenants were from Saint-Maixent and only 45 percent were Saint-Cyrians.[20] However, as Sarrail sadly noted, such a shift in junior officer recruitment meant but little when the entering students at both Saint-Cyr and Saint-Maixent held the same political attitudes.[21]

Sarrail conceded that his reform program at Saint-Maixent had little real impact. This was not surprising, since most of the students came from well-to-do conservative classes; Sarrail considered 35 percent of the 279-man class of 1903-4 as Bonapartist, clerical, or nationalist.[22] The large concentration of antirepublican students resulted, he felt, from the recruitment policy. In order to be eligible to take the entrance examinations for Saint-Maixent the noncommissioned officer had to be recommended by his commanding colonel or general; this method of selection tended to reinforce the existing conservative attitudes. Furthermore, the entrance examinations, Sarrail believed, favored the wealthy classes; the exams were heavily peppered with questions on literature and foreign languages, which inevitably gave an advantage to the *lycéen*, who in all probability had failed the exams for Saint-Cyr. Instead of a poor man's Saint-Cyr, where those from humble backgrounds could enter the officer corps, Saint-Maixent had become the last outpost for the would-be Saint-Cyrian.

To curb the heavy concentration of antirepublican students, Sarrail suggested that all sergeants, whenever they deemed themselves prepared, be allowed to present themselves for the entrance examinations. Sarrail further suggested that the examination questions be changed. Rather than emphasizing detailed factual questions on renowned battles and campaigns, Sarrail proposed that practical military questions be asked emphasizing information which an attentive candidate would have grasped in his years as a noncommissioned officer. He also urged that the questions center on topics of contemporary significance; he suggested such questions as the relationship of society to the military, the importance of nationalism in the creation of the European state system, and the factors contributing to German unification.[23]

After three years at Saint-Maixent, in February, 1904, Lieutenant Colonel Sarrail was summoned to Paris by Chamber President Henri Brisson and appointed military commandant at the Chamber of Deputies. His new position entailed attending all the Chamber sessions and insuring the personal safety of the deputies while the sessions were in progress. The assignment in Paris, normally a routine one, was enlivened by the most dramatic Chamber session since that of June 23, 1899, when at the height of the Dreyfus affair, Waldeck-Rousseau pleaded for all republicans to support the "Government of Republican Defense."

The session of October 28, 1904, opened when the nationalist deputy from the Meuse, Léonce Rousset, a retired lieutenant colonel and a frequent contributor to the conservative press, took the floor and set forth a bill of particulars against Sarrail. Relying on a series of recent articles in the Paris daily, *Le Matin*, Rousset first accused Sarrail of having written political comments on the records of two Saint-Maixent students. On one student's report, contended Rousset, the former head of Saint-Maixent had written: "He will make as good a Freemason as he would a Jesuit"; on the second: "Nephew of General Dodds; he depends solely on this relationship to advance." Rousset next charged Sarrail with being antinationalistic and antimilitaristic; he had undermined the traditional military virtues of discipline and sacrifice by permitting Pacifist Le Foyer to lecture the students on the benefits of peace and the dangers of professional armies. Rousset concluded this attack by implying that Sarrail had established a spy system at Saint-Maixent in which an instructor, a certain Lieutenant Mathieu, was the means by which the commandant gathered information concerning the religious and political opinions of the other students.[24]

War Minister André then took the floor and only weakly answered the charges. He gently criticized Sarrail for having inserted political comments in the two dossiers, but he quickly reminded the deputies that such a pecadillo in no way tarnished Sarrail's outstanding military qualities.[25]

No sooner had André completed his vague and insipid defense of Sarrail than the nationalist deputy from the Seine department, Jean Guyot de Villeneuve, directed a volley of attacks at the war minister himself, calmly producing irrefutable evidence that the War Ministry had organized an intelligence system whereby the political and religious views of the officers were collected. Acting on the instructions of General Percin, André's *chef de cabinet*, Captain Mollin was shown to have been in constant contact with the Freemasons. Each time that information was required concerning the religious or political views of an officer, Mollin would send the officer's name to Vadecard, the secretary-general of the Grand Orient. Vadecard, in turn, would write to the provincial lodge in the town where the particular officer was stationed; the local Freemasons, teachers, judges, businessmen, doctors, and cobblers would seek out the information on the particular officer and then transmit it to Mollin in Paris. The information, kept on a *fiche*, a form on which the reports were made, was later used to determine promotion lists.[26]

General André resigned a few days later, acknowledging that Mollin had indeed been authorized to gather information from the Grand Orient. André denied, however, that political sentiments without military competency could either assist or deter an officer's chance for promotion. He gave ample evidence that many colonels whose *fiches* had clearly marked them as reactionaries had been promoted to brigadier generals.[27]

Sarrail had been somewhat tainted by *l'affaire des fiches*. Not only were his activities at Saint-Maixent questioned in the Chamber only minutes before Villeneuve's startling revelations, but a week later *Le Figaro*, France's largest moderate republican daily, implicated him directly with the scandal. Specifically, editor Gaston Calmette claimed that the War Ministry, after receiving political and religious information from various sources—Freemasons, bureaucrats, and republican officers—forwarded to Sarrail those *fiches* that pertained to colonels tentatively proposed for promotion to brigadier general. Sarrail supposedly evaluated the disparate information and then, using a coded number, indicated on a special card whether that particular officer was politically reliable.[28]

In the ensuing three months *Le Figaro* daily published scores of documents and letters demonstrating that delation was rife within the officer corps. Irrefutable evidence showed that General Percin, Lieutenant Colonel Jacquot, Majors Pasquier, Paul Peigné, Paul Lemerle, Lejaille, and Captain Mollin had either revealed the political and religious inclinations of their fellow officers or had taken part in coordinating the thousands of *fiches* that flowed into the War Ministry. Yet *Le Figaro* never published evidence to substantiate its initial charge against Sarrail, nor for that matter did *Le Figaro* ever again mention Sarrail's name in connection with *l'affaire des fiches*.[29] *Le Figaro* seemingly realized that its case against Sarrail was, at best, tenuous, for when Sarrail was promoted in March, 1905, the newspaper praised the entire promotion list.[30]

On the other hand, as the Chamber debate of October 28 revealed, Sarrail did write political comments in at least two students' permanent dossiers. There was nothing surreptitious about Sarrail's method, since the dossiers were accessible to all of the cadets' future commanding officers. Furthermore, Sarrail did keep a personal political and religious file on all of the cadets in the 1903 class at Saint-Maixent and it is conceivable that he had the assistance of Lieutenant Mathieu in gathering the information; however, there exists no evidence that these personal files were transmitted to the War Ministry. While not unsympathetic to the War Ministry's method of ascertaining the officers' religious and political attitudes,[31] Sarrail did not take part in the *fiches* system. Many years later, when he had already become a bitter critic of Sarrail, General Emilien Cordonnier, a practicing Catholic and second in command to Sarrail at Saint-Maixent, wrote that Sarrail was not involved in any way with the organized method of gathering nonmilitary information concerning other officers.[32]

The nationalist Right was not satisfied that Sarrail had emerged relatively unscathed from *l'affaire des fiches*. On November 15, 1904, in a session devoted to budgetary problems, the nationalist deputy from the Doubs, Georges Grosjean, interrupted the discussion and accused Sarrail of having participated in the affair; he demanded that sanctions be taken against Sarrail. Henri Brisson, the president of the Chamber of Deputies and its presiding officer, quickly came to Sarrail's defense, claiming that the former commandant at Saint-Maixent had never taken part in acts of delation. Grosjean quickly withdrew his accusation.[33]

Henri Brisson was one of the outstanding parliamentarians of the Third Republic. He was the paradigm of radical republicanism: austere, tolerant, honest, anticlerical, and as premier at the height of the Dreyfus affair, frightfully aware of having an army unresponsive to the commands of the civilian government.[34] A lawyer by training, Brisson devoted his entire life to politics; a political journalist in the last years of the Second Empire, he was elected a deputy in 1871 and served continuously until his death in 1912; he was twice premier and nineteen times elected president of the Chamber of Deputies. Within the inner circles of the nonsocialist Left, no man's prestige and influence was greater than Brisson's.[35]

In February, 1904, as president of the Chamber, the Radical Brisson appointed Sarrail commandant of the Palais-Bourbon. For the next several years there existed an extremely warm relationship between the middle-aged republican officer and the Radical septuagenarian. Brisson's correspondence with Sarrail shows that he was captivated by Sarrail's energy, personal loyalty, and quiet devotion to republican France.[36] Consequently, Brisson effectively used his political power to promote Sarrail's fast-rising career. Writing to Sarrail in February, 1905, Brisson related a meeting he had had with Premier Emile Combes: "I told him [Combes] that I would consider what the War Ministry was preparing for you as a personal insult to me. I presented the situation to him as best I could and asked for either the Second Bureau or your leave of absence with the promise that you would be promoted colonel in March."[37] On March 24, 1905, Sarrail was promoted to colonel. He then served the next sixteen months as commander of the 39th Regiment at Rouen. When the 1906 elections resulted in another overwhelming victory for the Socialists and Radicals, Brisson was again elected president of the Chamber. He immediately summoned Sarrail to Paris for a second term as military commandant of the Palais-Bourbon. Sarrail only served ten months at the Chamber of Deputies, for Brisson persuaded Georges Picquart, war minister in the Clemenceau government, to appoint Sarrail director of the infantry in March, 1907.[38] The Radical leader's solicitous concern for Sarrail's career was once again demonstrated the following year when Picquart wrote Brisson: "I learned that you were worried about Sarrail's fate. I hasten to reassure you. Sarrail will be advanced at the very next promotion and will be retained in his present post. I am happy to acknowledge in this way the ability of this excellent officer."[39] A week later, on March 25, 1908, Sarrail was appointed brigadier general.

In a hierarchy still overwhelmingly conservative, if not reactionary, General Sarrail had become by 1908 the most prominent and powerful of the Andréists. Sarrail's rapid promotions at a time when officer promotions were agonizingly slow did not escape the attention of the Right. Each promotion within a bureaucracy which the nationalists considered their private domain brought an outburst of criticism. The nationalist press claimed that Sarrail was a *fichard*, that he owed his promotions to the Freemasons, and that he was responsible for the wave of antimilitarism sapping the morale of the army.[40]

At the same time it was obvious that because of his ambitious reform program at Saint-Maixent and his close identification with André and Brisson, Sarrail had become the favorite of the Left. When Radical Maurice Berteaux, André's successor at the War Ministry, announced the promotion list for 1905, *La Lanterne* and Georges Clemenceau observed that if the Left complained that several militant reactionaries had been promoted, Berteaux could easily retort: "But I have promoted Lieutenant Colonel Sarrail."[41]

Sarrail served in the War Ministry as director of the infantry from March, 1907, until March, 1911. The position was basically an administrative one, and other than routine matters such as introducing newer and more effective weapons, overseeing the military schools, and determining assignments and reassignments, he was involved in two important and controversial areas: strengthening the reserve units and drawing up advancement lists.

The question of reserves was inextricably bound to the wider scope of politics. The professional officer corps and the Right, champions of the permanent standing army, with its long-term service, had nothing but contempt for the reserves. The citizen called to arms was considered to lack discipline; his *esprit militaire* had supposedly been vitiated by exposure to civilian amenities. At best, the reserves were considered fit only for rear duty or as fortress troops. Until 1900 only a modicum of attention had been given to the reserves. The Dreyfus affair had shown the republicans the dangers of this professional army. Yet when the question arose of how best to break the autonomy of the army and thus reduce its danger to the state, only the Socialists offered a viable alternative to the permanent standing army. Reminiscent of the republican military program of the Second Empire, the Socialists wanted to abolish the active army and rely on a militia system. The Radicals of the post-Dreyfus years, despite their fear of the army, refused to countenance this radical step. Instead, as embodied in the 1905 recruitment law, which reduced universal military service from three years to two years, the republicans attempted to minimize the influence of the professional army while accentuating the civilian aspects of the country's defense. Two-year service for the conscript would hopefully prevent indoctrination of military values. Second and more important, the 1905 recruitment law minimized the role of the active army and insisted that the reservists be the principal instrument of the country's defense; the basic role of France's permanent standing army during peacetime was to be a school for the training of reserves.[42] The heavy reliance on the reserves as the key to national defense and the hope that the 1905 two-year law foreshadowed further reductions in military service, prompted one Socialist deputy to proclaim somewhat prematurely the beginning of a new era—*l'ère de civilianisme*.[43]

Two years later, at a time when the ethos of *civilianisme* was ebbing but had not yet evaporated, General Sarrail's task as director of the infantry was to bring the reserves up to combat strength. Displaying outstanding organizational abilities, Sarrail prepared the reserves for a major role in case of mobilization. Finding some reserve units with a plethora of officers and others with none, he arranged to have each regiment equipped with a minimum number of officers. Those units with special functions in case of mobilization were to be commanded by officers who had recently completed their active duty. The same pattern was applied to the territorial reserve, which in many instances existed only in skeletal form; territorial battalions were brought to full size.[44]

Sarrail's organizational ability laid the foundation for the most brilliant though abortive attempt to reformulate France's military strategy before 1914. General Victor Constant Michel, vice-president of the Superior War Council and commander in chief of the French army in time of war, presented a report to the war minister in February, 1911, explaining that the Germans could not pierce the French lines in Lorraine; instead, they would attack through Belgium. Thus, he wanted to stretch the French lines from Belfort to the Channel; in this way the expected German onslaught through Belgium could be countered. But in order to have the necessary manpower he proposed to double front-line effectives by attaching a regiment of reserves to every active regiment. When mobilization was ordered, the reserves, the very core of Michel's defensive plan, would fight side-by-side with the active army. Michel had complete confidence in the combat effectiveness of the reserves because of "the measures already taken by the [war] minister and those which are presently on the drawing boards for increasing the number and effectiveness of the reserve officers."[45] It was basically this emphasis on the reserves, however, that caused War Minister Adolphe-Marie Messimy and the military chiefs to reject outright Michel's strategy; the General Staff considered the reserves to lack cohesion and solidity and thus were a hindrance to the active army. Michel was quickly forced to resign his position.[46]

The greatest domestic political struggle since the 1906 church-state conflict was the one staged between the partisans of the two different types of army. In this struggle, which centered on the question of whether to strengthen the active army or the reserves, rightist military concepts emerged victorious. Moderate republicans, led by Raymond Poincaré and Louis Barthou, supported by nationalists, the General Staff, and several Radicals, succeeded in strengthening the active army in 1913 by increasing the length of service from two to three years. The 1913 three-year law was significant for several reasons. First, it presupposed that Germany, without employing her reserves, would cross France's eastern frontier and launch an immediate offensive. Second, it presupposed that France's only method of warfare was the *offensive à outrance*. Both assumptions, accepted as dogma in official military circles, meant there was little or no place for the reserves, since the reserves seemingly could not assemble quickly enough to ward off the expected German thrust nor could they wage an immediate offensive. Thus, the only military solution that suited the General Staff's plan of attack and, at the same time, neatly dovetailed with its conception of Germany's war plans was to increase the size of the active army; the conservatives reasoned that an added year's class under the colors, which would add 180,000 men to the standing army, was a necessity, for it would also increase the frontier forces and thus permit France to halt Germany's anticipated *attaque brusquée*.[47]

Although it is difficult to ascertain Sarrail's position on all the issues surrounding the 1913 three-year law, it is apparent that he disagreed with the bill's proponents on at least two counts. First, he opposed the three-year law because it minimized the role of the reserves. While it is not clear what role he was prepared to assign the reserves, Sarrail, supporting one of the basic premises of left-wing military strategy, believed that the nation in arms was the only feasible means of national defense. It is further clear that Sarrail, again siding with the Left, rejected the General Staff's contention that Germany's permanent standing army alone would launch a sudden attack. Sarrail and the Left believed that Germany would employ her reserves; consequently, there would be a delay before she could begin an offensive. It was during those few critical days, while Germany would be concentrating her manpower and matériel, that Sarrail would have begun the French offensive.[48] Sarrail's insistence on carrying out an offensive, however, separated him from one of the basic tenets of Radical and Socialist military strategy. The Left's strategy was strictly defensive; supported by heavy artillery and large fortress emplacements, regional reserve units would, so the Left argued, hold back the German invasion.[49]

Sarrail's overall strategy contained the same basic flaws as that of the High Command: failure to consider the use of heavy artillery, insistence on the offensive, failure to consider and to prepare for a German invasion through Belgium,[50] and lastly, believing in a short war, failure to consider the economic repercussions and dislocations of a war of attrition. In the last analysis, Sarrail's prewar strategy, as well as that of the General Staff, lacked those qualities that General Michel alone had demonstrated: boldness, prescience, and imagination.

Sarrail's most important and certainly his most controversial task as director of the infantry was to determine assignments and promotions. Technically, the war minister drew up the promotion tables; but with two or three thousand candidates Picquart and his successors, Generals Jean Brun and Berteaux, had little time and even less inclination to do so themselves. Thus, Sarrail composed and then submitted the promotion lists to the war minister for the latter's formal signature.[51]

Sarrail's initial step was to dismiss most of the previous members of the Directory of the Infantry. This action brought a congratulatory letter from André, who considered Sarrail his most prominent protégé: "Your arrival at the head of the Infantry and the changes which you have made in its personnel have clearly shown that the minister

[Picquart] has decided to follow a course which republican officers regretfully saw him hesitate to take."[52]

Sarrail's promotion policy favored those officers who were republicans and yet were professionally competent. He explained his promotion policy at the War Ministry as follows:

> I treated everyone equally. For example, I broke with the tradition of reserving all the favors for the same people; that is, for those who owed their careers solely to birth, fortune, or connections. . . . Also I did not yield to any imperative requests from any general whatsoever, or from any influential parliamentarian on the Right. . . . In matters of personnel, I have always considered the intellectual and professional value of those concerned. People could highly praise the ideas of any person to me, but never did I assign anyone any post whatsoever if that person were not militarily competent to fill it.[53]

Sarrail used two methods to determine an officer's political affiliation. A government circular had been sent to the prefects on January 13, 1905, two years before Sarrail became director of the infantry, requesting them to determine the political and religious attitudes of those officers in their particular department; Sarrail relied on these prefectural reports.[54] Second, he gave serious consideration to the demands of left-wing politicians, who frequently requested promotions or reassignments for officers of unquestionable loyalty to the Republic.[55]

Since promotion was the key to any serious attempt in rendering the army more democratic, it is not surprising to find Sarrail's promotion policy receiving sharp criticism. The Right realized that if control of promotions could be torn from Sarrail's grasp, it would guarantee that very few republicans would advance to the army's higher ranks. In March, 1911, the question of Sarrail's promotion policy came under heavy attack in the Chamber of Deputies. The nationalist deputy from the Meurthe-et-Moselle and Sarrail's former classmate at Saint-Cyr, Lieutenant Colonel Emile Driant, vociferously argued that there existed a crisis of morale within the army. Driant, who was instrumental in distributing to all the regiments a list containing the names of those officers purportedly belonging to the Freemasons, claimed that the crisis in military morale arose from the techniques by which officers were selected for promotion. Specifically, Driant accused Sarrail of basing promotions strictly on political considerations.

Worse yet, the traditional military ethic of honor, according to Driant, was being corroded by Sarrail's insidious technique of encour-

aging officers to furnish secret information concerning their colleagues. This ill-gotten information helped Sarrail to determine which
officers would be placed on the promotion tables. Driant claimed that
the only effective means to extirpate all nefarious political criteria in
military matters would be to emasculate the war minister of his power
and to resurrect the classification commissions. Only the field generals
were adequately prepared to judge an officer's ability.

Retired General Jean Pédoya, Radical-Socialist deputy from the
Ariège, agreed with Driant that there was a crisis in morale within the
army. But the source of this malaise resulted from painfully slow advancements and low salaries and pensions. Turning directly to the role
of political favoritism in military advancement, the knowledgeable
Pédoya retorted that conservative officers were advancing much more
rapidly than republicans. A few sessions later Pédoya, noisily
supported by the Left, eloquently defended Sarrail in the face of
Driant's hostility. The Radical-Socialist deputy emphasized that
Sarrail was an indefatigable worker, loyal, and of unimpeachable
character. Pédoya warned that whenever Sarrail was attacked, "I will
be there to defend him."[56]

Driant's accusations, as if by design, unleashed a barrage of press
attacks against Sarrail. Ernest Judet concluded a two-thousand word
article on Sarrail: "It would be necessary to devote one hundred
columns of *L'Eclair* to cite all the arbitrary and unjust acts of tyranny
that Sarrail has committed during his reign. On the other hand, it has
been the triumph of his friends, of mediocrity, of incompetence, and
of Freemasonry."[57] Readers of the nationalist press were reminded
that Sarrail represented everything that was pernicious in the gangre-
nous Republic. He was one of three high-ranking officers whose rapid
advancement was due to the patronage of the Dreyfusards. As befits
any man whose meteoric rise was due to political loyalties and not
loyalties to France, Sarrail preached the slogans of the dominant political parties; he had taught that the military spirit was dangerous to
democratic institutions; he spouted pacifism, humanitarianism, international cooperation, loyalty to the Republic, while emphasizing the
officer's new civilian functions. All this had supposedly undermined
the traditional warrior instinct of the army.[58]

Sarrail had his defenders. In addition to *La Lanterne*, the eminent
journalist, Marcel Brossé, while warning that the army was still a
great danger to the Republic, explained why Sarrail was the victim of
a violent press campaign: "Of all our generals he is one of the rare
ones who has enough character to assume responsibility for his acts

and reconcile them with his words. . . . Of course he is attacked with such violence only because of his republican opinions."[59]

Of all the press reaction in March, 1911, there was one of unusual significance. France's prestigious newspaper, *Le Temps*, a moderate republican paper of the *grande bourgeoisie* and one that usually refrained from intemperate criticism, unleashed a surprisingly harsh attack against Sarrail. Supporting Driant's basic charges, *Le Temps* claimed that the "maintenance of certain military personalities at the head of some of the great branches of the army gives a semblance of truth to the assertion that the famous method of General André, with its denunciations and its *fiches*, is not completely abolished."[60]

Le Temps's sharp criticism of Sarrail manifested the moderate republicans' increasingly conservative approach to military matters. Although the Radicals continued to control French politics for the next five years after the fall of Combes's Radical government in 1905, they refused to institute any far-reaching military reforms. Their reason for inaction is not difficult to discover: frequent industrial and agricultural strikes required the use of the army. Radicals, such as Georges Clemenceau, quickly appreciated the army's usefulness as an arbitrator in the bitter and bloody class warfare that engulfed France in the years after 1905.[61]

But by 1911 domestic strife was easily overshadowed by the heightening international tensions. The various international crises created a climate of opinion within France that slowly but perceptibly emphasized military preparedness. As a result of the increasing fear of Germany, all deputies except for a majority of Socialists and Radical-Socialists became extremely chauvinistic. The majority of republicans, rediscovering a new pride in the army, joined the nationalists in demanding that the armed forces be strengthened.[62] And as *Le Temps* explicitly stated, political considerations in military affairs only weakened the army.

Immediately following the 1911 Agadir crisis, War Minister Messimy reorganized the High Command, minimizing political considerations while hoping to improve military efficiency. Messimy, a Radical-Socialist and anticlerical, strengthened the independence of the General Staff. Rejecting André's careful efforts to subordinate the General Staff to the war minister, Messimy consolidated into one office—that of chief of the General Staff— the functions of the vice-president of the Superior War Council, who was generalissimo in time of war, and those of the General Staff, whose function was to plan the strategy in case of war. General Joseph Joffre was appointed to this newly created post. Although a moderate republican from a lower middle-class background, Joffre had a tendency to surround himself with conservative officers. Assuming his new position as chief of the General Staff, Joffre selected Edouard de Curières de Castelnau as his first assistant.[63] Castelnau, a passionate Catholic known as the *capuchin botté*, had been one of the three officers removed by André in his struggle with the General Staff in 1900.

Few politicians better reflected the Republic's nationalist revival than Alexandre Millerand, once a feared Socialist, but by 1912 conservative enough to be war minister in Poincaré's national republican government. Concerned solely with military efficiency, which purportedly could not prosper with political considerations, Millerand rejected André's legacy and followed Messimy's lead; he increased the autonomy of the army. This was best demonstrated in the question of military promotions: Millerand gave the military commanders almost unlimited authority to draw up the promotion lists. The periodic prefectural assessment of an officer's political reliability, which had played an important role in determining previous promotion lists, was abruptly terminated. In a further step, Millerand dramatically destroyed all the officers' political dossiers.[64] The accomplishments of André and Sarrail were demolished with such rapidity that for the first time in fifteen years, Ernest Judet praised a promotion list. Scrutinizing the names of generals recommended for promotion in 1913, he noted the new "spirit which has currently won out and is attempting to repair past errors."[65] However, there was one name on the list he regretted: General Sarrail, who had been named a corps commander.

In the three years before the war the national republicans, whether they be moderate or radical, and the Right dominated French politics; it was this coalition, greatly assisted by Joffre, which successfully passed the 1913 three-year law. With the Left in descent, Sarrail, the symbol of the Radicals' attempts to republicanize the army, could not maintain his powerful position in Paris as director of the infantry. Promoted a divisional general on March 27, 1911, Sarrail spent the next three years in the field: first at Reims and later at Mézières. In recognition of his outstanding work at Mézières he was appointed a corps commander in November, 1913; he served first at Bourges and then in May, 1914, he took command of the VI Corps at Châlons. Devoting most of his time to infantry maneuvers along the Meuse and Woëvre regions, Sarrail's responsibility was to direct France's *couverture*, or frontier troops, which, in case of war, were intended to check Germany's *attaque brusquée*.[66]

When Sarrail was forced to leave his powerful and prestigious position as director of the infantry in March, 1911, he considered his expulsion a welcome relief. The incessant personal attacks and the sudden death of his young daughter in 1908 made his last four years in Paris a time of anguish.[67] While the frequent attacks had failed to intimidate him, there is little question that after 1911, removed from his Paris position and with the conservatives possessing control of both the military and political apparatus, Sarrail deeply sensed his isolation, for "each day a new enemy enters the arena."[68] But, for the most part, he assumed the duties of field commander with his characteristic calm and confident demeanor. Happily married and extremely wealthy as the result of family inheritances, Sarrail had reconciled himself to spending the remainder of his military career in the field, determined "to prove that in any military situation given me I would do a good job."[69]

Although isolated within the military hierarchy, Sarrail kept in contact with his many friends. Occasionally he received encouragement from military colleagues. Upon his appointment as corps commander in 1913, General Percin reminded Sarrail that the promotion "was only a step . . . toward another goal—to a post where you will be able to restore things as they were before this wind of reaction."[70] Much more frequent, however, were Sarrail's contacts with his many political friends. The prominent Socialist, Albert Thomas, wrote Sarrail: "I want to continue the conversations we had at Reims. When shall I see you again? I need your advice . . . on a good number of points."[71] And throughout the late winter and spring of 1914, when Gaston Doumergue's Radical caretaker government held power, War Minister Joseph Noulens frequently consulted Sarrail concerning military promotions; Sarrail's recommendations were faithfully followed.[72]

It was only in mid-1914 that national attention, for the first time in three years, again focused on Sarrail. The Socialists and Radicals, forming a united front for the purpose of repealing the 1913 three-year law, made spectacular electoral gains in the national elections of June, 1914. Left-wing solidarity, however, did not survive the election. The newly formed Radical cabinet of René Viviani jettisoned the Socialists and drawing support from the moderates and non-socialist Left, promised to enforce the three-year law until international tensions eased. Nevertheless, it was clear that if many Socialists and Radicals were disappointed with Viviani's temporizing position on the three-year law, they at least wanted the government to replace those prominent military figures who had been associated with the nationalist revival of the previous three years. The rejuvenated Left demanded that Sarrail, the only army chief whom they unhesitatingly trusted, be returned to Paris either to replace Joffre or to head the War Ministry.[73]

On July 15 the parliamentary Left, Radicals and Socialists, demanded an investigation of the army. Leftist criticism of the army ostensibly dealt with purely military matters; specifically, several deputies claimed that France's military organization was slipshod and, as a result, there was a shortage of military supplies ranging from shoes to artillery. The Left suggested, somewhat vaguely, that the situation could be remedied by a reorganization of personnel. The leading nationalist deputy, Emile Driant, quickly moved to Joffre's defense, praising the general's organizational abilities and his choice of personnel. But the ever-alert Driant correctly analyzed the underlying reasons for the recent left-wing criticism of the army: "The real aim of the campaign . . . consists solely in changing the personnel of the High Command and substituting in its place a politico-military coterie which is standing ready in the wings. General Pédoya . . . told me: 'We want to replace General Joffre with General Sarrail.' "[74]

Viviani's ambivalence toward the three-year law had cost him the support of the Socialists; the government would have collapsed without sizable Radical support. Thus the Viviani government, wilting under intense behind-the-door left-wing pressure, had to accommodate the Radicals' demand that Sarrail be brought to Paris for an important appointment. Two days after the Chamber debate of July 15, War Minister Messimy summoned Sarrail to Paris. He begged the astonished Sarrail to tell his friends "not to attack Joffre." And in return, Messimy promised that Sarrail would replace Joffre the following autumn.[75]

Thus, on the very eve of World War I Sarrail had become the most politically powerful general in the French army. An uncompromising radical republican, Sarrail owed his rapid advancements within an extremely conservative bureaucracy to the Left, the victorious Dreyfusards who had assumed political power in 1899. Left-wing politicians, such as Brisson, Pédoya, and Thomas, were attracted to Sarrail because of his political attitudes and loyalty, his character, and his outstanding military record. By 1914 Sarrail had become both the symbol and the means by which the Left hoped to change the political orientation of the French officer corps, thus assuring that the army would actively defend the Republic against its domestic enemies. On the other hand, the nationalists, whether they be royalists, authoritarians, or republicans, considered the conservative professional army the embodiment of certain sacred and irrefutable values and thus never ceased claiming that Sarrail's attempts to reconcile the army with the Republic had weakened and demoralized the nation's armed forces. This accusation is without foundation. The French army's wartime performance in 1914 belies the charge that a few radical republican officers, of which Sarrail was the most prominent, had wrought havoc on the army. Furthermore, Sarrail had the respect of such eminent and politically diverse military chiefs as Philippe Pétain, Georges Picquart, and Marie-Adolphe Guillaumat. Upon his appointment as director of the infantry in 1913, Guillaumat wrote Sarrail that "in taking the Directorship of the Infantry my first thought could only lead to you . . . where your example will sustain me."[76]

Messimy's July, 1914, promise that Sarrail would soon be summoned to Paris as Joffre's successor was not realized. The outbreak of World War I a month later aborted all immediate plans to change the French High Command. Sarrail, one of the heroes of the Battle of the Marne, would only return to Paris in July, 1915—and Viviani's war government would then face its greatest political crisis, one that it could not overcome.

III. A Call to Arms

Sarrail's imperturbable nerves of steel during those trying days from September 6 to September 13, when he daily repeated "We must hold on," had a great effect on morale. . . . And the morale of the troops, responding to his appeal, carried the day.

—GENERAL ALFRED MICHELER

Only the barest military precautions had been taken; all furloughs were canceled; officers and noncommissioned officers were recalled to their units. Across the border, however, German military preparations progressed at a more rapid pace: patrols moved to the frontier; roads leading to France were barricaded; batteries were built; the garrisons of Trier, Sarrebourg, and Strasbourg were reinforced. The French could wait no longer—the first step of the French war plan, Plan 17, was put into effect on July 31, 1914: General Sarrail, commander of the VI Corps, was ordered to stagger his covering troops along France's northeastern frontier.[1]

Still confident that war would not break out, Sarrail and his chief of staff, Alfred Micheler, left VI Corps headquarters at Châlons and drove into the Woëvre, that hot dry plain situated between the Meuse Heights and the Moselle. Here in the Woëvre Sarrail supervised the placement of his three divisions, the 12th, the 42nd, and the 40th. By August 3, stretching from Damvillers, north of the redoubtable fortress of Verdun, to Pont-à-Mousson on the Moselle, the VI Corps was poised for its primary function: to thwart the anticipated German onslaught emanating from the fortified staging area of Metz-Diedenhofen, and in so doing, to allow the mobilization and concentration of the Third Army, which on August 1 had begun to proceed in an orderly fashion behind the Meuse Heights. The concentration of the Third Army was completed a week later with no difficulty, for contrary to the French High Command's calculations, the Germans unleashed no *attaque brusquée* against the French center. Putting the

[36]

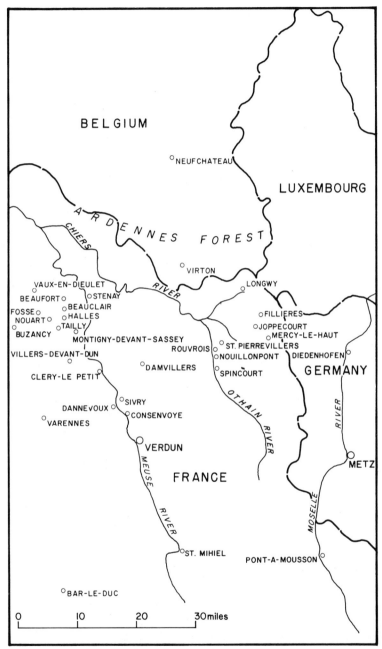

The Battle of the Frontiers and Retreat

Schlieffen Plan into effect, Germany's immediate objective was Liège and Brussels, not Verdun.

Ten days after the formal declaration of war, the five French armies assumed their positions in order from the First Army on the right to the Fifth Army on the far left. The First and Second armies, which comprised the French right wing, occupied that area to the right or south and east of the heavily fortified area of Verdun, while the Fourth and Fifth armies lay north and west of Verdun. The Third Army, commanded by General Pierre Xavier Emmanuel Ruffey and composed of the IV, V, and VI Corps, covered Verdun from the north and east. By August 17 Sarrail's VI Corps, which comprised the right wing of the Third Army, moved into position directly east of Verdun.[2]

Three days later the French army's right wing, the First and Second armies, absorbed defeats at Morhange and Sarrebourg in Lorraine. The German army's left-wing counterattack in Lorraine, coupled with its right-wing scythe-like movement through Belgium, could mean only one thing to the Grand Quartier Général (G.Q.G.)—the German center was weak. Thus on August 20 Joffre ordered his main attack to begin. Joffre's plans called for the five army corps of General Langle de Cary's Fourth Army to undertake the principle offensive action by striking north through the Ardennes Forest in the direction of Neufchâteau. On Langle's right the Third Army, also advancing through the Ardennes, had a dual mission: to support Langle's offensive and to protect the right flank of the Fourth Army. If the Third and Fourth armies were successful, the German center would have been forced to retreat eastward to the Metz-Diedenhofen area. Once the German center had given way, the German right or western wing, which had crossed the Meuse at Namur, would have been severed from the rest of the German armies and thus would have become an easy target for the French. To support the Third and Fourth armies' offensive, the First and Second armies on the right were to make only a secondary attack between Metz and the Vosges for the purpose of holding the German Sixth and Seventh armies and thus prevent them from taking in flank the French Third and Fourth armies. Lastly, the left wing, consisting of General Charles Lanrezac's Fifth Army, the expected British Expeditionary Force, and the Belgian army, was to move into Belgium in order to hold in check any German forces that might advance from the Meuse, and so gain sufficient time to allow the Third and Fourth armies' attack to become effective.

On August 21 the Third Army, expecting to meet a minimum of resistance, confidently began its northward trek to that pocket of heavily wooded land where the borders of Belgium, Luxembourg, Imperial Germany, and France were contiguous. Opposite the Third Army stood the German Fifth Army, commanded by the German crown prince, William. The Fifth Army, anchored at Diedenhofen, acted as the pivot of the German offensive, slowly moving at the center as the German right wing swung through Belgium in its attempt to envelop the French armies. On August 20 the German Fifth Army came south against Virton and Longwy. Two days later Ruffey's army, groping through dense fog and the heavy woods along the Franco-Belgian border, were caught off balance by the crown prince's huge army. The German Fifth Army, using the reserves in the front line, was composed of five corps instead of the expected three. Possessing not only front-line numerical superiority, but also combining well-concealed machine gun and artillery emplacements that unleashed a steady barrage against the French positions, the Germans in a three-day battle forced Ruffey's army to retreat. Sarrail's VI Corps was no exception; it took heavy casualties at Joppécourt, Mercy-le-Haut, Spincourt, Fillières, Nouillonpont, Saint-Pierrevillers, and Rouvrois on the Othain River. By August 24 the VI Corps had been forced to regroup on the western bank of the Othain.[3]

While Ruffey's Third Army was being badly battered, Langle's Fourth, Lanrezac's Fifth, and General John French's British Expeditionary Corps suffered severe defeats at Neufchâteau, Charleroi, and Mons. Recognizing that the Battle of the Frontiers, that is, the Third and Fourth armies' recent offensive, had failed and that the French left wing needed precious time to escape envelopment and to regroup, Joffre on August 25 ordered his left and center armies to retreat. Two days later Sarrail's VI Corps, fighting rear guard encounters, crossed the Meuse at Consenvoye, north of Verdun. For the first time in several days the VI Corps was out of range of the deathly German artillery.[4] The respite, however, was exceedingly short. The German advance continued.

On August 28, as the Third Army stretched along the right bank of the Meuse from Stenay southward to Verdun, the first units of the Duke of Württemberg's Fourth Army began crossing the Meuse north of Stenay. Ruffey, supported by General Augustin Gérard's II Corps (Fourth Army), decided to make a stand on the Meuse. For the next two days, heavy fighting occurred southwest of Stenay in the area of Beaufort, Nouart, Beauclair, and Montigny-devant-Sassey. But the German pressure was too much and when the Fourth Army's

II Corps retreated to Buzancy, the Third Army's left wing had to retreat from the Meuse.[5]

Apparently undaunted by the jolt, Ruffey ordered a counterattack for the morning of August 30. However, no sooner had the offensive begun than Joffre arrived at Varennes, Third Army headquarters. Convinced that Ruffey's nerves were failing, Joffre appointed Sarrail to replace Ruffey as commander of the Third Army.[6]

Ruffey and Sarrail had worked well together. Ruffey had been satisfied with Sarrail's performance during the Battle of the Frontiers. Before the war, Ruffey, himself a member of the Superior War Council, considered Sarrail eminently qualified to be a member of that august body.[7] Sarrail, for his part, admired the personal and professional qualities of his superior and was pleased to have been Ruffey's subordinate. Thus, when offered the position of Third Army commander, Sarrail hesitated; he believed that it was not appropriate to replace a man whom he respected. Sarrail asked Joffre for another command. The commander in chief gave little attention to such sentimental niceties and left.[8]

In the war's first month, as the French armies were retreating, Joffre sacked field commanders with monotonous regularity. Desperate shuffling of personnel inevitably produced questionable changes, such as the removal of Lanrezac as Fifth Army commander. But Joffre's appointment of Sarrail was a master stroke; for the next twelve critical days Sarrail was to be one of the outstanding field generals on the Western front. He made the right moves at the right time, combining boldness, imagination, and initiative with calculated restraint. Most important of all, Sarrail was calmly determined not to yield.

Assuming command of the Third Army on August 30, Sarrail ordered Ruffey's counterattack to continue. The Seventh and Eighth divisions (IV Corps), and the Tenth Division (V Corps), carrying the brunt of the attack, wedged forward and regained Montigny-devant-Sassey, Halles, Tailly, Nouart, and Villers-devant-Dun.[9] The Germans soon discovered that the retreating French were not yet beaten.

On August 31 Sarrail ordered the offensive to continue. He wanted the Seventh, Eighth, and Tenth divisions to maintain their drive northward, hoping to reach the Vaux-en-Dieulet–Beaufort line, just west of Stenay. After an initial early dawn advance, however, the French offensive was halted by a German counterattack. The enemy retook Beauclair, Halles, and Montigny-devant-Sassey. Although Sarrail absorbed heavy casualties throughout the day, he nevertheless managed to hold Fossé, Nouart, and Villers-devant-Dun, which had been captured the previous day. Further south, the VI Corps's 12th Division braced itself at Dannevoux and Sivry for the anticipated smash across the Meuse by the German Fifth Army's XVI Corps. Just north of Verdun, under the protection of the fortress's long-range artillery, the 65th, 67th, and 75th Reserve Divisions (Third Reserve Group), recently placed under Sarrail's orders, succeeded in gaining a solid foothold on the left bank of the Meuse. Holding a line in the north that stretched from Fossé southeastward through Nouart and Villers-devant-Dun to Clery-le Petit on the Meuse, Sarrail notified Joffre in the late evening of August 31: "Our offensive northward has met the enemy everywhere. The offensive will be resumed tomorrow morning."[10]

But the Third Army's northward offensive was not resumed on September 1. To the west of the Third Army, the Allied armies faced impending defeat as the massive German armies pushed through northwestern France and raced to envelop the Allied left. The G.Q.G. had no alternative—on September 1 Instruction Number IV ordered the Third, Fourth, and Fifth armies to retreat. The Third Army's withdrawal could extend, if need be, as far as Bar-le-Duc, twenty-seven miles south of Verdun. The next day, September 2, again attempting to escape the pressure of the German right wing, the G.Q.G. ordered a further withdrawal. Sarrail was given permission to draw back to Joinville, twenty-two miles south of Bar-le-Duc.

Sarrail was surprised to have received such orders. He was not aware of the gravity of the situation on his left, for the information he received was often contradictory. Second, to retreat twenty-five or fifty miles when he was more than holding his own on the Meuse made no sense to him. And third, to withdraw to Bar-le-Duc would have resulted in the isolation of Verdun and just how long the cluster of fortresses could have held out without reinforcements is a moot question. Therefore, energetically and at times abusively contradicting the violent objections of the G.Q.G. and General Georges Lebouc, Third Army chief of staff, Sarrail did not literally obey the orders to withdraw immediately all of his troops straight south. In a brilliant tactical maneuver that not only prevented the Germans from investing an isolated Verdun but also shaped the eastern front of the impending Battle of the Marne, Sarrail used Verdun as a pivot, keeping his right wing wheeling slowly on the fortified area as his left and center, keeping in close touch with the retreating Fourth Army, withdrew through the Argonne.[11]

The French retreat halted on September 5 when Joffre realized that the far right of the German tentacle was swinging east of Paris, thereby leaving its right flank exposed to the French Sixth Army. Joffre ordered the French to attack on September 6—and the Battle of the Marne began.

The major front of this momentous battle, which shaped itself toward the south into a pocket in which the Germans were concentrating, stretched 125 miles from the outskirts of Paris to Verdun. From Paris to Revigny, the German First, Second, Third, and Fourth armies opposed Joseph Maunoury's Sixth Army, the British Expeditionary Corps, Louis Franchet d'Esperey's Fifth, Ferdinand Foch's Ninth, and Langle's Fourth armies. The twenty-eight mile front from Revigny to Verdun, the extreme right of the Battle of the Marne, pitted Sarrail's Third Army against the crown prince's Fifth Army.

The crown prince's army was assigned the dominant role in the new tactical directives issued by Chief of Staff Helmuth von Moltke on September 5. Recognizing that the French army's left wing had escaped encirclement, Moltke abandoned the Schlieffen Plan. While the First and Second armies were to remain north of Paris, Moltke ordered the Third Army to continue its southward advance in an attempt to seize Troyes, fifty-five miles southwest of Revigny. The Fourth Army was directed to change its direction from the south to southeast in an attempt to take Vitry-le-François, twenty miles southwest of Revigny. More important, Moltke's September 5 directives ordered the Fifth Army to stop its due south advance and to strike southeast, break the contact between Sarrail's Third Army and Langle's Fourth Army on Sarrail's left, seize Revigny, and then to proceed nine miles southeast through the Revigny Gap, that clearing in a country of dense forest, to Bar-le-Duc. If the crown prince's tactics had been successful, the results would have been catastrophic for the Allies because a German breakthrough on the Revigny–Bar-le-Duc line would have left the Fourth Army's flank exposed and perforce would have meant a sizable retreat of the Anglo-French armies all along the southern one-hundred mile battle front as they would again attempt to escape envelopment. A German breakthrough at Bar-le-Duc would have cut off the Third Army from the rest of the Allied armies, and Sarrail would have had to fall back on Verdun, isolated in a sea of German armies. Third, if the crown prince had broken through Sarrail's army, General Auguste Dubail's First Army and General Castelnau's Second in Alsace-Lorraine, both facing east and holding off the German Sixth and Seventh armies, would have been exposed to a German attack from the west. Consequently, the Haute Moselle, the area between Toul and Epinal, would have been open to the German armies.[12]

On the eve of the battle, Sarrail's Third Army, stretching southwest

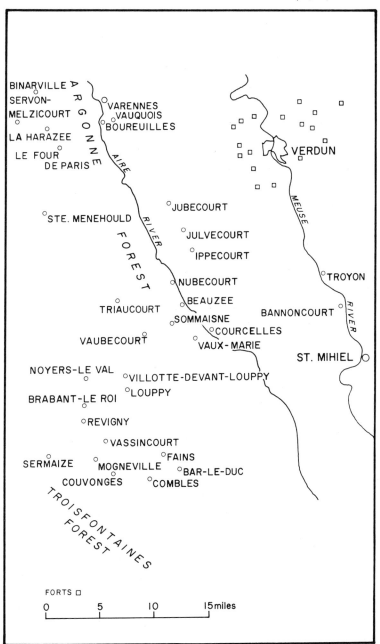

The Battle of the Marne and the Argonne

of Verdun, stood east of the German Fifth Army and faced northwest. With no knowledge of Moltke's September 5 directive, Joffre assumed that the crown prince's army would continue its southward course. On the morning of September 5 Joffre ordered Sarrail to prepare a flank attack from the east. Thus as the German Fifth Army prepared its major thrust at Revigny and Bar-le-Duc on the Third Army's left, Sarrail planned an attack on the Fifth Army's left wing in hopes of turning it. Consequently, while General Micheler's V Corps and General Victor d'Urbal's Seventh Cavalry Division covered Revigny from the north, Sarrail ordered the Third Army's center and right, General Martial Verraux's VI Corps and General Paul Durand's Third Reserve Group (65th, 67th, and 75th divisions), to carry the brunt of the offensive.[13]

However, the battle did not follow the pattern that Joffre and Sarrail had expected, for in accordance with Moltke's September 5 orders, the Fifth Army had deflected its course from the south to the southeast and, as a result, Sarrail's offensive developed into a frontal clash rather than a flanking attack.

In the dawn of September 6, before General Verraux's VI Corps could strike, General Fabeck's XIII Corps, General Mudra's XVI Corps, and General Gossler's VI Reserve Corps smashed against the VI Corps and Durand's Reserve Group. By evening the Germans had taken Triaucourt, Vaubécourt, Sommaisne, and Beauzée. The German advance would have been greater had not Durand's Third Reserve Group and the 72nd Reserve Division under the command of General Michel Coutanceau, the military governor of Verdun, stopped the Germans at Ippécourt, Jubécourt, and Julvécourt.

Although forced to give up three to four miles, Sarrail's attack in the north had held its own and had succeeded in tying down two active corps and one reserve corps, thus preventing the Germans from consolidating their forces in the Revigny–Bar-le-Duc area, which was their major goal. But while surprising the crown prince in the north, Sarrail was himself surprised in the south.

At dawn on September 6 General Charles Roques's Tenth Division (V Corps) held the Noyers-le Val–Brabant-le Roi line. Within a matter of hours Pritzelwitz's VI Corps, supported by the Fourth Army's XVIII Reserve Corps, moved through the French lines. General Roques was killed as the Germans overran the French positions. Revigny quickly fell into enemy hands and the Tenth Division, retreating eastward, was fortunate to regroup on the Villotte-devant-Louppy–Vassincourt line.

Sarrail's concern for his left wing turned to anxiety when the Fourth Army's II Corps, on the V Corps's left, could offer no assistance. Four miles southwest of Revigny, General Gérard's II Corps had lost Sermaize to the Duke of Württemberg's Sixth Army. Sarrail could do nothing except to beseech Micheler to hold on. Sarrail was fighting for time, until reinforcements arrived. The first units of the XV Corps, detached from Castelnau's Second Army, began arriving in the Bar-le-Duc area during the early morning of September 7.[14]

For the next four days, while the VI Corps and Durand's reserves fought a bloody stalemate with the German XIII and XVI Corps along a front stretching south from Nubécourt to Sommaisne and then eastward to Courcelles and Vaux-Marie, Sarrail attempted to stop the German drive through the Revigny Gap.[15]

The pressure on the Revigny Gap had become so great that on the afternoon of September 7 Joffre frantically reminded Sarrail of the unfortunate consequences that would ensue if the breach between the Third and Fourth armies were widened. Joffre emphasized that "it is your duty to make your action felt on the right of the Fourth Army."[16] Heeding Joffre's concerns, Sarrail prepared to utilize General Louis Espinasse's recently arrived XV Corps to counterattack the Germans in the Revigny Gap. Thus, he immediately ordered the XV Corps's 29th Division to be positioned west of Bar-le-Duc at Couvonges, Combles, and Fains, while Espinasse's 30th Division was placed east of Bar-le-Duc, prepared to move in any direction as the situation developed.[17]

In the humid dawn of September 8 the crown prince's VI Corps, in a concerted effort with the Duke of Württemberg's two right-wing corps, smashed Micheler's V Corps and the Fourth Army's right wing, Gérard's II Corps. The fighting was savage and the French were forced to give ground. Joffre was once again greatly concerned about a German breakthrough at Bar-le-Duc. In the evening of September 8 he authorized Sarrail, "if you judge it expedient, to withdraw your right, so as to cover your communications and to lend power to the action of your left wing." The commander in chief emphasized to Sarrail: "Do not allow yourself to be cut off from the Fourth Army."[18] Although receiving permission to break contact with Verdun by bringing all his forces south in order to assure the Third Army's liaison with the Fourth Army, Sarrail did not avail himself of this opportunity. Instead he ordered the XV Corps to counterattack; the 29th Division was to attack the XVIII Reserve Corps at Vassincourt; the 30th Division, to the immediate south of the 29th, advanced through the eastern section of the Troisfontaines Forest and attacked Mognéville. On September 10, as Gérard's II Corps maintained its position in the western sector of the Troisfontaines Forest, Espinasse's XV Corps succeeded in regaining Vassincourt and Mognéville. Contact between the Third and Fourth armies was once again firmly established. The crown prince's offensive against Bar-le-Duc had been broken.[19]

At a time when he was desperately attempting to stop the Germans at Vaux-Marie, Courcelles, and further south in the Revigny Gap, Sarrail had been plagued by difficulties elsewhere. The Third Army's right wing, anchored by Durand's Third Reserve Group, had been forced to withdraw to the Aire River. Punished by Mudra's XVI Corps, the reservists were forced back to such an extent that Sarrail's right wing no longer faced west, but north, and the Third Army's tenuous contact with Verdun had been severed.[20]

It now appeared that Verdun would be lost to the Germans, for on September 8 the crown prince ordered Strantz's V Corps, which was covering the eastern front of Verdun, to attack the Third Army from the rear. To ward off the German strike from the east, Sarrail quickly sent the Seventh Cavalry Division to meet Strantz's corps. If the Seventh Cavalry Division were not able to delay the V Corps on the Meuse until the outcome of the Battle of the Marne had been determined, Sarrail would have faced an extremely difficult situation: either to fight a hopeless two-front battle or to retreat southward. Sarrail rejected the first alternative. If need be, the Third Army commander was prepared to have his left wing pivot on Bar-le-Duc while his right wing, the Third Reserve Group and the VI Corps, retreated south to Toul. Verdun with its 75th Reserve Division would have to fend for itself.

Strantz, however, never crossed the Meuse. The Troyon fortress, strategically situated on the Meuse eight miles south of Verdun perimeter, fought magnificently for five days, successfully preventing the V Corps's Tenth Division from crossing. Foiled at Troyon, Strantz decided to cross the Meuse further south at Bannoncourt. Before the crossing could be undertaken, however, the V Corps suddenly received orders to withdraw. A crisis had developed on the far right of the German army, that very instrument that had been meticulously honed to bring instant success. As Kluck's First Army moved east of Paris, his exposed western flank was attacked by Maunoury's Sixth Army. This attack forced Kluck to reorganize his front by turning west, thereby leaving a gap between the German First and Second armies. A northward retreat was the only means to close the gap between these two armies and thus prevent the Anglo-French forces from cutting off Kluck's army. A retreat by the First and Second armies necessitated a similar withdrawal on the part of the Third, Fourth, and Fifth armies, for not to withdraw was to invite envelopment. By September 10 the Germans were retreating all along the Western front. The next day at noon Sarrail received two unforgettable telegrams: there was no opposition in front of the Fourth Army or the XV Corps.[21] The Battle of the Marne was over and the French had won the greatest strategic victory of the war.

Had the Duke of Württemberg cooperated with the crown prince's army more closely in the first days of the battle by concentrating additional manpower against the Revigny Gap instead of further west at Vitry-le-François, or had Strantz succeeded in crossing the Meuse, France's victory at the Battle of the Marne would not have occurred. But the success of the Third Army was predicated upon something more than luck. Sarrail had handled the tactical and strategical aspects of the battle extremely well; witness his judicious utilization of the XV Corps and his failure to heed Joffre's suggestion that the right wing of the Third Army be brought further south, a move that might have led to the loss of Verdun for the remainder of the war. But there was another ingredient that cannot be overlooked. The six-day battle, which was nothing less than a bloodletting slugging match, revealed that Sarrail possessed the necessary qualities needed to master this type of intense warfare. Never losing his nerve, quietly confident, and fully grasping the situation as it unfolded along the Third Army's front, Sarrail was able to inspire confidence through the ranks. General Micheler recalled that "Sarrail's imperturbable nerves of steel during those trying days . . . when he daily repeated 'We must hold on,' had a great effect on morale. . . . And the morale of the troops, responding to his appeal, carried the day."[22]

Now victorious, Sarrail's exhausted troops moved slowly northward until forced to halt when the German Fifth Army took positions in the northern Argonne. On September 15, with its headquarters at Verdun, the Third Army straddled the great fortress, its right wing (VI Corps, Seventh Cavalry Division, and 75th Reserve Division) in the Woëvre, its left wing (V and XV Corps) in the Argonne facing the German Fifth Army's XIII and XVI Corps and its VI Reserve Corps.[23]

On September 17 the G.Q.G. made a decision that determined the fate of the Woëvre for the next four years. Underestimating the German danger in the east, the G.Q.G. sent Castelnau's Second Army, which had been in the Toul area, westward to Picardy to join other French units in a futile effort to outflank the German right wing. The Second Army's VIII Corps (15th and 16th divisions), however, was left in the Woëvre and was assigned to Sarrail's army. As events would shortly demonstrate, the G.Q.G.'s action placed a heavy burden on both Sarrail's Third and Dubail's First armies, for their respective fronts would have to be dangerously lengthened in order to fill the gap created by the removal of Castelnau's army.

Confident that the southern Woëvre was lightly defended, the G.Q.G. ordered Sarrail to sweep the Woëvre in order "to drive those detachments still in the Woëvre back to Metz." Thus on September 19, while both the V and XV Corps held defensive positions in the Argonne and the Third Reserve Group remained on the Meuse Heights flanking Verdun from the north and east, Sarrail ordered the Seventh Cavalry Division to Nonsard, General Charles Vimard's 75th Reserve Division to Hattonchatel, and the VIII Corps's 16th Division to Woel. But no sooner had the military operation begun than the G.Q.G., influenced by Castelnau's statement of September 18 that "with the exception of the roads the Woëvre could be considered impassable," recalled the VIII Corps and reassigned it to the Fourth Army. The VIII Corps's 16th Division immediately returned to Saint-Mihiel in order to be transported to its new assignment. The removal of the VIII Corps meant that the 75th Reserve Division found itself isolated on the Thillot-sous-les-Cotes–Creue line. And opposite Vimard's division was not some insignificant unit from Metz, but the III Bavarian Corps, which was part of the newly formed Strantz army. The results were predictable: the 75th Reserve Division retreated westward to Lamorville, Spada, and Rouvrois, on the Meuse Heights, just north of Saint-Mihiel.

The III Bavarian Corps, supported by the II and XIV Corps, poured into the Woëvre. Sarrail quickly moved to stabilize his right wing. He ordered the VI Corps's 40th Division into Spada and Rouvrois. To the north of the 40th Division the 67th Reserve Division and the 12th Division were sent to Vaux-les-Palameix and Mouilly.

By the evening of September 22 the Third Army's right wing was well entrenched along the Mouilly-Spada line. But that was not sufficient, for there existed a seven-mile gap between Spada southward to Varneville, where the Seventh Cavalry Division and the left wing of the First Army were located. German troops were moving into this gap. Consequently, on the morning of September 22 Sarrail urged Joffre to order the First Army's XVI Corps to move northward to Saint-Baussant in order to hit the III Bavarian Corps as it moved

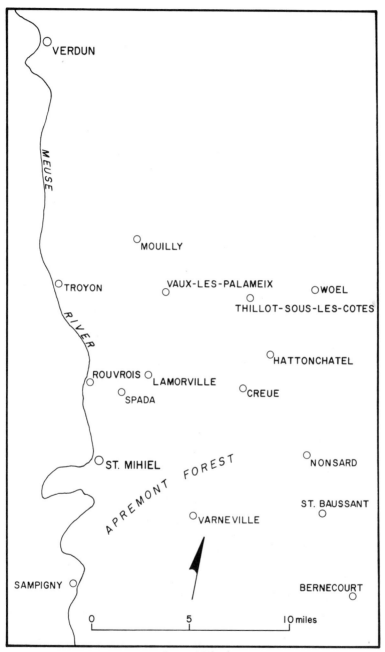

VERDUN

MEUSE

MOUILLY

TROYON

VAUX-LES-PALAMEIX

WOEL

THILLOT-SOUS-LES-COTES

RIVER

HATTONCHATEL

ROUVROIS

LAMORVILLE

CREUE

SPADA

ST. MIHIEL

APREMONT FOREST

NONSARD

ST. BAUSSANT

VARNEVILLE

SAMPIGNY

BERNECOURT

0   5   10 miles

Saint-Mihiel

westward toward Saint-Mihiel on the Meuse. Joffre immediately reiterated what he had told Sarrail two days earlier; namely, that Sarrail did not need assistance from Dubail's army because there was no significant German threat to the Woëvre. It was only in the very late evening of September 22 that Joffre awoke to the seriousness of the German thrust through the Woëvre. He immediately ordered the VIII Corps, which was at Sainte-Ménehould, to return to the Third Army. Likewise, Joffre notified Dubail that his XVI Corps should move north to assist the Third Army.[24]

The first units of the much-traveled VIII Corps arrived in the Verdun area on September 23. Sarrail, however, did not utilize both of the VIII Corps's divisions in the Woëvre. Faced with a major offensive spearheaded by the crown prince's three corps in the Argonne, Sarrail feared that the front between the Fourth Army and the left wing of the Third Army might be ruptured. Thus, he sent the VIII Corps's 15th Division to the Argonne to support the badly battered V Corps. Only the VIII Corps's 16th Division was sent to the Meuse. The 16th Division landed at Sampigny, six miles to the south of Saint-Mihiel and then pushed into Aprémont Forest, but its northward advance was quickly stopped by the III Bavarian Corps. On September 25 the Germans took the important communications center of Saint-Mihiel.

While the V Corps pinned down the Third Army's VI Corps in the north and the III Bavarian Corps slipped into the opening between the First and Third armies, General Dubail's First Army in the south rendered little assistance. It was a case of too little too late. Dubail sent the XVI Corps and the 73rd Division northward into the Woëvre in an attempt to hit the German flank marching west toward the Meuse. The 73rd Division was badly hit in the Haye Woods by Strantz's XIV Corps, and the XVI Corps and 64th Reserve Division, after successful encounters at Bernecourt and Saint-Baussant, were stopped at Nonsard, ten miles east of Saint-Mihiel. Although flanked from the north, west, and south, the Germans kept Saint-Mihiel until 1918.[25]

By late October open warfare with the opportunity to maneuver had ended. From Switzerland to the Channel trenches and reserve trenches were dug and redug, drained and redrained. And in front of these hideous pits, sheets of barbed wire were tautly strung on wooden poles. Penetration of a mile or two was possible, but a breakthrough was an impossibility; secondary lines of resistance prevented the enemy's assaults from cleanly penetrating the defenses.

The results of this kind of warfare—immobility at the cost of astronomical casualties—was nowhere more evident than on the Third Army's front. As of January 8, 1915, Sarrail's Third Army, incorporated into the Eastern Army Group under the supreme command of General Dubail, defended the area between the Aisne and the Meuse. The major part of Sarrail's front centered in the Argonne Forest. It was here, particularly in the region of Vauquois, Boureuilles, Le Four de Paris, and La Harazée, that for months on end the antagonists, separated only by barbed wire, engaged in a mutual killing match.

In this war of attrition Sarrail's successes and failures were modest. He recognized the futility of undertaking an offensive in the impassable Argonne; he only initiated an offensive when ordered to do so by the G.Q.G. or when it was necessary to respond to an unusually severe enemy attack. In February and March, the XV Colonial Division crept northward and in hand-to-hand combat, took most of the town of Vauquois. Destroying German positions in and around Vauquois had a certain tactical importance: the security of the Sainte-Ménehould-Verdun railroad was guaranteed and Vauquois, henceforth, could no longer serve as a staging area for German reserves moving westward into Champagne.

The success was short-lived. On June 20, 1915, the crown prince's Fifth Army unleashed an artillery barrage against General Emile Duchêne's XXXII Corps. Ten days later the Germans successfully stormed Duchêne's first line of defenses north of La Harazée on the road to Binarville and inflicted heavy casualties. Sarrail's response to the effective German attack of June 30 was to initiate an offensive of his own. Sarrail planned to have Duchêne's corps strike north of Le Four de Paris. Duchêne's offensive was to be supported in the eastern Argonne by the V Corps and in the western Argonne by the XV Colonial Division and XV Corps situated to the south of Servon-Melzicourt. The purpose of Sarrail's counterattack was to regain the crests situated to the east of the Binarville-La Harazée road.

On July 13, one day before Sarrail's offensive was to have begun, the Germans again seized the initiative and attacked the V Corps. Suffering heavy casualties, the surprised V Corps yielded four hundred yards along a 2,500 yard front and in the process surrendered the strategically important Hill 286, located two miles southwest of Boureuilles. The next day the V and XXXII Corps tried to recapture the lost ground. Here and there a few yards were regained, but Hill 286 still remained in enemy hands.[26]

Two days later, on July 16, Joffre requested Sarrail's immediate superior, General Auguste Dubail, to investigate the Third Army's operations of June 30 and July 13-14. Dubail's extremely ambivalent report, submitted to Joffre on July 20, criticized Sarrail's deployment of second-line troops on June 30 and July 14. Dubail contended that if on June 30 the XXXII Corps had been supported by five or six reserve battalions, "the consequences might have been very great." On the other hand, Dubail reported, the German attack of July 13 had been broken because Sarrail had quickly reinforced the V Corps with a reserve brigade.

The second aspect of Dubail's report dealt with the state of morale within the Third Army. While acknowledging that Sarrail had the respect of several of his generals, Dubail emphasized that a good deal of friction existed between Sarrail and many of his subordinate officers. The rift between Sarrail and some of his generals caused Dubail to recommend that Sarrail be relieved of his command and that he be given the command of a smaller army unit.[27] Two days later, on July 22, 1915, Joffre recalled Sarrail as commander of the Third Army.

From the moment Sarrail had assumed command of the Third Army, his relations with the G.Q.G. had been characterized by mutual distrust. One would have expected some tension if only because Sarrail's prewar political and military experience differed greatly from that of the officers who directed the G.Q.G. Yet it is surprising to find that personal and political concerns, much more than purely military considerations, played the dominant role in shaping this relationship.

Sarrail's basic allegation was that the politically conservative G.Q.G. did not want him to succeed; in fact, Sarrail suggested that his appointment as Third Army commander in August, 1914, was the result of politics—Joffre and the G.Q.G. wanted France's foremost republican general to share in the country's impending military collapse.[28] Sarrail also implied that the transfer of the Third Army to the Argonne in January, 1915, was determined by political considerations, for the Argonne could only be a defensive position, thus allowing no opportunity for a commander, republican, or otherwise, to distinguish himself.[29]

The entire question of personnel, a constant source of irritation between Sarrail and the G.Q.G., had a highly irregular coloration. Joffre accused Sarrail of predicating his promotion policy on political factors and, as such, asked Sarrail to consider "only the officer's moral and professional capabilities" when determining the promotion lists. There may have been some truth to Joffre's allegations, for Sarrail contended that the G.Q.G. was mistaken if it "believed that everyone acted as it did with regards to problems of personnel."[30] Yet there is evidence that perhaps modifies Joffre's accusations. Conservative Catholic General Cordonnier, upon learning of his promotion to corps commander in May, 1915, wrote Sarrail: "I am disturbed by the immensity of the debt of gratefulness which I owe those who have helped me [in my career], and I know that you were the first to propose me for an army corps."[31]

On the other hand, Sarrail maintained that many of his recommendations for promotion were relieved of their positions while those officers whom he did not recommend advanced rather rapidly.[32] For example, two of Sarrail's finest generals, Verraux and Espinasse, who had commanded adequately and at times brilliantly during the Battle of the Marne, were dismissed. Sarrail claimed that Major Férréol Bel, the G.Q.G. liaison officer attached to the Third Army, "took advantage of anything and everything to pursue systematically . . . the purging of all those who held prominent positions, and he replaced them with anyone who was affiliated with the holy chapel of the G.Q.G."[33] It is evident that, as General Dubail reported, mutual confidence at the staff level did not exist. Sarrail agreed: "The G.Q.G. and its followers on the corps' staffs knew what I thought of their way of doing things and of their military capabilities; they had no confidence in me. . . and I, for my part, could have no confidence in them."[34]

In the multitude of accusations, one fact is clear. The vast majority of field commanders who rose to prominence during the first two years of the war were of conservative political and religious persuasion and thus were no threat to Joffre's jealously guarded position because in republican France conservative generals, such as Castelnau, Franchet d'Esperey, Foch, Langle, Maud'huy, and Urbal, had no parliamentary support. Sarrail, on the other hand, was the most politically powerful general in France and was certainly a contender for Joffre's position.[35] Although probably ignorant of Messimy's July, 1914, promise that Sarrail would replace him as commander in chief, Joffre was undoubtedly aware of the July 15, 1914, Chamber debate in which Sarrail emerged as a rival for his position. Joffre was probably aware also of two anonymous memoranda circulating in left-wing parliamentary circles in March and June, 1915, which denigrated his leadership and called for Sarrail to assume command of the French armies.[36] And Joffre was very much aware that in the first half of 1915 liberal politicians were making frequent trips to Third Army headquarters at Sainte-Ménehould.[37]

Joffre, however, insisted that military considerations alone dictated Sarrail's dismissal. Joffre claimed that immediately following the Battle of the Marne Sarrail had not actively pursued the retreating German Fifth Army. Saint-Mihiel had been lost, according to Joffre, because Sarrail had neglected information that reported a large concentration of German troops moving into the Woëvre. And in the Argonne Joffre contended that French casualties were excessive because Sarrail had not established adequate defensive positions.[38] But action was taken against Sarrail, Joffre strongly claimed, only after careful consideration had been given to General Dubail's impartial and comprehensive report. Nevertheless, it is clear that Joffre was determined to relieve Sarrail of his command before Dubail undertook his inquiry. Joffre's letter to Dubail requesting the investigation clearly revealed the answer Joffre wanted: Dubail was bluntly told that Sarrail was incompetent and morale at Third Army headquarters would improve if Sarrail were relieved of his command.[39]

But in relieving the popular republican general, Joffre unfortunately miscalculated the strength of Sarrail's political support. Left-wing parliamentarians were not prepared to have Sarrail shunted into oblivion and, as a result, wartime France would witness her first direct confrontation between the government, the parliamentarians, and the High Command.

IV. L'Affaire Sarrail

I was . . . in truth the first . . . victim of the camarilla at the G.Q.G.
about whom the deputies were going to make a protest.
—SARRAIL, *"Souvenirs"*

In the late afternoon of August 4, 1914, Premier Viviani solemnly read President Raymond Poincaré's message to the Chamber of Deputies. Poincaré's message concluded with an unconcealed plea for a domestic political truce—a *union sacrée*—an end to the country's internecine partisan political strife.[1]

Later that historic day the National Assembly, stirred by the spirit of the *union sacrée*, hastily passed emergency legislation necessary for the nation's defense and then adjourned for six months, by which time the war was expected to end. The National Assembly's surprise adjournment sprung from its belief that the traditional political prerequisites of discussion, investigation, surveillance, and interpellation would, in the midst of invasion, only result in a debilitating chaos; consequently, the legislators temporarily abdicated their power and deferred to the executive authority, believing that a strong government, unhampered by Parliament, was alone capable of waging the war. The parliamentarians, in turn, expected the Viviani ministry to oversee the High Command.

In reality, however, no effective civilian control of the army existed; during the first year of the war Commander in Chief Joffre gained ascendancy over both the legislative and executive branches of government. A distressing aspect of Joffre's relationship with the government was his disdain for the parliamentarians; the G.Q.G., located at Chantilly, considered itself completely independent of the government and was determined that the government and the deputies should learn nothing of military events, thus obviating any possible civilian interference.[2]

[55]

Unfortunately the Viviani ministry received no cooperation from Joffre's nominal superior, War Minister Millerand, who never wavered from the basic principle that regulated his relations with the High Command: complete accord with the generalissimo. In practice this meant that Millerand was nothing more than Joffre's "echo." The war minister, "immobile as a statue and as impenetrable as a sphinx," supported the G.Q.G. in its campaign of silence; only with great reluctance did Millerand disclose the least significant military information to the other Cabinet members.[3]

When Parliament reconvened in December, 1914, moderate and left-wing representatives were determined to reestablish some degree of control over the military. The basic instruments used by the parliamentarians in the attempt to reassert their power were the Chamber Foreign Affairs Commission and the Army Commissions of the Chamber and Senate, which were to undertake secret and judicious investigations of all questions pertaining to national defense. Public parliamentary attack and interpellation were to be eschewed, for open public debate centering on controversial political and military questions would, it was feared, revive partisan politics, break the *union sacrée*, and undermine the Viviani government, thereby ushering in ministerial instability at a time when the Germans were deeply entrenched within the country.[4]

During the first half of 1915 Millerand and Joffre successfully hindered all the judicious attempts by the Chamber commissions to gather pertinent military information. Although the *union sacrée* was still respected, it was clear that by June the National Assembly was seething. Millerand's continued servility to the inaccessible Joffre slowly eroded parliamentary support for the Viviani government; the parliamentarians demanded that the government assume greater leadership in the faltering war effort. But Viviani refused to dismiss Millerand; the government had to appear united if only because unity was synonymous with the strength and determination necessary to wage war. In addition, to replace Millerand, extremely popular with the army, with a strong civilian war minister would have resulted in a collision with the G.Q.G., and Joffre would have resigned. Instability had to be prevented, for it could only encourage the enemy, frighten prospective allies, and dismay loyal allies.[5]

On July 20, 1915, Joffre informed the Viviani government that Sarrail would be removed as commander of the Third Army. Consternation arose within the Cabinet immediately. At the Cabinet meetings of July 20 and July 22 both the Left and the Right, with the exception of Millerand, agreed that Joffre's action was not justified. Conservative Finance Minister Alexandre Ribot noted that it was unfair to break Sarrail for the operations in the Argonne while no sanctions had been taken against General d'Urbal, who had commanded the fiasco at Arras. Perhaps General d'Urbal had not been removed because, as Undersecretary of State Abel Ferry suggested, he was a reactionary and an ultra Catholic. Furthermore, there was ministerial dissatisfaction with Joffre because he had carefully submitted Dubail's report in order to justify Sarrail's removal. Yet Joffre had not followed Dubail's recommendation to appoint Sarrail commander of the Army of Lorraine; instead, Joffre proposed to appoint Sarrail a corps commander.[6]

The government could not rescind Joffre's decision as urged by Democratic Left Minister of Colonies Gaston Doumergue and Radical-Socialist Minister of Public Instruction Albert Sarraut, for to retain Sarrail as commander of the Third Army would have resulted in Joffre's resignation. On the other hand, the Cabinet could not permit Joffre's decision to stand unaltered. The Cabinet realized that breaking France's most prominent republican general—the only one with large political support—would not only have exacerbated the existing tensions between the High Command, the government, and the Parliament, but would also have revived all the political passions that had accompanied Sarrail's prewar career. If the Left deserted the *union sacrée*, the Viviani government would collapse. Thus, for the first time during the war, political necessity forced the Viviani government to take "a step in military matters which nullified one of Joffre's decisions."[7] The Viviani government, reasserting its legal right to make military appointments, appointed Sarrail to replace General Henri Gouraud as commander of the French Eastern Expeditionary Corps assigned to the Dardanelles.[8]

On the evening of July 22 Sarrail received a telegram at his Third Army headquarters in Sainte-Ménehould, notifying him of his dismissal and ordering him to report to the War Ministry the following day. When he reported to the rue Saint-Dominique on the afternoon of July 23, Viviani and Millerand offered him the command of the Eastern Expeditionary Corps. Sarrail refused this new assignment, considering it a demotion. He offered to retire to his home at Montauban.[9]

Although humiliated by what he considered an unwarranted dismissal, Sarrail's actions belie those of a person who was prepared to resign meekly. Immediately upon his return to Paris on the morning of

July 23, Sarrail met with Louis-Jean Malvy, Radical-Socialist minister of the interior, and heatedly told the minister that "it is useless to keep talking about the superiority of civil power over military power and about the government's rights to oversee and even direct military operations when there are only words and no action." Perhaps this was simply a parting warning of a cashiered general. But more likely Sarrail, as well as anyone else, realized that if civilian control of the war effort were a reality, he would not be without a job. Furthermore, within twenty-four hours of his return to Paris Sarrail conferred with Paul Painlevé, leader of the Republican Socialist party, Radical-Socialist Deputy Pascal Ceccaldi, and Radical Left Deputy Joseph Noulens, apparently hoping that the politicians could save his position. What transpired at these hurried conferences is not clear, except that several Radical and Socialist deputies told Sarrail that they were determined "not to yield . . . to the whims of the Podesta of Chantilly."[10]

And Sarrail's supporters did not yield, for as the general observed, his demotion "had awakened the dozing Parliamentarians."[11] On the evening of July 23 a worried Viviani told Poincaré that "the Chamber is in an unbelievable state of agitation. [Maurice] Viollette,[12] on the one hand, and the Socialists, on the other, have tried to see me all day in order to protest the measure directed against Sarrail." The bewildered premier, having underestimated the unexpectedly strong parliamentary outcry, quickly reiterated a political fact of life: "We must live with the Chambers." Reacting hurriedly to the left-wing parliamentary pressure, Viviani dispatched Millerand and Doumergue to Chantilly on the morning of July 24 for the express purpose of persuading Joffre to give Sarrail the command of the Army of Lorraine. Joffre told the ministerial delegation that the request could not be granted because the command of the Army of Lorraine had already been given to General Augustin Gérard. The two ministers rushed back to Paris and informed the Cabinet of Joffre's decision.[13]

The Cabinet members were fully aware at their meeting of July 24 that "emotions are running high in the Chamber . . . [and] that on the Left there is a general outcry against Millerand and that in addition to Millerand [the Left] is aiming at the General in Chief and the government." Sarrail's resignation could not, therefore, be accepted. Desperately seeking to fend off the deputies, the Cabinet refused to allow any interpellation concerning the Sarrail affair. At the same time, the Cabinet, groping for a solution to the crisis, dispatched Sarraut to Sarrail's residence at the Hôtel du Louvre. Sarraut's instructions were threefold: to persuade Sarrail to reconsider his refusal to command the Eastern Expeditionary Corps; to emphasize the importance of the Dardanelles and the necessity of taking Constantinople as quickly as possible; and to suggest strongly that if Sarrail accepted the command, the manpower of the French Expeditionary Corps, which comprised but two divisions, would be increased.[14] Sarrail stubbornly refused the offer, maintaining that if the government still had confidence in him, he should be reinstated as commander of the Third Army.[15]

Immediately following Sarraut's visit on the evening of July 24, Pierre Renaudel, leader of the Socialist party, and Henry Franklin-Bouillon, chairman of the Executive Committee of the Radical-Socialist party and vice-president of the Chamber Army Commission, made hurried calls to Sarrail's residence. The deputies attempted to convince the general to accept the new post. They informed him that all attempts to rescind Joffre's decision had failed and that it was no longer possible for Sarrail to have a command on the Western front. In addition, Franklin-Bouillon promised that everything would be done to promote Sarrail's candidacy as supreme commander of the Anglo-French Eastern Expedition; many of the Radical-Socialists believed that Sarrail's appointment as Allied commander of the Eastern Expeditionary Corps would serve "as compensation . . . for the slur cast on his reputation by his removal from his command, and as a snub to General Joffre whom they hate."[16]

Later in the evening Sarrail's political supporters arranged a meeting between the general and Aristide Briand, minister of justice and Independent deputy from the Loire. Briand reiterated Sarraut's earlier message, claiming that the government had every intention of reinforcing its Dardanelles forces. But Briand did more than that: if the Eastern command were accepted, Briand assured Sarrail that he would attempt to prevent the G.Q.G. from undertaking further unwarranted and unjustified actions against him.[17] In addition, Briand may have done nothing to dampen the prospect that if England's consent were forthcoming, Sarrail would have the supreme command at the Dardanelles. Sarrail immediately agreed to accept command of an enlarged French Expeditionary Corps; however, he emphasized to Briand that he would assume the command "only after the increase had been carried out."[18] Sarrail would quickly discover that his skepticism regarding reinforcements was well founded.

The events of July 20-24 did much more than intensify the latent conflicts between the government, the High Command, and the left-wing parliamentarians. A new dimension was added to the French

political scene. Partisan political considerations, which had played the
dominant role during the events of July 20-24, were to become, in the
ensuing months, a key factor in French political and military life, and
in so doing, threatened to shatter the tenuous *union sacrée*. Reflecting
the quickly emerging partisan orientation of French wartime politics,
Socialist editor Gustave Hervé warned that since "the pride of the
whole Republican Party" had been unjustly disgraced, the Left would
adhere to the *union sacrée* only on certain conditions: Sarrail must be
given a new command and parliamentary control of the army must be
reestablished. Sarrail's demotion had revealed, at least to the Left, the
dangers of giving Joffre a free hand.[19] But as long as Millerand remained unresponsive to the politicians and as long as he continued to
shield Joffre from the investigating commissions, effective parliamentary control of the G.Q.G. was impossible. Thus, in the three weeks
following the Sarrail-Briand agreement of July 24, Radicals and
Socialists privately informed Viviani and Poincaré that Millerand must
be replaced by a minister more willing to support Parliament's wishes
before the High Command. However, as Poincaré noted, parliamentary control of the army could lead to a crisis within the High
Command, possibly forcing Joffre to resign.[20]

Addressing the Chamber on August 20, Millerand decided to answer his left-wing critics and for the first time *l'affaire Sarrail* emerged
in public parliamentary debate. To charges that he had abdicated to
the High Command, the war minister emphasized that Joffre had not
only been absolutely loyal to the republic, but that he was always in
the forefront of those who fought against attempts at personal power.
As regards parliamentary control, Millerand reasoned that to allow
military authority complete freedom of action in no way implied that
parliamentary control was being suppressed. But Millerand startled
the Chamber when he criticized those deputies who had discreetly in-
quired concerning Sarrail's dismissal. Some of these deputies, "not
afraid of interjecting political interests" into the issue, were "apparently unaware that they thereby created the most dangerous precedent by
authorizing themselves . . . to judge chiefs other than by their military
qualifications." Despite Millerand's provocative statement, the Left
refused to discuss *l'affaire Sarrail* in open debate. Franklin-Bouillon
reminded his colleagues that "everyone here, regardless of party or of
the political question[Sarrail affair], has no other concern than the nation's defense and an absolute victory."[21]

Yet there is little question that the war minister's "untimely refer-
ence to the Sarrail affair" aggravated the ever-widening gulf between

the government and its left-wing critics; by publicly alluding to *l'affaire*, Millerand "broke the agreement . . . between the Cabinet and the two groups of the extreme Left."[22] Frantically attempting to seal the cracks in the *union sacrée*, Viviani delivered an emotional speech to the Chamber on August 26 in which he beseeched the deputies to lay aside political differences and to unite until the war had been won.[23]

The fate of the Viviani government rested, however, not on patriotic platitudes, but on its ability to satisfy the demands of the left-wing parliamentarians in order that the *union sacrée* be maintained. But throughout the summer and autumn of 1915, the greatest obstacle to a politics of consensus and the preservation of the *union sacrée* still centered on General Sarrail.

On August 3, ten days following the Sarrail-Briand agreement, Millerand summoned the general to the rue Saint-Dominique in order to make plans for the Dardanelles campaign. Asked to present his "desiderata," Sarrail set forth three demands. First, there would have to be formed an army that would take the name of the Eastern Army. Second, Sarrail did not want to be under the orders of the British generals as had his predecessors, Generals Albert d'Amade and Henri Gouraud. Third and most important, he demanded reinforcements. In the following weeks he refused the suggestions of Millerand and Joffre that he depart for the Dardanelles to examine the field conditions; Sarrail feared that once he had left France without an extra four divisions, "not one gun, not one cannon would have been sent to me." Isolated in the eastern Mediterranean with no reinforcements, he would have accomplished nothing, a situation which, according to Sarrail, may not have displeased Millerand.[24]

Sarrail's request for reinforcements was certainly not unreasonable in light of the bizarre events occurring in the Dardanelles. In January, 1915, the British government of Herbert Henry Asquith decided to push its way through the Dardanelles by destroying the forts overlooking the Straits. It was expected that Constantinople would fall within a few weeks. In February the Turkish forts on the southern tip of the Gallipoli Peninsula were successfully silenced by the combined Anglo-French squadrons, but in mid-March the Allied navy incurred a spectacular defeat as it failed to reduce the forts overlooking the Narrows. Consequently, the Allies decided to employ ground troops and in mid-April General Ian Hamilton's divisions and the two French divisions under General d'Amade stormed the tip of Gallipoli and gained a beachhead, but could not dislodge the enemy. After the arrival of fresh troops, Hamilton ordered a second assault on Gallipoli in

early August. Ten days later the British acknowledged that their landing at Anzac and Suvla Bay had failed. Hamilton and Gouraud,
Amade's successor, once again called for additional manpower.[25]

After considering Sarrail's demands of August 3, Millerand again
summoned him to the War Ministry. On August 5 the war minister
told Sarrail that he was officially named commander of the French
Eastern Army. However, nothing was said of Sarrail's relationship to
the English command at the Dardanelles. Even more disquieting was
Millerand's ambiguity concerning the question of reinforcements; he
declared that Sarrail "would not go to the Dardanelles if the Expeditionary Corps were not increased." The war minister's statement,
according to Sarrail, was "in flagrant contradiction" with Briand's
earlier promise that the government would send reinforcements if
Sarrail promised to assume the Dardanelles command. The disap-
pointing conference concluded with Millerand's admonition to the
general: "Don't hang around with the deputies."[26]

Millerand's evasiveness concerning the question of reinforcements
was easily explained. Joffre refused to send four additional divisions
to the Dardanelles. On August 3 he formally set forth his reasons: the
Western front was not strong enough to permit any reductions from
that theater; the Dardanelles campaign had been a fiasco and there
was no guarantee that four additional divisions could change the outcome of the expedition; no adequate plans had been set forth for the
campaign, for, while asking "where are we going?", Joffre observed
that "we have not determined . . . either the landing spot, the final
objective to be sought, or the difficulties we shall face."[27] In addition,
the government's appointment of Sarrail as commander of the French
Eastern Army apparently hardened Joffre's opposition to release the
additional divisions.[28] After all, as he had said to Poincaré, "What do
you want to do in the Dardanelles? Launch an expedition for a
factious general?"[29]

But Sarrail was not the only one demanding reinforcements for his
Dardanelles campaign. Concerned that Sarrail might be associated
with an ill-fated campaign, left-wing deputies advised him "not to accept a command offered under conditions which make success impossible." They reminded him further that if he were to become entangled
in a military debacle, it would "give the worst enemies of France and
the Republic another opportunity to carry out their criminal maneuvers successfully."[30] The Left wanted Sarrail's reputation as one of
the victors of the Marne to remain unblemished so that if Joffre were
forced to resign, Sarrail could become commander in chief of the

French armies.[31] Thus in order to decrease the probability of failure, Radicals and Socialists once again intervened on Sarrail's behalf. On August 13, a delegation from the Chamber's Army, Navy, and Foreign Affairs Commissions, headed by their respective chairmen, Pédoya, Painlevé, and Georges Leygues, Democratic Left deputy from the Lot-et-Garonne, visited Poincaré. The deputies' message was simple—immediate reinforcements were needed for the Eastern Army. Undoubtedly aware that all three chairmen were not only ardent supporters, but also personal friends of Sarrail, Poincaré, accompanied by Viviani and Millerand, went to Chantilly the next day. The president told Joffre that the Chamber Commissions believed that a greatly expanded Eastern force was urgently needed. Joffre replied that he planned a major offensive in Champagne for mid-September and that he would need all necessary troops; however, once the offensive was completed he would send Sarrail the four additional divisions.[32]

Joffre's promise to send four divisions to the Dardanelles in mid-September did not satisfy the Left. On August 25 the Army, Navy, and Foreign Affairs Commissions addressed a letter to all Cabinet members denouncing the government's failure to send immediately four or five French divisions to the Dardanelles. Receiving no response from Viviani, the three commissions on August 27 adopted a resolution once again demanding that French reinforcements be sent to the Dardanelles.[33] Prodded by the persistent parliamentarians, Viviani and Poincaré emphatically told Joffre the next day that the immediate transport of reinforcements to the Dardanelles was indispensable. The commander in chief countered that he needed the four divisions for his upcoming offensive; if, however, the four divisions were not employed by September 20-22, that is, from five to seven days following his scheduled Champagne offensive, they would be sent to the Dardanelles.

At the Cabinet meeting of August 31 a letter from Painlevé was read. Viviani and Millerand were requested to appear before a meeting of the three Chamber Commissions in order to explain the government's policy in the Dardanelles. The Cabinet, responding to Painlevé's note, ordered the departure of four divisions for the Dardanelles by September 20 thus increasing France's Eastern Army to six divisions. Minister of Foreign Affairs Théophile Delcassé, member of the Radical Left party from the Ariège, promptly notified England that French reinforcements would be forthcoming and asked for transport assistance. No sooner had the British been informed of the French decisions, however, than Joffre notified Viviani that he could not release the four divisions on September 20 as he had earlier promised. The Champagne offensive was to be delayed until September 25; therefore, Sarrail's reinforcements could not be sent until early October. The government agreed to Joffre's latest decision if only because he once again threatened to resign if his views were not upheld.[34]

In light of the conflicting decisions of the previous days, an Anglo-French conference was held at Calais on September 11. The purpose of the conference, which was attended by Joffre, Millerand, Sarrail, General French, commander in chief of the British forces in France, and British War Minister Horatio Kitchener, was to determine exactly when, where, and how many French and British reinforcements should be dispatched to the Dardanelles. Although Kitchener wanted to pursue an active policy at the Dardanelles, the conference settled very little primarily because Joffre refused to send the four French divisions eastward until the forthcoming offensive in France had been undertaken. The French commander in chief maintained that if the offensive were successful, there would be no necessity to send the additional French troops to Gallipoli. If, however, the western offensive were unsuccessful, he tentatively agreed to begin dispatching four French divisions eastward on October 10; however, he strongly cautioned that if his offensive were to fail, all available manpower might be needed on the Western front, thereby depriving the Dardanelles campaign of French reinforcements.

Despite its inconclusiveness, the Calais Conference was both interesting and important. First, Franklin-Bouillon's July 24 promise to Sarrail had been fulfilled; at Calais, Millerand, obviously reacting to domestic political pressures, asked that Sarrail be given the supreme command of the Dardanelles expedition. Kitchener refused this request on the grounds that the British general at Gallipoli, Hamilton, not only had greater experience at the Dardanelles than had Sarrail, but that he had the larger number of troops under his command. In an attempt to reach a compromise on the question of command, the conferees, including Sarrail, agreed that if at a future date Sarrail's forces were to operate on the Asiatic side of the Straits while Hamilton remained at Gallipoli, the two commanding officers would have independent commands. Any differences that might arise between the two generals would be referred to their respective governments.[35]

Second, Calais introduced Sarrail to the British High Command; unfortunately it was not a successful debut. Whatever confidence

Kitchener may have had in Sarrail was quickly dissipated when Joffre told the British war minister that he "had no confidence in Sarrail."[36] In addition, Kitchener, who had previously been told that Sarrail had a good deal of political support from France's "extreme radicals,"[37] now discovered at first hand the impact of French domestic politics upon the Dardanelles campaign. The British government, which, upon receiving Delcassé's message of August 31, had been "amazed that, on the very eve of a joint major offensive on the Western Front the French Government should propose to add four divisions to the two they already had at Gallipoli," now learned at the Calais Conference that France's offer to send four divisions had been dictated largely by political considerations. It is not surprising that Kitchener "took a dislike" to Sarrail.[38]

Ten days after the Calais Conference Joffre notified the Cabinet that he could not promise that the four divisions intended for the Dardanelles could be sent there in mid-October; the expedition, according to Joffre, contained "serious risks of failure and might lead us to additional shipments of reinforcements that would endanger the very security of our national territory." A disbelieving Viviani, caught between the irreconcilable dictates of the High Command and the left-wing politicians, could only cry out: "The Dardanelles operations will not be carried out. The G.Q.G. does not want it because General Sarrail is the commander."[39] Viviani was correct on at least one point—Sarrail never went to the Dardanelles, for on September 22 King Ferdinand ordered the mobilization of the Bulgarian army, and a staunch member of the Entente, Serbia, once again facing extinction, asked the Allies to send military assistance.

Bulgaria's decision to join the Central Powers was but another painful reminder that Allied policy in the Balkans had been little more than a series of blunders. Throughout the first year of the war Delcassé and British Foreign Secretary Sir Edward Grey had many opportunities to induce the Balkan neutrals, Rumania, Bulgaria, and Greece, to join the Entente. But all of the proposals put forth by the Entente failed to entice the Balkan neutrals. Meanwhile, in the summer of 1915, Generals Erich von Falkenhayn and Conrad von Hötzendorf, the chiefs of the German and Austrian General Staffs respectively, decided that if Turkey were to be an effective ally, supplies and reinforcements would have to move freely through Belgrade and Nish to Constantinople; this meant that Serbia had to be defeated. Hence, on September 6 Germany and Austria signed a secret treaty with Bulgaria wherein the two Central Powers agreed to cross the Danube and the

Sava and attack Serbia from the north, while Bulgaria attacked the Serbs from the east. With Serbia eliminated, Germany could help hard-pressed Turkey, and Bulgaria would realize her old dream of a "Greater Bulgaria."

By September 20 the Serbian General Staff correctly guessed the imminent Austro-German-Bulgarian offensive. The Serbs thus proposed an immediate preventive strike against Bulgaria; if successful against Bulgaria in the east, the Serbs would then turn north to await the Austro-German blow. But on September 22, despite the Bulgarian mobilization order, Delcassé and Grey not only dissuaded Serbia from its preventive attack, but also unrealistically persisted in offering Serbian Macedonia to Bulgaria. Sofia, however, was committed to an irreversible policy.[40]

Bulgaria's mobilization directly affected Greece, for Greece was bound to Serbia by a 1913 treaty that stipulated that if either country were attacked by Bulgaria, Greece would supply 90,000 troops and Serbia would supply 150,000. In September, 1915, however, King Constantine and the Greek General Staff felt that they were not obligated to fulfill their terms of the treaty because Serbia, faced with an attack by Austro-German forces in the north, could not supply the 150,000 men needed to fight Bulgaria. But Greece's Liberal prime minister, the Ententophile Eleutherios Venizelos, recently victorious at the polls, asked France and England on September 22 to supply the 150,000 men; Venizelos assured the Allies that if they did so, Greece would honor her commitment to Serbia. On September 23 France agreed to Venizelos's request, and as an advance installment to what the Viviani government hoped would be the first of six French divisions sent to the Balkans, General Maurice Bailloud's 156th Division was ordered from Gallipoli to Salonika.[41] London quickly followed suit and transferred General Bryan Mahon's Tenth Division from the Dardanelles to Salonika. However, no sooner had the transfer orders been dispatched than on October 1 Venizelos informed the Allies that he would not authorize an Allied landing at Salonika.[42] Venizelos's pro-Entente policy was meeting resistance from Constantine, Greece's Germanophile king.

Meanwhile Sarrail, who had been spending the last several weeks preparing strategy for the prospective Dardanelles campaign, was notified on September 29 that he and a French brigade would be departing immediately for Salonika.[43] Requested to formulate a detailed plan of operations for his new mission, Sarrail promptly replied that with three brigades, that is, Bailloud's division and the recently assigned brigade from France, the French could only play a defensive role, holding at best a section of the Nish-Salonika railway. Sarrail, however, urged a much more ambitious project than this; if the French Eastern Army were comprised of at least three corps as "had been anticipated" and as Millerand "had alluded to," a massive offensive against Bulgaria could be undertaken. While 30,000 British troops remained in Greece protecting the line of communication between Salonika and the Serbian border, five or six French divisions could move into Serbia and then strike quickly northeastward to Sofia in order "to put Bulgaria out of commission."[44]

Joffre, however, totally opposed Sarrail's ambitious Balkan offensive. Reaffirming his Western orientation, Joffre argued that France was the principal theater of the war and that any operation in another area was secondary and therefore must be treated in the "most economical way." Nevertheless, he recognized that the Allies could not remain idle as Serbia was overrun. But it was England that was to have the mission of eventually supporting the military engagement of the Balkan powers; France should commit only two or three divisions to the Balkans "so that the French flag is represented in the Balkan peninsula just as it is now in the Gallipoli peninsula."[45] Allied strategy, according to Joffre, should be defensive; the Anglo-French troops should limit themselves to preventing the Serbs from being crushed by guaranteeing them an opening to the sea and possibly an area of retreat.[46]

Joffre's recommendations were fully adopted by the Viviani government, for after five weeks of fruitless negotiations with the commander in chief, it was obvious that a crisis within the High Command would ensue if the government continued to insist that more than three French divisions should partake in a secondary theater. Thus, on October 3, only hours after receiving Joffre's latest suggestions, Millerand sent Sarrail instructions concerning the scope of the Balkan expedition. The basic purpose of Sarrail's Eastern Army was a defensive one: to defend the lines of communication between Salonika and Serbia against Bulgarian attacks. The French government, hoping to save Serbia from annihilation, believed that if the Serbs could successfully retreat into southern Serbia and then form a defensive position there, they could be supplied from the sea by the Salonika-Nish railway.[47]

Joffre and the French government were mistaken, however, to believe that England was prepared to shoulder the burden of Sarrail's campaign. An Allied conference held at Calais on October 5 revealed that England had serious reservations concerning the entire Balkan project. Although agreeing to send five British divisions to the Balkans, Kitchener maintained that eight Allied divisions, 150,000 troops, could not rescue Serbia unless the Allies also had the military support of Greece. Kitchener and Arthur Balfour, first lord of the Admiralty, contended at Calais that England was sending five divisions to Salonika not to offer direct immediate military assistance to Serbia, but in response to Venizelos's earlier request that if the Allies supplied 150,000 troops, Greece would honor its prewar treaty with Serbia and thereby declare war against Bulgaria; therefore, when the five British divisions arrived at Salonika, they were to remain there until Greece had irrevocably committed herself to the Entente. Millerand, on the other hand, declared at Calais that French troops, once disembarking at Salonika, would immediately strike northward into Serbia without waiting either for English assistance or for Greece to forego her neutrality.[48]

There was also disagreement in Greece. On October 5, as the first British and French troops from Gallipoli were disembarking at Salonika and on the very day when the Allies were disagreeing at Calais on the exact role of the Balkan expedition, Venizelos was forced to resign. The Germanophile Constantine and his General Staff, opposing the Liberal prime minister's pro-Entente policy, reaffirmed Greece's intention to remain neutral.[49] Emboldened by Greece's declaration of neutrality, Bulgaria attacked eastern Serbia on October 7, while Austro-German troops attacked from the north. Serbia faced a hopeless situation.

Despite the sudden turn of events in Greece, the disunity within the Allied camp, and the obviously illegal act of landing troops in a neutral country, the French government was determined to undertake a Balkan campaign: Serbia had to be saved in order to prevent the establishment of communications between Turkey and the Central Powers; an Allied victory was desperately needed in the fall of 1915 when both the Dardanelles campaign and Joffre's latest offensive were faltering; the presence of Allied troops in the Balkans could possibly encourage neutralist Rumania to join the Entente camp; last, the Viviani government was fully aware that if the Balkan campaign were canceled, Sarrail would have been without a prominent field command and any abatement of the political crisis created by Sarrail's dismissal in July would have evaporated. Thus, Millerand notified Sarrail on October 6 that he was to depart immediately for Salonika with one brigade and a cavalry division; these forces together with the two undermanned French divisions at the Dardanelles destined for Salonika gave Sarrail three full French divisions, far fewer than the six to eight divisions that he had requested.[50]

Concerned about the manpower inadequacy of the Eastern Army, Radical-Socialist deputy from the Aisne, Léon Accambray, and Radical Left deputy from the Indre, Paul Bénazet, attempted to persuade Sarrail "not to throw himself into the Eastern hornet's nest." Nevertheless, Sarrail embarked at Marseilles on October 7, determined that "it could not be said that I shirked the most thankless duty." As he set sail for the Balkans with his scanty forces, fully aware that "many people would have wanted me to object so as to get rid of me definitively under this pretext," one thought appeared foremost in his mind: "The G.Q.G. and the war minister had achieved their goal—I was thrown out of France."[51] But he at least had received one consolation: as commander of the French Eastern Army, he would not serve under Joffre's orders; instead he would report directly to the war minister.

The government and the G.Q.G. badly miscalculated the political situation when they believed that *l'affaire Sarrail* would evaporate once Sarrail were given a command and sent out of the country. On the evening of October 6, as Sarrail was departing for Marseilles, Franklin-Bouillon, Pédoya, Painlevé, and Charles Chaumet, Democratic Left deputy from the Gironde, met with Viviani. The deputies demanded a major Balkan commitment irrespective of what England, Joffre, and the Westerners advocated, for to send Sarrail to the Balkans with three divisions was "absolutely insufficient and ridiculous"; the government was sending "Sarrail and his troops to the slaughter-house." As the deputies prepared to leave the conference, they gave the shaken premier open warning: "If you want to avert real trouble, you haven't a minute to lose in order to correct the mistakes of our diplomacy and to shake off your inertia and show some energy."[52]

Viviani scarcely needed a reminder that a Balkan army of several hundred thousand men was a prerequisite for the maintenance of the *union sacrée*. But Joffre would release no more than three divisions; thus Viviani once again turned to England for assistance.[53] On October 6 the Dardanelles Committee considered and then rejected French pleas for large-scale British military assistance for a Balkan campaign. Now that Venizelos had been forced to resign, the British High Command and most of the Cabinet, with the notable exception of Minister of Munitions David Lloyd George, agreed with Prime

Minister Asquith that the Balkan campaign was nothing more than "a wild goose affair"; to send Allied forces northward into Serbia without the support of Greece would be, according to Winston Churchill, "sheer madness," for "the communications of our force would run through and be at the mercy of Greece, which had a pro-German King, a pro-German Queen, and was about to have a pro-German Government." Thus, in an obvious repudiation of its agreement with France taken twenty-four hours earlier at Calais, the Dardanelles Committee decided on October 6 that no British troops, other than the advanced units of General Mahon's Tenth Division, which had been dispatched from the Dardanelles and had already arrived at Salonika, would be sent to the Balkans.[54]

On October 7, the day following his conference with Franklin-Bouillon, Pédoya, Chaumet, and Painlevé, Premier Viviani arrived in London and proposed that England supply 330,000 of the 400,000 men needed in the Balkans.[55] England again rejected the latest French proposals, maintaining that Greek cooperation was necessary before Britain sanctioned a sizable commitment to the Balkans.[56] Realizing that Viviani's plans for a large-scale Balkan campaign did not have Joffre's support, Kitchener immediately went to Chantilly to consult the French commander in chief and once again there was no agreement concerning the manpower requirements of the Balkan campaign. Kitchener claimed that 250,000 troops would be necessary to save Serbia and 400,000 men would be needed if the Allies should decide to carry out a major Balkan offensive. Joffre reiterated that the Allies could not afford to wage a major campaign in both the West and in the Balkans; he believed, however, that a combined Anglo-French force of 150,000 would be sufficient for a decisive defensive role, namely to assure Serbia's line of communication with Salonika.[57]

Kitchener promised to refer Joffre's plans to the British government for consideration but in the interim, the British war minister, in an attempt to minimize the obvious differences between the two countries, revoked his government's decision of October 6 and tentatively agreed to dispatch a few British divisions from the Western front to Salonika.[58] However, upon returning to London, Kitchener quickly discovered that the government would not support his Chantilly decision. Asquith told an October 11 meeting of the Dardanelles Committee that under no conditions would additional British troops be sent to the Balkans. Consequently, on October 14 Kitchener notified the Viviani government that two British divisions would be withdrawn from the Somme, but their destination would be Egypt—not Salonika.[59]

Poincaré's wry assessment of London's latest decision—"It is not the time for a trip to Egypt"[60]—was fully shared by Viviani. The *union sacrée* was again threatened. The only way that Viviani could alleviate the domestic political pressure was to assure the Left that Sarrail would not be defeated in the Balkans. An acute awareness of this basic political situation explains the premier's disingenuous announcement to the Chamber on October 12 that "France and England . . . have come to a complete agreement to send assistance to Serbia . . . [and] acting on the advice of their military authorities, agree as to the number of men required."[61] Viviani's statement, however, failed to dispel the widespread fears concerning the outcome of Sarrail's expedition. The next day, in the most acrimonious public parliamentary session since Poincaré's appeal for the *union sacrée*, left-wing deputies, led by Painlevé, focused upon the one issue that consumed them—Sarrail's Balkan expedition. Supported by Chaumet and Renaudel, Painlevé attacked the government for its failure to supply several new divisions for Sarrail's proposed Dardanelles campaign. Painlevé charged that if additional troops were not forthcoming immediately, Sarrail's Balkan campaign would be a disaster.[62]

In order to have unrestricted debate, Renaudel called for the Chamber to meet in secret session. His request was rejected by a vote of 303 to 190. Immediately following the rejection, the Chamber gave the government a vote of confidence; the tally was 372 to 9. But it is significant that more than one hundred left-wing deputies abstained from voting, for as Franklin-Bouillon stated, "a great number of my friends and I cannot at this time voice our confidence in the government."[63]

Despite the public vote of confidence, Viviani's appearance before the Chamber Foreign Affairs Commission on October 19 revealed that the government was in fact "at its last gasp."[64] Chairman of the commission Leygues began the discussion by sharply criticizing Viviani for not sending reinforcements to Gallipoli in late August. Leygues was convinced that if Bulgaria had known that 150,000 or 200,000 men were sent to Gallipoli, she would not have entered the conflict. But even if Bulgaria were not intimidated by the presence of 200,000 additional troops at the Dardanelles, these troops could have easily been shifted to the Balkans thereby rendering Serbia invaluable assistance. When Viviani lamely explained that reinforcements could not have been sent to the Dardanelles during the summer because of Joffre's upcoming Champagne offensive, an exasperated Franklin-Bouillon criticized the premier's inability to force Joffre to send several divisions eastward. Chairman Leygues concluded the lengthy session with a warning that there would be political repercussions unless Viviani forced Joffre and England to commit several hundred thousand troops to the Balkans.[65]

The insistent demand for reinforcements meant that the left-wing members of the Chamber commissions were keeping their promise to Sarrail. Alfred Margaine, Radical-Socialist from the Marne and member of the Army Commission, wrote to Sarrail in Salonika: "Let [the Army Commission] know what you are requesting [for your campaign]; let it be informed well in advance and in detail of the difficulties which you may face, and I am confident that it [the Commission] can put almost invincible pressure on the government."[66]

Once again, responding to unrelenting pressure, Viviani sent Millerand hurrying to London for the express purpose of persuading Grey to send several British divisions to the Balkans. Millerand's October 19 mission was no more successful than Viviani's had been two weeks earlier. Grey refused to commit more than the one division already at Salonika; however, England did agree that once those divisions taken from the Western front had concentrated in Egypt, the British government would reexamine the general Eastern situation.[67] Failure to secure British support was followed by disastrous news from the Balkans. On October 22 the Bulgarians took Kumanovo and Uskub, which meant that the Serbian army's communication with Sarrail was cut; the Serbs now faced encirclement.

On October 21 Viviani again asked London to commit more than one division to the Balkans.[68] Four days later, at a meeting of the Dardanelles Committee, Kitchener correctly analyzed the fundamental reason for France's latest request. There was certainly no military rationale for sending additional divisions to the Balkans, since Serbia was "practically done for"; instead, Kitchener believed that "the terms in which the note [Viviani's] was couched suggested that there was a political move behind it." General French readily concurred: "The whole story began" when following his dismissal as Third Army commander, Sarrail "worked up Socialistic influences to turn out M. Millerand, General Joffre, and the French Government. He had then been given a big command, and . . . the whole movement had been based on a desire to accentuate the importance of General Sarrail's command." Now that it was generally recognized that France's Balkan strategy was being shaped by domestic political pressures, the next question was what policy should London pursue. Lloyd George's suggestion that the French government might alter its Balkan policy if Sarrail were given a prominent command in Egypt or elsewhere was not realistic since Sarrail was then in Macedonia. Once again it was Kitchener who pinpointed the British dilemma: would "a refusal on our part to comply with French demands place the French Government in any political difficulty?" Lord Selborne, president of the Board of Agriculture and Austen Chamberlain, secretary of state for India, quickly dismissed the political implications of the problem, contending that it was senseless to embark upon a hopeless military campaign simply to save Millerand, Joffre, and the Viviani government. "It was more," retorted Kitchener. "It was to save the Alliance; that if we were to break with France the war would be over." Despite Kitchener's sense of urgency, the Dardanelles Committee continued to move extremely cautiously; although reaffirming its earlier decision that additional divisions concentrating in Egypt could be utilized for possible deployment elsewhere, it decided that pending further consultations between the Allied military chiefs, Britain would have no more than one division in the Balkans.[69]

The Viviani government was caught in a bind. Those left-wing deputies who had saved Sarrail in July and had forced the government to give him a new command, now demanded that his army be supplied with adequate forces. Despite Viviani's requests, London and Joffre had refused to grant the necessary troops; this lack of support meant that Sarrail's army apparently faced a calamity now that Serbia was being overrun. On October 25, the day before his scheduled appearance before Pédoya's hostile Army Commission,[70] Viviani told Poincaré that he was prepared to resign. Poincaré then asked Briand to form a new government.[71]

Although indicating that he would resign, Viviani, who still had a majority in the Chamber, apparently believed that he could restore the *union sacrée* and thereby save his government. Realizing that it would be several days before a new Cabinet could be pieced together, the premier made one last frantic attempt to gain British support for the Balkan campaign, evidently believing that if he could persuade London to commit several divisions to the Balkans, left-wing pressure would subside. In this last-minute attempt to save his government, Viviani received energetic assistance from an unexpected source— Joffre.

As early as October 23 Viviani explained to the commander in chief that "the Cabinet situation is critical."[72] Apprised of the intense political pressure generated by Sarrail's supporters who were demanding a large-scale Balkan campaign, Joffre now realized that if these demands were not satisfied, the government might collapse and consequently his position would be at stake. Joffre, the Westerner who for months had resisted all attempts to undertake large-scale operations in the Dardanelles and in the Balkans, now urged the English to dispatch four additional divisions to Salonika, which would have brought British strength there to five divisions. When the chief of the Imperial General Staff, General Archibald Murray, rejected the French commander in chief's request, maintaining that it was too late to save Serbia, Joffre left for London on October 28[73] and at a conference held the next day at 10 Downing Street, he requested that England send an additional four divisions to the Balkans in order to prevent the total collapse of the Serbian army. He emphasized that the five British divisions would play a limited defensive role in the Balkans; they would simply guard the railway leading from Salonika to the Serbian border while Sarrail's three divisions would move northward against Bulgaria in an attempt to reestablish communications with the Serbian army. When Joffre's military presentation won little support, he intensified the pressure: he made it be known that his retention as commander in chief of the French army, and even the permanence of the Alliance itself, would depend on the reply of the British government. London yielded to these threats; on October 30 Kitchener agreed to dispatch four additional divisions to Salonika with the understanding that if communication with the Serbian army were not opened and maintained, the Allied forces would be withdrawn.[74]

Joffre had succeeded in his mission. But before he could return to Paris with his victory, Briand had succeeded during the evening of October 29 in forming a new ministry—the Viviani government had become the first casualty of l'affaire Sarrail.[75] Both Premier Briand and his war minister, General' Joseph Galliéni, were longtime advocates of a massive Balkan campaign. And in the autumn of 1915 only a government headed by Easterners, a government committed not only to a Balkan campaign but one that possessed the apparent resolve to override Joffre and London's objections to an Eastern campaign, could have preserved the union sacrée.[76]

V. Vardar and Politics

There's an appalling amount to do here with five [British] divisions pouring in, in no sort of order: no plan, no policy: no answer to questions: Nothing known! . . . What they are all coming for—heaven knows, or anyhow the British Cabinet certainly does not.
— GENERAL PHILIP HOWELL *to his wife, Rosalind, November 27, 1915*

Rest assured that here we will continue to watch over everything concerning our dear Eastern Army with the most ardent solicitude.
— LEON BOURGEOIS *to Sarrail's brother, Maurice, January 3, 1916*

General Bailloud's 156th Division and Mahon's Tenth Division, dispatched from Gallipoli, began disembarking at Salonika on October 5, 1915. The unplanned haste of the expedition, accompanied by the diplomatic and political uncertainties in London and Paris, was immediately felt in Salonika. Bailloud was ordered to use the single track railway running alongside the Vardar River in order to establish contact with the beleaguered Serbian army at Nish. But no sooner had the 156th Division begun its journey than it was ordered to fall back upon Salonika and await the arrival of General Sarrail. General Mahon, taking orders directly from London, was also instructed by his government not to leave Salonika.[1]

Sarrail and the advanced units of the 57th Division sailed from Toulon on October 7 and arrived at Salonika five days later. Determined "to show that we came to accomplish something,"[2] Sarrail immediately requested permission from Millerand to cross the Serbo-Greek frontier. The request was approved. On October 14 Sarrail ordered a brigade of the 156th Division northward into Serbia with the limited objective of securing the Vardar railroad from Gevgeli to the

[75]

Strumitza Station. On October 19 Bailloud had established his head-quarters at the Strumitza Station, sixteen miles beyond the Serbo-Greek border and just west of the Bulgarian border. For the next seven days Bailloud, with some difficulty, deployed his forces east of the Vardar and drove the Bulgarians from Rabrovo and Tartali, thus guaranteeing the security of the railway from Gevgeli to the Strumitza Station.

After much pleading from Sarrail, on October 26, Mahon, whose command was completely independent of Sarrail's, received permission from Kitchener to cross the frontier; the Tenth Division, taking up positions between Kostorino and Lake Dojran, relieved the 156th Division and thus allowed Bailloud's division to move five miles further north through mountainous country to Gradec.

On October 23 Paris ordered Sarrail to move up the Vardar to establish contact in the north with the Serbs, who were near Uskub and Veles, and, at the same time Sarrail was reminded not to lose contact with Salonika. Sarrail sent General Paul Leblois's 57th Division up the Vardar, past Gradec, through the treacherous Demir Kapu defile to Krivolak, twenty miles southeast of Veles. By the end of October Leblois had secured the Krivolak railhead by taking Kara Hodjali, which overlooked Krivolak from the north. In addition, as General Charles de Lardemelle's 122nd Division began landing at Salonika on November 1, Sarrail immediately ordered it up the line beyond Krivolak to the Cerna-Vardar junction, fourteen miles south of Veles. But on the same day the Serbs lost Veles.[3]

On November 4, with only three French divisions and Mahon's Tenth Division at his disposal, Sarrail wired Galliéni: "It is necessary to increase the number of troops in order to do something here. . . . I am therefore again requesting that reinforcements be increased to four army corps."[4] But according to Joffre's London agreement of October 30, the terms of which were still unknown to Sarrail, the French would supply only three divisions to the Balkan campaign, the British five. However, the other four British divisions had not arrived. London, still not convinced that the Serbians could be saved, had yet to order to Salonika three of the four additional divisions that had been promised to Joffre on October 30.[5]

Sarrail could not wait until reinforcements leisurely arrived, for the Serbs were quickly retreating southwesterly toward Prilep. Therefore, Sarrail attempted an extremely risky maneuver. He ordered Leblois's 57th Division to leave the Krivolak railhead, cross the Cerna River, and strike westward in order to attack the left flank of the Bulgarian

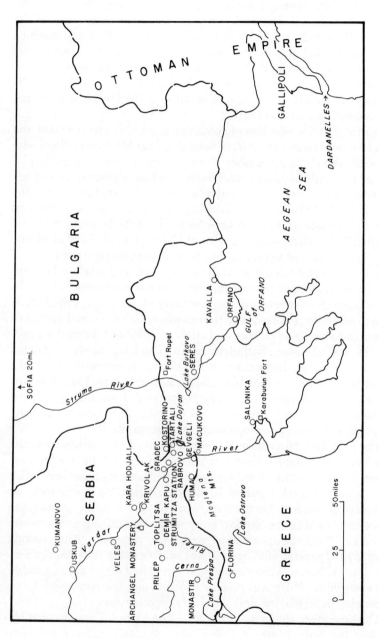

OTTOMAN EMPIRE

GALLIPOLI

DARDANELLES →

AEGEAN SEA

BULGARIA

SOFIA 20mi.

Struma River

Fort Rupel

Lake Butkovo

KAVALLA

ORFANO

GULF of ORFANO

SERES

Karaburun Fort

SALONIKA

KOSTORINO
TARTALI
Lake Dojran
GRADEC
RABROVO
GEVGELI
MACUKOVO

River

KUMANOVO

SERBIA

KARA HODJALI

KRIVOLAK

DEMIR KAPU
TOPLITSA
STRUMITZA STATION
HUMA
Moglena Mts.

Lake Ostrovo

ARCHANGEL MONASTERY

PRILEP

USKUB

Vardar

VELES

River

FLORINA

Cerna

MONASTIR

Lake Prespa

GREECE

Macedonia

0   25   50 miles

forces, which were advancing from Veles southward to Prilep in hopes of catching the fleeing Serbian army. Leblois, supported by Larde-melle's 122nd Division, could only advance two miles west of the Cerna. Three Bulgarian divisions, supported by artillery and machine guns, controlled the heights west of the Cerna from Archangel Monastery to Toplitsa. By November 12 it was evident that the French could not advance, despite attempts by both Leblois and Lardemelle to seize Archangel, which had to be taken if the French were to advance either due west or north.[6]

Fearful that Sarrail's line of communication was overextended and that he would be separated from Salonika, War Minister Galliéni telegraphed Sarrail on November 12 to prepare to retreat from Serbia. Sarrail promptly brought his offensive to a halt. However, he did not contemplate a hasty withdrawal from Serbia; he was hoping that the British 22nd Division, which had just arrived at Salonika, could be sent to Monastir in southwestern Serbia in order to support the retreating Serbs. After a defensive front had been established at Monastir, Sarrail planned to resume the offensive with his right wing.[7]

Later, a second cable from Galliéni, received by Sarrail on November 12, revealed that the war minister was not interested in Sarrail's latest suggestion concerning the possibility of sending a British division to Monastir and resuming the offensive. Galliéni urged Sarrail to return to Salonika as quickly and safely as possible.[8] Refused support by the war minister, Sarrail turned to Painlevé, newly appointed minister of public instruction in the Briand government: "For [the benefit of] France, the Republic, and the Eastern Army, I am delighted to see you a minister. I am counting on you. I am telling you this frankly so that I may overcome all the difficulties which arise each day: my only wish is for *immediate* reinforcements."[9]

The next day, November 13, Sarrail received new orders from the rue Saint-Dominique, giving him greater latitude: "You are the best judge of the conduct of military operations and until further notice you have complete freedom in deciding upon your offensive or defensive position within the framework of your mission, [namely] to come to the aid of the Serbian army while maintaining contact with Salonika."[10] Sarrail commented somewhat bitterly: "After having been invited to return to Greece, I was left free either to remain in Serbia or to withdraw when circumstances required it; I was responsible for everything."[11] He was prepared to shoulder the responsibility of remaining in Serbia, but only if he had reinforcements.

On November 16 the war minister asked Sarrail if it were possible to join the Serbs north of Prilep, approximately halfway between

Veles and Monastir. With the 122nd Division and two regiments of the 57th Division pinned down on the banks of the Cerna, Sarrail replied that it would be impossible to advance until reinforcements were forthcoming. Sarrail again asked for four army corps and warned that if he did not have 300,000 troops, the attempt to save Serbia would collapse.[12]

The lingering illusion of having additional troops was dispelled the next day when Lord Kitchener visited Sarrail at Salonika and in a long conference between the two men, Sarrail discovered "what had always been hidden from me; General Joffre had stated that he would not give me one man more than those I had; he had persuaded the French and English ministers that 150,000 men would be enough for the Balkans."[13] Crestfallen, Sarrail wrote to Painlevé:

I have just been notified . . . that no new unit would be sent to me. . . . I am not protesting. But when Serbia is defeated . . . I do not believe that anyone will be able to think that with three divisions it is possible to hold off the entire Bulgarian army and the Austro-German army in the East—not to mention the Greek army which is scattered between Serbia and Salonika. . . . General Galliéni has ordered me to make a study for a retreat of our troops from Serbia to Salonika. If I have no reinforcements, it is certain that we can do nothing but get out. . . . There is no sense in staying in Salonika and trying to transform it into an English colony; we have only to reembark.

I wanted to keep you informed. I am not complaining; but after what I was hoping for when I saw M. Millerand fall, I confess to you that I am greatly heartbroken. It was possible to do something, but because of the lack of troops and the lack of any decision taken in time, nothing will have been accomplished.[14]

Painlevé could do nothing for Sarrail, at least for the present.[15]

With no reinforcements and three Bulgarian divisions effectively blocking the French attempt to line up with the Serbs, Sarrail could do nothing but watch the remnants of the Serbian army flee further westward. On November 23, as the Serbs began their perilous escape over the snow-capped Albanian mountains to the Adriatic coast, Sarrail ordered his troops to withdraw from Serbia.

Holding off the Bulgarians with rearguard skirmishes while at the same time receiving invaluable assistance from the British Tenth Division, the French troops began their arduous slide down the Vardar. By December 12, after two weeks of marching and intermittent fighting, the Allied divisions successfully crossed into Greece. Paris immediately ordered Sarrail to begin building an entrenched camp at Salonika.[16]

As the orderly and successful retreat to Greece was under way, Sarrail had asked Galliéni: "What role will fall upon our troops? Are they going to remain idle around Salonika? Or will they be solely concerned with setting up a temporary stronghold there? Or will they, on the contrary, have to prepare for a new engagement, be it in Thrace, in Bulgaria, or in some other spot?"[17] Field Marshal William Robertson partially answered Sarrail's question: "Of all the problems which brought soldiers and statesmen into conference during the years 1915-17 the Salonika Expedition was at once the most persistent, exasperating, and unfruitful."[18]

By temperament a conciliator, Aristide Briand possessed those attributes needed for a successful career in parliamentary politics—he was suave, adroit, eloquent, opportunistic, and above all else, supple. In his inaugural speech to the Chamber on November 3, Briand revitalized the *union sacrée* as he reaffirmed his Eastern predilections. The premier assured the deputies that France would not abandon Serbia.[19]

Three weeks later Briand clarified his Balkan policy. Addressing a joint session of the Chamber's Army and Navy Commissions on November 27, the premier announced that despite the failure to save Serbia, which after all had been the original purpose of the expedition, France was going to remain at Salonika; the presence of Allied troops would keep Salonika out of German hands as well as encourage neutralist Greece and Rumania to join the Entente. But other than remaining at Salonika, the premier was extremely uncertain as to the Allies' future course in the Balkans. While insisting that 150,000 troops, three French and five British divisions, were capable of defending the vital port town against an imminent Bulgar-German attack, he readily recognized that the 150,000 troops were insufficient to launch a Balkan offensive. He was hoping, however, that in the coming months reinforcements drawn from Italy, England, and the remnants of the Serbian army would substantially increase the eight divisions already committed to Salonika, thereby permitting the Allies to undertake large-scale offensive operations in the Balkans.[20]

Certain aspects of Briand's policy statements received a tepid reception from several left-wing deputies. Charles Chaumet, chairman of the Navy Commission, requested that the separate French and English Eastern commands be abolished and that Sarrail be named commander in chief of the Allied Eastern Army. Briand replied that the British would say to the French: "Agreed! Unified command. You have 60,000 men there and we have 90,000. We shall assume the command. What shall I answer?" Chaumet retorted: "Then increase your troops so that you have the command." Maurice Bernard and Marcel Cachin demanded that the Eastern Army be increased to 300,000 men; eight Allied divisions could not possibly hold Salonika against 400,000 enemy troops. Briand declared that it was impossible to remove additional troops from the Western front. When the premier asserted that military specialists from the G.Q.G. had reassured him that 150,000 well-entrenched troops could defend Salonika, Radical-Socialist Accambray suggested that perhaps these specialists were no more knowledgeable than those who had advised the government during the Dardanelles imbroglio. Accambray urged Briand to ask Sarrail and not the G.Q.G. specialists whether Salonika could be held with 150,000 troops. The premier promised that additional troops would be forthcoming if Sarrail requested them.[21]

Earlier in closed-door session, Socialist Vaillant had asked Briand if England were in full support of Briand's Balkan policy. The premier reassured the deputy that the British and French governments had a common Balkan policy.[22] Briand, however, had been less than candid.

Briand, in his initial relations with the British government concerning the question of the Balkans acted quickly and energetically. At an Anglo-French conference held at Paris on November 17, Briand brusquely reminded Prime Minister Asquith that three of the additional four divisions that had been promised to Joffre at the October 30 London Conference had not yet been ordered into the Balkans. Thus far England had not fulfilled the terms of the October 30 agreement, believing that it was too late to save the Serbian army irrespective of how many Allied troops were sent into the Balkans. Briand, on the other hand, considered England's dire pessimism unwarranted. The premier and Joffre maintained at the Paris Conference that if England were immediately to dispatch all the divisions that had been promised two weeks earlier, there existed a realistic possibility that the Serbian army could be rescued. England temporarily bowed to French demands and agreed to release the additional divisions for action in the Balkans. But Balfour reminded the French representatives of another aspect of the October 30 London agreement. If Sarrail were to fail to establish communications with the Serbian army, serious consideration would be given to evacuating the Balkans.[23]

Two weeks later, when Sarrail's withdrawal was underway and it had become obvious that Serbia could not be saved, the British government, in accordance with the October 30 agreement, recommended that Salonika be immediately evacuated.[24] Briand, however, was determined to remain at Salonika. Not to do so would have led to a domestic political crisis similar to the one that had forced the Viviani government to resign. To settle the obvious differences between Paris and London a conference was summoned on December 5 at Calais.

At Calais the French delegation, headed by Briand and Joffre, presented its arguments for remaining at Salonika: Greece and Rumania could be pressured to join the Entente; Serbia would possibly desert the Entente unless the Allies made a greater effort on her behalf; Italy and Russia had aspirations in the Balkans and if France and England allowed Germany to have a free hand in the Balkans, the Entente's solidarity could be seriously endangered; the 150,000 Allied troops would not only protect Salonika but would keep 400,000 Bulgar-German troops pinned down in the Balkans rather than freeing them for action on the Western and Russian fronts. Briand's persuasiveness was to no avail; Kitchener and Asquith stood firm. The French had no choice but to agree to Asquith's demand that the evacuation of the 150,000 troops at Salonika be immediately undertaken.[25]

But Briand was not dismayed. He was quite aware that all the Allied General Staffs would be meeting at Chantilly on December 6 in order to plan strategy for the upcoming year. Joffre would be presiding at the Chantilly Conference and, not surprisingly, one of the key items on the agenda would be the Salonika question.

Briand carefully prepared the groundwork for the Chantilly Conference. On December 2 Poincaré issued a decree stating that Joffre had been promoted from general in chief of the Armies of the North and Northeast to rank of commander in chief of the French armies; this meant that, whereas previously Sarrail had taken his orders directly from the War Ministry, his Eastern Army was now under Joffre's direct control. Briand explained the basic reason for Joffre's new appointment:

There is no doubt that General Joffre has considerable prestige and authority abroad and there is reason to take into account [the fact] that if the theater of Eastern operations had not been under his orders . . . General Joffre would have been singularly weakened for the conduct of the conference, [and] he would not have had the authority which it was indispensable for him to have in order to voice an opinion and have it accepted.[26]

As France's new generalissimo, Joffre did a splendid job of supporting Briand's Eastern policy at the Chantilly Conference. When General Murray attempted to justify Allied evacuation of Salonika by pointing out that 150,000 troops could neither stop a Bulgar-German attack against Salonika nor persuade Rumania to join the Entente,

Joffre immediately called upon the Russian, Italian, and Serbian representatives; all insisted that the Allies remain at Salonika. England was clearly isolated. For the second time within two months the Entente was undergoing severe strains from within.[27]

Shaken by the deadlock, War Minister Kitchener and Foreign Secretary Grey hurried to Paris on December 9 for yet another conference with Briand and Joffre. At the Paris Conference nothing was said of abandoning Salonika; instead, the British representatives agreed that for the time being the Allies should remain at Salonika.[28] Briand had emerged with his greatest wartime diplomatic triumph, and England was committed to a campaign that all her generals and most of her politicians detested.

Successful as it may have been, there was one aspect of Briand's recent policy that disturbed several left-wing deputies: the December 2 decree, which promoted Joffre to the rank of generalissimo. Minister of Public Instruction Painlevé grudgingly accepted Joffre's recent appointment, believing that Sarrail would receive reinforcements more easily if Joffre were made responsible for the Balkan front.[29] Such acquiescence, however, was not to be found elsewhere, for, as Deputy Margaine wrote to Sarrail, Briand's government "will suffer for what has been done against you."[30]

There was left-wing apprehension when Briand appeared before the Chamber Army Commission on December 18. Briand's assertion that the basic reason for Joffre's recent promotion—to improve France's bargaining position at the recently held Inter-Allied Conference at Chantilly—did not satisfy Léon Accambray and Abel Ferry. Accambray, who had recently called for Joffre's replacement by Sarrail, observed that the December 2 decree appeared to have greatly restricted Sarrail's power and initiative. Further attempting to discredit the December 2 decree, Accambray and Ferry raised the question of civilian control of the army. The two deputies emphasized that whereas previously Sarrail had reported directly to the war minister, the government, by increasing Joffre's power to include Sarrail's Eastern Army, was abdicating control over the High Command.

Briand promised that Sarrail would receive the government's complete support. The premier emphasized that although Joffre was commander in chief of the French army, he was still responsible to the war minister.[31] The premier technically was correct. But the Left's concern over the December 2 decree arose from considerations other than strictly constitutional ones: past experience had demonstrated that Joffre was less pliable to left-wing political pressure than was the civilian Cabinet.

Upon being appointed generalissimo, Joffre lost no time in planning a lightning two-stage attack against Sarrail: first, to remind Sarrail that the Eastern Army was in fact subordinate to the G.Q.G., and second, to reduce effectively Sarrail's power as commander of the French Eastern Army. On December 12 Galliéni wrote Joffre: "The government insists that you ask General Sarrail . . . the following question point-blank: 'Apart from all political and diplomatic considerations, do you think you can put up a lasting resistance with 150,000 men [at Salonika]?' " Joffre rejected the war minister's request. The generalissimo told Galliéni that General Castelnau would be sent to Salonika to determine whether 150,000 troops were adequate to defend the port.[32]

The archclericalist Curières de Castelnau, appointed chief of staff by Joffre only a few days earlier, arrived at Salonika on December 19 for a five-day inspection tour of the defensive organization of the entrenched camp. During the inspection tour, the new chief of staff recommended that 150,000 troops, three French and five British divisions, would be sufficient to hold Salonika. Upon concluding his inspection, Castelnau sent a formal report to Sarrail that emphasized that the Eastern commander should create an additional reserve division and he should construct another line of surveillance posts on the slopes north of Salonika in order to prevent enemy infiltration along the valleys. It is important to note, however, that throughout the report there is a nagging, sometimes condescending tone, as if Castelnau were lecturing a cadet. For example, Sarrail was reminded that telephone lines should be placed either on thin poles or in shallow trenches so as to maintain their preservation; he was also told to move his headquarters to the outskirts of Salonika where he and his officers would lodge in a permanently guarded enclosure.[33]

Sarrail was furious when he received Castelnau's report. "It was the seizure of the Eastern Army by the G.Q.G."[34] He immediately wrote Painlevé:

I cannot accept having orders which contain me, deprive me of all initiative, ruin my authority, even impose on me to change the position of my generals, etc., etc. I find it strange that a general [Castelnau] who has not lived through the hours which I have just spent in Salonika, who knows nothing of what has happened, and who goes to the front in order to find troops there whose recent efforts he knows nothing about, is so bold as to award, blame, or praise, to give directives ex cathedra. . . .
Please, Mr. Minister, have such anomalies stopped.[35]

Sarrail was not the only one outraged. So were the politicians. And, as a result, Joffre's second stage offensive against Sarrail would collapse.

On December 23, while Castelnau was in Salonika, Joffre wrote to Kitchener and pointed out that because an enemy attack against Salonika was a distinct possibility there should be a single commander for the eight Allied divisions situated there.[36] Kitchener agreed that there should be a unified command but, as he had consistently stated during the past two weeks, he would not permit British troops to be placed under Sarrail's command. Therefore, Kitchener suggested that the Supreme Allied Commander of the Eastern Army be either Franchet d'Esperey or Louis-Hubert Lyautey. Mahon and Sarrail would still maintain command of their respective armies, but they would take orders directly from the new Allied commander of the Eastern Army. Joffre eagerly accepted Kitchener's recommendation.[37]

When the Joffre-Kitchener proposal was submitted to the Cabinet on December 28, Poincaré recorded that there were "heated objections especially on the part of Painlevé and Léon Bourgeois."[38] Painlevé and Minister of State Bourgeois brought pressure to bear upon Briand, for as Bourgeois wrote to Sarrail's brother: "Rest assured that here we will continue to watch over everything concerning our dear Eastern Army with the most ardent solicitude."[39] Faced with a political crisis, the elastic Briand gave way to left-wing pressure and promptly informed England of "all the difficulties which the appointment of a general having authority over General Sarrail and General Mahon would create for the French government."[40] London understood Briand's difficulties;[41] on January 5, 1916, Kitchener agreed that Sarrail would assume command of the Allied Eastern Army.[42]

On January 8 Sarrail received a New Year's greeting from Painlevé:

First of all, let me send you my very hearty congratulations—or rather I should congratulate *us* concerning the distinction which has been bestowed upon you. . . . Oh! that was hard: a day of fighting. But they finally yielded; they had to yield, and that is crucial. Having yielded once on a matter which they had their hearts set on so much, they will always have to yield. . . . You are now the Commander in Chief of all the Allied forces in Salonika. The fury of our enemies only better points out their disappointment. You have in the government men who will not let you be touched under any pretext.[43]

Painlevé's letter touched upon yet another subject that in recent days had been a further cause of friction between Sarrail and the G.Q.G.

General Leblois, selected by Sarrail the previous October to command the 57th Division, had distinguished himself during the successful retreat from Serbia; consequently, in early January Sarrail recommended that he be selected a *grand officier* of the Legion of Honor. At the same time that Sarrail was submitting his recommendation on Leblois's behalf, the G.Q.G. ordered that Leblois be placed on inactive service. During his inspection tour of Salonika, Castelnau had reported to Chantilly that Leblois had not yet set up his defensive fortifications.[44]

Sarrail was stunned when informed of Leblois's recall; he claimed that Leblois was being broken because the general's brother, Antoine Leblois, had been one of Alfred Dreyfus's attorneys two decades earlier. Determined to reverse the G.Q.G.'s decision, Sarrail called upon Painlevé for assistance.[45] The letter of January 8 revealed that the minister of public instruction had been successful: "Your excellent colleagues strove to attack you by way of Leblois. . . . Luckily I was prepared, and I think that the debate—which was extremely bitter— was not to the advantage of my opponents. . . . As I write you, the question of decorations for the officers . . . is not yet settled, but I hope very much that Leblois (who is now saved) will be promoted." Painlevé concluded his interesting letter: "Do not fail to let me know the needs of your expeditionary corps (manpower, cannons, etc.) . . . . Our success in the East is essential. Nothing must be spared."[46] Sarrail immediately availed himself of Painlevé's latest offer.

After Sarrail had completed the retreat to Salonika, he requested two additional divisions; 40,000 additional troops would be needed if the Allies were to hold Salonika. Joffre, supported by Castelnau's report, refused all of Sarrail's requests, maintaining that the three French and five British divisions situated in the fortified environs of Salonika were sufficient to stop a Bulgar-German assault on the port city. On January 17, 1916, Sarrail sent yet another telegram to Joffre, once again requesting two additional French divisions. On January 17 a cable from Chantilly again informed Sarrail that immediate reinforcements would not be forthcoming; Sarrail was to consider "this decision as definitive." Joffre's cable concluded with a rebuke, reminding Sarrail "to correspond with the government only through my intermediary."[47]

Meanwhile in Paris on January 17 the politicians were again preparing to settle the latest Joffre-Sarrail conflict. Following a late evening meeting with Lieutenant Paul Bouët, Sarrail's son-in-law and staff officer, who had just arrived from Salonika, Painlevé dashed off the following letter:

Bouët visited me and disclosed the critical situation in which General Sarrail finds himself. . . . He [Bouët] asks me to tell you immediately that it is necessary to consider his information "as a real cry of alarm" from General Sarrail. The *immediate* dispatch of a division is essential, not to mention the considerable number of troops which should follow this division. But there is no time to lose and M. Bouët thinks that tomorrow morning at the Cabinet meeting you should insist on the urgency of these measures.[48]

The Cabinet met the next morning and War Minister Galliéni notified Joffre of its decision: Joffre was ordered to send the 17th Colonial Division to the Eastern Army immediately.[49] Once again the generalissimo had been overridden.

"Your position here [in Paris] is excellent," Painlevé confidently wrote to Sarrail. "They have abandoned the campaign against you, which each time becomes a retreat with losses—all of which does not mean that we must be lulled to sleep."[50] Sarrail's political supporters had demonstrated on several occasions in recent months that they were insomniacs when Sarrail's welfare was at stake. Despite the generalissimo's protests and intentions, an increasingly large-scale commitment to the Balkans had been undertaken, and Sarrail had been appointed commander of the French Eastern Army and later commander in chief of the Allied Eastern Army. It is clear that the civilian-military relationship had undergone perceptible changes since July, 1915, when Sarrail had been removed as commander of the Third Army.

VI. A House Divided

The moment I receive the order, believe me, I will . . . try to do something useful.

—SARRAIL to Painlevé,
April 15, 1916

Sarrail waited for a Bulgar-German attack against Salonika. By the end of February, 1916, he had made the necessary preparations: a well-fortified, seventy-mile-long defensive line of machine guns, trenches, and barbed wire stretched from the Gulf of Orfano to the Vardar River. But the enemy halted on the Greek frontier. German Chief of Staff Falkenhayn had succeeded in his basic Balkan mission; namely, to destroy Serbia and thus insure communication with Turkey. He was not prepared, however, to attempt to throw Sarrail's Eastern Army into the Aegean. It was wise, so Falkenhayn reasoned, to have eight Allied divisions inactive in Macedonia rather than have them on the Western front.[1]

Now that Serbia lay defeated and the enemy refused to cross the Greek frontier, the purpose of the Eastern Army was again questioned. Again the Allies were badly divided. In the early months of 1916, Briand, Joffre, and London put forth three varying strategic concepts concerning the possiblities of Sarrail's army. Briand, a long-time advocate of a Balkan campaign, believed that if Sarrail had 400,000 men or twenty divisions, a major offensive against Bulgaria would be feasible. But in the spring of 1916 there were only four French and five British divisions at Salonika. The Serbs, who were being regrouped at Corfu and would be arriving at Salonika in June, would add six more divisions. But who would supply the other five divisions needed for Briand's offensive? The premier hoped that Italy and England would furnish the remaining 100,000 troops. Even if an offensive were not possible with 400,000 men, Briand believed that

[88]

Sarrail could still play a significant role; twenty divisions in Salonika might be sufficient to make the Bulgar-German army fear an offensive, thereby preventing enemy troops from being shifted to the Western front. Furthermore, the presence of a large number of Allied troops at Salonika could possibly encourage neutralist Greece and Rumania to support the Entente.[2]

As he clearly told the newly appointed chief of the Imperial General Staff William Robertson in February, 1916, General Joffre believed that to have any opportunity of success Sarrail would need 600,000 to 700,000 men; an offensive would be "impossible" with anything less than thirty divisions, but to place 600,000 Allied troops in the Balkans was a chimera. Joffre, however, was prepared to support Briand's demand that Sarrail be supplied with twenty divisions if a simple increase in troops would persuade Rumania to join the Entente. But, as Joffre noted, once the six Serbian divisions arrived in June, there would be only fifteen Allied divisions at Salonika. England, according to Joffre, would have to furnish the remaining five divisions, since the four French divisions already at Salonika were the most that could be spared from the Western front.

In mid-February Westerner Robertson, who had replaced Kitchener as the government's principal adviser on military strategy, forcefully presented Britain's Balkan position. He agreed with Joffre that a minimum of 600,000 troops was needed for an offensive and believed that to place thirty divisions in the Balkans was an impossibility. Robertson, however, rejected Briand's and Joffre's contention that to increase the Salonika forces to 400,000 could persuade Rumania to join the Entente. The best way to prevent the Germans from attacking Rumania was to crush the Germans on the Western front. Robertson wanted to return all five British divisions to the Western front once the Serb divisions had arrived at Salonika. The Balkan campaign, as Robertson envisaged it, should be limited to the occupation of Salonika by the Serbs; nothing more—for as he emphatically stated to Joffre, "I studied the Balkan question for many years. This region is hell."[3]

The German attack on Verdun in late February made it imperative that the nine Allied divisions at Salonika be utilized to apply pressure on the enemy; thus the generalissimo ordered Sarrail to submit a detailed study of how the Eastern Army could immobilize the German divisions located in the southern Balkans. Sarrail's plan of operations, submitted on March 7, proposed a major offensive involving twenty-one divisions against the 350,000 Germans and Bulgarians entrenched in the mountains of southern Serbia and Bulgaria: the Serbian army, on the left, would attack in the direction of Monastir in southern Serbia; the British, in the center, would move between the Vardar and Lake Dojran; and the French, on the right, would assume the major effort by moving up the Struma River while simultaneously attacking north of Lake Dojran. Sarrail was quick to point out that his ambitious offensive could take place only when the Serbs and additional reinforcements had arrived. However, if Joffre wanted an attack in March or April, that is, before the six Serbian divisions and further reinforcements were forthcoming, Sarrail was prepared to undertake the only operation possible: a series of demonstrations or local engagements.[4]

Sarrail told General Mahon that an impending offensive was a distinct possibility. Mahon, who had recently been informed by Robertson that the British troops were to remain on the defensive, promptly notified London of Sarrail's plans. A badly shaken Robertson immediately sent a cable to Joffre, emphasizing that London had not agreed to an offensive. Robertson was informed by Joffre on March 10 that the generalissimo had simply asked General Sarrail "to conduct a study emphasizing the conditions under which the troops under his [Sarrail's] command would be able to take up the offensive in the event that certain circumstances favorable to such an action should arise in the Balkans."[5]

On the same day that he was denying serious plans for an offensive in the Balkans, Joffre sent Sarrail extremely fluid orders concerning the role of the Eastern Army. The mission of the Eastern Army was to detain as many enemy troops in the Balkans as possible. To fulfill this mission Sarrail was ordered to threaten or bluff an attack against the enemy, to prepare an offensive limited to the Greek-Serb-Bulgarian borders, and to prepare for a major offensive against Sofia. Ten days later Joffre was more explicit: nothing was said of a major offensive. The role of the Eastern Army was to threaten an attack so that the enemy would not transfer troops from the southern Balkans to the Western front.[6]

The very thought of an offensive greatly upset the British. At a late March meeting in Paris, Asquith, Grey, Kitchener, and Robertson presented a closely reasoned argument rejecting a Balkan offensive and instead requested the withdrawal of Allied troops from Salonika. The British contended that there was no sound military reason for keeping five British and four French divisions in the Balkans, since nine divisions were far more than was needed for the defense of

Salonika; on the other hand, nine divisions were not adequate for an offensive, for as Robertson emphasized, 600,000 to 700,000 troops, according to French calculations, would be needed for a successful offensive. Therefore, now that the French were suffering considerable losses at Verdun, the C.I.G.S. (chief of the Imperial General Staff) strongly recommended that one British division be withdrawn from Salonika and sent to the Western front.

Logical as it may have been, the British presentation won no converts. Sidestepping the basic issue of whether a Balkan offensive could be launched with less than 600,000 men, Briand and Joffre focused upon the British request to withdraw a single division. While the premier countered that the addition of one division to the Western front would be of minor significance to the defense of Verdun, Joffre claimed that the German thrust against Verdun had been successfully thwarted and that "if troops were withdrawn from Salonika now it would appear as if he had failed at Verdun, with the result that the moral effect which had been recently gained would be lost." However, in what appears to have been an afterthought and one that reflected his distaste for a Balkan campaign, the generalissimo stated that if a division were withdrawn, "it ought to be a French division."[7] Encountering a wall of resistance, the British once again gave way and Robertson grudgingly notified Mahon that there was a possibility that "circumstances may justify us later on in changing our purely defensive policy for limited offensive measures."[8]

Meanwhile, Sarrail continued his preparations. He notified the G.Q.G. on April 7 that the Eastern Army was prepared to undertake a demonstrative offensive—a "bluff"—if that was all that Joffre wanted. However, if the Allies intended to launch a major Balkan offensive, additional troops would be needed. Sarrail agreed with Robertson, Joffre, and Mahon that four French, five British, and six Serb divisions were not enough to dislodge the German and Bulgarian troops massing on the Greek frontier. Sarrail correctly pointed out that unlike the Western front, the Balkans still offered an opportunity for large-scale movement and maneuvering. Thus he energetically requested that additional troops be sent immediately so that a major offensive could be undertaken before the enemy had become solidly entrenched in Macedonia.[9]

Joffre was not convinced by Sarrail's arguments. On April 20 the generalissimo, unequivocally rejecting a major offensive, clarified his previous orders: Sarrail was to begin preparations for a demonstrative operation along the Greek-Serb-Bulgarian borders.[10]

Joffre's strategic concept of a demonstrative operation quickly gave way to Premier Briand's demand for a major offensive. Ten days later, on April 30, Joffre forwarded to Sarrail a telegram that War Minister Pierre Roques had sent to the G.Q.G. Roques announced that Sarrail would not receive reinforcements; with four French, five British, and six Serb divisions that would shortly be arriving at Salonika, Sarrail was to prepare plans to attack the enemy armies at the Greek frontier, and if successful, "pursue them in the general direction of Sofia."[11] Sarrail quickly submitted his plans for an offensive; they were basically the same as those of March 7, except that in an attempt to narrow his front now that he would only possess fifteen divisions, Sarrail wanted the Serbs, on the left, to concentrate their main advance against Huma, just west of the Vardar, instead of moving against Monastir; the British, in the center, were to be employed between the Vardar and Lake Dojran and were simply expected to keep the Bulgarian troops from shifting against the Serbs and the French; on the right, the four French divisions were to attack northeast of Lake Dojran with the hope of quickly moving into the heart of Bulgaria.[12]

Between April 20 and 30 Easterner Briand had obviously convinced Joffre to agree to an offensive. In the spring of 1916 Joffre was being severely criticized for the Verdun slaughter, and his sudden conversion to a Balkan offensive was undoubtedly an attempt to placate Briand.[13] The premier may have been victorious in his struggle with the generalissimo concerning the role of Sarrail's army, but it is clear that Briand had not succeeded in obtaining from Joffre the necessary means to accomplish a successful offensive, for Roques's April 30 telegram had ordered Sarrail to prepare an offensive with but fifteen divisions. Yet in the preceding ten weeks Sarrail had requested at least 400,000 troops and Joffre and Robertson had deemed thirty divisions the minimum requirement for a successful offensive. It was understandable that Joffre had no intention of reinforcing the Eastern Army while the fate of Verdun hung in the balance, but what was disturbing was that at no time during the spring of 1916 did he hold out the possibility of ever sending additional French manpower eastward. It is not surprising that when Sarrail realized he was to lead a major offensive with but 300,000 men, his first thought was that "at Salonika as with the Third Army, it was necessary that I not have a victory."[14] He may have been correct.[15]

In late April Briand had a much more immediate problem than finding an extra five to fifteen divisions for Sarrail's army. The premier had to persuade England to commit its five Salonika divisions to an offensive. Joffre was to be the means by which Briand hoped to persuade England to undertake an offensive. On April 25, five days after declaring that a large-scale Balkan offensive was not possible, Joffre wrote to Robertson, and for the first time, advocated a major Balkan offensive. The generalissimo pointed out that when the six Serbian divisions arrived in June, the fifteen Allied divisions, 300,000 troops, would be on a numerical equality with the enemy and therefore Sarrail should have no other mission "than to attack the enemy with all its forces assembled on the Greek border." This offensive would possibly induce Rumania and Greece to join the Entente, while at the same time force Bulgaria to sue for peace. But if these goals were not reached, at least several German and Bulgarian divisions would be pinned down in the Balkans and consequently could not be transported to the other fronts.[16]

On May 17 the British War Committee replied to Joffre's April 25 note point by point: the possibility of Rumania and Greece intervening on the side of the Allies was too uncertain to justify a Balkan offensive; the Bulgarians were superb fighters and would not collapse; the Allies did not possess the overwhelming superiority of troops and artillery needed to break the strongly entrenched Bulgarian lines; the Bulgarians and Germans would remain in Macedonia regardless whether the Allies attacked or did not attack. In conclusion, the War Committee not only rejected a May 13 French request that two British divisions be diverted from Egypt to Salonika, but also categorically opposed any kind of Balkan offensive, whether a major one or of the "limited" variety; the best policy to be pursued was to send the bulk of the Allied Balkan troops to the Western front, leaving only a few divisions necessary for the defense of Salonika.[17]

But there were several other factors not stated in the May 17 note that reinforced Robertson's aversion to a Macedonian offensive. General George F. Milne, who had replaced Mahon in early May as commander of British forces at Salonika, had written that a Balkan campaign would be a dubious undertaking: there were inherent difficulties in coordinating an offensive that would involve three different nationalities; and the Serbs, who had taken severe losses the previous autumn, would be of "doubtful quality." Second, as the C.I.G.S. noted, Briand had counted upon Russia and Italy to supply several divisions to the Balkan campaign; by mid-May both these Allies had refused French overtures to send manpower to Salonika and had instead suggested that the Allies concentrate on the main fronts, not on "eccentric operations." Third, Robertson, after several personal meetings with Joffre, had good reason to believe that the generalissimo had no confidence that a Balkan campaign would succeed. Joffre had evidently not forgotten the politico-military crisis of the previous summer and autumn that had centered upon General Sarrail; according to the C.I.G.S., Joffre, against "his better judgment," was advocating a Balkan offensive "in order not to oppose his Government, which is committed to the enterprise and fears the political consequences in France at its abandonment."[18]

But there was another reason that made Robertson doubtful of the efficacy of a Balkan campaign: he had no confidence in Sarrail. The British were fully aware that it was not Joffre, but the politicians who had been responsible for Sarrail's appointment as commander of the Eastern Army. This explanation, however, omits one important aspect of the problem; namely, the generalissimo and his staff officers deliberately and effectively undermined Sarrail's military effectiveness: Robertson was "convinced by his French friends that S[arrail] is a bad general."[19] Obviously the G.Q.G., led by General Maurice Pellé, had not forgotten Sarrail's prewar career: "People know with what hatred—a hatred which in certain respects is justified—the officers of the G.Q.G., who formerly were thwarted by General Sarrail when he was Director of the Infantry, hound this same general."[20] Unquestionably there was also a good deal of resentment within the G.Q.G. because of the politicians' intervention on Sarrail's behalf. Not only was the name of Sarrail synonymous with civilian control of the military, but his Eastern Army had been created solely by the politicians; Sarrail and his army, both bearing the left-wing parliamentary label, were never accepted by the G.Q.G.[21]

Rebuffed by England's note of May 17, Briand quickly used another technique in his attempt to lure England into a Balkan offensive. On May 21 the premier wrote to London that French politicians and public opinion demanded a Macedonian offensive.[22]

Was there, in truth, any great demand for a Balkan offensive during the first half of 1916, a time that saw all of France's energies concentrated upon Verdun? There was certainly no pressure from the Left. There is little question that left-wing deputies wanted Sarrail to launch an offensive, but not until he had considerably more than the four French, five British, and six Serb divisions; 300,000 troops were not sufficient.[23]

While evincing only sporadic interest in the Eastern Army during the first half of 1916, several left-wing deputies did suggest that reinforcements for the Eastern Army were not forthcoming because Joffre and the G.Q.G. "sought above all to put General Sarrail in a bad position."[24] When several deputies requested that the December 2, 1915, decree be revoked so that Sarrail would no longer be under Joffre's command, Briand quickly refuted the notion that Sarrail was not receiving the G.Q.G.'s full cooperation. Testifying before the Army Commission in April, the premier reminded his critics that it was he who had convinced Sarrail to assume command of the Eastern Army in July, 1915; that it was he who was responsible for Sarrail's promotion as Allied commander of the Eastern Army in January, 1916, and that it was he who had nominated Sarrail for the Grande Croix of the Legion of Honor. All of these acts, Briand asserted, demonstrated that he would not allow Sarrail to be damaged by personal rivalries. Briand reassured the deputies that Joffre had personally promised the premier that he would no longer be hostile toward Sarrail. While emphasizing the newly founded harmony between Chantilly and Salonika, Briand promised that Sarrail would be given all the means needed to carry out his mission.[25]

There was, however, one sector of the French political spectrum during the first half of 1916 that did grow restless over the Eastern Army's inactivity—the Right. As early as January *L'Action française* wrote that "some people seem to be impatient at the immobility of General Sarrail's army. . . . We hope at any rate that he will not let himself be hemmed in and that he will be able to rout the small line of Bulgarians he has in front of him."[26] But it was only at the end of May that a press campaign of any dimension began. While *L'Echo de Paris* announced that the French public was holding high hopes for the Balkan expedition, *La Libre Parole*, which "every day [was waiting] to hear that we are marching towards Sofia," claimed that Sarrail "has considerable forces at his disposal and there has been enough time to provide him with everything necessary for a vigorous offensive."[27] The Right even offered an explanation for Sarrail's long months of inactivity at Salonika: "They say that General Sarrail does not want to move and that the government is afraid of beginning any trouble with him."[28]

Although concerned about Briand's May 21 message, London was not convinced of its validity. On May 26 England rejected the premier's note, reminding Briand that the question of operations at Salonika was one in which military considerations should be the decisive factor; if political considerations were to dominate the Balkan question, any hope for victory would be imperiled. But in deference to Briand's request Grey invited the premier to London for a conference.[29]

Despite its emphatic refusals to undertake an offensive, London feared that it would inadvertently be drawn into a Balkan offensive.[30] Particularly distressing to Whitehall was that General Mahon had "entirely subordinated himself from the first to the masterful personality of General Sarrail, so that latterly he was hardly informed, much less consulted regarding what was done."[31] And Sarrail concurred, noting that Mahon "always helped me in the often difficult operations—even before London had given its authorization."[32] Hereafter, British troops would no longer be commanded by "Sarrail's double"; Robertson removed Mahon in early May and replaced him with General George Milne. The C.I.G.S. wanted "a disciplined brute" to resist—firmly but politely—Sarrail's preparations for an offensive.[33]

No sooner had the change in command taken place than Robertson wrote Milne on June 3 that General Mahon had been notified the previous January 10 that Sarrail was to be the supreme commander of the Balkan forces but only for those matters directly pertaining to the defense of Salonika.[34] Milne, who had believed that Sarrail was in supreme command of all Balkan military operations,[35] now discovered that other than in those questions concerning the defense of Salonika, he had an independent command taking orders directly from Robertson. Sarrail, as well as the French government, was immediately reminded of the limitations placed upon the French commander's prerogatives; Milne informed Sarrail on June 6 that since he was only under Sarrail's command on matters relating to the defense of Salonika, the English commander could not take any action, without orders from London, which might involve British troops in offensive operations.[36]

Robertson's latest attempts, however, to force France to scuttle her plans for an offensive had no appreciable impact, for Sarrail not only refused to withdraw his advanced positions but he promptly cabled Joffre that he was prepared to fulfill his April 30 orders, employing, if need be, only Serb and French troops.[37] Easterner Briand, emboldened now that he had recently gained the support of Russia for a Balkan offensive,[38] bluntly warned London on June 8 that there would be an offensive, even if British cooperation were not forthcoming.[39]

On June 9, in response to England's May 26 invitation as well as to the bizarre situation in the Balkans where Sarrail and the Serbs were preparing for an offensive while England was a bystander, Briand and

Joffre traveled to London and once again urged the British to undertake a Balkan offensive. Briand stressed that Italy had agreed to send one division to Salonika while Russia would be dispatching slightly more than a brigade; thus the Allied Eastern Army would soon consist of approximately sixteen divisions. The French delegation maintained that while sixteen divisions would not be capable of taking Sofia, Sarrail would possess adequate manpower to cross the Greek frontier and make substantial progress against the Bulgarians; if the Allies achieved a minor success, Greece and Rumania might find it expedient to join the Entente. Both Briand and Joffre emphasized that failure to attack immediately would result in forfeiting the initiative to the enemy. The Bulgarians could then choose the time and place for an offensive.

The British rejected the French demand for an offensive maintaining that the Allies lacked the manpower and weapons, particularly artillery, for a successful Balkan campaign.[40] Even Lloyd George, an Easterner, was not convinced of the French argument, for, as he observed of Joffre's performance, "It was difficult to believe that he was convinced even by his own eloquence. He was urging an attack with forces devoid of the armament necessary to achieve their purpose, and he made no suggestion that the equipment should be strengthened up to the point of effectiveness. It was one of the most cynical performances I have ever listened to. . . . He was relying upon our turning his proposal down."[41] Although refusing the French request, the British did grant one significant concession. Other than agreeing to increase the equipment of their Balkan forces, they promised to examine the possibility of a Macedonian offensive if there were a significant change in the Balkan military and diplomatic situation.[42]

On June 17 Sarrail received an interesting directive from Joffre. He was informed that at the recent conference in London, England had agreed to have her Salonika forces fully equipped by July in order to participate in an eventual offensive. Second, in contradictory orders reminiscent of Joffre's March 10 orders, Sarrail was ordered to remain poised on the Greek frontier in order to keep the enemy under the threat of an offensive, and at the same time, he was to be prepared to carry out this offensive. If the Bulgar-German forces were to remain on the defensive, he was to seize any favorable opportunity for action against them; however, the generalissimo warned Sarrail to abstain "from any operations likely to draw the main body of the Allied forces into a premature offensive until the governments concerned have arrived at their decision on this question." Joffre concluded his message by inexplicably stating that all the Allied troops at Salonika for "operations between the sea and the Greek frontier" had been placed under Sarrail's command.[43]

Stunned by the generalissimo's latest instructions, London four days later reiterated to the French that it had not yet agreed to undertake an offensive in the Balkans; the equipping of British forces with heavy artillery and the necessary animals needed for mountain warfare could not be completed until November; in addition, the French were reminded that Milne was under Sarrail's command only for those questions concerning the defense of Salonika and not for all military operations between Salonika and the Greek frontier.[44]

On June 25 Joffre cabled Sarrail that England had refused to partake in an offensive. Sarrail's mission therefore was twofold: to assure the defense of Salonika and to threaten but not undertake, an offensive so that enemy troops in Macedonia would not be transferred elsewhere. These clear-cut directives became blurred, however, for in the same dispatch Joffre forewarned Sarrail that a sudden change in the Balkan diplomatic and military situation might necessitate an immediate small-scale offensive launched, if need be, without British support.[45]

Sarrail was fully prepared to defend Salonika against an enemy offensive, to bluff an offensive, to initiate a full-scale offensive with Sofia as his destination, or to develop a small-scale offensive in order to keep the Bulgarians pinned down in the southern Balkans. For the present, however, Sarrail could do nothing but wait; the Eastern Army's strategy would have to await the outcome of the Allies' diplomatic offensive currently taking place in neutralist Bucharest.

The relationship of Greece to the Entente was yet another aspect of the Balkan situation that greatly concerned Sarrail and the Allies. In October, 1915, King Constantine, after repudiating Greece's treaty obligations to Serbia and forcing the legally elected Ententist Premier Venizelos to resign, declared that Greece would pursue a policy of benevolent neutrality. In early November, however, Constantine's hand-picked premier, the pro-German Skouloudis, announced that the Greek army would disarm the Allied troops once they reentered Greece from Serbia. Briand and Grey quickly responded and on November 23 they demanded that Greece rescind her orders to disarm the retreating Allies. As an Allied squadron sailed into Greek waters, Skouloudis accepted the ultimatum.[46]

A unified Allied Greek policy was short-lived. During the first few months of 1916, just as they could not agree upon the military role of the Eastern Army, France and England had a divergent Greek policy.

London did not want Constantine to intervene on behalf of the Allies. England simply wanted Greece to pursue a policy of benevolent neutrality, fearing that if Greece were to ally herself with the Entente, the Allies would be obligated to assume the responsibility of defending her against the Central Powers. That would have meant a Balkan military commitment which the British government wanted to avoid.[47] Briand also expected Constantine to follow a policy of benevolent neutrality. But unlike England, Briand was hoping that Constantine would eventually join the Entente;[48] as the premier and Joffre had stated throughout the spring of 1916, one of the basic results that France hoped to achieve by a Balkan offensive was to convince Constantine to render military support to the Entente.[49]

Constantine's actions from October, 1915, to the spring of 1916 strongly suggested that not only was Briand's fundamental Greek strategy built upon illusions, but that Constantine was not following a policy of benevolent neutrality. Venizelos's dismissal in October, Skouloudis's pretensions in November, the Greek government's warning to Sarrail in December that Greece would not oppose Bulgarian and German troops if they were to cross the frontier and lay siege to Salonika, Constantine's refusal to allow Sarrail unhampered use of the Macedonian railways, the constant harassment of the Eastern Army such as jamming the air waves and curtailing road transportation, a General Staff headed by General Dousmanis and Colonel Mataxos, both pro-German, and a relentless press campaign in Athens that extolled the Central Powers while denigrating Sarrail and the Entente— these actions did not bespeak a policy of benevolent neutrality.[50]

Greece's hostility placed Sarrail in a difficult position. On the one hand, he had been instructed by Paris to pursue a conciliatory policy toward Constantine; on the other hand, mistrusting the Greek government's duplicity, Sarrail believed that his primary concern was to secure the safety and well-being of the Eastern Army. The contradictions of such a situation, seeking security for the Eastern Army while appeasing Constantine, quickly became apparent. In late December, immediately following an enemy air attack against Salonika, one that heightened the expectation that the city would soon be the object of a full-scale attack, Sarrail ordered French and British troops into the enemy consulates at Salonika. Presenting Briand as well as Constantine with a fait accompli, Sarrail arrested the accredited diplomats,[51] thus assuring that if Salonika were to be under siege, the diplomats of the Central Powers could not carry out acts of espionage against the Eastern Army. A month later, when a German submarine torpedoed a British ship near the Salonika port, Sarrail, receiving prior permission from Briand, forcibly seized from the Greek royalists the Karaburun Fort, which overlooked the main seaway into Salonika; henceforth Allied ships entering Salonika would be adequately protected.

But Sarrail insisted that further measures were necessary if the security of the Eastern Army were not to be jeopardized. He considered it intolerable to permit royalist troops to move freely throughout northern Greece, including Salonika, whether it be in December and January when an enemy attack was expected or in the early spring of 1916 when he had been ordered to make preparations for an offensive across the Greek frontier. Thus Sarrail made several recommendations: he wanted Briand to demand that Constantine either demobilize his army or remove the royalist troops from Salonika; he sought permission to declare a state of siege at Salonika, and he advocated that the Allies seize the Greek railroads, press, and postal and telegraphic systems.[52] Briand as well as Joffre rejected any suggestions to take stronger action against Constantine, a potential ally.[53] The government cautioned Sarrail in January and February that any measures infringing upon Greek sovereignty should not be taken without explicit instructions from Paris.[54]

On May 26 a Bulgarian division crossed the Greek frontier and advanced about ten miles toward Fort Rupel, an impressive military installation perched high above the Struma, which commanded the major entrance to Bulgaria from eastern Macedonia. The Greek fort responded to the invasion with artillery. But Constantine had no intention of resisting, for in previous negotiations with the Bulgarians he had promised Fort Rupel to the Central Powers; therefore, he ordered the garrison commander to surrender Rupel to the Bulgarians.[55]

Constantine's surrender of Fort Rupel greatly disturbed the Allies, so much so that on June 1 Briand granted Sarrail permission to declare a state of siege and the general promptly assumed control of Salonika's police, railroad, press, telegraph, and mail service.[56] But the Allies' immediate response to the surrender of Fort Rupel was more significant not for what the Allies did but for what they failed to do. On May 29 Venizelos approached the British and French ambassadors at Athens and set forth an intriguing plan. He explained that the Bulgarian occupation of Rupel proved that collusion existed between Constantine and Germany; however, Venizelos did not propose that the Greek king be deposed, for that might lead to civil war. Instead,

Venizelos suggested that he go to Salonika, remove the royalist authorities there, establish a provisional government, and then make an appeal to Greek patriots to join the Allies against the Bulgarians.[57]

The French government was prepared to sanction Venizelos's scheme.[58] On May 29 the French ambassador to Greece, Jean Guillemin, wrote Sarrail that the general would shortly be informed of some "very important events in the wind." On the same day, the French military attaché at Athens, Colonel Paul Braquet, arrived in Salonika and told Sarrail that everything should be done "to foster" Venizelos's plans.[59]

There is no question that Sarrail would have been willing to support Venizelos's plans. The French commander had written Paris two months earlier that the Allies were being hoodwinked by Constantine's duplicity. Sarrail believed that the Allies should support Venizelos, for the wily Cretan, who had been illegally deposed as prime minister, wanted to render military assistance to the Entente.[60] Consequently, Sarrail rendered moral assistance to the Venizelists in the late winter and spring of 1916 despite repeated messages from Paris that he should pursue a conciliatory policy toward Constantine and not become involved in Greek internal political affairs. For example, Sarrail publicly attended social functions at Salonika with prominent Venizelists. These social affairs were uneventful except that on several occasions the Venizelists told Sarrail of their "more or less feasible revolutionary plans." Although Sarrail "always turned a deaf ear" to these plans,[61] he had assisted the Venizelists in other ways. On May 28, when the Greek chief of police at Salonika sent a considerable number of gendarmes to prevent the Venizelists from holding a demonstration to protest the recent Bulgarian occupation of Fort Rupel, Sarrail ordered French troops to the meeting; the presence of French troops "gave courage to the demonstators and overawed the local gendarmery," thereby assuring that the Venizelist meeting took place. When several people complained that the meeting had been held "under foreign auspices," Sarrail explained that French troops had been sent in order "to prevent a breach of the peace."[62]

Despite his sympathy for the Venizelists, Sarrail refused to assist Venizelos on May 29 and the few critical days thereafter. The only directives that Sarrail had received from Briand were those of June 1 in which the premier authorized the general to take all the measures needed to guarantee the security of the Eastern Army. Sarrail believed that these instructions were too vague to justify open intervention on behalf of the Venizelists; he immediately wrote Guillemin asking for further directives that either implicitly or explicitly would allow him to assist the Venizelist coup.[63] But Sarrail never received these directives because on June 2 England formally vetoed Briand's suggestion that the Allies consent to Venizelos's plans.[64] The Foreign Office feared that Venizelos's project could be successful only if supported by Allied "guns and bayonets"; London believed that if Greece were to have a revolution, it should "only come about through the agency of the Greek peoples themselves."[65] Without French and British support Venizelos made no attempt to establish a provisional government at Salonika.[66]

Despite Venizelos's failure to ignite a revolt, there remained a slight chance in June that Constantine would be overthrown. Convinced of Constantine's "obvious collusion with the enemy" ever since the Rupel incident, Briand, supported by Russia, pressed England to take stronger action against Constantine.[67] On June 21 the Allies submitted a note to the Greek government demanding that the Greek army be demobilized, the pro-German Skouloudis be replaced by a non-political "business ministry" headed by Zaïmis, and that the Chamber be dissolved and new elections be held. Meanwhile, France and England were preparing a landing at Piraeus in the event that Constantine did not accept the demands. Sarrail was certainly hoping that Constantine would either refuse or delay answering the Allied ultimatum. If such had been the case, Constantine would have been deposed; however, the Greek king immediately accepted the June 21 note.[68] The Allies appeared victorious but Sarrail agreed with Colonel Braquet's appraisal of Constantine's apparent capitulation: "The king has just swindled the Entente again."[69]

As the summer of 1916 began in Salonika, it had been seven months since the Allied armies had retreated from Serbia and other than keeping Salonika safe for the Allies, the Eastern Army had accomplished very little. During the winter and spring of 1916 Sarrail had been instructed to threaten a small-scale offensive as well as to prepare a limited offensive; both plans were intended to keep the enemy forces pinned down in Macedonia. Yet he had also been ordered to prepare a full-scale offensive with Sofia as his destination. There had, of course, been no offensive because England not only opposed Briand's plans for an offensive but she also wanted to leave the Balkans. Parallel to their different respective Balkan military strategies was their conception of the role that Greece should play. Briand was hoping that a Balkan offensive might induce a Constantine-led Greece to join the Entente whereas England, fearful that Greece's entry into the Entente camp would drag the Allies into a full-scale Balkan campaign, sought nothing more than benevolent neutrality from Constantine. Despairing of the Allies' vacillating and fruitless military and diplomatic policy, Sarrail wrote to one of his political supporters:

Will there be an offensive? Will this time come? In my opinion, no. . . . The English do not want an offensive in Macedonia. They always balk. . . .
As for our conduct toward the Greeks, it is the same thing; we rely on the king, the court, the Greek army, that is, on the Germanophiles. . . . They are only waiting for a favorable opportunity to join up with the Germans and Bulgarians. . . . As long as Constantine remains king, we have everything to fear. Before even considering an offensive, it is necessary to make him unable to inflict any damage.[70]

Receiving a similar letter, Painlevé wrote Sarrail that "your hour will come, and it will be glorious, greater and more glorious than your deeds at Verdun."[71] But if Sarrail's hour were to arrive, London and Paris would first have to agree upon a common Balkan policy. And this they did.

On July 4 Rumania's prime minister, Ion Bratiano, highly impressed by the successful Brusilov offensive and Italian counterattacks in the Trentino, informed the Allies that he was prepared to join the Entente provided that the Eastern Army would protect Rumania by attacking Bulgaria. Six days later, on July 10, London notified Paris that should Rumania intervene on behalf of the Entente, England was prepared to cooperate in offensive operations at Salonika.

On July 15, notifed that negotiations were taking place with Rumania, Sarrail was asked by Joffre to submit plans with the aim of engaging the Bulgarian army on the Greek border thus making it impossible for the enemy to move north against Rumania. He promptly forwarded his plans to the G.Q.G. On the left, the six Serbian divisions stretching from Florina to just west of the Vardar were to make their main attack in the direction of Huma; in the center, two French divisions (the 17th and the 122nd) and two British divisions (the 22nd and the 26th) were situated between the Vardar and Lake Dojran. While the two British divisions were to hold a defensive position, Sarrail hoped that the 122nd Division could be successful at Macukovo, just east of the Vardar, and that the 17th Division could break through west of Dojran. On the right, from Lake Dojran to the Gulf of Orfano, the five remaining Anglo-French divisions were to remain on the defensive.

On July 23 the Allies met the Rumanian military representatives at Paris, and it was decided that Rumania with 150,000 troops would begin an offensive south of the Danube on August 7. Now that the Allies had a concrete commitment from Rumania, Joffre on July 23 sent an extremely important cable to Salonika. Sarrail was informed that London and Paris had settled the thorny question of command. Sarrail was to be the commander in chief of the Allied Eastern Army. Other than consulting Milne on the employment he proposed to make of the British troops, Sarrail was to determine the missions, the objectives of the campaign, the zones of action, and the dates on which each action was to commence. Second, Joffre's July 23 message, which had received Robertson's approval, clearly defined the goals of the Allied armies at Salonika. Sarrail was to prepare for an offensive, tentatively set for August 1, one week before the anticipated Rumanian offensive, in order to contain the Bulgarian troops in Macedonia so that the mobilization of the Rumanian army could take place without fear of an attack on its southern frontier; later, when Rumania, assisted by Russia, began her operations south of the Danube, which meant an offensive against Bulgaria, the Allied armies at Salonika would combine with the Russo-Rumanian army in an attempt to destroy the enemy.

However, there would be neither an August 1 offensive nor any attempt to coordinate an attack from Salonika with the Russo-Rumanian thrust south of the Danube because on July 25 Rumania rejected the two-day-old Paris agreement. Rumania refused to take the field by August 7 and requested a delay of ten days. More important, she refused to declare war against Bulgaria. Hoping to satisfy her irredentist aspirations, Rumania proposed to hold a defensive position on the Danube against Bulgaria while launching an attack with heavy Russian assistance westward into Transylvania against Austria-Hungary.[72]

Rumania's tergiversation was not the only disconcerting factor in late July. Sarrail, as commander of the Allied Eastern Army, directed the five British, six Serb, and four French divisions as well as the one Italian division and one Russian brigade that were to arrive at Salonika in early August.[73] Joffre believed that direct command of French troops and supreme direction of all Allied operations placed an extremely heavy responsibility on the same authority. Consequently, during the forthcoming offensive Sarrail would not be able to devote the necessary time to the conduct of operations of the French army. The generalissimo, therefore, took a highly irregular step. On the eve of the offensive he decided that a new commander for the French divisions was needed. But, according to Joffre, since none of the generals currently at Salonika was qualified to assume such a command, he asked Sarrail to choose one of three generals for the new post: Henri Berthelot, Marie-Adolphe Guillaumat, or Emilien Cordonnier.[74] Sarrail selected Cordonnier as the commander of the French Eastern Army. The new commander arrived in Salonika on August 11, knowing little of the topography and nothing of the strategy of the proposed offensive.[75]

With 325,000 men of five nations under his command, Sarrail waited for news regarding the signing of a military convention with Rumania. On August 17 the Entente agreed to Rumania's demands; she would attack Austria-Hungary, not Bulgaria, by August 28. In return for Rumania's entry into the war the Allies guaranteed to facilitate her mobilization and concentration by having Sarrail's Eastern Army undertake an offensive on August 20. Chantilly notified Sarrail on August 18 that in forty-eight hours he was to attack the Bulgarian forces at the Greek border, thereby permitting Rumania's mobilization to take place in a relatively secure and orderly fashion.[76]

Although the August 18 directive said nothing of attempting to reach Sofia nor of ultimately linking up with the Russo-Rumanian forces, Joffre had certainly not precluded the possibility that the scope of the forthcoming offensive could be broadened. On August 11 the British and French governments had formally agreed that while the immediate purpose of Sarrail's forthcoming offensive was to contain the Bulgarians in the southern Balkans, this limited objective did not exclude any new objectives that might present themselves in the course of the operations except those imposed by a lack of resources.[77]

The August 18 cable ordering Sarrail to attack, however, arrived too late—the enemy had already seized the initiative. On August 17 the Bulgarian First Army overwhelmed the Serbian forces on Sarrail's western wing and within the next few days had captured Florina and forced the Serbs to retreat twenty miles southeasterly to the banks of Lake Ostrovo. In the east the Second Bulgarian Army came down the Rupel Pass into the Struma valley and advanced toward Seres forcing French detachments to fall back on the right bank of the river, while on the extreme right, the Bulgarians advanced into Greek Eastern Macedonia, eventually taking Kavalla. As Sarrail watched his army reeling on both wings, he received a note from Painlevé: "Here finally the great historic hour is ringing for you and the Eastern Army. The best wishes of all republican France accompany you."[78]

Sarrail, however, would need more than republican France's moral support, for on August 25 Joffre was once again preparing to send Castelnau to Salonika for the purpose "of finding out exactly what was happening to the Eastern Army."[79]

VII. For Whom the Bell Tolls

The hour of immanent justice will soon ring for your enemies.
—ALBERT FAVRE to Sarrail
November 27, 1916

[Sarrail's] aim at establishing the Serbs in Monastir has been unsuccessful, and I have grave doubts of its chances of success this year,
though he assures me to the contrary.
—MILNE to Robertson
October 30, 1916

On August 20, as the Bulgarians crushed the Allied wings in the east
between the Struma River and Seres and in the west at Lake Ostrovo,
Sarrail called a conference of Allied commanders and presented a new
plan. He would no longer concentrate his main attack on both sides of
the Vardar. Instead, once the Bulgarian attack on the flanks could be
halted, Sarrail proposed to stand on the defensive on the right and
center, that is, on the Struma and Vardar fronts, while reinforcing and
then attacking with his left wing; Sarrail hoped that the six Serbian
divisions, which would carry the brunt of the Allied offensive, could
bend the enemy lines in a frontal assault. To the Serbian left, west of
Lake Ostrovo, the Franco-Russian divisions under General Cordonnier's command were to be the flanking wing, which hopefully would
turn the Bulgarian right flank. If all went well, the Serbo-Russian-
French forces would take Florina, move into Serbia, then take Monastir; from Monastir Sarrail planned to move north to Prilep and then
to Veles on the Vardar; if he could reach Veles, the major Bulgarian
line of communication that ran along the Vardar would be cut, and
consequently those enemy divisions on the Serb-Greek frontier would
be forced to retreat.

During the next three weeks, while the French 17th and 122nd divisions, one Italian division, and five British divisions bombarded the Bulgarians from the Vardar River eastward to the Gulf of Orfano for the purpose of immobilizing the enemy so that it could neither reinforce its right wing nor send troops northward to the Rumanian front, Sarrail moved troops and artillery westward: the 156th Division was sent to reinforce the Serbs southwest of Lake Ostrovo; Leblois's 57th Division, slowly replaced by the lone Italian division on the northeastern front between Dojran and Lake Butkovo, was also dispatched westward and took positions between the 156th right and the Serbian left at Lake Ostrovo; the newly arrived Russian brigade, under General Dieterich's command, joined with the 156th left.

On September 12, as his center and right pursued energetic action against the enemy, Sarrail unleashed his offensive. The Franco-Russian troops, the Serbian Vardar and Morava divisions, and the Serbian First Army, composed of the Danube and Drina divisions, moved northward against the Bulgarians.

The initial stage of the offensive was successful. The Serb Drina division gained a foothold on the uppermost ridges of the 8,000-foot Kaimakchalan Mountain. Meanwhile, the Franco-Russian troops, outnumbering the enemy by three to two, moved straight north, but not quickly enough. Sarrail beseeched Cordonnier almost daily to hasten the advance, for if the flanking movement were to be successful, speed was essential.[1]

By September 17 Armensko and Florina had been taken. But the fifteen-mile Franco-Russian northward advance was quickly stopped on the Florina–Lake Prespa line, for the Bulgarians had rushed several battalions from its eastern front to the northern outskirts of Florina; between Lojani and Petorak, Cordonnier encountered a solidly entrenched wall of Bulgarians. By September 19 Cordonnier believed that his lack of heavy artillery was preventing advancement. Sarrail dispatched reinforcements and again urged Cordonnier to maintain pressure on the enemy: "There is no question about the numerical superiority of the Franco-Russian army, [but] it [this superiority] may only be temporary; it must therefore be exploited immediately. Let me remind you that you must pursue your offensive operations very energetically so as to push the enemy back before a possible arrival of its reinforcements." Upon receiving Sarrail's latest message, Cordonnier issued new directives to his staff: "The first phase of operations is completed. . . . Tomorrow, September 21, preparation for driving back the Bulgarians and marching on Monastir will begin."[2] Cordonnier was correct; the first phase of the offensive was terminated—in both the Balkans and in Paris.

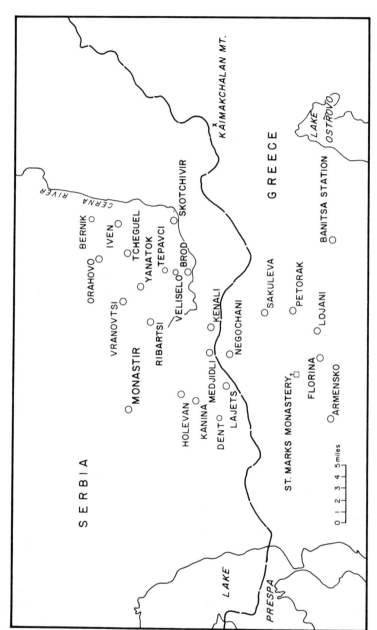

Three months earlier, in June, 1916, Sarrail was informed by Deputy Léon Abrami that "in the Parliament, your friends on the Left remain completely faithful to you, and when the question of J[offre's] successor has been posed (in the corridors), only one name has counterbalanced Pétain's (very popular)—yours." But, Abrami continued, "within the government it has been another story." The person whom Sarrail had most to fear was Philippe Berthelot, the premier's *chef de cabinet* as well as confidant to Joffre. As a "friend of Joffre and of several others at Chantilly,"[3] Berthelot championed the G.Q.G.'s desire to relieve Sarrail of his command. In addition, Berthelot had done much to shape Briand's Greek policy of appeasing Constantine. Sarrail had warned the government that such a policy was bankrupt; events, particularly the Rupel incident, had revealed that he was correct. Berthelot, however, never forgave Sarrail "for having clearly and correctly analyzed Greek affairs."[4]

As early as the spring of 1916 Berthelot had played an important role in fabricating and disseminating rumors concerning the Eastern commander: he was a Bulgarophile; he had blatantly disobeyed government directives by writing to Prince Alexander of Serbia, notifying him that the Serbian army should not embark at Salonika but at Santi-Quaranta; he had openly supported the Zionists, hoping to win the support of the concentrated Jewish population at Salonika. These stories reached such proportions that in March, Minister of State Charles de Freycinet, particularly disturbed by Sarrail's purported letter to Prince Alexander, proposed that Sarrail be recalled. But "here again it was Painlevé who saved the situation by revealing the forgery and requesting an inquiry in order to establish the author [of the letter]." But Freycinet persisted until Painlevé was more explicit: "If they touch Sarrail, I will resign and I will initiate a crisis by revealing everything."[5]

More important than being a mere rumor monger, Berthelot, ambitious and of a "pushing and intriguing nature,"[6] eventually succeeded "in setting Briand against" Sarrail, for by late August, at a time when Sarrail's army had been thrown on the defensive by the surprise Bulgarian attack, Briand had decided that the time was ripe "to give Joffre a hand" in relieving Sarrail of his Eastern post.[7] The Briand-Joffre understanding led Lord Reginald Esher to report from Paris on August 21 that "Sarrail is being watched with malicious intent over here. A series of slight checks would lead to his inevitable suspension. I am not sure that a brilliant victory . . . would be at all welcomed in high quarters."[8]

At a Cabinet meeting of August 26 Briand and War Minister Roques supported Joffre's latest recommendation that Castelnau be sent to Salonika for another fact-finding mission. Immediately Sarrail's "rue de Valois Cabinet friends objected that he being the only real republican general in high command, it would not be advisable to deprive him of his command."[9] Radical-Socialist Minister of the Interior Malvy, who previously had not supported Sarrail, protested: "Any other, but not Castelnau." The minister of armaments in both the Viviani and Briand governments, Socialist Albert Thomas, also supported Sarrail; the minister maintained that "his almost daily contact with Chantilly had allowed him to realize that among all the concerns of the gentlemen in Joffre's entourage," there was one that held top priority: "to take revenge against Sarrail." Thomas urged the Cabinet "not to take such a dangerous step." However, it was Paul Painlevé and Léon Bourgeois who most effectively defended Sarrail within the Cabinet. Painlevé asked the premier: "What are you looking for? A dispute, that is, a crisis affecting the High Command? That is a sure way of provoking one. What did C[astelnau's] first inspection of Salonika produce? . . . Let's get to the point . . . ; if you are again trying to bounce Sarrail, then say so and let's discuss [it]—putting our cards on the table. What do you hold against him? What do you reproach him for?"[10] When Painlevé and Bourgeois claimed that Sarrail was being recalled because he was a republican, Minister of Colonies Doumergue snapped: "One cannot speak of any political persecution of General Sarrail. It is because he is a republican that he has a command. Politics has served him. Anyone else in his position would have been removed a long time ago."[11] Attempting to restore a semblance of harmony, Briand took two steps to mollify the Left. First, he agreed to delay Castelnau's Salonika trip, and second, the premier stipulated that when Castelnau did go to Salonika, he could not remove Sarrail without first receiving the government's permission.[12]

The crisis appeared to be over. But instead it was only now that "the dishonesty was fully revealed."[13] Briand and Berthelot, plotting their strategy carefully, were doggedly determined to cashier Sarrail. First, "the Censor . . . received an order from the Premier to let through all articles attacking Sarrail."[14] And the conservative and right-wing press, receiving its instructions at secret meetings with Briand and Berthelot,[15] initiated the first sustained wartime press campaign against a French military figure. The sole purpose of the two-week campaign was to discredit Sarrail in order that his removal could be publicly justified. On September 2 *La Libre Parole* wrote: "Never, in fact, has it [Sarrail's army] had a finer opportunity to smash Bulgaria. And yet, Sarrail does not seem to move." Sarrail possessed more than enough men and equipment, continued *La Libre Parole*, and "he even has an appreciable superiority over his adversaries. Under these circumstances there is no reason for any more hesitation. . . . To hesitate now would be a crime because any loss of time would enable the enemy to draw up new formations. . . . General Sarrail must not allow our enemies to withdraw; he must rout them before they have taken up positions from which it would be harder to oust them."[16] And on August 31 *L'Echo de Paris* complained that Sarrail's recent offensive had yet to produce any "positive results." *L'Echo de Paris* was hoping that Sarrail would be "anxious to justify his military reputation and the confidence which the government has placed in him."[17]

Briand arranged to hold a Cabinet meeting on September 7; the date was opportune because Painlevé, Thomas, and Bourgeois would not be in Paris. With a rump Cabinet Briand intended to select General Henri Gouraud as the new commander of the Allied Eastern Army; Sarrail would have been appointed governor of Indo-China. The premier was prepared to justify his dismissal of Sarrail by revealing that Rumania demanded the general's immediate recall.[18] In early September Rumania maintained that Sarrail's failure to launch an offensive on August 20, as the Allies had promised, had permitted several Bulgarian divisions to move from the southern Balkans to the Rumanian front, thus making it easier for the Austrians to capture Rumania's Danubian stronghold of Turtucaia and then proceed through the Dobruja.[19] Berthelot encouraged Rumania's deepest fears, for he supposedly told the Rumanian ambassador, " 'It is true, Sarrail does not want to march; he does not want to leave his entrenched camp; he let the Bulgarian army escape northward.' "[20]

Briand's plans, however, went awry. Painlevé had a fair insight into the premier's machinations. Poincaré notified him of Berthelot's statement to the Rumanian ambassador, and the minister of public instruction knew who had instigated the press campaign against Sarrail. Therefore, Painlevé, Thomas, and Bourgeois rearranged their schedules enabling them to attend the important September 7 Cabinet meeting. It is not surprising that when Painlevé entered the room Briand blanched. The premier, "sensing that Painlevé is going to raise cane with him, does an about-face and turning toward Roques says, 'Why General! That press campaign is still being waged? . . . That is inexcusable, etc., etc.' " Briand promised that the campaign would cease and the next day the Censor suspended *La Libre Parole*.[21]

Exactly what Painlevé said at the September 7 Cabinet session is not clear. But whatever he said was effective, for Briand and Joffre, meeting three days later, agreed on the untimeliness of planning General Sarrail's removal—at least for the immediate future.[22] Perhaps Painlevé reiterated what he had told Poincaré on September 6: "If the maneuver [Sarrail's removal] is carried out," he would resign and then "expose the whole affair in the Chamber."[23] The result would have been the collapse of the Briand government. Perhaps Painlevé made no threats, but instead simply defended Sarrail against the bizarre attacks. It is likely that Painlevé commented upon the press campaign which "under the Censor's eye" claimed that Sarrail's army outnumbered the enemy two to one; this distortion "has made the public believe that the Eastern Army's march on Sofia was only a military parade and that General Sarrail only had to push in order to put down a superficial resistance. Fact is far removed from this pipe-dream." It is even more likely that Painlevé focused upon one of the major criticisms recently leveled against Sarrail; namely, as of September 7 the Eastern Army had not yet become "seriously engaged." But how could Sarrail have initiated an offensive when he needed time to maneuver his troops to the western wing? The minister of public instruction correctly pointed out that Sarrail's plans to reinforce the Ostrovo front and then unleash an offensive on September 12 had been approved by both the G.Q.G. and the government. Last and most important, Painlevé demolished Briand's basic argument for relieving Sarrail. Were Bulgarian troops, in fact, moving north from Macedonia to the Danube, as Rumania and Briand had claimed? Despite the fact that Sarrail's army would be on the defensive from August 20 to September 12, Painlevé correctly stated that "until now the Salonika army has fulfilled the mission which it was assigned by holding back all Bulgarian forces which were in front of it. For it has been shown, by Rumanian intelligence itself, that all Bulgarian divisions which attacked on the Danube had for months been stationed in this area and that until now neither Bulgarian nor German troops from the Salonika front have been brought back toward the Danube."[24]

The latest dispute centering on General Sarrail was not solely an intra-Cabinet struggle. While most of the Radicals and Socialists knew little of the intricate military and political details, they had read the right-wing press. And the Left agreed that "this campaign has had a very bad effect on the country."[25] Hervé and Le Radical warned that the union sacreé was once again threatened: "Since all the attacks against Sarrail came from newspapers which before the war we regarded as right-wing, we in leftist circles wondered whether it were not a new attack on the *union sacreé* and whether Sarrail were not just a victim of old political grudges."[26]

Socialist Paul Poncet pursued the matter further. Addressing a public session of the Chamber on September 22, Poncet asked: "How does it happen that, with censorship regulations, such a vicious campaign against the commander of one of our armies could have been carried on for several days?" As his left-wing colleagues applauded, the Socialist from the Seine strongly suggested that the press campaign against Sarrail appeared to have received the government's approval. Making every effort to end the controversy, Briand repeated several times that Sarrail enjoyed the full and complete confidence of the government. The premier guaranteed his left-wing critics that Sarrail would be "protected from unjust attacks."[27] Poncet was pleased with Briand's statements. The latest Sarrail controversy—one that had been settled at the September 7 Cabinet meeting—subsided. But not for long.

Meanwhile, in Macedonia, the Allied left-wing advance had been brought to a halt by September 20. Sarrail's immediate objective was to break into the fifteen-mile long valley leading north from Florina to Monastir; therefore, he ordered an attack upon the Bulgarian positions covering the entrance to this wide valley. During the next week the Franco-Russian attacks were stopped by Bulgarian artillery and reinforcements, which had been hurried westward from the British sector of the Eastern front. Further east the Serbs were doing no better as they and the Bulgarians seesawed on the upper crests of Kaimak-chalan.[28]

Sarrail was not discouraged. On September 27 he ordered the Franco-Russian troops to prepare for a massive attack against the enemy positions. The attack, which Sarrail warned should be pursued with the greatest energy, was scheduled for September 30. Cordonnier grumbled at the orders. He wrote Sarrail that since the enemy was dug in all along its front, a heavy artillery bombardment of several days duration would be needed before the attack could be unleashed. Cordonnier further explained that on September 30, the date set for the next offensive, he would have neither adequate manpower to undertake the offensive nor sufficient artillery to destroy the enemy's defensive positions; thus any opportunity for victory would be remote. Sarrail agreed to delay the Franco-Russian offensive until October 3, but he warned Cordonnier that if he did not attack then, he would be replaced. Again, Cordonnier balked. He maintained that the

October 3 offensive should be delayed until intensive artillery bombardments against enemy positions had taken place. Sarrail was furious, for at the time Cordonnier was refusing to obey orders, Joffre was urging the Eastern Army to undertake an immediate offensive. Further north, the Rumanian counteroffensive was to begin on September 30 and the Eastern Army was ordered to pursue its attacks in the direction of Monastir-Prilep in order to hold the enemy troops in Macedonia so that the Rumanian offensive could have a chance to succeed. Receiving Cordonnier's second refusal, Sarrail raced to the front and on September 30 the two commanders had a short conference at Banitsa Station; Sarrail ordered Cordonnier to assume an offensive on October 3 with the purpose of taking Saint Mark's Monastery, one mile north of Florina, or to resign his command. Cordonnier agreed to the ultimatum.[29]

On October 3, as the Franco-Russian troops prepared to resume their latest offensive, the Bulgarians withdrew nine miles north to their extremely well-fortified basic line of defenses that ran along the Greco-Serbian frontier. The principal line of defenses—trenches, bunkers, and barbed wire, which the Bulgarians had constructed during the past eight months—bisected the Florina-Monastir valley, a few miles south of Monastir. If Monastir were to be taken, the Allies would have to drive the enemy out of Medjidli, Lajets, Negochani, and particularly Kenali, the very heart of the Bulgarian defensive structure. And this is what Sarrail intended to do.[30]

On October 6 he ordered an attack on Kenali. Cordonnier believed that Sarrail was slightly demented to order an offensive directly against Kenali; a flanking movement through the mountain passes would have been better. But Cordonnier said nothing: "I had to obey."[31] However, the Russian general, Dieterich, submitted a formal note to Sarrail, explaining that the assault would fail because the Allies did not have adequate artillery to dislodge the enemy. Sarrail rejected Dieterich's protest and for the next three days the Serbian Vardar division and the Franco-Russian troops stormed the Bulgarian trenches, but to no avail. Still hoping that the pivot of the Bulgarian defenses would crumble, Sarrail ordered yet another attack on the Kenali-Medjidli line; on October 24 the Franco-Russian forces suffered two thousand casualties while gaining no more than two hundred yards.[32]

In the late afternoon of October 14 Sarrail arrived at Cordonnier's command post near Sakuleva and "in front of more than fifty officers I told him my way of seeing things."[33] Sarrail emotionally claimed that Cordonnier's troops "have not left their trenches"; the only ones to attack and to capture prisoners were the Serbs. Cordonnier calmly told Sarrail that the casualty figures easily revealed that "my troops have left their trenches. Compare the number of dead," Cordonnier continued, "and you will see who has attacked."[34] Sarrail stormed out of the room and immediately cabled Joffre that Cordonnier be recalled.[35] On October 20 Cordonnier sailed for France—a ten-week veteran of the Macedonian front.

There were several reasons which explain Sarrail's peremptory dismissal of Cordonnier. Sarrail had been fully informed of what had occurred in Paris in late August and early September,[36] and he was convinced that Cordonnier, a longtime friend,[37] was now the "G.Q.G.'s man":

Of all the documents I possess one sure fact emerges: to all my pleas General Cordonnier offered passive resistance. Why? Was the position I had given him . . . too much for him? I do not think so. He liked to imitate General Bonaparte in his attitude, his gestures, and speech too much for one to imagine that his procrastination originated from any lack of confidence in his own military talent. In my opinion one must seek the cause . . . in the desire to please the High Priests of Chantilly. . . . The G.Q.G. wanted to get rid of me and as early as September 26 Cordonnier already believed he was to replace me.[38]

Sarrail also considered Cordonnier militarily incompetent. Cordonnier's attacks were poorly executed; bringing to the Balkans "the strategy of the French front,"[39] he simply moved too slowly and cautiously, failing to appreciate that the key to Sarrail's strategy, the western envelopment movement, depended upon speed. Sarrail's appraisal appears to be correct; by advancing too slowly, Cordonnier had "wasted a golden opportunity"[40] particularly immediately following the capture of Florina when "reconnaissance must have shown that the Bulgars were holding the line with a rear-guard only, and that they had no prepared line of defence before that through Kenali." In addition to allowing the Bulgarians to retreat unhindered and giving them the necessary time to pour reinforcements into their western defensive positions, the Cordonnier-led assaults of early October left much to be desired. He seemed "to consider it his duty to lead his skirmishing line into action, regardless of the fact that, by doing so, he allows the whole conduct of the operations to pass out of his hands," and as a result there was seldom a coordinated attack.[41]

Sarrail, however, must shoulder some of the blame for the October failure to crack the Bulgarian lines. Instead of ordering an attack into the strength of the enemy's defensive positions, especially when it became apparent that the enveloping movement was not progressing as quickly as expected, better results may have been forthcoming had he held a defensive position in front of Kenali and diverted a couple of French divisions a few miles eastward in order to support the Serbs who were making some progress in their attempts to gain control of the bend of the Cerna.[42]

Cordonnier's failure to move quickly and confidently, his frequent complaints that he lacked sufficient artillery and manpower, and his insistence that the enemy was too well entrenched to permit an advance, were manifestations of an attitude that was also prevalent in the Italian, Russian, and British High Commands, namely, a deep-seated pessimism concerning the outcome of Sarrail's offensive.[43] It appears that only the Serbs and Sarrail believed that the offensive that was then underway would be successful.

Certainly General Milne did not believe that Sarrail's plan to envelop the Bulgarian flank could succeed. To attempt to take Monastir and then advance northeasterly to the Vardar with the purpose of cutting the enemy's line of communication was "a scheme which would be difficult of accomplishment were the whole Bulgarian Army in full retreat"; the mountainous terrain with an almost total lack of roads and the communication problems inherent in such a situation would prevent an advance. There were other reasons, however, why there could be no advance: the Eastern Army, according to Milne, with slightly more than sixteen divisions, did not have enough men; the British commander believed that if the Eastern Army possessed twenty-four divisions, the enemy "may be forced back"; and with twenty-nine divisions, "the odds are in our favor."[44]

Sarrail did not have to be reminded that more men were needed; he had requested twenty-one divisions seven months earlier and they were not forthcoming. But Sarrail had been ordered to attack and with his limited manpower he was attempting to take advantage of the strategical possibilities as they existed in August and September. He had complete confidence that an enveloping movement swiftly executed could be successful. Milne's failure to share Sarrail's confidence in the strategical possibilities, his failure to appreciate Sarrail's ferocious determination to take Monastir, and his underestimation of the Serbs' fighting abilities,[45] led the British commander to state in early October that with a minimum of ten additional divisions, there was a "fair hope" that Monastir could be taken.[46] Three weeks later Milne declared that without the additional manpower he had "grave doubts" that Monastir could be taken, for "to force a strong line with inferior troops is difficult of achievement."[47] These sets of attitudes, whether emanating from Milne, Dieterich, or Cordonnier, may have accounted for Admiral Norman Palmer's mid-October observation that Sarrail "is *the* only officer" in the Balkans."[48]

Certainly Joffre did not appreciate Admiral Palmer's appraisal. On October 16, the day that Sarrail requested Cordonnier's recall, Joffre received a preliminary report of Sarrail's campaign from Major Edouard Requin, the G.Q.G.'s liaison officer attached to the Eastern Army. Requin's report criticized Sarrail for the "violent scene" with Cordonnier, substantiated Cordonnier's claim that the Allied artillery preparation for the October 14 offensive had been totally inadequate, and claimed that Sarrail was incapable of leading the Allied armies. Requin concluded his report by recommending that an immediate investigation was needed, "which would undoubtedly lead to a big shake-up in the High Command in Salonika." Joffre decided to heed Requin's suggestion that Sarrail be recalled. Thus the generalissimo again asked the Briand government that Castelnau be sent to Salonika in order to conduct an investigation of Sarrail's command. If, as was expected, the investigation proved unfavorable to Sarrail, Castelnau would replace Sarrail as commander of the Allied Eastern Army.[49]

The next day Joffre was blandly informed that the French government had rejected his latest proposal because it was thought that the sending of Castelnau to Salonika would result in the "weakening of General Sarrail's authority."[50] However, on October 25 the Cabinet did sanction an on-the-spot investigation of Sarrail. At Painlevé's request, however, it was decided that an immediate investigation would be conducted by War Minister Roques. Joffre was uneasy when informed of the Cabinet's decisions despite the fact that Roques had been appointed war minister the previous March on Joffre's own recommendation and that both men had been classmates at the Ecole Polytechnique and campaigners together in the Far East. Joffre believed that an investigation directed by the war minister was an infringement upon the conduct of his command. After all, the December 2, 1915, decree had explicitly put Sarrail under Joffre's orders. But there was another reason for Joffre's anxiety. He feared that the affable Roques would placate the politicians. Briand, in turn, reassured the generalissimo "of his desire to get rid of Sarrail according to a plan which he had drawn up." The premier emphasized that "I have my plan. And if, as I expect, the inquiry is unfavorable to Sarrail, I will take the responsibility of firing him."[51]

Joffre and Briand had a good deal of international assistance in their attempt to unseat Sarrail. In mid-October, Italy and Russia, strongly suggesting that Sarrail be removed as commander of the Eastern Army, flooded Paris and London with the same basic complaint: Sarrail was devoting more time to Greek politics than to military operations. Particularly infuriating to Italy and Russia was the role that Sarrail had played in the Salonika revolution of August 30-31.[52]

The Greek imbroglio had once again surfaced as a major question in late August, at a time when the Bulgarians had attacked the Eastern Army and Sarrail was regrouping his forces for a counterattack. By August 26 Briand had reached the conclusion that Constantine had not fulfilled the terms of the Allied note of June 21, that Greek military authorities were informing the enemy of Sarrail's troop deployment, and that the Germans in collusion with the Greek General Staff were preparing to invade Thessaly. On August 30 Briand informed London that the security of the Eastern Army dictated that the Allies seize control of Greek ports, railways, postal and telegraph services; the premier was preparing to send a French brigade to Athens to enforce his demands. Although Grey succeeded in persuading Briand to renounce his plans to land troops as well as to reduce his demands upon the Greek government, the French government ordered the Allied fleet, under the command of Admiral Dartige du Fournet, to sail into the Bay of Salamis during the night of August 31; some Austrian ships were seized and the Greek fleet was blockaded. Without consulting the British, the French admiral took it upon himself to enter into direct negotiations with the Greek government. Two days later the French admiral's demands, which included the expulsion of enemy agents from Greece and Allied control of Greek postal and telegraph service, were readily accepted by the Greek government.[53]

Meanwhile, on August 30, while Venizelos was still in Athens, a revolution broke out in Salonika. Colonels Zimbrakakis and Mazarakis established a Committee of National Defense and urged the royalist garrison in Salonika to repudiate Constantine's neutralist policy and join the Allies in driving the Bulgarians from Greek soil. Supported by about 750 gendarmes and two hundred civilians, Colonel Zimbrakakis led the revolutionaries to Sarrail's headquarters. After conferring with Sarrail, Zimbrakakis announced to the crowd that General Sarrail would welcome those Greek troops who wished to join the Allies.

In the early dawn of August 31 the revolutionaries surrounded the two thousand-man royalist garrison and demanded that the troops surrender. The royalists did not comply despite a short but heavy exchange of gunfire. Sarrail then reinforced the badly outnumbered Venizelists with fifteen hundred French infantry and cavalry in addition to machine guns, trench mortars, and airplanes. At midmorning Sarrail arrived on the Champ de Mars parade ground, a buffer area between the insurgents and royalists, and announced that "I don't want to mix myself up between Greek and Greek, but I will not have shooting going on in the streets of this town which is my base and headquarters."[54] To assure tranquility Sarrail ordered the royalist garrison to surrender before noon; the royalists did so and were either interned or sent to Athens. The revolution was over and the Committee of National Defense immediately assumed the administration of Salonika. Five weeks later, when Venizelos arrived at Salonika to assume command of the provisional government, he was publicly welcomed by Sarrail. Greece now had two governments: Constantine's in Athens and Venizelos's in Salonika. Only the former, however, had diplomatic recognition.

The obvious question is how deeply was Sarrail involved in the formulation and planning of the August 30 revolution? Unfortunately, the question cannot be answered satisfactorily. The British consul at Salonika commented that "I cannot say how far the present movement was engineered by General Sarrail, but it certainly could not have succeeded without his protection."[55] On the other hand, Captain Jean Frappa, staff officer and confidant to Sarrail,[56] asserted that Sarrail, and particularly some of the staff officers, were responsible for the revolution: "Officially we had no hand in the movement, but I think that behind the scenes General Sarrail had provoked it and helped it. Everything, they said, had been organized and prepared in the offices of Captain Mathieu."[57] Although recognizing that "a revolutionary movement has a chance of succeeding only when the authorities in power either tolerate it or support it," Sarrail denied that he had manipulated the events of August 30-31. In fact, despite being informed of the revolutionists' plans beforehand, he was "surprised when on August 30 the planned movement finally took place." As for his decisive military intervention of August 31, Sarrail claimed that military reasons dictated his actions: the presence of Greek troops at Salonika had been a constant source of concern for him. He had informed Paris in the preceding months that should the Eastern Army be threatened by an enemy attack he would insist on the departure of all Greek troops from Salonika. When the Bulgarians finally launched a full-scale invasion in mid-August, Sarrail promptly took advantage of the Venizelist uprising to rid Salonika of all royalist troops.[58]

There is little question that Sarrail and Mathieu were implicated in the Salonika revolution. Yet it would be difficult to dismiss the role of naval Commander Henri de Roquefeuil in the events of August 30-31. Roquefeuil, chief of French intelligence in Greece, had frequently warned Paris throughout the summer of 1916 that if the security of the Eastern Army were not to be jeopardized, Constantine and his pro-German entourage must be deposed; this mission, Roquefeuil insisted, became even more imperative once Bulgaria had attacked the Eastern Army in mid-August.[59] Roquefeuil's messages reached such an ominous crescendo that Briand warned him on August 22 "not to commit any imprudence."[60] The next day Roquefeuil assured the French government that he had no "intention of fomenting revolutions."[61] On August 25 he informed naval Minister Marie-Jean-Lucien Lacaze that the Venizelists were preparing a coup at Salonika but that "nothing will happen," for the Venizelists lacked the energy and courage to carry through with their plans. The entire Venizelist movement was simply "too much smoke and not enough fire."[62] Roquefeuil, however, was prepared to stoke the fire. Four days before the Salonika revolution occurred, he wrote to Sarrail and Mathieu that he was leaving for Larissa in order "to prepare the movement"; Roquefeuil asked Mathieu and Sarrail to inform the Venizelists at Salonika that "[we] have unlimited resources for the Committee of National Defense." Meanwhile, the chief of French intelligence was preparing to meet that evening with a Venizelist agent "in order to arrange the details."[63] It is not surprising that on September 1, without specifically referring to the recent events at Salonika, Constantine bitterly complained to France of Sarrail's "attitude" and Roquefeuil's "activity."[64]

Several strands of evidence suggest that although not entirely prepared for the revolution at Salonika, Briand was not altogether displeased that the Venizelists had been successful: it will be recalled that Briand had sanctioned Venizelos's June plan to create a provisional government at Salonika; one of Briand's late August plans, which London had successfully rejected, was the landing of French troops at Athens and it may have been that Briand was hoping that a French invasion might have encouraged popular demonstrations in Athens, thereby forcing Constantine to abdicate;[65] although warning Guillemin and Sarrail not to interfere in Greek domestic politics, the French government formally notified Sarrail on September 1 that it approved the measures taken by him during the recent events at Salonika;[66] despite Briand's statement to England on September 5 that France had no intention of overthrowing Constantine or encouraging the Venizelist movement,[67] the premier raised no objections when in the ensuing weeks Roquefeuil smuggled Venizelos out of Athens so that the Greek politician could organize his forces in the neighboring islands, or when Roquefeuil's agents assisted Venizelists to reach Salonika from southern Greece, or when French naval forces accompanied Venizelos when he left Athens for Crete;[68] lastly, Roquefeuil's uninhibited support of the Venizelists earned him a promotion to the rank of navy captain, a promotion that Roquefeuil interpreted to mean that the government had been more than "satisfied with the naval mission."[69] If not yet ready to antagonize the Allies by insisting that Constantine be deposed, Briand by late September was nevertheless prepared to consider Venizelos as a serious alternative to the Greek king.

The results of the August coup were profound. First, the Entente had a new ally. Second, Sarrail's support of the revolutionists made any chance of a rapprochement between Constantine and the Allies more remote. More important, Sarrail's support of the Venizelists alienated the other Entente members.

Angry about Sarrail's role in the August coup,[70] Russia was incensed when Sarrail publicly welcomed Venizelos when the Greek leader arrived at Salonika in early October. Petrograd believed that the public reception served to give quasi-official recognition to the provisional government, thereby strengthening the Venizelists at the expense of the royalists.[71] This is precisely what Russia sought to avoid, for if Venizelos were to gain complete political control of Greece, his plans for a "Greater Greece" might hinder Russia's postwar territorial aspirations in Asia Minor.[72] Petrograd, however, was prepared to sanction Constantine's removal if the Greek king were to become a dire threat to the Eastern Army's security. But Russia would have preferred that he be replaced by a Romanov, not Venizelos.[73]

Italy's complaints against Sarrail were also rooted in tangible concerns. Fearing Venizelos's irredentism, Italy wanted Greece to remain neutral. If Greece did not join the Allies, she obviously would not have participated in the postwar territorial settlements and Italy would have been free to satisfy her territorial aspirations in both the Balkans and Asia Minor.[74] Sarrail's role in the sudden emergence of Venizelos as a threat to Constantine was not the only aspect of the Salonika revolution that Italy found disconcerting.[75] Rome suspected that there was a direct relationship between the events of August 30-31 and French intentions in the Balkans, particularly as they pertained to the question of Albania.

Essad Bey Pasha had assumed control of Albania immediately

following the outbreak of the war. When the Austrians occupied Albania in February, 1916, Essad and 800 of his followers were rescued by the Italians and taken to Naples. Rome's actions, however, were not altogether altruistic. Italy, which in 1915 had been promised postwar control of a large segment of Albania in return for joining the Entente, intended to keep Essad under very close scrutiny, so much so that Minister of Foreign Affairs Sidney Sonnino proposed that Italy be the only country to have an ambassador assigned to Essad's Neopolitan court; the Italian ambassador would serve as a convenient intermediary between Essad and the other Allies. Essad, however, did not want to be a captive of the Italians and sought to return to the Balkans. Briand concurred, believing that once an Allied Balkan offensive were undertaken, Essad could play an important role by inciting the Albanian Moslems to rebel against the Austrians. When Briand initially suggested his plan to the Italians in July, 1916, Sonnino refused to allow Essad to leave Italy.[76] However, as a result of assurances from Briand that France had only a military and not a political interest in Essad, Italy reluctantly but bitterly consented to allow the Albanian leader to depart for Salonika in mid-August.[77] As Essad sailed out of the Bay of Naples on a French naval vessel, Joffre informed Sarrail that he should greet Essad with a rousing welcome, one that would appreciably increase Essad's prestige and demonstrate that the Albanian chief "was able to conquer the feeling of the Allies, especially France."[78] Anticipating the deployment of Essad's troops on the Eastern Army's left wing,[79] Sarrail greeted Essad on August 27 with a full-scale military ceremony.

Sarrail's elaborate reception of Essad and the Eastern commander's role in the successful revolution a few days later at Salonika greatly intensified Italy's fear of French intentions in the Balkans.[80] Rome acted as if she feared that France were going to use Essad and Venizelos as a means to ease Italy out of Albania, if not out of the Balkans altogether.[81] Thus, Italy acted promptly: on September 3 Sonnino demanded that Essad not be allowed to leave Salonika;[82] on September 27 the Italian minister of foreign affairs denounced the "extraordinary honors" that Sarrail had bestowed upon Essad a month earlier;[83] two days later Rome informed Paris that if Essad entered Albania, he would no longer be under Sarrail's orders, but would be placed under the direct control of the commanding general of the Italian corps at Valona;[84] and on October 2, in a move designed to assure Italy's future claims in Albania, Sonnino ordered a detachment of Italian troops transferred from the Albanian port of Valona to

Santi-Quaranta in southern Albania.[85] Briand, who had been warned a month earlier that continued French support of Essad Pasha could lead to a serious split with Italy,[86] now understood the meaning of Italy's latest maneuvers. The premier cabled Salonika that Essad must not be allowed to enter any area where he might come into contact with the Italians.[87] Essad promptly took up residence in Salonika and Franco-Italian tensions concerning Albania abated, at least for the time being.[88]

Sarrail's reputation as a liberal and anticlerical,[89] his support of the pro-Entente Venizelist movement, and his stirring reception of Essad Pasha, which appeared to signify to the Italians that France had ulterior designs in the Balkans, help to explain why the Italian government, in an attempt to discredit Sarrail, gave undue importance to a relatively minor incident involving the Eastern commander and General Petitti, commander of the Italian division at Salonika. In late September, without consulting Petitti, Sarrail ordered a French division, which was at the time east of the Vardar and on the Italian division's left flank, westward in order to bolster Cordonnier's enveloping movement. Petitti claimed that the removal of the French division meant that the Italian division's left flank would be dangerously exposed. Petitti communicated the situation to General Luigi Cadorna, commander in chief of the Italian army, who, in turn, protested to Joffre that if there were no change in Sarrail's "conduct," the Italian division would be withdrawn from Macedonia.[90] Sarrail was not the only one perplexed that the incident had been unnecessarily magnified; so was Petitti, who expressed "surprise at [the] importance given it."[91]

In late October England decided to support the Russian and Italian suggestions that Sarrail be relieved of his command. There was a general consensus within the British government that Sarrail's dismissal would remove a source of friction within the Entente camp.[92] His support of Venizelos's antidynastic movement in Greece had antagonized London, as well as Petrograd and Rome.[93] Also, the slow advance of the Eastern Army's offensive appeared to confirm British suspicions that Sarrail was not capable of leading a multi-nation campaign.[94] General Milne had written Robertson the previous July that although Sarrail was a "strong man with big outlook [sic] and ideals and great brain power," the Eastern commander was "resentful of opposition and control and this leads him to be impatient with those who do not agree with him. He is not open to argument once he has come to any conclusion but is inclined to show dislike of those whom he considers have stood in his way." Sarrail, Milne had concluded, was a harsh taskmaster, but he "does not lead and he does not understand or make allowances for the different mentality of the nations with which he has to deal."[95]

There was yet another factor, perhaps the most important one, which encouraged London to concur with the Italian and Russian position: the French government had made it known that it would "like to get rid" of Sarrail[96] and therefore wanted England to recommend that Sarrail be relieved of his post.[97] It was not the first time that France had made such a request; during the previous July Robertson had received a "hint that the French would like to have a hint from him that we did not like General Sarrail." Robertson had rejected the suggestion, believing that the French "should do their own dirty work."[98] Three months later, however, the C.I.G.S. was prepared to support the French request. There may be a good deal of truth to Painlevé's observation that it was no accident that the Allied suggestions for Sarrail's removal arrived in Paris at precisely the time when Joffre was preparing another investigation of the Eastern commander. Painlevé added:

This persecution against General Sarrail increases in proportion as the moment approaches when it is feared that his [Sarrail's] energy may achieve some results. In Rome, Petrograd, [and] London there exists a conspiracy in which representatives of the G.Q.G. and some agents of the Ministry of Foreign Affairs are collaborating in order to obtain documents entitled "Boomerang," which ascribe some documents originating from Chantilly as coming from the Allies.[99]

On November 3 Lord Bertie handed Briand a memorandum that stated in very general terms that England and Italy were dissatisfied with Sarrail's recent military performance and that Russia was distressed with the role that Sarrail had played in Greek domestic politics. The Allies wanted a new Eastern commander. Briand was "quite satisfied" with the memorandum.[100] And well he should have been; the Allies' demand for Sarrail's recall, together with the forthcoming Roques report, which Briand expected to be critical of the Eastern commander's recent political and military activities, may have been sufficient to have ended Sarrail's wartime career.[101]

As Joffre had noted, Briand was extremely confident of the outcome of the Roques investigation. But even more confident was Painlevé, and for very good reason. He appears to have known the tenor, perhaps even the substance, of the Roques report even before the war minister had arrived in Salonika to undertake the investigation. On October 28, the day that Roques departed for Salonika, Painlevé wrote Sarrail that when Roques returned from Salonika, his report would "meet the *unanimous* approval of the government and that that will be the end of intrigues which have lasted only too long."[102] And in the next few days Painlevé twice reminded Sarrail to give Roques the exact technical information requested, such as the number of troops wounded, sick, as well as the number of the Eastern Army's front-line and second-line troops. Painlevé emphasized that if Roques possessed a precise account of what was occurring in the Balkans, it would be advantageous "for our cause." Hopefully, Roques's trip would "once and for all put an end to the intolerable intrigues by Paris and its suburbs [Chantilly] . . . and that the government [would] finally be capable of making a decision . . . concerning the troops necessary for the Eastern Army."[103] It is not surprising that Sarrail greeted Roques's arrival with complete confidence.[104]

Roques did not disappoint Sarrail and his political supporters. Upon completing his ten-day inspection of Salonika, the war minister issued his report in mid-November. The report praised Sarrail's military abilities, claimed that he had the support of the Allied generals at Salonika, and vindicated his role in Greek domestic politics. Roques made three recommendations: Sarrail should not be recalled; the Eastern Army must have thirty divisions if the Allies were to advance into Bulgaria; and the December 2, 1915, decree should be rescinded, thereby removing Sarrail from Joffre's command.[105]

Briand and Joffre were stunned. "Despite Major Requin's reports . . . , despite complaints from the Russians, Italians, and English, [and] despite the very distressing impression created in the whole Eastern Army by the violent discussions between Sarrail and Cordonnier," Roques had unexpectedly defended Sarrail and in so doing created a situation that Briand had not anticipated. The premier believed that Roques was only going to Salonika to gather "evidence supporting the generalissimo's criticism concerning Sarrail."[106] But Painlevé, in some spectacular political infighting, had circumvented Briand's plans. Most significant, however, left-wing deputies immediately realized that the Roques report was, in fact, a liability to the government, for the war minister had vindicated Sarrail, and in so doing, had indicted Joffre and those who supported him, particularly Briand. As Radical-Socialist Deputy Maurice Bokanowski pithily told Sarrail: "With old man Roques on our side, we are going to be able to go from the defensive to the offensive."[107] Briand and Joffre, who had casually and unrealistically staked their careers upon the uncertain shoulders of War Minister Roques, would quickly discover that Bokanowski was not engaging in idle chatter.

In addition to the Roques report, the Left had yet another reason to rejoice in mid-November. Sarrail had captured Monastir, the first important Allied victory in two years.

On October 16, the day when Joffre decided to send Castelnau on another mission to Salonika, Sarrail was still having difficulties near Monastir. The Franco-Russian forces were a few miles south of Monastir while on their immediate right, the Serbs were fighting to gain the left bank of the Cerna River. And for the next three days, while the Franco-Russian troops made no attempt to advance, the Serbian Morava and Vardar divisions (First Army) and Danube division (Third Army) took Brod, Veliselo, and Skotchivir.

On October 20, when the Serbs were making progress, Sarrail greatly modified his strategy. He adopted Cordonnier's suggestions and decided to forsake another direct smash on the well-fortified Kenali-Medjidli line. While the French 57th and 156th divisions and the Russian brigade, now under Leblois's command, maintained an artillery barrage on Kenali westward to Lajets and Medjidli, the Serbs were instructed to attack the enemy east of Kenali.

On October 27 the offensive was resumed. But the four-day offensive begun in rain and fog, made little progress—and understandably so. Beginning in late October the Germans began pouring battalion after battalion, most of them rushed from France, into the Tcheguel-Kenali area. The Bulgarians were cracking, but the Germans were determined to keep Monastir.

Within the next ten days Sarrail regrouped his forces. On November 10 he ordered another offensive. Again, he was pinning his hopes on the Serbs, for while the French and Russians continued to shell the Kenali defenses, the Danube, Morava, and Drina divisions, shoulder to shoulder over an eight-mile front, pushed straight north through rain, fog, and snow. In the heaviest fighting of the campaign the Serbs succeeded in taking Tcheguel, Tepavci, and Iven, and by the evening of November 14 the Bulgar-German troops were forced to retreat four miles northward along the Ribartsi-Vranovtsi-Orahovo line. Meanwhile the French renewed their attack on the Kenali defenses; on November 14 the 17th and 156th colonial divisions cut their way through barbed wire and, using hand grenades and bayonets, fought their way through the flooded trenches to the enemy's third and last line of defenses. By the late evening of November 14 the Bulgarians retreated from the Kenali defenses and took positions on the western slopes of the Monastir valley along the Dent-Kanina-Holevan line. Kenali had finally been taken, but it was still five miles to Monastir.

The Allies maintained their relentless pressure. Again it was the Serbs, particularly the Vardar, Morava, and Danube divisions, which did the most damage. From November 15 to 18 the Danube division took Bernik and Hill 1378, the commanding height in the region, fifteen miles east of Monastir; the Morava and Vardar divisions seized Yanatok, Vranovtsi, and Orahovo, ten to twelve miles east of Monastir; the French 17th Colonial Division, recently attached to the Serbian First Army, took Ribartsi, six miles east of Monastir. During this four-day period, while the Serbs and the 17th Colonial Division were striking north and east of Monastir, Sarrail ordered the French 57th and 156th divisions, and the Russian brigade to move directly on Monastir from the south. Bending before the Allied pressure, the Bulgarians and Germans began their retreat to the northern heights overlooking Monastir. On the morning of November 19 French and Serbian cavalry entered Monastir unmolested.[108]

Sarrail immediately received what must have been a gratifying letter. It was written by General Milne: "I offer you in the name of the troops under my command our warmest congratulations on the success you have achieved in Monastir. Your wonderful determination to overcome difficulties and the magnificent courage shown by your troops are the admiration of us all."[109] Sarrail, for his part, was less than enchanted with the British performance during the three-month offensive. He and the Serbs found it "extraordinary that an army as large as the British army did not attempt something."[110] Nevertheless, upon taking Monastir, Sarrail issued an order of the day in which he warmly congratulated all of the national contingents that had taken part in the offensive. However, he reserved his greatest praise for one particular army, the Serbs. But, as he reminded his troops, Monastir was only a "prelude."[111] Now that the Allies had a foothold in southern Serbia, Sarrail wanted to continue his way northward.

For the next three weeks, despite repeated efforts to break the enemy lines in an attempt to reach Prilep, the Eastern Army could advance no further. There is little question that the Bulgarians had been badly broken and were holding on desperately; had it not been for eighteen German battalions thrown against the Allied left wing, Bulgaria might have collapsed. But if Sarrail were to advance beyond Monastir, he needed immediate reinforcements, for the Eastern Army's left wing had suffered more than forty thousand casualties during the three-month campaign, almost as many as the enemy.[112] On November 19, however, when Monastir had fallen, Sarrail did not have the three or four fresh divisions that he needed.

Sarrail had taken Monastir without the moral support, certainly without the material assistance, of the Italian, British, and French High Commands. From October, 1915, to September 12, 1916, when Sarrail's offensive began, the British and French had failed to agree on fundamental issues. Should there in fact be an Allied army in the Balkans? What was to be its purpose? How many men should Sarrail have? Should the Eastern Army engage in an all-out offensive to Sofia, or simply a holding action? None of these questions was wholeheartedly agreed upon even by September 12. But what is remarkable is that the Allies displayed the same enervating indecision, the same lack of foresight, and the same reluctance to support the Eastern Army quickly and decisively even when Sarrail's offensive had all the appearances of a successful campaign.

On October 2, two weeks after Florina had fallen and the Bulgarians had withdrawn to their Kenali defenses, Joffre informed Briand that no sizable French reinforcements would be sent to the Balkans. Joffre maintained that since there was no indication that Germany or Austria would send significant reinforcements into the Balkans, Sarrail and Rumania would have adequate manpower to accomplish their respective missions.[113] Although finding no military necessity for sending additional French troops to Sarrail, Joffre found it convenient in early October to ask Robertson and Italy's Cadorna to reinforce the Eastern Army. Joffre pointed out to the other Allied military chiefs that if the Eastern Army were increased, it would not only achieve more decisive results on its own front, but would draw a substantial number of enemy divisions from the sagging Rumanian front. He therefore requested Italy to send two divisions eastward from the relatively quiet Trentino front and England to divert two of her eight Egyptian divisions to Salonika. Cadorna promised but a single brigade, whereas Robertson on October 8 rejected Joffre's suggestions, claiming that not a single soldier could be spared from Egypt and the Suez Canal.[114]

The War Committee met on October 9 to discuss Joffre's latest requests. No agreement could be reached, if only because France's recommendations produced one of the most bitter military-civilian confrontations of wartime England. War Minister Lloyd George argued that Rumania was floundering and it was imperative that additional divisions be sent to Salonika. Referring to Milne's recent appraisal that twenty-four divisions were needed in Macedonia, Lloyd George claimed that if Sarrail possessed twenty-four divisions, Sofia could be reached and the Allies would then be in position to supply Rumania with urgently needed artillery and ammunition. Robertson, on the other hand, assumed a diametrically opposite position. Explicitly rejecting Milne's opinion that twenty-four divisions were needed, Robertson claimed that the Eastern Army needed no reinforcements because it was effectively fulfilling its designated assignment—to prevent the Bulgarians in Macedonia from withdrawing to the north. More revealingly, Robertson maintained that the Eastern Army had no role to play in the forthcoming attempts to rescue Rumania. He believed that the means to save Rumania were twofold: the "best way" to assist Rumania was to continue the Allied offensive in France; and second, it was Russia, strategically located to the north of Rumania, which could successfully send thousands of troops southward in order to stabilize the Rumanian front.[115] Robertson was placing his bets on the wrong horse—two months later the Austro-German army, marching with ease over the Russo-Rumanian forces in Transylvania and the Dobruja, entered Bucharest.

The next day Joffre shook London with a new message. Believing that with four additional divisions, two British and two Italian, the Eastern Army would be able to crack the Kenali defensive positions and then advance deep into Serbia, thereby easing the pressure on Rumania, Joffre announced that the original role of the Eastern Army had been extended; the Eastern Army, whose original role was to cover the mobilization and concentration of the Rumanian army, was now to cooperate with the Russians in the decisive defeat of the Bulgarians.[116]

At a meeting of the War Committee on October 12 Robertson bitterly opposed Joffre's latest plans, maintaining that four additional divisions would not be sufficient to enable the Eastern Army to inflict a crushing defeat upon Bulgaria. The C.I.G.S. reiterated that "the function of our force [Eastern Army] was to contain the Bulgars, and not to push forward." Robertson read the latest cables from Petrograd, which indicated that Russia was rendering adequate assistance to Rumania; therefore, there was no need for the Eastern Army to break the Bulgarian lines in an attempt to save Rumania. He reassured his colleagues that if Rumania "made her dispositions properly she ought to be all right. She was different from Serbia. She had a larger army and three railway lines."[117]

Robertson's arguments were heeded at least partially. On October

12 the War Committee refused to sanction the new role that Joffre had unilaterally assigned to Sarrail's army; yet, in what was a haphazard, half-hearted, even ludicrous attempt to compromise the differences between Robertson and Lloyd George, as well as those between London and Paris, the War Committee decided to send approximately one division to Salonika,[118] not with the purpose of reinforcing the Eastern Army so that it could push its way into central Serbia, but because there was "a risk that, if the Allied army is not reinforced, it may not even be able to fulfill its original role, and Bulgarian troops may be withdrawn [from Macedonia] for operations against Rumania."[119]

The failure to supply Sarrail with additional divisions during the inital stage of his offensive greatly agitated much of the French Left. On October 17 left-wing members of the Chamber Army Commission told Briand that Sarrail did not have the necessary manpower because Chantilly was dictating the government's Balkan policy. Furthermore, "it is known that the person who directs operations from Chantilly . . . is not exactly sympathetic to the person who commands over there [in Salonika]."[120]

Briand, whose ascent to the premiership had been greatly aided because of his reputation as an Easterner, readily agreed with his left-wing critics that the G.Q.G. had imposed its views upon the government. When the premier stated that Joffre refused to commit additional French troops to the Balkans, Radical-Socialist Accambray assailed Joffre and the Westerners for failing to realize that the Balkans offered the Allies strategic and tactical possibilities. Accambray emphatically reminded Easterner Briand that "it is necessary that you be careful not, as you have done till now, to rely exclusively on the military for the care of conducting the war, even from the military standpoint." Joffre should only be "an agent [for carrying out operations] and it is the government which should oversee military operations."[121]

The pressure generated by the Army Commission evidently stiffened Briand's resolve to oppose Joffre. At an Anglo-French conference held at Boulogne on October 20 the premier maintained that the Allies must "push forward from Salonika" in an attempt to save Rumania. The Eastern Army should be strengthened from sixteen to twenty-three divisions. Briand "begged" England, which had promised an additional division a week earlier, to commit yet another division; furthermore, he wanted Italy to add two divisions and Russia one. But most surprising of all, there was a radical change in

France's position concerning the question of French reinforcements; Briand brushed aside Joffre's objections and promised that two French divisions, the 11th and 16th Colonial, would be sent to the Eastern Army.[122]

Asquith was correct when he commented at Boulogne that although France and England wanted to assist Rumania, the two countries differed as to the means. The prime minister recalled that in mid-August, that is, on the eve of Rumania's entry into the war, France and England had agreed that the first objective of the Eastern Army—to contain the Bulgarians in Macedonia so as to facilitate Rumania's mobilization—would not prevent any further objectives being considered, such objectives being limited only by the matériel at the Allies' disposal. Yet it is clear that England never seriously considered the latter part of this agreement, for as Asquith readily admitted, his government had proceeded on the assumption that the object of the Salonika operations was to keep the bulk of the Bulgarian army pinned down in Macedonia. Now, in a desperate attempt to save Rumania, France wanted to extend the role of the Eastern Army, namely, to cooperate with the Russians in hopes of defeating the Bulgarians. England, Asquith asserted, could not agree to this, for the Eastern Army needed an additional ten or fifteen divisions if it were to inflict a decisive defeat on the Bulgarian army. Therefore, London considered that the role of the Allied forces at Salonika should remain as heretofore, namely, to continue their present attack with the object of holding the main part of the Bulgarian army in Macedonia. However, as a sop to Briand, Asquith did promise to give immediate consideration to the French request that England contribute another division to the Balkans.[123]

The War Committee met on October 24 to discuss Briand's latest request for an extra division. In an atmosphere of penetrating gloom, the War Committee read the cables from Bucharest, which revealed that the Rumanian disaster was imminent. And Milne's reports from Salonika, if not correctly analyzing the military situation, at least added to the misery of the politicians and generals: the Serbs were a "demoralized mob"; the Eastern Army's offensive was disorganized; there was little likelihood that Monastir would be taken. In anger, disgust, and frustration, a dispirited Lloyd George summarized the twelve-month existence of the Eastern Army: "The Salonika enterprise had broken down because it had been treated as a political question: by the French as political on account of Sarrail, and by us as political on account of the French. It had never been treated as real."

The war minister thought that it was now too late to send reinforcements to Salonika. In a sharp indictment of the Westerners, who
controlled both the War Office and Chantilly, he maintained that if
reinforcements had been sent two months earlier, the Bulgarians may
have collapsed.[124] Lloyd George's appraisal was correct on all points
except one: the Eastern campaign had not broken down, as the taking
of Monastir would demonstrate.

Once again the C.I.G.S. refused to send an extra British division to
the Balkans, maintaining that "these reinforcements would increase
the danger of our being drawn eventually into major operations . . .
which . . . would be a very grave and perhaps fatal strategical error."
Nevertheless, the War Committee overrode Robertson's objections
and agreed on October 24 to send the 60th Division to Salonika, thus
bringing the number of British divisions there to seven. The politicians
agreed with Robertson that due to the lateness of the year and the
strength and defensive positions of the Bulgar-German forces, an extra
division would have no real military value. Nevertheless, it was felt
that the sending of an additional division would placate the French
and Russian governments, as well as bolster the morale of the faltering
Rumanians.[125]

During the next three weeks Joffre, prodded by Briand, attempted
to obtain futher reinforcements from London and Rome. Echoing
Briand's recent Boulogne policy statements, Joffre wrote to Robertson
on November 3 that with twenty-three divisions Sarrail would be able
to threaten Bulgaria by delivering a vigorous offensive in the direction
of Sofia.[126] Robertson rejected Joffre's latest pleas, despite having received on October 30 Milne's observation that Sarrail's offensive
could "at any moment cause a break-up in the Bulgarian Army."[127]
Strongly supported by his government, Robertson again adamantly
maintained that "nothing could be worse" than adding additional divisions to the Balkan campaign. More than twenty-three divisions
would be needed to reach Sofia; therefore, the Eastern Army must
restrict itself to the limited role of keeping the Bulgarians pinned down
in the southern Balkans.[128] Likewise, in late October and November,
Italy refused to make further commitments beyond the single brigade
promised in early October, believing that whatever reinforcements the
Allies could send to the Balkans "will always be too weak to assume
the offensive."[129]

If not entirely successful, Joffre and Briand had at least succeeded in
reinforcing Sarrail's army with one Italian brigade, two British, and
two French divisions, thereby increasing the Eastern Army to twenty-

one divisions. However, when the Eastern Army was preparing for its final thrust against Monastir in mid-November, only a few British battalions and the Italian brigade had arrived. The British 60th and the French 11th and 16th divisions encountered transportation difficulties and consequently were not put ashore at Salonika until early December. By then it was too late; not only was the enemy hurriedly and successfully reinforcing its right wing north and east of Monastir, but the Macedonian blizzards and freezing temperatures prevented any further military action in the mountainous Balkans.[130] The Eastern Army's next offensive would have to wait until the following spring.

On November 21 Deputy Bokanowski informed Sarrail that "if the capture of Monastir pleases the French, it delights your friends." Bokanowski did not underestimate the importance of Sarrail's victory. Monastir not only confirmed the thesis of the recently issued Roques report, but Sarrail's victory stood in such glaring contrast to the recent Verdun, Somme, and Rumanian disasters that even some of Joffre's supporters were beginning to doubt their "idol's ability."[131] Armed with Monastir and the Roques report, the Left now believed that it was opportune to move against Joffre and Briand. Consequently, on November 21 and 23, Radical and Socialist deputies requested the opportunity to interrogate the premier on such questions as the abrogation of the December 2, 1915, decree, the reorganization of the High Command, and the lack of reinforcements for the Eastern Army.[132] Because these topics were not only controversial, but of a military nature as well, it was deemed prudent to discuss them not in public session, but in camera; the Chamber therefore voted to convene in secret committee with the first session to begin November 28.

Meanwhile, Briand, receiving the cooperation of Joffre, who fully understood the implications of the Roques report, braced himself for the upcoming secret session by taking two steps: first, he sent Chief of Staff Castelnau to Russia for a December inter-Allied military conference and then arranged to have him replaced upon his return; second, he immediately assigned to field commands both Lieutenant Colonel Férréol Bel, head of the G.Q.G. personnel bureau, and General Maurice Pellé, the G.Q.G.'s policy adviser for the Eastern Army.[133] Whether such measures could pacify the government's left-wing critics and thus preserve the *union sacrée* was doubtful. Sarrail's longtime friend Albert Favre was not mollified. On the eve of the secret Chamber session, the Radical Left deputy from the Charente-

Inférieure wrote to Sarrail: "I want to tell you, dear General, that you have in the Chamber a devoted, earnest, energetic, and disciplined battalion which will not allow you to be mistreated with impunity any longer. The hour of immanent justice will soon ring for your enemies."[134]

The first session of the most critical parliamentary debate hitherto held in wartime France was called in the afternoon of November 28. Briand presented some of the diplomatic background leading to Rumania's entrance into the war, emphasizing that Rumania had blundered when she insisted upon moving west against Austria rather than south against Bulgaria. The premier then turned to the question of the Eastern Army and focused upon the problem of Sarrail's manpower shortage. The Eastern Army did not have reinforcements because England refused to support the campaign, and second and somewhat surprising, the premier claimed that it was not Joffre, but the malarial conditions in the summer of 1916 that had prevented the sending of additional troops to Macedonia. Briand's basic contention, however, was that Sarrail did not need more than the 300,000 troops already at Salonika because "never, at least for this year, did the Allies conceive of undertaking in Salonika . . . an operation capable of bringing about important strategic results." The premier emphasized that with 300,000 men Sarrail had accomplished his principal objective, namely, to keep the Bulgarians and Germans who were in Macedonia from moving north against Rumania.

No sooner had Briand finished his introductory statements than Radical Left Deputy Camille Picard asked: "And what about Sarrail?" The premier conceded that there had been "difficult moments" for Sarrail and the government; however, Briand dared anyone "to say that the government has committed the smallest act of injustice toward him [Sarrail]."[135]

Several deputies were not convinced. Seeking wider political support for Sarrail and conversely greater opposition to Joffre, the Left arranged to have a right-wing deputy, Charles Meunier-Surcouf, launch the session's first sustained attack against the generalissimo.[136] It is surprising that a conservative would defend Sarrail. However, Meunier-Surcouf had just returned from Salonika, where he had conducted an investigation of the Eastern Army. Upon his return, on October 25, he drew up a report, perhaps filed with one of the Chamber commissions or simply circulated informally within the Chamber, which lavishly praised Sarrail's military leadership and political conduct in Greece.[137]

At the secret committee of November 28 Meunier-Surcouf made one basic charge: Joffre, as supreme commander of the French army, had failed to give adequate material and moral support to the Eastern Army. Why, Meunier-Surcouf mused, has the Eastern Army "not been treated like the other armies."[138]

Victor Augagneur, Republican Socialist from the Rhône, followed Meunier-Surcouf to the speaker's podium and promptly accused the premier of undertaking a political double cross. As minister of justice in the Viviani government, Briand had consistently advocated not only an energetic Eastern policy, but he had strongly urged the submission of the High Command to the government. But no sooner had the Easterner become premier than he issued the December 2, 1915, decree, which transferred direct control of the Eastern Army from the War Ministry to the Westerner Joffre. Augagneur maintained that the December 2 decree allowed Joffre to determine the government's Eastern policy, with the result that Sarrail did not have adequate troops for the long, sustained thrust deep into the northern Balkans, which was needed if Rumania were to be saved.[139]

The second and third sessions were the highlights of the ten-day secret committee. Léon Abrami, who previously "had not dared address the Chamber for fear of appearing to carry your [Sarrail's] colors," now "sensed that the Chamber was waiting for me and that I could tell everything; [therefore] I did tell everything."[140] Abrami, as did Augagneur, focused upon the major reason for much of the left-wing disillusionment with the Briand government. Briand as a minister in Viviani's government had espoused a full-scale Balkan campaign; when Briand became premier it was expected that he would pursue an energetic Eastern policy and, if need be, impose his policy upon the G.Q.G. Briand's Eastern plans, however, were aborted the day he appointed Joffre to be generalissimo; the December 2, 1915, decree meant that the government had abdicated the military direction of the Balkan campaign to the G.Q.G. Longtime hostility between Sarrail and the G.Q.G. guaranteed that the Eastern Army would never receive the men and artillery that were needed for an effective offensive. It is true, Abrami continued, that the two new divisions were currently preparing to disembark at Salonika, but "can you confirm, M. Premier, that in order to obtain them, you did not run into repeated refusals from the G.Q.G. Can you assure us that you have not once again had to overcome the obstinate resistance of the G.Q.G.?" If the Eastern Army were to be successful, Sarrail must be assured full independence from Chantilly. Abrami warned that many politicians would not support the Briand government unless the December 2 decree were abrogated.[141]

No sooner had Abrami completed his two-hour address than the Chamber witnessed a thirty-minute demonstration reminiscent of prewar days. Radicals and Socialists surged to the podium to congratulate the fiery little Radical: "Caillaux, Renaudel, Thomson . . . everybody," Abrami wrote Sarrail, "was grouped around me. . . . Never have your friends been more numerous and more determined. My great joy was to witness it." Abrami had indeed "celebrated Monastir in my own way."[142]

Briand finally answered his critics. The premier's response was revealing, if only because he refrained from discussing the basic questions that had been raised. He devoted the greater part of his discussion to a detailed account of the Rumanian fiasco. Briand's basic thesis was that he and Joffre had done everything humanly possible to persuade Rumania to attack south into Bulgaria, but Rumania, supported by Russia, insisted on moving west into Transylvania; Briand had to accept Rumania's demands, for this was the sine qua non for Rumania's entry into the war. The premier was quick to point out, however, that once Rumania declared war, France fulfilled her part of the bargain by pinning down all the Bulgarians present on the Macedonian front.[143]

On November 30, as the third session opened, Briand gingerly touched the Sarrail question. The premier admitted that tensions did exist among the upper echelons of the army, but all of Sarrail's requests had been met. He recounted that when Sarrail requested the Legion of Honor for Leblois, it was granted; when Sarrail asked for reinforcements, the increases were granted. However, Briand did admit that concerning the question of reinforcements, he had to overcome serious difficulties. The premier, who had no intention of bringing Joffre into the discussion, claimed that it was London alone that had created the obstacles and Briand recited his year-long frustrating attempts to have England supply the Eastern Army. He assured the Chamber that he had done everything possible to give the Balkan campaign the "importance which it was to have" and that "if the state of [its] manpower and matériel . . . made it impossible for it to assume . . . an important strategic operation . . . it was perfectly capable . . . of accomplishing the essential task to which it was to apply itself, and until now, it has carried out."[144]

A few moments later, in response to Renaudel's request for additional information and clarification concerning the Eastern Army's manpower difficulties, War Minister Roques addressed the Chamber. He presented a summary of the Eastern Army's numerical strength and claimed, just as he had done two weeks earlier in his now famous report, that despite being undernourished, Sarrail's army had done a first-rate job. And to the frequent and sustained applause of the Left, the war minister continued to praise Sarrail: the Eastern Army's morale was superb, the Allied commanders respected Sarrail, and Sarrail's attitude was excellent. Roques concluded the session by admitting that friction had existed between Sarrail and the generalissimo; however, the government, acting as a referee between the two generals "had constantly seen to it that things happened as they should happen."[145] And, of course, the war minister three weeks earlier had played no small role in making sure that "things happened as they should happen."

Writing to Sarrail, Albert Favre and Abrami summarized the first three sessions of the secret committee: "I assure you that you are well avenged, for they talked only about you. All the speakers . . . praised you to the applause of all the parties on the Left."[146] There is little question that the *union sacrée* was once again badly disrupted. Although Briand "felt the storm," he "does not dare drop [Joffre] yet." Nevertheless, "all the parties on the Left are determined to obtain the abrogation of the [December] decree. . . . If he does not give it to us, B[riand] will be in the minority."[147]

But where would Sarrail's political friends gain the necessary supporters to overthrow the Briand government? First General Roques's recent speech, according to Albert Favre, "has increased the quality and number of those whom you [Sarrail] already have in the Chamber. Your position has been very much strengthened to the detriment of your persecutors, whose reputation and influence, I dare say, have proportionately declined."[148] Second and more significant, Abrami shrewdly observed that Sarrail's supporters, who were responsible for initiating the secret committee, had opened a Pandora's box. The Left was gaining the support of conservatives and moderates—but not because the non-Left supported Sarrail. It was simply that after twenty-eight months of a costly and inconclusive struggle, France was suffering from war weariness: "Every day the opposition grows: [there are] crises in transportation, in coal, in food, in the merchant marine, and manpower. . . . On the other hand, it is felt that the morale of the French soldiers demands new men who will give the army at least the illusion of new methods."[149] Abrami was correct, as the secret sessions of December 1, 2, and 3 revealed. During these three calm sessions several left-wing, center, or right-wing deputies, all critical of Briand's management of the war effort, proposed that the government manufacture additional submarines, torpedo boats, tanks, ammunition, and heavy artillery, that it increase mining and food production, that it undertake a more intensive aeronautical program and increase naval patrols to escort the merchant fleet, that it utilize dirigibles, not on the Western front, but as a means to scout German submarines, and that it rescind the eight-hour workday recently introduced in the state-owned munition factories.[150]

On December 3 Briand invited Joffre to lunch and the two men discussed politics. Briand, as Joffre later recalled, explained that the attitude of the Chamber was causing him great uneasiness and that in order to restore the *union sacrée* and save the Cabinet, the High Command would have to be reorganized. Briand appealed to Joffre's "patriotism to save the government by accepting the changes." Fully informed of the political realities, Joffre agreed to Briand's plans for reorganization. Joffre, relinquishing day-to-day control of the French armies on the Western front, was to assume the newly created post of technical adviser to the government. It was agreed that Joffre's control would extend over both the commander in chief of the North-East armies and the commander in chief of the Eastern Army.[151]

The next day Briand appeared before the seventh session of the secret committee and in a vague and circumlocutionary speech announced that Joffre, with his international prestige and influence, was to be the new technical adviser to the government. In addition, Briand casually announced that the December 2, 1915, decree would be rescinded.[152] Sarrail would now be independent of Chantilly, but the abolishment of this decree did not mean that he would be independent of Joffre, for the previous day Joffre and Briand had agreed that Sarrail would be subject to the new general commander in chief's orders.

Whereas the Right and Center greeted Briand's remarks with applause, the Left devoted the session of December 5 to a bitter attack upon Joffre and the premier's reorganizational scheme. Renaudel charged that Joffre was no longer competent to lead the war effort: the Artois, Champagne, and Somme battles had been failures; the defense of Verdun had been grossly mismanaged; there was a shortage of heavy artillery as well as an unnecessary wastage of ammunition; the military hospitals were not adequately staffed; the war of attrition was a miserable failure as Joffre had employed French youth as fodder. But Renaudel's fundamental concern was "what will be the role of the man who is no longer the generalissimo?"[153] Briand refused to answer the question.

Briand's reticence only increased the left-wing pressure. Speaking for the Radicals, Joseph Noulens demanded a clarification of Joffre's new status. More specifically, Noulens asked whether Joffre's new post was "purely advisory . . . or does it confer effective authority" over both Sarrail and the future commander in chief of the Western front? Briand responded that while Sarrail would receive his directives from the government, Joffre would assist the government in determining these directives; however, for the execution of these directives Sarrail would have "full autonomy and be free to dispose of personnel and equipment under government control."[154]

Immediately, and almost in unison, Renaudel, Abel Ferry, and Pierre Masse asked the same question: would Joffre continue to sign the battle orders? Making every effort to save Joffre, Briand refused to answer the question, claiming that all the necessary information concerning the reorganization of the High Command had been furnished. The premier declared that "I have told the essential point: the autonomy of the commands will be fully guaranteed and the government will unfailingly exercise its control over all matters."[155] The Left greeted Briand's comments with marked disapproval. And for the second time in eight days, the president of the Chamber was forced to proclaim: "The session is suspended."

Briand had been quite explicit. His government would survive or collapse on the basis of his ambiguous plans for reorganization. On December 7, after completion of the hearings of the secret committee, Briand succeeded in winning a vote of confidence of 344 to 160.[156] The *union sacrée* was again under great pressure.

Briand offered his resignation to President Poincaré the following day. Poincaré refused to accept it, maintaining that Briand still had the support of the majority of the Chamber. The resignation rejected, Briand then reshuffled his Cabinet, the important change taking place in the War Ministry where General Roques, whose report had done much damage to the government, was dismissed. Briand, attempting to appease the Left, offered the War Ministry to Painlevé. Painlevé's terms for accepting the War Ministry were steep. He insisted on the dismissal of Joffre and the guarantee that Sarrail would be completely independent of any military body other than the War Ministry.[157] Briand refused these conditions and Painlevé refused to partake in Briand's new Cabinet.

During the next few days Briand succeeded in forming a new

government without difficulty, but more important, the premier realized that if some semblance of the *union sacrée* were to be restored, his recent December 3 agreement with Joffre would have to be altered. Groping for a compromise solution, Briand issued the December 13 decree, which somewhat clarified his reorganizational plans for the High Command; General Robert Nivelle was to be the new commander in chief of the French armies on the Western front, but of more significance, General in Chief Joffre, no longer general commander in chief, was appointed "technical adviser to the government for the direction of the war."[158]

But would the formation of a new Cabinet and the December 13 decree appease Briand's parliamentary critics? Briand received his answer when the Chamber convened in the afternoon of December 13. The moderate republican from the Seine-et-Oise, André Tardieu, immediately demanded Briand's resignation, claiming that the Rumanian debacle was a prime example of the government's blundering foreign policy. The conservative from the Alpes-Maritimes, Ernest Lairolle, focusing upon the December 13 decree, demanded that the ineffectual Joffre be dismissed; to have Nivelle as commander in chief on the Western front and Joffre as general in chief would result in overlapping responsibilities, debilitating delay, and unnecessary confusion. But it was Maurice Viollette who unleashed the most telling blows against the premier. The Republican Socialist deputy claimed that the basic question concerning the reorganization of the High Command was simple: would Nivelle and Sarrail be autonomous or would Joffre be the intermediary between them and the government? Viollette feared that if Sarrail were to receive his orders from Joffre, "everything will continue as in the past."

Supported by repeated left-wing applause, Viollette next criticized the failure to include Painlevé in the new Cabinet. Viollette noted that in Briand's previous government Painlevé had been the only man "who had the courage to battle perseveringly against the whims of the High Command." And if France has not "already had a disaster in the East, if a plot hatched against the leader of this army has not succeeded, we owe it to him [Painlevé]." Moreover, why was General Roques no longer the war minister? Was Roques dismissed, Viollette innocently asked, because "the report that he made on the Eastern Army was not the one that Chantilly expected?"[159]

Although Briand received a vote of confidence of 314 to 165,[160] the premier had few alternatives. On December 18 the government informed Joffre that it would be his responsiblity to send the government's decisions to Nivelle with the words "By Order," indicating that he was acting in the name of the government. A few days later Sarrail was formally notified that all decisions and suggestions that he received from General Joffre would be signed with the words "By Order," indicating that the former generalissimo was simply acting in the name of the government. Not only was the December 2, 1915, decree formally broken, but Joffre was now nothing more than a glorified messenger boy. He was no military adviser as the December 13, 1916, decree had stipulated, for he learned on December 21 that he had not been consulted when General Nivelle decided to change drastically France's 1917 operational plans. Realizing that he was being stripped of all power, Joffre personally handed his letter of resignation to Briand on December 26. The premier read the letter and, with relief, said, "You are right." A few moments later Joffre walked out of the room, convinced that Briand "felt that my resignation was a rather pitiable conclusion to political agitation which he had not known how to control."[161] No longer could it be said that Chantilly ruled France. Hereafter France's wartime military leaders would play a subordinate role to the civilian government.

The relationship between the politicians and the High Command had undergone profound changes during the last eighteen months. Several of General Sarrail's political supporters, such as Renaudel, Painlevé, Franklin-Bouillon, Viollette, Pédoya, Chaumet, Leygues, Thomas, and Bourgeois, had played a major role in this changing relationship. At various times during the previous eighteen months these politicians had successfully negated all of Joffre's attempts to have Sarrail dismissed and had arranged Sarrail's appointment as commander in chief of the Allied Eastern Army. They had forced the Viviani government to undertake and adequately supply a Balkan commitment and had pressured Briand to increase French manpower in the Balkans and to rescind the December 2, 1915, decree. Finally, strengthened by the Roques report and taking advantage of the National Assembly's growing dissatisfaction with Joffre's handling of the Verdun, Rumanian, and Somme fiascos, many left-wing politicians decided in late 1916 that the time was ripe to prevent Sarrail from being "mistreated with impunity any longer."[162]

Why did so many politicians support Sarrail? Certainly there were practical political considerations. Many Radicals, Republican Socialists, and Socialists, such as Noulens, Favre, Augagneur, Picard, Poncet, Abrami, Bénazet, Cels, Bernard, Vaillant, Bokanowski, and Dalbiez, may have considered Sarrail a convenient means to strike at the High Command.[163] But there were other powerful wartime politicians, such as André Tardieu, Georges Clemenceau, Paul Doumer, Republican Union party senator from Corsica, and André Maginot, Democratic Left deputy from the Meuse, who opposed the political pretensions and military strategy of the High Command. These politicians certainly did not rally to Sarrail's support; some, among them Clemenceau, were fervently opposed to a Balkan campaign. The fundamental reason for Sarrail's support, it would seem, is to be found in the ideological affinities between Sarrail and much of the French Left. Painlevé, Margaine, Accambray, Bourgeois, Thomas, and Renaudel defended Sarrail during the war for the very reasons that Brisson, Pédoya, and the radical press had done so before the war. Sarrail represented what much of the Left thought the French officer corps should be: competent, patriotic, and devoted to the ideals of the Republic. At both Saint-Maixent and as director of the infantry, Sarrail had attempted to change the fundamental political attitudes and ideals of the officer corps: at Saint-Maixent by educational means and as director of the infantry by predicating promotions on military competency and political criteria. In addition, Sarrail, agreeing with many Socialists and Radicals, had been one of the few generals in prewar France to stress the importance of the reserves in a forthcoming war. He therefore opposed the 1913 three-year law, the immediate prewar issue that divided the French Left and Right, whereas the High Command had little confidence in the reserves and relied instead upon a large standing army as the basis of France's defense program. Perhaps the radical academician, Albert Mathiez, best summarized the basic reason for much of the Left's support of Sarrail when he wrote the general in early 1916: "You are the only general whom the war has shown to be on our side."[164] And as events revealed, if the *union sacrée* were to be maintained, the French war governments had to make certain basic concessions. Sarrail must not be cashiered, and his command must be adequately supplied in order to prevent a defeat that could possibly justify a dismissal.

There is still another question that must be asked, but that is more difficult to answer. Why did Joffre dismiss Sarrail in July, 1915, and continue his attempts to have Sarrail removed as commander of the Eastern Army? Basically, Joffre claimed that Sarrail was militarily incompetent. Yet when one compares Sarrail's performance with that of any other French commander, particularly Castelnau's, during the first critical weeks of the war, and when one realizes that Sarrail took

Monastir without adequate support, one may have to admit that Joffre's criteria for what constituted military competency contained serious shortcomings. There may, however, have been other reasons that explain Joffre's hostility toward Sarrail. The radical republican general, with his increased political support as a result of the 1914 elections, was the only general in mid-1915 who could have been a rival for Joffre; it is possible that Joffre decided to strike against a rival, believing that he could do so with impunity. Yet personal rivalries do not fully explain why the generalissimo persistently undermined Sarrail's position as commander of the Eastern Army and effectively blunted the potential of the Balkan campaign. It may very well have been that Joffre's feelings toward Sarrail were encouraged and nurtured by Castelnau and the politically conservative G.Q.G. The High Command deeply resented Sarrail, if only because his political supporters had succeeded in overturning several of its decisions, thereby greatly increasing civilian control of the military. Moreover, the G.Q.G., like many of the politicians, had not forgotten Sarrail's prewar career. Sarrail and his supporters believed this to be the case. But if political factors were to override military considerations, then the conservative republican Joffre, the Rightist Castelnau, and the G.Q.G. had badly underestimated the domestic political situation. Sarrail may have had little influence within the G.Q.G., but the radical republican general possessed the appropriate kind of power—political power—when it was needed.

In addition to Joffre, the December, 1916, crisis claimed yet another victim. Early in January, 1917, Briand recognized that the *union sacrée* had been irreparably damaged and that he could neither heal nor conceal the animosity, passion, and mistrust engendered by the recent crisis. The premier admitted that his government had outlived its usefulness and that it would be only a matter of time before he would resign.[165] When in mid-March War Minister Lyautey angered the Chamber by tactlessly refusing to answer questions concerning the deficiencies in France's aviation program, Briand, although maintaining a majority in the Chamber, took the opportunity to resign. And unlike the previous December, Poincaré accepted the resignation and called Alexandre Ribot to form a new government.

The year of 1916 had not been an easy one for Sarrail either. A poignant letter to his younger brother reflected the hopes and uncertainties of France's most politically powerful general:

And 1917 is almost here. And I am writing to you. What is there to say? What is there to hope for? What is there to prophesy? I had happy moments during 1916, but also many sad ones. What will happen to you, to me, to the country in the new year? You cannot imagine all my thoughts both about the past and the future. And yet, despite everything, despite the shattered illusions, despite the heartaches, I cannot bring myself to the point of not still cherishing some hopes—even when I find myself alone, even when I think that if ever I return to Montauban, it will be to ride in my own funeral procession.[166]

Sarrail was overly pessimistic. In March, 1917, when Ribot replaced Briand as premier, the new war minister would be Paul Painlevé, and in September, 1917, Painlevé would succeed Ribot as premier. Sarrail's position was apparently still secure.

VIII. Success and Setback

In the autumn of 1916, while Sarrail's offensive was in progress, Constantine sent royalist troops with artillery into the northern provinces
of Thessaly and Epirus. The presence of royalist troops at the rear of
Sarrail's army alarmed the Allies. They requested Constantine to
withdraw his troops southward and to surrender a good share of his
war matériel. On November 21 Constantine formally refused to surrender the military equipment. A week later, following a cordial
meeting with the Greek king, admiral of the French Mediterranean
Fleet Dartige du Fournet felt that the Greek king would peacefully
surrender the military equipment if faced with a show of strength.
Therefore, on December 1, under Dartige's command, three thousand
Allied sailors, expecting no royalist opposition, disembarked at
Piraeus and advanced to Athens for the purpose of confiscating the
royalist arsenal. Greek troops, however, surprised the Allied landing
party and inflicted more than two hundred casualties upon the sailors.
The next day royalist troops and reservists wantonly attacked Venizelists. Only when Allied artillery shells landed near the Royal Palace
on December 2 did Constantine call a halt to the fighting and agree to
surrender a few cannons.[1]

Agitated by the events at Athens, Sarrail, who was still conducting his offensive north of Monastir, immediately cabled Chantilly on December 2 that it was intolerable to permit the continued royalist concentration in Thessaly. To prevent the possibility of a simultaneous frontal attack from the Central Powers and a royalist attack against the Eastern Army's western flank, Sarrail proposed that the Allies undertake an immediate offensive against Larissa where the Greek royalists were concentrating. If the strike against Larissa were successful, Sarrail wanted to move further south against Athens, for it was imperative "to put Greece out of commission."[2]

For the first time since his arrival at Salonika Sarrail's suggestions concerning royalist Greece were readily accepted by Briand. The events of December 1 and 2 at Athens convinced Briand that not only had all hopes of Constantine's joining the Entente evaporated, but that the Greek king had become a menace to the Eastern Army's existence. Thus on December 4 the premier suggested to the other Allies that Constantine be deposed.[3] The next day Joffre informed Sarrail that the "political aim pursued by the government, if it is adopted by the Allies, is to depose the King and put Venizelos in power." Therefore, Sarrail was to prepare "to render the King and all his supporters powerless by force."[4] Two days later, in order to assure that any military action against Constantine would be successful, Joffre dispatched two additional French divisions to the Balkans, thereby increasing the Allied Eastern Army to twenty-three divisions of which eight would be French.[5]

The Allies, however, rejected Briand's recommendation that Constantine be deposed. England, Italy, and Russia, the latter two anti-Venizelist, claimed that Sarrail did not possess adequate troops to engage both Constantine and the Bulgar-German forces.[6] The three Allies were not prepared to supply the necessary reinforcements. On December 7, when Joffre requested London and Rome to increase their Balkan commitment by two and four divisions respectively so that the Eastern Army would have enough manpower to undertake a rapid strike against royalist Greece while thwarting a possible German-Bulgarian attack from the north,[7] Cadorna and Robertson rejected the request and suggested that the Eastern Army could extricate itself from the possibility of a simultaneous Constantine-Bulgar-German attack by retreating to Salonika, which could be defended.[8] If enemy pressure became too great upon Salonika, the C.I.G.S. believed that the Eastern Army could evacuate the Balkans, as the collapse of Rumania in early December meant that all future Allied offenses originating from Macedonia would be fruitless.[9]

For the sake of Allied unity Briand did not pursue his demand that Constantine be deposed. However, the premier was successful in urging the other Allies to agree that some measures must be taken to assure the Eastern Army's security. On December 8 France and England imposed a naval blockade of Old Greece, one that was intended to last until Constantine had given some indication that he was no longer hostile to the Entente. On December 14 the Allies presented a note to Constantine demanding that all royalist troops and matériel be transferred from northern Greece to the Peloponnesus.[10]

Although Briand had succumbed to the Allies' pressure, he was not prepared to tolerate a hostile Greece. On December 12 the premier wrote to Paul Cambon, French ambassador to England, that if Constantine did not withdraw his troops from Thessaly, Sarrail would be ordered to seize Larissa, the French fleet would take Volo and bombard the other Greek ports, Athens would be occupied by French troops and a French "military administration would be temporarily set up in Greece . . . while [at the same time] demonstrating an absolute desire to respect the [Greek] dynasty."[11]

Although Constantine accepted the Allies' December 14 note, the crisis did not ease. On December 19 France intercepted a message from William II to his sister, Queen Sophia of Greece, in which the kaiser stated that "Tino's [Constantine's] intervention with his main forces against Sarrail's western flank will lead to victory in Macedonia. May our cooperation bring success! You can count on every assistance from me now and in the future. A part of your army ought to prevent enemy landings at Athens and in the Gulf of Corinth."[12] Briand and Joffre were shaken by this latest disclosure.[13] Joffre immediately notified Sarrail that if royalist troops were not withdrawn from Thessaly, the Eastern commander must "put Greece out of commission."[14] Fearing that Sarrail's latest instructions would lead the Allies to a complete rupture with Greece, London demanded an immediate conference with France.[15]

At the London conference of December 26-28 the French representatives, supporting Sarrail's view of the Greek situation, claimed that the evacuation of Thessaly by the Greeks was not being carried out in accordance with the Allies' note of December 14 and thus the Eastern Army was in danger of an attack by the Germans in front and by the Greeks in the rear. To prevent a two-front attack France again recommended that England send two additional divisions to the Balkans and that the Allies make the necessary preparations to undertake an attack on the Greeks in Thessaly. On the other hand, the British representatives, led by England's new prime minister, David Lloyd George, Robertson and Foreign Secretary Arthur Balfour, stated that according to reports received by them, Germany would abstain from a major offensive against the Eastern Army and that the royalist evacuation of Thessaly was being carried out; thus Sarrail needed neither additional troops nor a free hand against Constantine.[16]

For three days France, which wanted a more aggressive policy toward Constantine, and England, which still had hopes that the Greek king would follow a policy of benevolent neutrality, sought to compromise their differences. Although agreeing with Balfour's opinion that "it was absurd to try to be logical in regard to the situation in Greece, [for] the system that was forced upon us there was neither coherent nor intelligible,"[17] the conferees ended the impasse by agreeing to send military representatives to Greece who would report on the manner in which the Greek government was conducting its promised withdrawal from Thessaly. If this report were unfavorable, Sarrail would then be permitted to propose the course of action that he considered necessary.[18]

No sooner had the conference concluded than London learned that French troops were concentrating near Kozani for an apparent strike at Larissa. In reply to England's request for an explanation of Sarrail's activities the French government claimed that the diversion of French troops to Kozani was a precautionary move, since royalist activity in Thessaly seemed to indicate that Constantine had not foregone the possibility of attacking the Eastern Army. Not satisfied with France's interpretation of what was occurring in Greece, England vociferously protested that France was not agreeing to the decisions recently taken at the London Conference.[19] Briand again heeded the protests. Sarrail was reminded on January 1, 1917, not to undertake military action against Greece without prior authorization from Paris and London.[20]

In light of the divergence of views concerning the Greek question it was decided to summon an Allied conference. In the first days of January, 1917, Briand, Sonnino, Lloyd George, Robertson, Cadorna, Milne, and Sarrail met in Rome for the purpose of attempting to reach an understanding concerning two basic Balkan questions. What was to be the future role of the Eastern Army? What was to be the Allied position vis-à-vis Constantine's Greece?

At the Rome Conference Sarrail once again stated that he feared an attack by Bulgar-German troops from the north and a simultaneous royalist attack from the south. He maintained that Constantine had not adhered to the Allied note of December 14 that had called for the withdrawal of troops and ammunition from Thessaly; in the northern provinces royalist reservists were living as civilians and large stores of weapons were hidden in schools and churches. Sarrail proposed that he be allowed to undertake "police action" against Greece without formally declaring war against Constantine. Sarrail wanted to move into Thessaly, confiscate all weapons, and intern all the royalist troops. Lloyd George, in a personal interview with Sarrail, rejected the general's proposals, fearing that Allied military action would precipitate open civil war between royalists and Venizelists as well as arouse American public opinion, which might draw parallels between Germany's invasion of Belgium and Sarrail's proposed "police action" against neutral Greece. With reluctance Sarrail accepted England's proposals that the Allies issue yet another ultimatum to Constantine, one that reiterated their previous demands of December 14. The Greek king accepted the Allies' January 8 ultimatum to move men and supplies to the Peloponnesus. How effectively he intended to fulfill its demands remained to be seen, for he appreciated that Italy, Serbia, Russia, England, and France had conflicting aspirations in the Balkans, and concerted action against the Germanophile Constantine appeared remote.

As a means of deciding upon a unified military strategy the Rome Conference was a failure. Both England and Italy maintained that the Eastern Army should remain on the defensive. Believing that the Balkan front was overextended, they urged Sarrail to withdraw from Monastir, which was under constant enemy barrage. Sarrail, supported by Briand, Russia, and Serbia, refused to desert Monastir. Although agreeing to remain at Monastir, England and Italy refused Briand's impassioned pleas to dispatch eastward three additional divisions, which would have strengthened Sarrail's army to twenty-six divisions. Sonnino contended that all available Italian manpower was needed on the Austrian frontier, while Lloyd George maintained that British shipping was inadequate to transport additional British troops to the Balkans. As the prime minister readily appreciated, without additional divisions there could be no offensive. When the three-day conference was concluded, no agreement had been reached concerning the question of further reinforcements for the Eastern Army nor had its precise role for the new year been defined. Sarrail was "disgusted by the conference. There was talk. But no decision was made. They tried to deceive one another unnecessarily. It was just another conference." He correctly asked "Where do we go from here?"[21]

After returning to Salonika, Sarrail received his 1917 directives from War Minister Lyautey: Sarrail's army could not remain inactive when the Allies unleashed their forthcoming offensive on the Western front. Consequently, the Eastern Army's mission was to keep the enemy troops in Macedonia from being shifted to the principal fronts. Sarrail was requested to submit a plan of operations that, if agreeable to Lyautey, would be forwarded to London for consideration.[22]

On February 8 and 9 Sarrail submitted plans for a spring offensive; his army, composed of twenty-three divisions, would attack a slightly larger enemy force at five different points. The British were to attack on the Struma and also west of Lake Dojran; the Serbs, again carrying the brunt of the offensive, were to attack in the Moglena Mountains, to the east of the Cerna River, and if successful, move sharply eastward, thereby taking the Bulgarian defense fortifications along the Vardar in the rear. Further west, from the bend of the Cerna to Monastir, French and Italian divisions would attack in the direction of Prilep; on the far left, French units were to move between Lakes Prespa and Ohrid in an attempt to seize Resan, which lay eighteen miles west of Monastir. The destination of Sarrail's offensive was to be Sofia.[23]

Upon receiving these ambitious plans, Lyautey reminded Sarrail that "the goal of the Eastern Army must remain proportionate to its resources."[24] The Eastern commander replied on February 19 that the goals of his offensive, in accordance with the war minister's suggestions, would be greatly reduced in scope. Sarrail would simply contain the enemy in the southern Balkans since "my role is merely to facilitate a favorable result along the other fronts."[25] Three weeks later, in early March, Sarrail was informed that not only had England accepted his plans for an offensive, but that at a recent Anglo-French Conference held at Calais, the role of the Eastern Army had been clearly defined. Briand and Lloyd George agreed that it was not possible to envisage the taking of Sofia or any other kind of large-scale operation originating from Salonika without a simultaneous Allied advance from the northern Balkans. Since Rumania and Russia could no longer render appreciable assistance in the Balkans, it was decided that the "decisive defeat of the Bulgarian army is not a practical objective . . . [therefore] the mission of the Allied forces in Salonika is to hold the enemy forces presently found there and to take advantage of attacking the enemy, if that seems opportune."[26]

Sarrail scheduled his offensive for April 24 and 26. Three British divisions were to launch the offensive by attacking along the Vardar–Lake Dojran front. Two days later, from the Vardar to Lake Prespa,

The Southern Balkans

the French 30th and 122nd divisions, the Serbian First and Second armies, the French 11th, 16th, and 17th colonial divisions, the Italian 35th Division, and two Russian brigades, and the French 57th, 76th, and 156th divisions would undertake the major portion of the offensive. The forthcoming offensive had no specific destination, such as Sofia or Prilep; Sarrail thought it best not to specify a certain goal "so as not to face a defeat if this point is not reached."[27] At best, the Serbs, whom Sarrail was counting upon to break the enemy lines, would advance northward and then cut eastward into the Vardar valley. At worst, the basic objective of the offensive would be met, namely, to prevent the enemy's withdrawal from the southern Balkans.[28]

During the night of April 24 the British 22nd and 26th divisions, packed tightly together along a two-mile front along the western fringes of Lake Dojran, raced out of their trenches into the Jumeaux Ravine with the intention of taking the nearby heavily fortified ridges. The British attack was easily repulsed by superior Bulgarian fire power, particularly machine guns and howitzers, and then by infantry counterattacks. Further west, at Macukovo, the 60th Division, also attacking at night, reached the first line of enemy trenches and then discovered that the battlefield was bathed not only in blood but also in light, as searchlights succeeded in making the attackers easy prey for enemy crossfire. Influenced by the British failures and the heavy snowstorms west of the Vardar, Sarrail postponed the major portion of his offensive, scheduled for April 26.

On May 5 Allied artillery flashed all along the Monastir-Dojran front. The Eastern Army's spring offensive began three days later. The British results were similar to those of April 24-25; further west, in the Moglena Mountains, the Serb Second Army attacked the lower portions of the Dobropolje Mountain and six days later were still one thousand yards from the summit; to the Serbs' left, in the bend of the Cerna, the single Italian and two French divisions were stopped. Further west, the 57th and 156th divisions failed to seize the hills overlooking Monastir.

Concerned by the apparent futility of the offensive, Painlevé, war minister in the newly created Ribot government, strongly suggested on May 14 that the offensive be halted. But Sarrail attempted yet another effort to pierce the enemy lines, and three days later the 11th, 16th, 57th, and 156th divisions again attacked. All these attacks were repulsed and on May 21 Sarrail finally terminated his offensive. Although Sarrail had fulfilled the role assigned to his army—to retain the enemy in the Balkans, thus preventing its dispatch to the other fronts—his offensive must be classified a major disappointment, since, at a cost of fourteen thousand casualties, no appreciable territorial gains had been made.[29]

Several reasons explain the Eastern Army's failure to achieve a tactical victory. The offensive was poorly coordinated: Sarrail had made no attempt to withdraw troops from one part of the line in order to concentrate them in another sector with a view to attacking in depth and achieving a breakthrough. Instead, the offensive was simply "pin-pricks everywhere and not even synchronised."[30] Field leadership within the various armies was slipshod as French and Italian infantrymen sometimes attacked without adequate artillery support and British artillery accidentally fell upon British troops.[31] In addition, unlike the previous fall's offensive where maneuvering was possible, the spring of 1917 offensive was basically a case of attacking fully fortified positions, elevated and well defended. If these entrenched positions were to be taken, superiority of manpower and of artillery was needed. The Eastern Army did not possess these necessary prerequisites.[32] Lastly, Sarrail blundered when he expected the Serbs to carry the brunt of the offensive. Well before the spring offensive began, he was aware that the heavy losses taken during the 1916 offensive had created a problem in morale for the Serbs.[33] Yet Sarrail persisted in thinking that the Serbs could repeat their outstanding performance of the previous year. However, when the 1917 offensive began, the Serbs' First Army with its four divisions refused to leave the trenches, despite Sarrail's pleas to do so.[34] Not only had the Serbs been badly decimated by the 1916 fall offensive, but the Serbian High Command had been shaken by a recent domestic political crisis. Several high-ranking Serbian officers were arrested in December, 1916, and early 1917 and charged with conspiring to establish a military dictatorship. These officers had a good deal of support within the officer corps, so much so that the Serbian Third Army was abolished, its three divisions attached to the First Army, and a good number of its officers interned in Tunisia.[35] Rather than risk testing the weakened loyalty and sagging morale of its military machine, the Serbian High Command deemed it best to refrain from fully partaking in Sarrail's latest offensive.

Although the buoyant hopes for the May offensive had not been remotely reached, Sarrail had at least one consolation by June, 1917. Constantine was deposed and Venizelos became the prime minister of a unified Greece, thus removing the possibility that the Eastern Army would be attacked by a hostile Greece. The political turn of events at Athens was surprising when one considers the divergent views that the Allies held throughout 1916 on the Greek question. Italy had been violently anti-Venizelist; the czar had warmly supported Constantine. Briand, although at first believing that Constantine would support the Allies, had become increasingly suspicious of the king's intentions and, as a result, had recommended stern action against Greece. England had successfully resisted French demands that stronger action be taken against Constantine, hoping that the Greek monarch would eventually pursue a conciliatory attitude.

During the first three months of 1917 the breach between Paris and London widened. The source of this friction was the Allies' January 8 demand that Constantine withdraw all his troops to the Peloponnesus. Supported by reports from Sarrail and other French military and diplomatic personnel in Greece, Briand maintained that although thousands of Greek troops were withdrawing from Thessaly, there was ample evidence that Constantine was sending weapons, furloughed officers, reservists, and paramilitary groups into Thessaly. The continued presence of royalist forces in Thessaly, according to Briand and Sarrail, posed a threat to the security of the Eastern Army; therefore, the premier proposed to London in January and February that not only the Allies maintain their blockade of Greece, but that Sarrail be permitted to move into Thessaly in order to seize Larissa and the port city of Volo. The Allied occupation of these cities, "accompanied by formal guarantees for the future with respect to Greek sovereignty and the present Government, would result in removing any inclination on Greece's part for a possible attack in liaison with our enemies."[36] On the other hand, Lloyd George, relying upon reports filed by Milne and General G. F. Phillips, who had been sent to Greece to oversee the royalist withdrawal from Thessaly, came to the conclusion that Constantine was fulfilling the terms of the recent Allied ultimatum and that remaining reservists in Thessaly posed no substantial threat to the Eastern Army. Thus the British government not only rejected Briand's request concerning the occupation of Thessaly, but also suggested that the blockade of Greece be lifted.[37]

The divergent, if not contradictory, reports submitted by the British and French military representatives on the manner in which the January 8 ultimatum was being fulfilled led London to draw two conclusions. First, France wanted to occupy Thessaly for political reasons, not military reasons. The occupation of Thessaly was purportedly the first step in France's design "to bring Greece under their exclusive or at least predominant influence."[38] Lord Robert Cecil, acting British foreign secretary, commented in May that "the actions and language of several of the French agents in Greece during recent months have raised a suspicion . . . that [an] influential section of French opinion is anxious to utilise the present opportunities to secure for France something like the permanent protectorate of Greece."[39] Second, whether in Whitehall, the Foreign Office, or at the British Embassy in Athens, there arose the uneasy suspicion that Sarrail was not only a willing agent for France's imperialistic designs, but that he was determining if not dictating Briand's Greek policy. Concerning the French proposal to occupy Larissa and Volo, Balfour wrote that "General Sarrail is suspected of using a perfectly legitimate desire to secure the safety of his left flank as an antimonarchial instrument."[40] The British Admiralty and General Staff believed that "the French proposal may have mainly a political bearing since it may be an excuse for an extension of their sphere in Northern Greece. . . . It is almost certain that one, if not the chief of General Sarrail's objects in this was to intervene more effectively in Greek affairs."[41] More specifically, England feared that the occupation of Volo, one of Sarrail's "schemes," would have given France an opportunity "to pick a quarrel with Greece,"[42] thereby giving the Eastern commander a convenient excuse to overthrow Constantine while undertaking the complete occupation of the country.[43]

But why, the British reasoned, should Sarrail recommend the Allied occupation of Greece if there were no military necessity for such a move? Guesses were quickly forthcoming: France wanted a postwar "stepping stone" to the Middle East; Sarrail, "a member of the Financial Democratic Party" was "engineering a scheme for the French Freemasons and Jews to make money"; the Eastern commander's "personal dislike of King Constantine had unreasonably coloured his whole attitude with a desire for revenge"; and Sarrail wanted to enhance his prestige with a victory against Constantine as a first step to the eventual overthrow of the French Republic.[44]

Were the British fears justified? There is no evidence to suggest that during the first three months of 1917 France had any intention of using the royalist threat in Thessaly as a means to gain permanent political or economic control of Greece. French military, diplomatic, and political leaders emphasized that their proposal for sterner action against royalist Greece was predicated upon immediate military requirements and not ulterior political motives.[45] French intelligence activities and the role of the Allied Commission of Military Control during the winter of 1917 appear to substantiate the French contention.

In January, under Roquefeuil's direction, France greatly expanded its intelligence network in Greece. The basic reasons for the reorganization were twofold. Following the events of early December at Athens, Constantine had badly disrupted the French secret service by arresting scores of French agents, most of whom were Greek nationals.[46] Second, the December massacre at Athens demonstrated, at least to the French, that war between Constantine and the Entente was imminent; therefore, all information concerning the location and quantity of royalist troops and supplies would be invaluable.[47] Roquefeuil, Commander Emmanuel Clergeau, newly appointed naval attaché in Greece, their agents, and the French diplomatic corps scattered throughout Greece sent daily reports to Salonika and Paris during the first months of 1917. These reports contained information such as the names of royalist sympathizers, claims that the royalists were not fulfilling the terms of the January 8 ultimatum and that the paramilitary leagues as well as the Greek General Staff intended to attack the Eastern Army, the names of royalist officers sympathetic to the Entente, detailed accounts of royalist troop movements, the temper of the local press, the location of royalist troops and supply depots in northern Greece, and the strength and location of the royalist paramilitary organizations.[48] The only apparent exceptions to the Intelligence Service's function as a fact-gathering agency were Roquefeuil's suggestion for a military strike against royalist Greece,[49] Clergeau's recommendations that the Allied blockade not be lifted until royalist Greece complied with the January 8 ultimatum,[50] and Clergeau's modest attempts to persuade a few Greek politicians to support the Entente[51] and his more successful attempts to subsidize a few Greek newspapers, thus establishing a convenient Allied propaganda organ in Athens.[52] Nevertheless, the overwhelming collection of evidence strongly suggests that if Sarrail or Briand were motivated by other than military concerns, it was an extremely well-kept secret.

London's apprehension concerning French intentions in Greece also centered upon the activities of the Allied Commission of Military Control. Following Constantine's acceptance of the Entente's January 8 ultimatum that royalist troops and war matériel be removed from northern Greece, the Allies established the Allied Commission of Military Control as a means to supervise the royalist withdrawal to the Peloponnesus.[53] England suspected that Sarrail was using this organization as an instrument for either French aggrandizement in Greece or as a means of provoking a war with Constantine.[54]

The British representative to the Allied Commission of Military

Control was General G. F. Phillips. However, the chief of this organization was General Jean Cauboue, who received his orders directly
from Sarrail. Roquefeuil served as Cauboue's adjunct on the commission. Roquefeuil assigned several of his intelligence agents to the
commission. With its liberty to move throughout Greece to check
Constantine's compliance with the January 8 ultimatum, the Commission of Military Control offered a convenient means by which
French intelligence personnel could roam freely throughout the country. "We shall limit our investigations," Roquefeuil wrote Lacaze, "to
military and related questions."[55]

Sarrail emphasized to Cauboue in mid-January that the commission
was to have "a purely military character" and that its basic function
was to oversee the royalist military withdrawal.[56] Sarrail·also told
Cauboue that Constantine must fulfill exactly the terms of the January
8 ultimatum. There could be no exceptions, for as Sarrail explained,
"all [royalist] demands should be rejected outright."[57] This meant that
Sarrail wanted every piece of war equipment and every royalist sailor
and soldier except those needed to maintain domestic order to be sent
to the Peloponnesus. In the following months Sarrail, acting through
Cauboue,[58] tolerated neither royalist procrastinations nor Constantine's attempt to arrange a compromise on the number of royalist units
to be withdrawn.[59] When Constantine asked whether a small number
of his troops could remain in Athens, Sarrail wrote Cauboue: "When
people begin to talk . . . one always ends up by being swindled. I
think that we have been dupes for too long. I do not therefore agree to
maintaining a single sailor at Athens or Piraeus. You can tell that to
the Greeks and to the Control Commission and even state, if you
wish, that you do not share my point of view but that you are forced
to carry it out."[60]

Sarrail was prepared to oppose Constantine, London, or anyone
else on the fundamental question of royalist withdrawal to the
Peloponnesus. When Briand questioned whether Cauboue's demands
upon royalist Greece were unduly harsh,[61] Sarrail successfully assured
Paris that Cauboue's demands were "the minimum that could be
requested."[62] When General Léon Bousquier, Braquet's successor as
military attaché at Athens, supported the claims of General Phillips
that royalist troops in Thessaly posed no serious threat to the Eastern
Army and that Sarrail was making unnecessarily stiff military demands upon the Greeks,[63] the Eastern commander prevailed upon
Lyautey to have Bousquier recalled.[64]

Sarrail's stringent instructions to Cauboue, as well as his recommendations to Paris that the Allies should occupy Thessaly and maintain their blockade of Greece, sprang not from any sinister intent to create a French protectorate in Greece nor from any desire to provoke a war with Greece so as "to keep himself in the public eye, to draw attention to Salonika and to prevent it being regarded as a side show."[65] Fear of Constantine's intentions explains Sarrail's action. British military attaché General W. E. Fairholme was correct when he observed in March that "General Sarrail, in advocating more drastic demands, is acting in perfect good faith, and not with a view to gratifying personal ambition or furthering French political aims."[66]

Did Sarrail, as the British maintained, have an undue impact upon Briand's Greek policy in the winter of 1917? Certainly Sarrail's claim that the continued presence of Greek royalists in Thessaly constituted a major threat to the Eastern Army was a factor in influencing Briand's increasingly anti-royalist policy. Moreover, there was no one in the French military and diplomatic delegation in Greece who successfully opposed Sarrail's assessment of the royalist threat in northern Greece: Cauboue, Roquefeuil, and Clergeau substantiated Sarrail's judgment of the situation in Thessaly. Guillemin did likewise, willingly deferring to Sarrail on all questions concerning the military security of the Eastern Army.[67] Bousquier was the only prominent French official to disagree with the prevailing opinion concerning the situation in Thessaly and he was recalled. Yet, in the last analysis, the major determinants in molding Briand's increasingly hostile policy toward royalist Greece were not Sarrail, Roquefeuil, or Guillemin, for the premier had successfully rejected on several occasions during the previous fourteen months their proposals that stronger action be taken against Constantine. The decisive factor that convinced Briand to recommend Constantine's abdication, the Allied occupation of Thessaly, and the continued Allied blockade of Greece was the royalist attack of the Allied troops on December 1 and 2 at Athens. The events of early December, 1916, had convinced Briand that royalist Greece had become a serious threat to the Eastern Army's security; thus the premier had suggested as early as December 4, 1916, that Constantine be deposed and on December 12 the premier warned that Constantine's hostility might force France to assume control of Greece.[68] Briand's recommendations during the winter of 1917 for direct military action against Constantine were not of course implemented because Rome, Petrograd, and London refused to sanction the premier's plans. Briand heeded the advice of the other Allies, for not to do so would have placed a severe strain upon the alliance.

Unfortunately for Constantine, by the end of March the international political situation was changing: Briand and Nicholas II were no longer in power. Premier Ribot and War Minister Painlevé, upon assuming power in March, 1917, made it abundantly clear that Briand's policy of "undue mildness" toward Greece would no longer be tolerated. Notified of the new French government's determination to take "a stronger line" against Constantine,[69] the Foreign Office, convinced that the "rather intermittent check which we have hitherto been able to place upon General Sarrail's ambition will now be removed," postulated what was considered to be the crux of the problem: "Are we, or are we not, going to allow the French to assume a Protectorate in Greece?"[70]

Convinced that Constantine was violating the January 8 ultimatum and that the royalists presented a threat to Sarrail's army, Ribot and Painlevé wasted no time preparing what was hoped to be a decisive blow against the Greek king. On April 7 Paris notified Sarrail to undertake secret preparations for a move on either Larissa or Athens, or both. Sarrail immediately replied that he was preparing his spring offensive. He cautioned that to direct Allied divisions against Greece at that time would entail suspending the offensive. Painlevé persisted; on April 26 the war minister asked whether it would be unduly dangerous to wait until the offensive were completed before striking against Thessaly and Athens. Sarrail responded that he could move easily against Larissa, but lack of troops dictated that ground operations against Athens be postponed until the offensive had been completed.[71]

On May 7, just as the Eastern Army's offensive began, Painlevé wrote Sarrail that "the essential thing now is to be sure of Greece before June 15, Look into it, think about it, and tell us energetically what you think possible and reasonable. You will be followed."[72] On May 21, the same day that Sarrail was calling a halt to his spring offensive, Painlevé notified the Eastern commander that "in order to settle the Greek question at once, there is reason, if our Allies give us a free hand in Greece, to combine operations in Thessaly with a landing in the Athens area." And not surprisingly, Sarrail immediately concurred that it was necessary "to eradicate the Greek king and his dynasty; only at this price will we have the freedom to concern ourselves with Bulgaria."[73] He further told Painlevé not to worry about what "England and Italy have said, now say, or will say, [but rather] confront them with a fait accompli and let me direct operations without concerning myself with the Allied legations."[74]

On May 28 Ribot and Painlevé traveled to London and successfully persuaded Lloyd George that Constantine must be deposed. Consequently, in early June, acting on behalf of the Allies, Charles Jonnart arrived in Greece and issued an ultimatum to the Greek king demanding his abdication. This ultimatum was supported by two of Sarrail's divisions: one commanded by General Paul Venel moved into Thessaly, the other commanded by General Charles Regnault landed at the Isthmus of Corinth on June 10 and then proceeded to Athens. Encountering for the first time a determined and united Allied front and with much of his army bottled up in the Peloponnesus and thus unable to threaten the Eastern Army, Constantine abdicated on June 11 in favor of his son, Alexander. Two weeks later, with French troops in the Greek capital, Venizelos returned to Athens from Salonika to assume his former position as prime minister of a united country, committed to the Allied cause. However, it would take several months to purge the Germanophiles within the officer corps as well as to mobilize, equip, and transport two hundred thousand troops. In mid-1918 the Greek army would be prepared to play a decisive role in the last and most successful offensive of the Balkan campaign.[75]

Several factors explain England's surprising decision at the London conference of May 28-29 to depose Constantine. First, London was convinced that reconciliation between royalists and Venizelists was impossible.[76] Second, England found itself isolated on the question of maintaining Constantine in power. The czar had been deposed in February, and in mid-April Italy gave France a free hand against Constantine with the understanding that the Greek dynasty would be maintained; in return Italy was promised postwar concessions in Asia Minor.[77] Third, London's fears concerning France's long-range intentions in Greece were somewhat alleviated when the Ribot government agreed in April to London's frequent request that Sarrail no longer be affiliated with the Allied Commission of Military Control. Hereafter, a committee composed of Allied representatives would share supreme control over this commission.[78] Furthermore, in early May General Fairholme reported a frank conversation held with French Military Attaché Braquet. Braquet explained that France had "no special interests of her own" in Greece. However, looking ahead to the postwar period when France would be seeking allies, Braquet stated that since the northern Balkan states in the postwar era would probably be under Germanic or Slavic influence, it was imperative that "Greece should be both friendly towards France and strong." Evidently

England did not find France's plans objectionable even though a "friendly" Greece meant that the German-oriented Constantine could not be tolerated. A "strong" Greece, which England also sought, was synonymous with an independent Greece.[79] English apprehension was further assuaged in late May when France agreed that a seasoned diplomat, Charles Jonnart, not Sarrail, would carry out the forthcoming negotiations with Constantine concerning his abdication. The British believed that Jonnart would "provide a counterweight to the intrigues and impulsiveness of General Sarrail and his subordinates."[80]

There was yet another reason for England's acquiescence to French demands. England's agreement to Constantine's abdication was the price that Lloyd George had to pay for the removal of British troops from Salonika. As early as April 17 the English prime minister had warned Ribot and Painlevé that if Sarrail's forthcoming offensive were to fail, Britain would drastically reduce her manpower in the Balkans. At an Anglo-French conference held in Paris on May 5, the very eve of Sarrail's May offensive, Lloyd George was more explicit. Although he had always been in favor of the Salonika expedition, he announced that Britain's shipping was not adequate to supply both the Balkan and Palestinian campaigns. Thus, the prime minister announced that the Balkan campaign should be reduced to nothing more than an entrenched camp surrounding Salonika. The British would therefore begin withdrawing one division and two cavalry brigades on June 1; however, Lloyd George promised to reconsider his decision to withdraw the troops if Sarrail's imminent offensive were to result in an overwhelming victory so as to assure that "before the end of May Bulgaria would come to terms."[81] This meant that Lloyd George, who was fully aware of the limited objectives of the Eastern Army's forthcoming offensive, had unilaterally assigned a new mission to Sarrail's army, one that was not only unrealistic,[82] but incongruous with the prime minister's previous policy statements. For example, at the Rome Conference the prime minister, readily recognizing that Sarrail's troops "were far from being a good specimen of an average French Army . . . [and] were far below strength," refused to reinforce the British Balkan contingency, maintaining that a shortage of ships prevented the transport of troops to Salonika. Yet, as the prime minister realized, without additional troops, the Eastern Army could not advance beyond Monastir.[83] Likewise, at the Anglo-French Calais Conference in late February Lloyd George had agreed that the Bulgarians could not be defeated. Therefore, it was agreed by the Allies that the purpose of Sarrail's spring offensive was not to reach Sofia, but to retain the enemy divisions in the Balkans so that they would not be diverted to the other fronts.

The sudden shift in British policy, dramatically put forth at the May Paris Conference, was the result of an uneasy agreement between the Easterner Lloyd George and his chief of staff, the Westerner Robertson. If Sarrail's May offensive did not force Bulgaria to seek peace, the prime minister promised to reduce England's commitment to the Balkans, a suggestion that received Robertson's enthusiastic support. For his part, Robertson had to consent to send those troops released from the Balkans not to the Western front but to Palestine in order to assist General Edmund Allenby against the Turks. Robertson disliked a Palestinian campaign almost as intensely as he did the Balkan one, but at least those British Balkan troops sent to Palestine would not only make a greater contribution to winning the war than the Eastern Army, but they would "enjoy a better climate and be under British control."[84]

At the Paris Conference the French vehemently protested the British decision, but to no avail. The French representatives then shrewdly tied the question of troop withdrawal to the political situation at Athens. Painlevé and Ribot argued that the Allies must be certain of having a friendly Greece before weakening their forces at Salonika. Although asserting that Constantine had fulfilled his promise to evacuate Thessaly, Lloyd George was prepared to comply with French requests. It was agreed at the Paris Conference that once the Eastern Army's forthcoming offensive had been terminated, Sarrail should be permitted to occupy Thessaly.[85] And three weeks later at the London Conference, when it was obvious that Sarrail's recent offensive had not forced Bulgaria to seek peace terms, Lloyd George conveniently decided that Constantine had become a threat to the security of the Eastern Army. Consequently, as a quid pro quo for the withdrawal of British troops, the prime minister agreed to French demands for deposing Constantine.[86]

While making final arrangements to remove Constantine, France and England were shaken by two unexpected events. On June 3 Italy proclaimed a protectorate over Albania and six days later Italian troops in southwestern Albania poured into northern Greece. Italy's moves were inspired by a sinking fear that her postwar territorial aspirations would not be satisfied.[87] In the previous April at the Allied conference held at St. Jean de Maurienne, Italy had sanctioned deposing Constantine. In return, Sonnino was promised portions of the Turkish Empire, such as Smyrna and its surrounding territory.

However, in the ensuing weeks London and Paris appeared to be re-
neging on their promises. Ribot and Lloyd George insisted that Italy
would receive Smyrna only when Russia, which had not attended the
recent conference, sanctioned the St. Jean de Maurienne agreement
and this the Russian provisional government refused to do.[88] Even
more significantly, Lloyd George declared in May that the postwar
zones of influence in Asia Minor would be determined by whichever
country made the greatest wartime contribution to the defeat of
Turkey.[89] This stipulation obviously repudiated the recent St. Jean de
Maurienne agreement, since Italy, unlike England, had no troops in
the Middle East.

Bitterly resenting being finessed out of its apparent gains in Asia
Minor,[90] suspecting France's ulterior motives concerning the future of
Greece,[91] and deeply fearing French intentions in Albania because
France had not only supported Essad Pasha in 1916, but had recently
taken the initiative in creating the independent Albanian state of
Koritza,[92] Rome suddenly decided to solidify its territorial ambitions
in the Balkans. As a first step toward this goal, Rome proclaimed the
unity and independence of all of Albania, while emphasizing that
Albania was henceforth under the aegis and protection of Italy. Paris
was notified by Sonnino that Italy had proclaimed a protectorate over
Albania because France had been responsible for the creation of the
autonomous Albanian state of Koritza,[93] which was under the protection of French military authorities. Italy was correct and once again
Sarrail found himself in the middle of an international dispute.

In the autumn of 1916 while Sarrail's offensive was underway, a
detachment of French troops in a precautionary move to assure that
no Austrian troops would threaten the left flank of the Eastern Army,
advanced into the southern Albanian province of Koritza. On December 10, 1916, fourteen Albanian representatives, consisting of seven
Christians and seven Moslems, with Thermistocles Germeni as president, created an Administrative Council and proclaimed Koritza an
autonomous Albanian province. The new state acted as if it were an
independent nation, for it minted its own coinage, printed its own
stamps, and introduced its own flag.

On December 13 Rome notified Briand that French military authorities had been responsible for the creation of the newly independent state of Koritza. Briand, who knew nothing of what had occurred
at Koritza, promptly asked Sarrail for the details concerning the
recent events at Koritza.[94] On December 15 Sarrail replied that French
troops, under the command of Colonel Henri Descoins, had moved

into Koritza in order to guard the Eastern Army's left flank. More important, the Eastern commander asserted that French military authorities had played no role whatsoever in the creation of the new state.[95] Greatly assured by Sarrail's dispatch, Briand assumed that the matter was closed.[96] However, in February, 1917, Italy once again complained that French military authorities had played a significant role in the creation of Koritza.[97] And a month later Rome notified a startled Briand that the December 10, 1916, protocol declaring Koritza an autonomous political entity had also stated that the new state was to be under French protection; furthermore, the proclamation had been signed by Colonel Descoins, which strongly indicated that he had been the author of the document.[98]

Briand immediately assured Sonnino not to become apprehensive, for France had no designs on Koritza or Albania. Then the premier asked Sarrail to explain exactly what had happened at Koritza.[99] Sarrail responded on March 21, declaring that on the previous December 10 Albanian delegates had proclaimed the independence of Koritza and had asked to be placed under French protection; Colonel Descoins complied with the wishes of the local population. Sarrail explained that he had "always let the population do what it wanted; . . . it does not behoove me to meddle in the Greek and Balkan internal political question. Koritza wanted to be independent: now it is."[100]

It is thus not surprising that when Briand resigned as premier in March, 1917, he was under the impression that the creation of an independent Koritza had been due solely to the initiative of the local inhabitants.[101] Unfortunately Sarrail had not given a truthful account of the events surrounding the Koritzan affair. Colonel Descoins and Sarrail had not been passive spectators in Koritza's sudden emergence as an independent state. On December 6, 1916, Descoins had informed Sarrail that several Albanian nationalists believed that although it was currently unrealistic to attempt to create an independent Albania, an independent Koritza could be created if the occupying French military authorities rendered assistance. Sarrail cabled Descoins on December 8 that the Albanian nationalists should be supported.[102] The next day Descoins wrote to Sarrail from Koritza: "Complete order in the city. The arrests and deportations [of Greeks] which I have been quietly carrying out for several nights are producing excellent results. All necessities are taken care of so that the event can take place tomorrow."[103]

Why did Sarrail sponsor the creation of an independent Koritza? He wanted peace and tranquility in an area where the left wing of the Allied Eastern Army was carrying out operations.[104] Following the establishment in August, 1916, of the provisional government at Salonika, Venizelists as a first move in attaining a greater Greece, moved into Koritza. Immediately Albanian nationalists, subsidized by Austria, began to wage guerilla warfare against the Greeks. Consequently in November Sarrail ordered Descoins to expel the Venizelists from Koritza.[105]

Continued large-scale disturbances in Koritza would have hindered French military operations in southern Albania. It was imperative that French troops remain in Koritza, if only to prevent the possibility of the Austrians, who were in northern Albania, from turning the Eastern Army's left flank. Furthermore, a peaceful and politically stable Koritza under French control would have discouraged the Austrians from moving into southern Albania; the Eastern Army's left wing, if it were so desired, could link up with the Italian troops concurrently occupying Valona in western Albania; and with tranquility assured in Koritza, fewer French troops need be committed to southern Albania.[106]

Sarrail and Descoins believed that Thermistocles Germeni was the one political leader who could guarantee a peaceful stable Koritza.[107] Germeni was not only pro-Entente but he had a good deal of popular support in southeastern Albania.[108] Of course, any opposition that Germeni and his Albanian followers might have encountered had been conveniently crushed by Descoins, and, as a result, on December 10, 1916, Koritza had "a completely peaceful revolution."[109] But this is all that Sarrail anticipated. He evidently had not expected that Descoins's activities would result in the creation of a political body called the Administrative Council. Nor had Sarrail expected that the Administrative Council's December proclamation would include a formal declaration of independence, Descoins's signature, and an unequivocal statement that Koritza henceforth would be under French military protection.[110]

The events of December 10 continued to reverberate well into 1917. No sooner had Ribot become premier in March than the Italians again raised the question of Koritza. Ribot informed War Minister Painlevé that as a sop to Italy Descoins should be recalled.[111] Painlevé disagreed, maintaining that it appeared that Sonnino no longer attached any importance to the Koritza affair.[112] Ribot hotly responded that the affair was not closed and demanded that Painlevé uncover the mysterious details surrounding the sudden emergence of Koritza as an independent state.[113]

While Ribot awaited Painlevé's response, Italy on June 3 proclaimed a protectorate of Albania, justifying its action by stressing that France had been responsible for creating the independent state of Koritza. Frantically cabling Rome that the emergence of an independent Koritza had been "a purely military situation which involves the intervention of only French military authorities and which in no way involves a political creation by the French government," Ribot bitterly denounced Sonnino's recent decision.[114] He reminded Sonnino that Rome's action contradicted the Treaty of London, signed by Italy, France, England, and Russia in April, 1915. This agreement stipulated that postwar Italy would receive direct control of Valona and the neighboring territory. It was also agreed at London that southern and northern Albania could be reserved for Montenegro, Serbia, and Greece. If at the postwar peace conference, a central portion of Albania were reserved for the establishment of a small autonomous state, Italy could direct its foreign policy. Obviously, as Ribot pointed out, Italy's claim to have a protectorate over all of Albania exceeded the terms of the London Pact. Rome's protectorate could only apply to a state carved out of the central portion of Albania. But that state had not yet been created if only because mid-1917 was no time to hold the Allied postwar peace conference. Furthermore, Italy had no future claim to Koritza, since that province was situated in southern Albania. For all of these reasons, Ribot cautioned Italy to await the postwar peace conference, a suggestion that wartime Rome did not heed.[115]

Now that the question of Koritza had surfaced so dramatically, Ribot reminded Painlevé that a comprehensive account of the events surrounding the origin of Koritza had not yet been forthcoming.[116] Painlevé, who had not been overly eager to probe the question of Koritza, wrote to Sarrail and while asking for details concerning the events of December 10, told the Eastern commander that Descoins must be recalled.[117] Sarrail replied immediately that he had relieved Descoins, but he remained reticent concerning the significant events in Koritza. He claimed that he had no information to add beyond that of his March 21 dispatch.[118]

Ribot was furious. On July 17 he again demanded to know exactly what had occurred at Koritza during the previous December.[119] Responding to Paris's latest request for clarification, Sarrail languidly explained on July 20 that the present situation in Koritza was the same as that of the previous December 10. Seven Christians and seven Moslems had formed an Administrative Council. This council then proclaimed their country's independence. The Administrative Council "does what it wants," but in order to protect the security of the French troops in Koritza, the French military commander there guided and directed the Administrative Council. Sarrail concluded his verbose but uninformative report by stressing that the occupation of Koritza was "a military necessity for us."[120]

Although still not resolved, the question of Koritza was over-shadowed in the summer of 1917 by a more immediate problem. In early June, while two French divisions prepared to occupy Thessaly and Attica as a means to support the Anglo-French ultimatum that Constantine resign, Paris and London were stunned to discover that Italian troops, under the command of General Giacinto Ferrero, were advancing from Albania into southern Epirus in northern Greece. Fearing France's intentions in the Balkans, the Italian invasion was intended to demonstrate to Paris that France would not be allowed to have a free hand in Greece unless Italy's Adriatic claims were assured. Sonnino emphasized to Ribot that if the French occupation of central and southern Greece were simply a temporary maneuver, then the Italian occupation would also be of short duration.[121] Paris was not concerned with Sonnino's thinly veiled suggestion that Italy would have to be compensated if France intended to establish permanent control over Greece. France never had such plans. What greatly agitated Paris was the possibility of a clash between the Venizelists and the invading Italians. Following frantic orders from Paris, Sarrail carefully established a neutral zone south of Janina between the Italian, French, and Venizelists, and as a result, an explosive confrontation between the Allies was averted.[122] By late August tensions had eased considerably, for by then the Venizelists had effective control of the Greek state and consequently Sarrail's divisions in Thessaly and Attica were withdrawn to Macedonia. Once this was done, the Italians withdrew their troops from northern Greece.[123] Although the latest crisis between Rome and Paris had been overcome rather easily, the seeds for continued friction still existed, for French troops remained in Koritza. And Italy, as she had demonstrated on more than one occasion, could react strongly if she thought that her position in Albania were threatened.

During the summer and autumn of 1917 Sarrail's army failed to launch a full-scale Balkan offensive. Several factors explain the relative inactivity of the Eastern Army. The British, as they had promised at the Paris and London conferences of the previous May, began reducing their forces in the Balkans. Unfortunately, the British withdrawal of one division and two cavalry brigades, which began on June 1, was only an initial step. Thoroughly disenchanted with the Balkan campaign, Lloyd George proposed at an Allied conference held in Paris on July 25 that a second British division be sent to the Palestinian front. The British maintained that an offensive from Salonika could only bring concrete results if it were combined with a full-scale attack by Russia and Rumania in the northern Balkans. To expect assistance from either of these two countries in mid-1917 was unrealistic. Therefore, the Eastern Army would henceforth play a defensive role in the Balkans; and, as Lloyd George and Balfour stated, a further reduction of manpower would not hinder the Eastern Army from fulfilling a defensive role.

Like the Serb and Russian representatives, the French violently opposed the British request. They maintained that a further withdrawal would not only symbolize the Allies' intent to desert the Balkans, but could possibly invite the Germans to launch a major Macedonian attack, once the Gallician campaign had been completed.[124] The British persisted, arguing that in order to prevent the possibility of a disaster in Mesopotamia, it was imperative that immediate reinforcements be sent to that theater. On August 7, at an Allied conference held at London, the French government, upon receiving assurances that England would not withdraw all of her troops from the Balkans, agreed to the withdrawal of a second British division. Albert Thomas, minister of armaments in the Ribot government, bitterly observed that for two years the various French governments "had been trying to draw the British Government away from their [British] General Staff in order to get troops to Salonica." Now the Ribot government "had to fight to keep the troops bit by bit at Salonica in opposition to the British General Staff."[125] Indeed, after a long and bitter struggle, Robertson had finally defeated the Easterners.

The British reduction of troops was not the only problem encountered by Sarrail in the summer of 1917. The Eastern Army was on the brink of disintegration. The Russian troops, affected by events in their homeland, were no longer a reliable force. The Serbs requested to be withdrawn from the front lines. The Serbian army, as it had demonstrated during the spring offensive and as its chief of staff readily admitted in August, needed time "to recover physically and morally and to prepare itself in every respect in order to carry out any new missions which could devolve upon it."[126] The French 242nd Regiment (57th Division), which had been in Macedonia without respite since October, 1915, mutinied in July, demanding furloughs. The potentially explosive situation was smothered within hours when Sarrail and Generals Charles Jacquemot and Paul Grossetti promised immediate leave to the men; ninety of the mutineers, not appeased by the promises, were quickly and bloodlessly disarmed and imprisoned.[127] Morale within the French army had been broken to such a degree that the possibility of launching a full-scale offensive in the immediate future was impossible. Sarrail wrote the war minister in mid-July, "I am willing to consider the wishes of our Allies, which, moreover, boil down to relying always on the French, but I also wish to protect the strength, discipline, and morale of the French army. We are not servants."[128]

To replace the two recently departed British divisions and cavalry, to bolster, if not replace the entire Serbian army, to replace the 57th, 122nd, and 156th divisions, which were being furloughed to France as quickly as transport facilities would allow, and to supply the superiority in manpower needed for a successful breakthrough, the Eastern Army would have needed at least fifteen additional divisions. New replacements could obviously not be supplied by Kerensky, nor by Italy, which at best was an unwilling partner in the Balkan campaign, and in mid-1917 needed all available manpower on her northern borders, nor by England, which had given up on the Balkan campaign.

France herself could send no appreciable assistance. Although Painlevé was war minister in the Ribot government until September and prime minister from September to November, 1917, it was utterly impossible, even unthinkable, for him to have supplied Sarrail with 300,000 fresh troops. In the spring of 1917 the Nivelle offensive, one of the costliest and most senseless offensives undertaken on the Western front, had resulted in widespread mutinies within the French army and consequently all available manpower was needed to reinforce the sagging French front.[129] In November the Italian front had collapsed and Painlevé had to rush four French divisions southward in order to stabilize that front. Therefore, reflecting the Allies' acute shortage of manpower and its weakening morale on both the Macedonian and Western fronts, France's Balkan policy in the summer and autumn of 1917 was a replica of the Allies' western policy. The Eastern Army, Painlevé wrote Sarrail on August 13, should "prevent any withdrawals of the Bulgar-German troops on the Macedonian front; it could achieve this result through local attacks at selected spots with a reduced number of infantry troops supported by as large an artillery concentration as possible."[130] Upon receiving this directive, Sarrail understandably replied: "I can do no more for the moment."[131] Just as there would be no further major offensives on the Western front until the Americans arrived in 1918, there would be no major Balkan offensive until the spring of 1918, by which time not only would the Serbs and French be reinvigorated, but more important, 200,000 fresh Greek troops would be in the field.[132]

With approximately twenty-three divisions, of which three were Greek, Sarrail fulfilled his orders: to keep the enemy bogged down in Macedonia. Throughout the summer and autumn of 1917 the Balkan front from Lake Dojran to Monastir was characterized by the constant strengthening of defensive positions, endless artillery duels, and frequent raids, always limited but occasionally costly. At no time was there a concerted Allied attempt against established positions. There was, however, one exception to this war of immobility. Seeking a lightly fortified area in which to maneuver, Sarrail decided to penetrate the wooded mountains north of Koritza. Led by General Jacquemot, Leblois's successor as commander of the French Eastern Army, those units of the 57th and 156th divisions not on leave advanced to the southern tip of Lake Ohrid, situated on the Albanian-Serbian border, and on September 10 surprised a small contingent of Austrians at Pogradec, capturing the town and several hundred prisoners. A few days later Essad Pasha and five hundred of his followers carried out a successful raid in the Skumbi valley, behind the Austrian lines.[133] No sooner had the Jacquemot-Essad thrust into central Albania been completed than Paris hurriedly warned Sarrail that the newly conquered territories north of Koritza must be under the control of French military authorities. Under no circumstances was Sarrail "to take any political initiative liable to create any incidents like that one at Koritza which had such deplorable consequences."[134] Paris then braced itself for the anticipated difficulties with Italy.

On September 28 Rome informed Paris that it was astonished that Essad Pasha had taken part in the recent offensive. Italy claimed that in October, 1916, Briand had agreed that Essad would remain at Salonika and not enter Albania. Ribot, minister of foreign affairs in the recently formed Painlevé Cabinet, replied that no such promise had been given. Briand had simply promised to keep Essad out of the Italian military zones in western and southwestern Albania; and this had been done. However, because Pasha had a good deal of popular support with the Moslems in central Albania, he had been permitted to partake in Jacquemot's recent offensive.[135] Ribot's explanation only intensified Rome's demand that the Italian 35th Division situated on the Cerna be allowed to occupy the Lake Ohrid area. "For reasons of political necessity," Premier Painlevé was prepared to allow an Italian brigade to occupy Koritza, if not Pogradec.[136] Sarrail, however, successfully urged Paris to reject the Italian plan. He emphasized that French troops and not the Italians must comprise the Eastern Army's left wing because Italy's presence in eastern Albania would result in violence between the Italians and Albanian nationalists. The Italians, Sarrail maintained, would not resist Austrian military pressure if it were forthcoming and would be tempted to flee westward to Valona, thus leaving the Eastern Army's left flank exposed.[137] And lastly, the Albanian sector of the Balkan campaign was the only one that offered Sarrail an opportunity "to maneuver and do something, a maneuver that I [Sarrail] alone can carry out with the French, who, listening to my orders, are always ready to face up to the stress of necessities and are not hypnotized by postwar political aims."[138]

Italy, however, was not the only one interested in the fate of Albania. In early October Venizelos casually but fruitlessly suggested to Painlevé that Greece be given Koritza and Pogradec so that France would have an excuse to reject Italy's requests to occupy these areas.[139] In late September, first Serbia and then the Essadists asked Sarrail that they be given exclusive control of the civilian administration of Pogradec. Following his directives from Paris, Sarrail refused the request.[140] Undaunted, the Serbs then asked Sarrail if Serbian troops could be transferred from Macedonia to Pogradec. Sarrail also rejected this suggestion. French troops alone would occupy and administer Pogradec "in order to prevent friction among the Greeks, Italians, Serbs, . . . and the Albanians, whether they be the followers of Essad or not."[141]

Meanwhile Sarrail decided to continue the advance northward along the western shores of Ohrid with the intention of reaching the lightly defended city of Struga, situated on the northern edges of the lake. The capture of Struga would have been significant for several reasons. The route between Elbassan, a major Austrian supply depot thirty-five miles west of Ohrid, and the area east of the lake would have been cut. Control of Struga would have placed the Eastern Army in a superb position to pressure the Bulgar-German right flank, particularly those troops north of Monastir. Sarrail's basic mission was to prevent the enemy from transferring units to the other fronts and a move on Struga would have greatly assisted this assignment, for there was ample evidence that the Central Powers, surprised by General Jacquemot's victory at Pogradec, were sending battalions from the Rumanian front into the Lake Ohrid-Prespa area.[142] But no sooner had Jacquemot begun his move on Struga than on October 20 Sarrail was notified by Premier Painlevé to stop all military action north of Pogradec: "An offensive in Albania seems inopportune from the political point of view because of the conflicts which it would cause among the Allies."[143]

Indeed, as Sarrail noted, there were "too many appetites"[144] coveting Albania, and, as a result, the only successful action in the summer and fall of 1917 had been curtailed not by the enemy, but by the Allies. Nevertheless, the failure to take Struga and the Eastern Army's limited military operations during the latter half of 1917 should not obscure one important point: Sarrail had successfully fulfilled the August 13 directives. There were more enemy troops on the Macedonian front in December than there had been in August.[145]

IX. Swing to the Right: Recall

*I am completely indifferent about the Paix-[Séailles]-Mathieu Affair.
. . . We must find something else for my enemies.*
                                        —SARRAIL to Jean Decrais,
                                                September 9, 1917

In September, 1917, Radical-Socialist Alfred Margaine informed
Sarrail of two important points. First, the British had demanded that
Sarrail be recalled.[1] Margaine was correct, for on June 6, immediately
following the May offensive, Lloyd George wrote to Premier Ribot
that the British, Serbian, Russian, and Italian commanders at Salonika
complained that in one way or another Sarrail's recent offensive had
been poorly planned and coordinated; consequently, Sarrail should
be recalled.[2]

Although much of the criticism leveled against Sarrail's management of the spring offensive was valid, it may have been that the
attacks served as a convenient smoke screen for shortcomings to be
found elsewhere. Certainly the Serbs who refused to leave their
trenches had not distinguished themselves during the 1917 spring offensive. Nor had General Milne, although he was quick to suggest that
the offensive had failed because Sarrail, in response to Paris's frequent
warnings that military operations against Greece were imminent, had
kept two French divisions in reserve where they remained inactive
during the entire offensive.[3] It appears that the British commander had
been plagued by the same self-doubts and brooding pessimism that
had characterized his performance during the 1916 offensive. His un-
inspired and lackluster leadership during the May offensive led naval
Captain Alfred Stead to observe: "[Milne] shelters himself behind the
orders he receives from Sarrail with whom he has not even tried to
cooperate. Before commencing the offensive he said that the task
allotted to him was impossible—result thousands of casualties. He re-

gards the whole expedition as a fiasco and his only desire is to clear out of the country."[4]

On June 7 the Ribot government discussed Lloyd George's request; once again, Poincaré recorded, it was "the eternal Sarrail question." Not surprisingly, it was Painlevé who defended Sarrail from London's criticism. The war minister emphasized that an army composed of several nationalities always posed exceptional difficulties for its commander and Sarrail's Eastern Army was no exception. Ribot, on the other hand, was sympathetic to England's recommendations.[5] Nevertheless, the premier had to reject Lloyd George's request because, as Painlevé cautioned London, if Sarrail were recalled, "it would bring down the Ribot government with a crash—and the Alliance with it."[6] London did not forget Painlevé's warning. Two months later when the War Cabinet again seriously considered requesting that Sarrail be removed, it refrained from presenting its demand to Paris, fearing that the Ribot government could not recall Sarrail without becoming involved in a serious political crisis—one that could possibly result in the fall of the French government.[7] Robertson was correct when he complained that as long as Painlevé held a Cabinet position, Sarrail would not be ignominiously sacked.[8]

Second, Margaine informed Sarrail that the general's political supporters were disappointed that with Painlevé's advent to power as war minister and then as premier in September, Sarrail had not been given a prominent position on the Western front, possibly as commander of a combined Franco-American army. Highly critical of Painlevé, Margaine told Sarrail that "none of the attempts we have made to get you out of Salonika has succeeded." Each time that Margaine approached Painlevé or fellow Cabinet member Léon Bourgeois about the possibility of bringing Sarrail to the Western front, the deputy received the same reply: "It was indispensable to keep you [Sarrail] there [Salonika]."[9]

There is no question that Painlevé had seriously considered assigning Sarrail to an important position in France. Immediately after the crisis of December, 1916, when Joffre had been forced to resign and the Briand government was tottering, Painlevé, acting through an intermediary, asked Sarrail exactly what position he wanted. The general replied on January 20, 1917: "I am entirely at Painlevé's disposal. If he has no particular idea about the role to give me, he could appoint me Chief of Staff of the Army and General Director of Personnel and Matériel. . . . If he thinks that that is too much, [then] Chief of Staff of the Army with a decree assigning me the personnel bureaus including the generals."[10] In mid-April, after becoming war minister, Painlevé notified Sarrail that he would be appointed to "a high position in France." But not immediately. The appointment could come only "later when he [Painlevé] would be in a stronger position to impose his will." In the meantime the war minister cautioned Sarrail "not to create any difficulty and to be patient."[11] Sarrail replied that "no difficulty will be raised by me. I wish only that the Eastern Army no longer be treated as a pariah."[12] And as the months rolled by, Sarrail waited. But later never arrived for the Eastern commander, although in September it was rumored that if England persisted in demanding Sarrail's recall from Salonika, he would return to France as commander in chief of the French army.[13] Without specifying the exact reasons, Sarrail fully appreciated that Painlevé was encountering insurmountable difficulties that prevented the general's return to Paris. The minister was "buffeted by events" and "hemmed in by circumstances."[14] It is not difficult to discern the events and circumstances that prevented Sarrail's appointment in 1917 to a higher position.

Commander in Chief Nivelle, despite serious doubts raised by Painlevé and several army commanders, ordered a mighty offensive in April, 1917. Instead of breaking the Hindenburg Line, waves of French troops charged into uncut barbed wire and protected German pillar boxes. Nothing was gained and there were ninety thousand casualties within the first few days of the offensive. By mid-May the futility of Nivelle's offensive resulted in large-scale mutinies with several units on the verge of disintegration. Painlevé desperately sought a remedy for the gravest internal crisis encountered by the French army. Sarrail was not the remedy that Painlevé sought. The war minister, more than any other politician, knew that Sarrail did not have the confidence of the G.Q.G. To have placed a controversial general, one whose entire career was closely associated with the political Left, at the top of a conservative hierarchy would have been folly. In time of crisis Painlevé turned to "the almost unanimous choice of the army" and in mid-May appointed Philippe Pétain commander in chief of the army and Ferdinand Foch as his chief of staff. With more frequent furloughs, better food, firing squads, and prison sentences, discipline was effectively restored. To assure that there would be no future mutinies, Pétain and Painlevé repudiated past basic military strategy. There would be no further large-scale, frontal assaults; France would remain on the defensive, stockpiling matériel while awaiting the 1918 arrival of the one million American troops.[15]

The mutinies, the psychological shock of the Nivelle disaster, the large-scale spring and summer labor strikes and demonstrations, together with an obsessive fear of Bolshevism, combined to produce a massive impact upon French domestic politics. The ultra Right, guided by Daudet's *L'Action française*, the Pétain-led G.Q.G., moderate republicans encouraged by Poincaré, and a good many radical republicans inspired by former Dreyfusard Georges Clemenceau, believed that the mutinies and strikes were caused by home-front pacifists, defeatists, and spies. Consequently, in the late spring and early summer of 1917 the Right, and moderate and radical republicans coalesced, as they had done in 1911 following the Agadir crisis, and demanded that the Ribot government repress the various subversive elements.[16]

The conspiracy theory was categorically rejected by the Ribot government. The Ribot government maintained that three years of low wages, inflation, and long working hours, together with wide-scale disillusionment stemming from the costly Nivelle offensive, had been the basic factors responsible for the spring strikes and mutinies. Under no conditions would the government unleash a witch hunt against well-known pacifists and left-wing trade union officials.[17]

In early August home-front hysteria was fueled by France's first and most sensational wartime scandal, an apparent case of espionage involving *Le Bonnet rouge*. Miguel Almereyda, a disciple of Gustave Hervé, had spent his prewar years as a militant anarchist-pacifist. In 1913, receiving financial assistance from Charles Paix-Séailles, a young oil tycoon and editor of the antimilitarist *Le Courrier européen*, Almereyda founded his own antimilitarist newspaper, *Le Bonnet rouge*. By the spring of 1916 Almereyda began receiving financial support from German agents, who were hoping to convert *Le Bonnet rouge* into a German propaganda sheet. In mid-July, 1917, the government, hounded by nationalists' demands for repression, suppressed Almereyda's *Le Bonnet rouge*. The entire affair, limited in scope, would have evaporated. But on August 4 military police raided the editorial offices of the defunct *Le Bonnet rouge* and confiscated six letters and three government documents. Almereyda was promptly arrested for possessing material pertaining to the defense and security of the country. On August 14 he was found strangled in his solitary prison cell.[18]

The nine letters and documents found on the premises of *Le Bonnet rouge* involved General Sarrail. Five of the letters were written in the spring of 1916 by Captain Mathieu, an aide to General Sarrail, and were addressed to Sergeant Paix-Séailles, who at the time was fulfilling his military obligation as a clerk in Painlevé's Ministry of Public Instruction. In these five letters Paix-Séailles was informed not only of the number of Allied troops, but that England did not want a Balkan offensive and that France should support Venizelos while forcibly deposing Constantine. Emphasizing a theme that was reiterated throughout all of the letters, Mathieu wrote that the Eastern Army, which had been ordered to prepare for an offensive in the spring of 1916, did not have sufficient manpower because Joffre and the G.Q.G. wanted "to make it impossible for Sarrail to do anything and then to accuse him of incompetence."[19] The G.Q.G. would leave "no stone . . . unturned so as to cause the General utter defeat. . . . The important thing is to ruin S[arrail]."[20] To make sure that "this criminal state of things ceases," Mathieu urged Paix-Séailles to mobilize political support for Sarrail: "I am depending on your concerted action with Viollette . . . [and] Painlevé etc."[21] And another letter concluded: "Show this letter to our friend J[oseph] C[aillaux]."[22] Paix-Séailles more than obliged. He gave the original letters to Almereyda while sending copies to the secretary of the League of the Rights of Man, the editor of Le Radical, Painlevé, Viollette, Hervé, and Caillaux.

Mathieu also sent Paix-Séailles three government documents and a copy of a June, 1916, letter from Sarrail to the Radical Joseph Noulens,[23] all of which were found in the offices of Le Bonnet rouge. The first document, dated May 2, 1916, and written by Sarrail for War Minister Roques, presented the Greek domestic political situation; Sarrail emphasized that it was necessary to overthrow Constantine.[24] The second document, written by Joffre and dated June 12, 1916, notified Sarrail that at the June 9 London Conference the British had opposed a Balkan offensive; therefore, the Eastern Army was to remain on the defensive.[25] The third document, dated June 14, 1916, and with the word "secret" stamped at the top of the page, was sent to Sarrail by the French ambassador at Athens. Guillemin, presenting the details of the London Conference, emphasized that although England had rejected an offensive, she had promised to study the possibility of a future offensive if circumstances in the Balkans were to change.[26]

One month following the discovery of these letters and documents, Sarrail received a letter from Captain Mathieu, who was on leave in Paris at the time. Mathieu related the recent events and then added:

In May or June of 1916 I gave a friend who has numerous acquaintances both in the Press and in the Parliament certain

facts which were to allow the cry of alarm to be sounded concerning the manpower of the Eastern Army.
1. I did this without consulting you. . . . .
2. I knew that you were crudely forbidden to bring up the question of manpower and matériel again.
3. I knew, as do so many others, that everything would be done to prevent you from having a victory in the East.
Was I wrong or was I right? I was right. . . . What I did, I would not hesitate to do again, should the need arise. . . .
Lastly, I swear [?] that I wrote neither to Le Bonnet rouge nor to its editor, whom I did not know.
This letter has as its aim only to establish responsibilities in the event that it is judged that responsibilities should be sought. . . . Whatever may happen, now I have a clear conscience.[27]

When informed of the details of the recent scandal, Sarrail believed that his political and military enemies would need much more than the *Bonnet rouge* affair to end his career.[28] Sarrail's confidence that he could escape the scandal unscathed had been bolstered by a mid-August letter from Painlevé in which the war minister assured Sarrail that "once again you have my full confidence."[29] Furthermore, Sarrail's position within the Ribot Cabinet had been greatly strengthened when Charles Chaumet, "a proven friend," had been appointed naval minister in early August. Sarrail was assured that Chaumet's appointment "can only be advantageous to you personally, to those around you, and to the Eastern Army."[30] In reality, however, the *Bonnet rouge* affair was more damaging than Sarrail had initially suspected.

Although the exact content of most of the nine letters and documents was never made public, their general nature was no secret. And when correct knowledge was lacking, guesswork sufficed. In conservative political circles it was bruited about that Germany's possession of the documents and letters had been responsible for the 1916 defeat of Russia and Rumania in Moldavia and that it was Sarrail himself who had given the documents to Almereyda.[31] The rumors reached such proportions that at a War Committee meeting in late August Painlevé heatedly protested against the attempts some people were making to link the names of Almereyda and Sarrail.[32] The general, however, was not the only victim of recent events. The *Bonnet rouge* scandal appeared to have substantiated the nationalists' claims that the Ribot government, which had eschewed a policy of repression, had been excessively lenient toward spies and defeatists. Consequently, first Malvy and then Ribot resigned.[33]

On September 13 Painlevé became France's premier. During his two months as premier Painlevé was plagued by a spate of scandals. All of these scandals, involving espionage or unlawful dealing with the enemy, discredited the government. The nationalists, whether monarchists or republicans, quickly became disenchanted with Painlevé, maintaining that he was not taking a hard line against the defeatists: he refused to arrest Joseph Caillaux, the leading proponent of a negotiated peace; the premier refused to impose a more stringent press censorship; he supposedly hindered the investigation of the Bolo Pasha spy case. Painlevé's permissiveness toward the defeatists, so the nationalists claimed, resulted from his attempts to protect his political friends.[34]

In reality, Painlevé was presiding over the dissolution of the *union sacrée*. For not only were the nationalists deserting him, but he also lost the support of the Socialists. The majority of Socialists abstained from giving Painlevé a vote of confidence following his September 18 inaugural address to the Chamber. They were upset not only because as war minister in the previous government Painlevé had supported Ribot's refusal to grant them passports to travel to the International Socialist Conference at Stockholm, but also because Painlevé insisted that the anti-Stockholmist Ribot serve in the new government as minister of foreign affairs. During his premiership, the Socialists were angered because Painlevé had not forcefully defended Malvy in early October when the former minister of the interior was slanderously accused by journalist Léon Daudet of having given military secrets to the Germans. Likewise, several left-wing Socialists, influenced by the Russian Revolution, demanded that Painlevé renounce or at least modify France's annexationist war aims, something that no premier could realistically do in 1917.[35]

On November 13 Painlevé became the first and only wartime premier not to receive a vote of confidence from the Chamber. Georges Clemenceau, who had played a major role in the nationalist revival, immediately assumed the premiership. Supported by the Right, moderates, and a good number of the Radicals, Clemenceau promised the Chamber that permissiveness toward pacifists and traitors would end.[36] And in the ensuing months advocates of a negotiated peace, such as Caillaux, were imprisoned. Those who were supposedly soft on defeatists, such as Malvy, were hounded, and spies such as Mata Hari, were executed.

Now that French politics had swung to the Right, Sarrail's position was extremely vulnerable, just as it had been in 1911. And no one knew it more than he, for on November 15, two days following Painlevé's overthrow, Sarrail wrote to the former premier: "I learn that serious events have occurred in the Chamber of Deputies. I think, I hope that, despite everything, you will remain at the rue Saint-Dominique. For the Eastern Army that would be a necessity, especially under the circumstances which we face."[37] Sarrail's apprehension was well founded. Critical of Sarrail's military accomplishments and dismayed that he had been implicated in the *Bonnet rouge* scandal, Clemenceau announced at a December 6 French War Committee meeting that "Sarrail cannot remain [in Salonika]. He will even have accounts to settle when he returns to France, for he left everything unfinished and has accounted for none of his actions. He will be placed at the disposal of the commander in chief." Pétain, perhaps fearing the political repercussions of such a move, refused the assignment. Clemenceau quickly snapped: "Don't worry. If you want, I will take on this responsibility myself."[38] On December 10 the premier notified Sarrail that the government, "basing itself on considerations of a general nature, has arranged your recall to France."[39]

Clemenceau's decision was warmly welcomed by London. On November 14 Robertson had submitted a memorandum to the British government, stating that "partly out of consideration for the French government" London's previous requests that Sarrail be removed had never "been pressed home." But now that the Painlevé government had just been toppled, the C.I.G.S thought the moment opportune to demand that Sarrail be recalled.[40] Lloyd George concurred and immediately asked Clemenceau to remove Sarrail as commander of the Eastern Army.[41]

Clemenceau also discovered that Sarrail had engendered the enmity and distrust of the other Allies, for in fulfilling his military mission the Eastern commander had become an unbearable and seemingly unbreakable obstacle to the aspirations of Serbia, Italy, and Venizelos in Albania.[42] Sarrail's recall was not only an attempt by Paris to remove a frequent cause of friction among the Allies, but was also intended to demonstrate that France had no territorial ambitions in Albania. No sooner had the Eastern commander been recalled than the Clemenceau government abolished the independent state of Koritza, a political entity that owed its existence to Sarrail.[43] On February 11, 1918, Koritza reverted to its status as an Albanian province, the native governing Administrative Council disappeared, and French military authorities assumed complete control of the administrative and political institutions of the newly integrated territory. France was to remain

in Koritza until a postwar peace conference could untangle the question of Albania's future.

If the Allies were not unduly upset by Sarrail's recall, neither was
he. In fact, a letter to his brother reveals that the general was in good
spirits:

> Yesterday I received a wire informing me that because of
> considerations of a general nature I was dismissed. I am there-
> fore going to return to France. The exile is over. I shall settle
> down and no longer move. Find me . . . an apartment with
> two bedrooms, living room, dining room, kitchen, and bath.
> The neighborhood matters little. . . . I shall have an un-
> pleasant conversation with Clemenceau, but once this moment
> is over I shall no longer think about anything. . . . I am very
> well. You will see. Naturally I have aged a lot—but this is per-
> haps pretentious—not intellectually; my white hair still be-
> comes me—that which is left of it.[44]

Sarrail arrived in Paris on December 28. This time there was no *affaire Sarrail*.[45] Several reasons explain the politicians' failure to support Sarrail. Painlevé, Bourgeois, and Thomas, who had defended
Sarrail as Cabinet members, had been swept from power as French
politics moved to the Right. The political effectiveness of the Radical-
Socialists had been greatly reduced as they were placed on the defensive and badly divided as a result of the treason charges leveled
against some of their parliamentary members, notably Joseph
Caillaux, Louis-Jean Malvy, and Louis Turmel. The Socialists not
only lacked any influence in Clemenceau's nationalist-oriented government, but they were divided by the question of whether to follow
Leninism or to support France's war effort, an issue far more important than one concerning Sarrail's fate. Also, several of Sarrail's former supporters, such as Hervé, Abrami, Leygues, and Albert Favre,
found it expedient to adjust to the new political climate and they en-
thusiastically joined the Clemenceau parade. Last and perhaps most
important, in the heavy atmosphere of repression that followed Clemenceau's assumption of power, many left-wing deputies, such as
Viollette, Accambray, Margaine, and Painlevé, although greatly ad-
miring Sarrail,[46] undoubtedly considered it politically unwise to
defend publicly a general who had not only been tainted by the war's
most sensational scandal, but who had not had a victory since November, 1916.

Whatever opportunity there may have been for the Left to rally to
Sarrail's assistance was dashed by the Caillaux affair. Radical-Socialist Deputy Joseph Caillaux advocated a negotiated peace with Germany.[47] During the war he had maintained casual acquaintanceships

with the German ambassador to Brazil, German agents such as Paul Bolo Pasha and Frank Minotto, and staff members of *Le Bonnet rouge*. Although there was no evidence that Caillaux had committed treason, the Clemenceau government asked the Chamber on December 11, 1917, to suspend Caillaux's parliamentary immunity so that he could stand trial. The case against Caillaux was intended to demonstrate Clemenceau's determination to continue the war to a victorious conclusion. Readily admitting that he had been guilty of imprudence, Caillaux claimed that he was being persecuted for his ideas and not for his acts.

In early January, 1918, Italian authorities in Florence seized the contents of a bank safe belonging to Caillaux. The safe contained jewelry, money, and a document, written by Caillaux himself, entitled "Rubicon." This document, written over a period of several months in 1915, outlined a program that Caillaux supposedly would have attempted to implement if he were to become a wartime premier. According to the "Rubicon," the president would have most of the political power while the Chamber and Senate would be reduced to advisory bodies. An executive, with the powers of a dictator, would silence political opposition, nationalize the railways, curb religious instruction, and institute old-age pensions and unemployment compensation. Caillaux also wanted to undertake some significant military changes, the most notable of which was the selection of General Sarrail as generalissimo of the French army.[48]

That Caillaux's 1915 "Rubicon" should have mentioned Sarrail as generalissimo was not surprising. On the eve of the war the Left had almost succeeded in arranging to have Sarrail succeed Joffre. In mid-1915 left-wing deputies other than Caillaux had mentioned Sarrail as a possible successor to Joffre. However, what is revealing is that the Caillauxists included Sarrail in their future plans. In February, 1917, Paix-Séailles wrote Sarrail a rambling, ambiguous, and patronizing letter in which he shrewdly observed that the poilus had become disillusioned with the war effort and would rebel if forced to undertake any more senseless offensives. The poilus' rebellion could initiate a civil war between those who wanted peace and those who wanted to continue the war. Under such circumstances Sarrail should "not be astonished that the hopes for the internal reorganization [of the country] center around the head of the Eastern Army."[49]

No evidence exists that suggests that Sarrail was willing to support the Caillauxists' vague plans for "internal reorganization," whether it be in 1915 or 1917. If even the slightest evidence suggested otherwise, it would certainly have been used against Sarrail in 1918 or in the immediate postwar years, when he led an active and controversial public career. Clemenceau did not think that Sarrail was implicated with Caillaux's schemes. In April, 1918, the Clemenceau government offered Sarrail the position of military governor of Paris. Sarrail refused the offer, preferring to remain in retirement. As military governor he would have had to sign the state's formal charges of treason against Caillaux. Sarrail wanted no part of Clemenceau's witch-hunt tactics.[50]

Sarrail's rejection of the government's offer was predictable, for upon his return to Paris four months earlier, he had indirectly repudiated the nationalists' political tactics. In January, 1918, Mathieu was on trial at the Palais de Justice for his role in the *Bonnet rouge* affair. The court had to decide one basic question: could the nine letters and documents have assisted the enemy, assuming that Almereyda or German agents had sent copies of the material to Germany? General Cordonnier, the chief witness for the prosecution, maintained that the documents and letters were responsible for the unexpected and successful August 17, 1916, Bulgarian strike against the Eastern Army's flanks. The enemy knew the numerical strength of the Eastern Army; Mathieu's constant references to the fact that Sarrail did not have sufficient manpower to undertake an offensive and Joffre's June 12 telegram ordering Sarrail to undertake no offensive allowed the enemy to choose the time and place for an offensive. Lastly, Mathieu's statements that the G.Q.G. wanted Sarrail to fail and Sarrail's depressing letter to Noulens reflected a malaise within the upper echelons of the Eastern Army, thereby encouraging the enemy to attack.[51]

Sarrail was the witness for the defense. Not intimidated by the repressive atmosphere that gripped France and determined that his political and military detractors should not have the opportunity of seeing him find a scapegoat for any of the Eastern Army's shortcomings,[52] Sarrail stated that none of the material found on the premises of *Le Bonnet rouge* could have assisted the enemy. First, the enemy did not need Mathieu's letters to discover the troop strength of the Eastern Army. Constantine's officials could have stood on the Salonika docks and simply counted the troops as they disembarked. Second, any information contained in the letters and documents pertaining to the Eastern Army's exact role, that is, whether to undertake an offensive or to remain on the defensive, was not only useless, but could have confused the enemy, since Joffre's orders were constantly changing. In the early spring of 1916 Sarrail was ordered to prepare for an offensive; Joffre's June 12 telegram ordered the Eastern Army to remain on the defensive; during the following month, when Rumania decided to join the Entente, Sarrail was ordered to undertake an offensive. Lastly, when asked for his opinion of Mathieu, Sarrail stated that his former staff officer was "an excellent soldier," one who had "served well in the Eastern Army" and had demonstrated "the qualities of a superior officer." Sarrail's testimony was effective. Convicted of negligence, Mathieu received a suspended sentence of ninety days.[53]

Sarrail's defense of Mathieu was the general's last wartime public appearance. Placed on the inactive reserve list on April 6, 1918, it appeared that the career of one of the most controversial figures in modern French history had ended. However, such would not be the case. When the Radicals and Socialists emerged victorious in the parliamentary elections of 1924, Sarrail would again emerge as an international figure and French domestic politics would once again be shaken by *l'affaire Sarrail*.

X. Politics:
French and Levantine Style

Your insults do not touch him [Sarrail].
—RENE CHAVAGNES, *Chamber
session, December 20, 1925*

Persuaded by Alphonse Aulard to enter politics, Sarrail stood for election to the National Assembly in November, 1919.[1] One of those representing the Republican Socialist party in the Seine's second electoral
district,[2] Sarrail campaigned on a program that included the introduction of short-term military service, democratic reform of the French administrative bureaucracy, and the implementation of Wilsonian ideals,
such as the welcoming of Germany into the international community, a
world order predicated upon the League of Nations, and general disarmament supervised by the League.[3] Sarrail and most of the left-wing
candidates, however, were easily defeated as the National Bloc, a coalition of right and center parties, won the elections in a landslide. Fear of
Bolshevism, distrust of Germany, and concern that the Treaty of Versailles was too mild led Frenchmen to elect the country's most conservative Chamber since 1871.

Following his political setback, Sarrail pursued an active career for
the next five years as a lecturer, journalist, and member of the central
committee of the League of the Rights of Man.[4] He publicly and frequently commented upon a wide range of contemporary military and
international affairs. Neither trenchant nor original, his views were
consistently liberal. His viewpoint was at once realistic and idealistic,
pessimistic and optimistic; and for good reason, for his ideas were both
the reflection of and a reaction to the staggering impact of the recent
war. For example, Sarrail suggested that postwar France no longer possessed the human and material resources of a great power. Advising

[185]

retrenchment, he criticized France's Versailles decision to occupy the Rhineland and the National Bloc's 1923 decision to occupy the Ruhr. These actions, he maintained, were militarily useless, gave German nationalists an opportunity to attack the humiliated Weimar Republic, disrupted the German economy, and were a financial drain to France at a time when expenditures were needed for the reconstruction of the war-ravaged country.[5] And Sarrail was not more sanguine concerning the French officer corps. He warned that the professional officer corps had emerged from the war with its traditionally antidemocratic values and attitudes intact. Not only did the professional army pose a latent threat to the Republic, but the army had an undue influence upon the National Bloc's foreign policy; witness the government's decision to pacify Syria, which together with Lebanon had been given to France as a mandate.[6] Under the guise of a mandate, France's occupation of Lebanon and Syria was, according to Sarrail, nothing more than "pure imperialism." Lashing out at the National Bloc's policies in the mandate, Sarrail claimed, "We [France] have contributed in Syria to the wealth of a handful of financiers and merchants . . . ; we have played into the hands of all the religious congregations over there; we have worked for them and not for France; we, the descendents of those who fought the French Revolution, have supported religious absolutism and antidemocratic principles with force."[7] Sarrail maintained that if France had any hope of playing a key role in Middle Eastern policies, it behooved her to terminate her pro-Catholic policies and to gain the support of the Moslems, a majority in the mandate, by granting them political and economic concessions.[8]

France's postwar military strategy and organization, however, were the foremost questions that dominated Sarrail's attention. He believed that if a major war occurred, it would be impossible for the combatants to break enemy lines and a long war of attrition would ensue. Thus the only logical strategy to adopt was one of defensive warfare. Since defensive warfare could only be waged by the masses, the basis of France's national defense must rest upon the reserves, not the professional army, whose basic peacetime function would be to train conscripts. Specifically, Sarrail favored a military organization similar to that proposed by the Socialists. The recruit would receive three months of basic instruction and then serve seven months on the frontiers; in case of war the frontier troops were not to be an offensive striking weapon, but simply serve as a protective screen allowing the reserves to join their units in an orderly fashion. Upon completing his tour of duty on the frontiers, the recruit would then enter the reserves.[9]

Sarrail's military theories contained significant ramifications. First, his tenacious insistence that the next war would be a defensive one prevented him from considering other alternatives. The result was the stifling of his imagination, so much so that he tended to be skeptical of the efficacy of offensive weapons, such as tanks and airplanes, believing that modern military equipment could effectively blunt the latest offensive innovations.[10] Even more revealing, Sarrail explicitly recognized that the heart of his proposed national defense program— the militia—could guarantee neither the peace of Europe nor France's security. France's security and preservation would have to rest upon the shoulders of the League of Nations. Pleading for an end to nationalism, he wanted each state to allow the League to supervise the reduction of all national armies and war matériel. The League alone would possess a large-scale professional army and acting as an international police force, it could punish any aggressor.[11]

Although the genesis of Sarrail's ideas concerning the basic questions of strategy and military organization can be found in his prewar career, there is little question that the experience of World War I had reinforced and accentuated his basic ideas. The war had revealed to Sarrail that the reserves had been the equal of the professional soldier, that the strategy of the offensive had been a failure, and that France had suffered a staggering disaster and thus was neither psychologically nor economically prepared to maintain a large professional army poised to unleash an offensive.[12] Unfortunately, during the interwar years Socialists, republicans, and the Right, as well as the General Staff, read the same basic lessons from the recent war. By the late 1920s politicians and generals accepted the fundamental premise that a future war would be one of attrition; therefore, France would have to wage a defensive struggle while relying upon the reserves. France's interwar military strategy and organization were shaped according to these principles. The year 1940 would demonstrate several things, one of which was that offensive warfare was not yet outmoded.[13]

In the national elections of May, 1924, the Cartel des Gauches, an alliance between the Radical, Republican Socialist, and Socialist parties, won a decisive victory as the French electorate voted against the National Bloc's inability to curb inflation, its program of increased taxation, and its foreign policy, particularly the costly occupation of the Ruhr. Edouard Herriot, leader of the Radicals, became premier in June and within the next several months his government opened diplomatic relations with Soviet Russia, promised a more democratic tax structure, attempted to enforce and broaden the state's laic laws, and ac-

cepted the Dawes Plan as a first step toward assuming a more sympathetic attitude toward the Weimar Republic. Furthermore, in a move
designed to condemn the iniquitous political policies of Clemenceau's
wartime nationalist government, the cartel steered a bill through the
National Assembly placing General Sarrail on the army's active list.[14]

Now that Sarrail was once again on the active list there was some
hope among left-wing politicians that he would be appointed to the
nation's highest military body, the Superior War Council. However, it
appears that Sarrail's well-known views concerning reduced military
service raised the specter of several generals resigning from the Superior War Council if he were appointed to that body. Rather that risk
a politico-military confrontation, Herriot sought an important assignment for Sarrail elsewhere.[15] In November General Maxime Weygand, a devout Catholic and admirer of Maurice Barrès, was surprised
to discover that he was no longer high commissioner to the Levant.[16]
The cartel selected General Sarrail to replace Weygand as France's
high commissioner in Syria and Lebanon.[17]

Once again politics had played an instrumental role in Sarrail's re-
emergence as a public figure. No sooner had the cartel swept to victory in May than Accambray had written Sarrail that "our friends are
thinking very much of you now."[18] And immediately following
Sarrail's appointment as high commissioner, Socialist Deputy Henri
Barabant informed the general that "I have worked with many of our
friends in order that the republican general whom we admire and respect . . . may assume a position for which he is more qualified than
anyone else."[19] Sarrail had demonstrated on several occasions during
the previous twenty-five years that he could survive and even prosper
in the rough and tumble world of French politics. But it remained to be
seen whether at the age of sixty-nine, he still possessed the mental
acuity and physical stamina to survive in the smoldering and strife-
torn world of Levantine politics.

In the wartime scramble for portions of the Turkish empire, France
and England agreed to divide the Fertile Crescent between themselves.
The Sykes-Picot agreement of May, 1916, gave France control of
Syria. However, French plans to occupy Syria encountered a good
deal of resistance in the immediate postwar period. Stressing the 1915
pledge of Britain's Henry McMahon, which had promised the Arabs a
large independent state in return for Arab military assistance against
the Turks, Syrian nationalists led by Emir Feisal refused to accept the
Sykes-Picot agreement. In June, 1919, the Syrian National Congress in
Damascus rejected all political control by foreign powers; and on

March 8, 1920, Emir Feisal accepted the National Congress's offer to become king of an independent Syria. Syria's declaration of independence and the enthronement of King Feisal were immediately rejected by France. On April 25, 1920, the Allied Supreme Council met at San Remo and partitioned the Ottoman Empire, granting France the mandate of Syria and Lebanon, and Great Britain the mandate of Palestine and Iraq. French General Henri Gouraud, who had been in Lebanon since the preceding autumn, demanded on July 14 that Feisal accept the San Remo decisions. Feisal refused the ultimatum; thereupon Gouraud marched on Damascus and easily crushed the hastily assembled, poorly trained, and ill-equipped forces of King Feisal. France had her mandate.[20]

France as a mandatory power was to have acted on behalf of the League of Nations. Her basic function was to educate, guide, and assist the less developed territories toward eventual self-rule. Yet, in reality, the French violated the spirit of the mandate, doing very little to encourage independence or to forge a sense of national unity amongst the various religious and ethnic groups.

A far-flung French bureaucratic machine, directed by the high commissioner, who had unfettered legislative, executive, and military power, effectively stifled all local initiative and political freedoms. Although each of the states had a governor, he was appointed by the high commissioner. Although each state had an elected representative council, the native legislative bodies had little power, for it was the high commissioner who supervised, initiated, or vetoed all legislation emanating from the native assemblies. The public services, such as the Departments of Public Health, Roads, Agriculture, and Education, were also regulated. The official hierarchy was composed of Syrians and Lebanese, but all important assignments were filled by French nominees with French advisers or liaison officers attached to them. France was thus able to control every branch and every level of the local administration.

Stifled politically, the Moslems also resented France's pro-Christian policies. The Christians, numerically overwhelmed by the Moslems everywhere except in Lebanon, were France's only supporters in the Middle East. France immediately reciprocated this friendship: she not only prevented the integration of Moslem Syria and Lebanon, but in 1920, to the great dismay of Syrian nationalists, Gouraud doubled the territorial boundaries of Lebanon at the expense of the neighboring Moslems.

There were additional reasons for native discontent. The middle class suffered economic hardship as a result of France's insistence that the local currency be pegged to the constantly fluctuating and quickly depreciating franc. The merchant class resented the import tariff regulations that favored French-made goods. Syrians of all classes resented the threat to the supremacy of the Arabic language. Immediately following the successful June, 1916, Arab revolt against the Turks, Arabic had replaced Turkish as the sole language of national life. But with the imposition of the French mandate a few years later, the French language was not only taught in all state schools, but in many cases superseded Arabic in the local courts of justice. Last, the Syrians resented being treated as second-class subjects by the French administrators. Turkish rule may have been corrupt and inefficient, but the Arab, for the most part, was treated as an equal, not as an inferior. There is little doubt that the French officials were psychologically and socially remote from the native population. Many of the French officials, including the high commissioners, were military men whose previous background as World War I commanders or colonial administrators in Africa or Southeast Asia had not prepared them to deal with their basic political function in Syria. Lacking knowledge of the local laws, customs, traditions, and language, the French administrators all too frequently considered Syria nothing more than a colony.[21]

From the crushing of Feisal's government in 1920 until the end of 1924, several acts of violence had occurred against the French. Regardless of the new roads, a greater number of law courts, better trains, and educational benefits that France brought to the mandate, the Syrians, especially the intelligentsia, never accepted the mandate system, considering it nothing more than a convenient means to mask French imperialism. Yet despite the frequent outbreaks of violence and the dramatic rise of Syrian nationalism, which thrived almost exclusively on an intense hatred of France, the mandatory power was oblivious to the widespread animosity and resentment directed against it. When Sarrail arrived in Lebanon, Syria was a tinder box of alienation, disillusionment, and smoldering discontent, needing but a spark to set off a massive explosion.[22] Unwittingly, Sarrail would help to supply the spark.

General Weygand departed from Beirut on December 5, 1924. He received a rousing send-off. Thousands of Lebanese Christians lined the streets and cheered as he proceeded through the town to the harbor where he boarded the boat for Marseilles. The only ones who felt little regret at Weygand's departure were the Moslems.[23]

When Sarrail arrived at Beirut on January 2, 1925, he received a lukewarm reception from the Christian population. Such a response was not altogether unexpected because when Herriot had announced Sarrail's appointment as high commissioner the previous November, the Catholic episcopacy in Lebanon, as a symbol of national mourning, had ordered a minute of silence in all Roman Catholic schools.[24] The Roman Catholics and Maronites feared that the appointment of a freethinker and political liberal meant that France no longer intended to wholeheartedly support Catholic interests in the Middle East. If the Catholics were frightened, the Moslems were delighted with Sarrail's appointment, believing that it foreshadowed a more realistic and enlightened era in French-Moslem relations. Thus, it was not surprising that when Sarrail arrived at Beirut it was the Moslems who formed the National Reception Committee and gave the new high commissioner his most enthusiastic reception.[25]

Following the general instructions that he had received from the Herriot government, Sarrail initially undertook a more liberal political and religious policy than had his predecessors. Believing that the mandate was neither a colony nor a protectorate and therefore should have greater experience in self-government,[26] Sarrail immediately announced that Weygand's appointee as governor of Lebanon, General Charles Vandenberg, would be replaced and the Lebanese Representative Council would elect a Lebanese national to be the new governor. Specifically, Sarrail wanted the Representative Council to elect three candidates. Upon Sarrail's approval of two of these candidates, the council would select its governor.[27] However, a few days later Sarrail informed several Lebanese deputies that he would not permit the president of the Representative Council, Emile Eddé, to become a candidate for governor. Sarrail was rejecting Eddé in an attempt to reduce the political influence of the Catholics. The Jesuit and Maronite clergy had actively supported Eddé's candidacy as governor, so much so that the clerical Eddé could count upon the support of twenty-six of the twenty-nine deputies in the Representative Council.[28]

On January 12 Sarrail summoned the council to hold its elections for governor. But in order to forestall an acrimonious debate on the part of Eddé's resentful partisans, Sarrail forbade any public discussion concerning the proposed candidates. The council promptly refused the high commissioner's restrictions. An irked Sarrail dissolved the council and appointed the French bureaucrat Léon Cayla as interim governor. Sarrail hoped that future elections would produce a more cooperative body.[29]

While the difficulties with the Representative Council were occurring, Sarrail was also involved in a dispute with the Lebanese Catholics. The traditionally close ties between France and the Catholics had been symbolized by a ceremony, one that even the Ottoman Empire had been forced to recognize. When the French representative had arrived at Beirut, either as consul-general in the prewar days or as high commissioner under the mandate, he had attended certain liturgical honors on his behalf at the local cathedral. Sarrail received an invitation to this traditional ceremony.[30] However, he refused to attend. Following Herriot's instructions, Sarrail was demonstrating to the Christians, as well as to the Moslems, a minority in Lebanon but a majority throughout the rest of the mandate, that henceforth the Christians would no longer receive favored treatment from France.[31]

Sarrail's gesture, so contrary to Weygand's statement to the Maronite Patriarch that "my mission only began when your Blessedness gave me your benediction,"[32] brought forth a storm of protest. Monsignor Giannini, apostolic delegate in Syria, wrote Sarrail that the pope would be notified of the high commissioner's actions and that France's traditional role as protector of the Christians "will have expired."[33] But what was surprising was the impassioned response in France to Sarrail's innocuous Lebanese policy. The attacks leveled against Sarrail as well as the intensity with which he was defended in French political circles sprang not only from his long and close association with the Left, but also from a bitter religious struggle that was poisoning contemporary French public life, the battle between Catholics and the cartel.

The religious policy of the National Bloc had been extremely favorable to the Catholic church. Diplomatic relations were reestablished with the papacy; many religious congregations, dissolved by the law of 1901, were quietly allowed to return to France; and those religious orders, excluded from teaching by the law of 1904, were allowed to resume their previous duties. The newly regained provinces of Alsace and Lorraine were allowed to maintain both the 1850 Falloux Law, which had given the church a preeminent position in the educational structure, and the Concordat of 1801, although both the Falloux Law and the Concordat had been banished from the rest of France. The law of 1905, which had stipulated that church property would be administered by secular administrative councils, was greatly altered. The National Bloc passed legislation that allowed the bishops and other ecclesiastical dignitaries to control the local administrative councils, thus assuring the church control of its property.[34]

Assuming power in mid-1924, Premier Herriot promptly set forth a program that included the severing of diplomatic relations with the Vatican, the stringent enforcement of the laic laws, which would have entailed the eviction from France of all unauthorized religious orders, the repudiation of the Concordat of 1801 and the Falloux Law in Alsace and Lorraine, and the implementation of the laic laws in these provinces.[35]

The cartel's laic policy, however, met an immediate wave of Catholic resistance. Resolutions passed by Alsatian municipal and departmental councils as well as large-scale protest rallies held at Strasbourg, Mulhouse, and Colmar made it quite clear that any attempts to secularize the recovered provinces would lead to bloodshed. In September the French cardinals sent the premier a letter warning him against undertaking an anticlerical program. The following month Cardinal Charost called for the faithful to take action against the forces of evil. Encouraged by the papacy, a bevy of militant Catholic lay organizations was formed to arouse public opinion against Herriot's religious program.[36]

This highly explosive and deeply suspicious atmosphere helps to explain the vitriolic response to the July, 1924, announcement that the Herriot government was considering the possibility of placing Sarrail on the army's active list. The conservative and right-wing press wasted little time reminding its readers that Sarrail, France's least competent wartime commander, was an Andréist, a *fichard*, a sectarian, a Freemason, and a political intriguer who had had extremely close ties with *Le Bonnet rouge*.[37] When Sarrail was appointed high commissioner to Syria and Lebanon in late November, apprehension within Catholic right-wing circles greatly increased as it was feared that the appointment of a freethinker meant that the Herriot government was preparing to pursue an anticlerical campaign in Lebanon.[38] Sarrail's initial Lebanese policy two months later convinced the Right that its worst fears had been confirmed.[39] On January 23, 1925, during a Chamber debate focusing on the government's controversial proposal to break diplomatic relations with the Vatican, several right-wing deputies, Anatole Biré, Achille Fould, and Jacques Poitou-Duplessy, raised the question of Sarrail's refusal to attend the traditional liturgical ceremony held for the French representative at Beirut. Obviously surprised by the deputies' question, Herriot declared that he did not yet possess enough information to give a detailed account of the incident, but, as far as he knew, Sarrail had simply declined a mass offered to him in his private status rather than one offered as part of the traditional honors bestowed upon the French representative.[40]

The Right, however, had no intention of letting the matter drop. A week later the first bitter postwar parliamentary debate concerning Syria took place. Biré angrily explained that France had traditionally been the protector of the Christians in the Levant. Yet, the Herriot government, Biré claimed, had selected an anti-Catholic as high commissioner, one who had refused to attend a mass, had been publicly welcomed by the Syrian Freemasons, and had dismissed the conservative and Catholic General Vandenberg as governor of Lebanon.

Désiré Ferry, vice-president of the ultranationalist League of Patriots and deputy from the Meurthe-et-Moselle, observed that the events of the previous two months appeared to reveal that the cartel was indeed introducing a pro-Moslem policy in the mandate. First, Sarrail was not only an anticlerical who had refused to attend the liturgical ceremony, but he had permitted the hitherto banned Syrian nationalist newspapers to resume publication and had allowed the Syrian National School, a center of Arab nationalism, to reopen. Second, Weygand, who had successfully pacified Syria, had been recalled. Why, Ferry asked, had Weygand been removed? And looking at Herriot, the right-wing deputy answered his own question: "Admit it, it was a question only of obtaining a job and a salary for General Sarrail." Herriot responded immediately. He delivered a passionate speech declaring that Sarrail's wartime record had not warranted his dismissal in 1917. Sarrail had been a victim of Clemenceau's nationalist policies. The premier elaborated: "The truth is that just when we are being accused of having taken a partial policy toward General Sarrail, we have, on the contrary, reestablished justice—justice which had been infringed upon with no regard for the rights of a great general who was struck and held in disfavor only because while being ardently French he is also sincerely republican. The French government has redressed an injustice."

But the right-wing attacks remained unabated. Joseph Brom, deputy from the Haut-Rhin and a member of the extremely conservative Republican Union party, shouted that Sarrail was under the control of the Freemasons. Marquis Henri de la Ferronnays, Right deputy from the Loire-Inférieure, claimed that Sarrail's policies were diametrically opposed to those of General Weygand. Obviously provoked, Herriot suggested that the right-wing deputies were purposely exaggerating the significance of Sarrail's failure to attend the mass because it gave them an additional instrument to strike at the government's domestic religious policies. Furthermore, Sarrail's French critics, according to Herriot, may have been receiving a good deal of assistance from elsewhere. The outcry concerning the mass incident had been "provoked by the party of the former high commissioner [Weygand]," that is, by the Maronites, who were determined "to oppose systematically the success of Sarrail's mission" in order to serve the church's current struggle within France. Despite the pressures exerted in France and Lebanon, Herriot declared that his government would not be intimidated. Sarrail would remain as high commissioner and he would pursue a policy of religious impartiality.[41]

Criticism in the Chamber and press of Sarrail's initial Lebanese policies was but one aspect of the Right's unrelenting attack against the cartel's religious policies. Throughout the early part of 1925 the attacks against the government became more ugly and foreboding. In February the National Catholic Federation and some left-wingers clashed in the streets of Marseilles. In March the French cardinals denounced Herriot's proposed religious policies as well as all aspects of the secular state, such as divorce, separation of church and state, and the absence of mandatory religious instruction in the schools. Calling for a "war on secularism," the cardinals declared that petitions and even strikes should be used to break the cartel's religious program. The cardinals warned Herriot that "we possess the troops, our organization is set. The hour has never appeared so opportune in perhaps fifty years. To let it pass by without taking advantage of it seems that we would be betraying Providence."[42]

Herriot reeled under the pressure. The government dropped plans to secularize Alsace and Lorraine. Although the Chamber voted to abolish the French embassy at the Vatican, Herriot announced that a French representative, not of ambassadorial rank, would remain at the Holy See. Although the Chamber voted in March the stringent application of the existing laic laws, the government made no serious effort to dissolve the unauthorized religious orders.

Herriot capitulated elsewhere. When the apostolic delegate in Syria ordered the removal from the Beirut Cathedral of the armchairs traditionally reserved for the French representative, Herriot wrote to Monsignor Giannini on March 4 that the French government "had no intention of renouncing in the East either the duties or the rights which it derived from a long tradition sanctioned by international treaties and recognized by the Holy See."[43] And three weeks later the premier ordered Sarrail to return as quickly as possible the visit that the Patriarch of Lebanon had made to him two months earlier. On March 30

Sarrail, donned in full-dress uniform, returned the long-delayed visit.[44] Forced to choose between the Christians or the Moslems, Herriot, harassed by the militant Catholics, selected the former. At precisely the time when the Herriot government was discovering that it was impolitic to fulfill its religious program, Sarrail was moving in the opposite direction. In late March Sarrail advocated the introduction of secular schools in Lebanon and brushing aside Herriot's explicit instructions that no electoral changes should be undertaken in Lebanon without the French government's prior consent,[45] the high commissioner issued a decree that made elections to the Lebanese Representative Council more democratic by substituting direct voting for the traditional two-stage system of elections. But much more significant, in an attempt to instill a sense of national unity whereby the Lebanese inhabitants would regard themselves as citizens of a country and not as members of any particular religion, Sarrail's decree abolished the traditional Lebanese electoral process whereby the various religious groups were allotted proportional representation, a practice that had tended to accentuate if not foster differences within the community. Sarrail's proposals to eradicate confessionalism in the electoral process and to introduce secular education drew sharp attacks from all Lebanese religious groups. The Maronites feared that if voting were not along religious lines, they would lose their dominant political position. The minority sects feared that if proportional representation were abolished, they might lose whatever political influence they possessed.[46] But it was the French domestic political situation, not the Lebanese prelates, which would determine the outcome of Sarrail's latest reform measures.

In mid-April, 1925, the Herriot government resigned when the Senate rejected its financial program. Supported by Socialists and Radicals, Paul Painlevé once again assumed the premiership. However, the Socialists quickly became disenchanted with the new premier when he rejected their extremely controversial plan to levy a tax on capital. Consequently, in an attempt to gain moderate republican support while at the same time convinced that France could ill afford the luxury of an unending politico-religious crisis and that issues such as rescuing the franc and curbing inflation were far more vital to the country's welfare than the religious one, Painlevé jettisoned whatever remained of the cartel's original religious policy. France would maintain its ambassador at the Vatican; Briand, who a few months earlier had strongly opposed breaking diplomatic relations with the Holy See, was appointed minister of foreign affairs; and Painlevé publicly promised that the laic laws would not be introduced in Alsace and Lorraine without the consent of the local population.[47]

The impact of the new government's religious policy had reverberations in Beirut. By late April Cayla publicly denied that France had ever intended to introduce secular schools in Lebanon.[48] Three weeks later, in an attempt to appease the French Catholics while acknowledging that it was politically unrealistic to abandon the Lebanese Christians in favor of very uncertain and in fact extremely improbable Moslem support, Briand ordered Sarrail to abrogate the proposed electoral measures.[49] Sarrail quickly restored two-stage voting and confessional representatives as the keystones of the Lebanese electoral process.

In Syria as in Lebanon Sarrail's initial programs, while more liberal than those of Gouraud and Weygand, produced nugatory results. Sarrail attempted to win Moslem support for the French mandate. Yet his policies were too moderate for the Syrian nationalists whose initial enthusiasm for Sarrail quickly waned as it became apparent that Arab independence would not be forthcoming.[50] For example, in an attempt to encourage a modicum of self-government, Sarrail promised in February, 1925, that following the forthcoming elections to the Syrian Representative Assembly in October, the Assembly would be granted much greater powers, such as the right of legislative initiative and effective control of the governor's ministers.[51] Second, Sarrail immediately permitted the native governor of Syria, Soubhi Bey, to have a good deal more freedom in shaping the country's administrative and political policies than he had enjoyed previously.[52] But the nationalists were not satisfied with these measures. They wanted the Representative Assembly dissolved and elections held immediately, not in October as Sarrail had promised.[53] Furthermore, many Syrians wanted a nationalist to be governor of Syria, not Soubhi Bey, whom the nationalists considered a self-seeking politician because he had faithfully served the Turks and later Gouraud and Weygand.[54]

In an attempt to encourage greater political participation on the part of the Syrian Moslems and at the same time to appease the nationalists who resented French rule, Sarrail suggested to several Syrian politicians the formation of an organized political party, which hitherto had been banned in Syria. In February various nationalist groups formed the People's party. But dismissing Sarrail's plea for moderation, the new party, headed by Abd-al-Rahman Shahbander, put forth a program of national sovereignty, the unification of Syria, and a democratic government. If implemented, the program would have ended France's control of Syria. Sarrail did not have to wait long to assess the impact of the organization whose formation he had encouraged. Lord Balfour, author of the famous wartime declaration that Great Britain favored the establishment in Palestine of a national home for the Jews, visited Damascus on April 8. Serious rioting, fanned by members of the People's party, immediately broke out and Sarrail was forced to use Algerian troops to repress the demonstrators when nationalist ringleaders began to surge toward the city's Jewish quarters.[55]

But it was not Sarrail's fruitless religious and political policies in Lebanon and Syria that would create the greatest difficulty for France. The Jabal al Druze, inhabited by fifty thousand people, was a mountainous desert area south of Damascus. The Druzes had several distinguishing characteristics. Having broken with Islam in the eleventh century, they practiced an esoteric religion. Their society was a feudal one. They were warriors and fiercely independent people, having rebelled on several occasions against the Turks.[56] France quickly recognized that the Druzes had a special position within the mandate; in 1921 an agreement was reached between France and the Jabal al Druze, whereby the latter was recognized as an independent state and guaranteed not only the right to have a native governor and representative council, but also independence even if there were a subsequent union or federation of the rest of Syria. In return for these prerogatives, the Druzes recognized the mandate, accepted French advisers, and permitted French troops to be garrisoned at the Druze capital of Suwayda.[57]

When the native governor died in 1923, the leading Druze families could not agree upon a successor. Therefore, in September, 1923, the Jabal al Druze Representative Council elected Captain Gabriel Carbillet as the new governor. Carbillet, "whose mentality and methods seem to be better suited to North African conditions than to the peculiar and delicate conditions of the Druze community,"[58] immediately attempted to transform the Jabal al Druze's feudal society. He introduced a more equitable judicial system and built roads, schools, aqueducts, and irrigation systems. But his greatest impact was in the area of property rights. Traditionally, much of the land in the Jabal al Druze was communal property. The common lands were redivided every three years. The leading families received one-third of the land, usually the third that had been best cultivated during the previous triennial period, whereas the peasants, who were expected to cultivate the chief's estates, received the poorer lands. This feudal structure, against which the peasants had rebelled twenty years earlier, stifled all economic initiative. In an attempt to increase the peasants' initiative, which hopefully would lead to greater economic productivity, Carbillet secured land tenure for the peasants by permitting them to have legal possession of what had formerly been communal property if they planted grape vines on the land.

The rapid attempt to modernize a feudal society created a revolutionary situation. Although by mid-1925 relatively few peasants had taken advantage of Carbillet's land reform project, the chieftains feared the program. The Druze chiefs reasoned that any reduction of communal property would reduce their traditional one-third share of the land. Even more frightening was the specter that even if somehow the chiefs could maintain their sizable estates, there would not be sufficient manpower available to work the land, for if a large number of peasants became owners of private property, they would not be willing to return to the chief's lands as wageless laborers.

But the feudal chieftains were not the only ones dissatisfied with Carbillet's programs. Ironically, so were the peasants. In order to build the roads and irrigation systems Carbillet resorted to forced labor. The peasants frequently worked on road construction for two or three months before being allowed to return to their homes. Sometimes 10 percent of a town's available manpower was pulled from its traditional occupations and forced to construct aqueducts. Moreover, not only was the Carbillet-imposed *corvée* far more excessive than anything the Druzes had experienced under Turkish rule, but the governor was an extremely zealous taskmaster, frequently punishing both commoners and notables who found compulsory and unpaid labor distasteful.[59]

In December, 1923, some of the Druze clans threatened to kill Carbillet unless he vacated his position.[60] In April, 1924, dissatisfied with Carbillet's policies and encouraged by Arab nationalists, a few of the Druze chieftains, spearheaded by the prominent Atrash family, prepared to lead a revolt against the French. Although there were sporadic outbreaks of violence, the rebellion was stillborn. Several factors explain the failure. French officials quickly arrested a few of the ringleaders. Carbillet persuaded many of the wavering Druze chiefs not to support what appeared to be a futile rebellion. And last, several of the dissident leaders lost their nerve when they feared that popular support would not be forthcoming. Although easily throttled in 1924, Druze discontent did not subside.[61]

In April, 1925, a Druze delegation led by several members of the

Atrash clan visited Sarrail at Beirut and complained of Carbillet's administration and, in accordance with the 1921 agreement, requested that a native governor replace Carbillet. Sarrail refused the demands, claiming that the 1921 agreement was of no practical significance, something that General Weygand had implicitly recognized the preceding year when he had refused a similar demand set forth by the Atrash lords. And in June and early July Sarrail refused to meet with Druze delegations that had come to Beirut seeking to have Carbillet dismissed and his programs curtailed.[62] Sarrail believed that had he met with the Druze representatives, it would have been interpreted to mean that their complaints against Carbillet were justified.[63] Not wishing to "give the appearance of abdicating before these agitators,"[64] and equally convinced that Carbillet's reforms had been impressive, Sarrail saw no reason why Carbillet should be dismissed.[65] Sarrail's stubborn refusal to meet with the Druzes and his insistence that Carbillet remain as governor led several Druze chieftains to conclude that the high commissioner was "in his dotage."[66] Although greatly exaggerated, there is little question that Sarrail was showing "distinct signs" of his age. It had been noted several months earlier that he was frequently irritable and eschewed close involvement with administrative details, something that in his younger days had been his forte.[67]

Meanwhile on June 2 Captain Antoine Raynaud, the provisional governor of the Jabal while Carbillet was spending a leave of absence in France, warned Sarrail that if a revolt were to be averted, an inquiry concerning the Druze allegations should be promptly initiated. Sarrail dismissed the recommendations while suggesting that Raynaud did not understand the Druze political situation. In early July, following a religious ceremony at Suwayda in which shots were fired at French officials, Sarrail selected Major Tommy Martin to replace Raynaud as governor of the troublesome state and, reversing his previous position, the high commissioner ordered Martin to investigate the accusations leveled against Carbillet. However, without waiting for Martin to complete his investigation Sarrail decided upon an unfortunate course of action. On July 11, in an attempt to isolate the Atrashes from their partisans, Sarrail invited five leading Atrash chieftains to Damascus under the pretext of discussing their grievances; three of the chiefs arrived at Damascus and were placed under house arrest. Sultan al-Atrash, who had shrewdly refused to accept the French invitation, now realized that he was a marked man. He considered armed rebellion his only recourse to restore Atrash domination in the Jabal al Druze.[68]

On July 18 Sultan al-Atrash and his followers fired on French aircraft. Two days later he seized Salkhad, the second largest town in the Jabal. Sarrail immediately ordered Captain Gabriel Normand to recapture Salkhad. However, Carbillet, who had just returned from France, advised Sarrail to rescind the orders, for if Normand and Sultan al-Atrash were to engage in a bloody clash, all opportunity for a negotiated compromise would evaporate. Agreeing with Carbillet that negotiations with Sultan al-Atrash might be fruitful, Sarrail promptly instructed Normand to return to Suwayda. Sarrail's latest orders, however, arrived too late. On July 21 at Kafer, six miles south of Suwayda, Captain Normand's 166-man column of French-led Syrian and Algerian troops was overwhelmed by Sultan al-Atrash's forces. Normand's troops were decimated. Thereupon, Atrash lay siege to Suwayda, a siege that would endure for sixty-five days.[69]

While the deeper causes of the Druze rebellion lay in the seething discontent engendered by the policies pursued by Carbillet, who utterly failed to respect the strong feudal traditions of the Druzes or to take into account their long tradition of resistance to external authority, the immediate cause of the uprising was Sarrail's insensitivity to the Druze demands that Carbillet be dismissed and his programs rescinded.[70] With tact and political flexibility Sarrail might have staved off the rebellion. Yielding the shadow of power for its substance, he could have given the Druzes a native governor and, as was the usual case in a mandated territory, attached French advisers, with all the real power in the advisers' hands.[71] But this policy was rejected and one of repression adopted. However, when Sarrail failed to make the necessary military preparations to carry out a policy of repression, thus allowing the initiative to pass to the rebels, he and his advisers in Beirut and Damascus revealed a tragic unfamiliarity with the situation as it existed in the Jabal al Druze.[72]

Despite warnings from Raynaud and Martin, Sarrail had not believed that an armed insurrection was imminent.[73] Had he thought so, he would have diverted most of the fourteen thousand French troops at his disposal into Suwayda and Salkhad before taking direct action against the Atrashes. Even following the immediate defeat of Norman's column, Sarrail failed to appreciate the scope and intensity of Druze and Moslem discontent. He and Major Henri Dentz, chief of the French Intelligence Service in Syria, considered the Atrash attack upon Normand's troops as an isolated event.[74] Supported by Dentz, Sarrail believed that the Druze insurgents could easily be crushed.[75] Thus he permitted a battalion of Algerian troops stationed in Syria to depart on July 30 for Morocco, which was then in the throes of the Abd-el-Krim-led revolt.

Sarrail thought that the anti-Carbillet movement was extremely limited in scope, being nothing more than a power play on the part of the Atrashes, who wanted to seize political control of the Jabal not only as a means of demolishing Carbillet's reforms, but also in order to reassert control over the rival feudal families. With the exception of the Atrashes, many of the Druze feudal families appeared satisfied with Carbillet. Furthermore, Sarrail believed that the anti-Carbillet movement had been encouraged by Captain Raynaud, who, aspiring to become permanent governor of the Jabal, was using the Atrashes as a means to discredit Carbillet.[76]

Evidence exists which suggests that some aspects of Sarrail's analysis were not incorrect. French intelligence agreed that Raynaud, motivated by "personal ambition" was attempting to replace Carbillet.[77] It is also true that the Druze National Assembly, comprised of representatives from several of the prominent familes, passed several resolutions throughout the winter and spring of 1925, praising Carbillet's reforms while, at the same time, criticizing the Atrashes for spearheading the campaign against the governor. And even immediately following the Atrash capture of Salkhad and the massacre of Normand's troops, the religious chiefs and several of the tribal factions in the Jabal refused to join the rebellion.[78] However, as events would quickly demonstrate, the Druze notables as well as the Syrian Moslems would remain quiet only if the French could quickly crush the Atrash-led uprising. This Sarrail failed to do.

In an attempt to lift the siege of Suwayda and to crush the rebellion before it could spread, a relief column of three thousand troops under General Roger Michaud's command gathered at Ezra and then set out on July 31 for Suwayda, twenty miles to the southeast. Michaud's column encountered difficulties immediately. Water arrangements proved inadequate as the water wells along the route were dried up. Insufferable heat left the troops "practically unable to move a limb after two or three hours in the field," a situation which revealed that the physical condition of the troops was substandard.[79] Without meeting Druze opposition, Michaud's troops successfully staggered into Burs-el-Hariri. The next day as his troops moved out of Burs-el-Hariri, Michaud foolishly permitted his main striking force to become separated from the supply column that was comprised of Syrian and Malagasy troops. Sultan al-Atrash immediately attacked the supply convoy. On August 2 and 3 the striking force of the column was attacked at Mezran, only seven miles from Suwayda. The results were calamitous. The French suffered eight hundred casualties. A Malagasy battalion guarding the supply column panicked and was slaughtered in its attempt to flee. Major Jean Aujac, commander of the battalion, committed suicide. Some two thousand rifles, twelve machine guns, large amounts of ammunition, and one battery of mountain artillery were captured. Suwayda remained under siege as Michaud was forced to return to Ezra.[80]

Sarrail immediately cabled Paris for reinforcements while warning that the latest Druze victory could have "great repercussions."[81] Sarrail was correct—even more correct than he imagined.[82] Sultan al-Atrash's spectacular success of August 2 and 3 changed the entire complexion of the rebellion. The revolt quickly spread through Syria as hitherto quite distinct social and economic classes with traditionally antagonistic political, religious, and economic goals joined forces in order to combat a common enemy. Feudal Druze chiefs who resented Carbillet's administration but who had initially refrained from open opposition to France now joined the rebellion. Many anti-Christian Arabs, heartened that the Christians' protectors had received an unexpected jolt, now believed the moment opportune to settle some agelong scores. Bedouin tribesmen encouraged rebellion if only because anarchy allowed them an opportunity to plunder. Peasants and unemployed artisans, driven by poor harvest results, hoped that an uprising would ameliorate their conditions. Nationalists, never having accepted the mandate and deeply resenting France's political, financial, and administrative policies of the past five years, now believed the time opportune to forge an independent and sovereign Syria. As a result, there would be an alliance without precedent in Syrian history, as middle-class, Western-educated intellectuals joined forces with the feudal, separatist, insular Druzes to create in the Jabal a provisional national government, one demanding democracy, the unification of Syria, independence, and the withdrawal of all foreigners.[83]

Sarrail's fourteen thousand-man Army of the Levant, composed of Senegalese, Malagasy, and Algerian units as well as one French battalion, had great difficulty maintaining order for a seventy thousand square mile area. Nor were the six thousand-man auxiliary troops, mostly Syrian volunteers, of much help, as they often deserted or simply refused to fight. By early September, reinforcements, spearheaded by the Foreign Legion, arrived at Beirut and under the leadership of General Maurice Gamelin, who had replaced Michaud, another attempt was undertaken to relieve the besieged French garrison at Suwayda. The Druze capital was successfully reached in late September, but because of a shortage of supplies, especially water, and an insecure line of communication, Gamelin had to evacuate the city. The Druzes remained unsubdued.[84]

Meanwhile, events in Syria were not going much better. On August 24 a mixed force of fifteen thousand Druzes and Bedouins, counting upon the support from within Damascus, raided the Syrian capital. When Damascene support for the Druze-led attack was not forthcoming, three squadrons of Spahis, assisted by airplanes, were able to stop the invaders.[85] Nevertheless, by late September the French had gradually lost control of the open country between the Jabal and Damascus. Railroad lines were cut, railroad stations were destroyed and, in isolated villages, the Moslems turned against the Christians.[86]

Sarrail's difficulties did not go unnoticed in France. During the ten weeks that followed Captain Normand's defeat in late July, the right-wing press reacted strongly to the deteriorating situation in Syria. Unfortunately, the Druze-Syrian rebellion did not stimulate the French Right to raise substantive questions concerning France's previous colonial policies. If penetrating questions had been forthcoming, they would have led to a deeper understanding of the causes of the 1925 revolt and, consequently, might have offered France a series of alternative policies that in time she could have profitably implemented not only in the Middle East, but also in Indochina and North Africa. Instead of discussing the broader implications of the Syrian rebellion, a discussion that would have raised the prospect that greater independence would have to be granted to the Arabs, the French Right focused exclusively upon Sarrail, and displaying partisan vindictiveness, attacked him with a mixture of truths, exaggerations, and falsehoods. The Right, "making no attempt to conceal their pleasure in being able to revenge themselves upon one of the hated 'Rue de Valois' generals,"[87] erroneously claimed that Sarrail, Freemason, sectarian, and sender of secret wartime information to Le Bonnet rouge, was now deliberately concealing information from the Painlevé government concerning the seriousness of the rebellion.[88] But the primary right-wing accusation was that Sarrail alone had been responsible for the rebellion and if he were recalled peace would be immediately restored to the mandate.[89] Relying upon classified documents supplied by French military and colonial officials in Damascus, Henri de Kérillis, editor of L'Echo de Paris, produced irrefutable evidence in late September and early October to demonstrate that on the eve of the Druze revolt Raynaud and Martin had informed Sarrail that the

Druze complaints against Carbillet were justified and that if Carbillet's programs were not changed, a rebellion could be forthcoming. Sarrail dismissed these warnings just as easily as he had dismissed the Atrash requests that a Druze replace Carbillet as governor. Kérillis also pointed out that nothing better revealed Sarrail's heavy-handed approach to the Druze problem than the high commissioner's July decision to invite five of the Atrashes to Damascus so that he could arrest them. There was a good deal of truth in Kérillis's claim that the Druzes, encountering "nameless insults and harassments," had been driven to revolt by Sarrail's unrealistic intransigence.[90]

Equally damning but more controversial was Kérillis's accusation that Sarrail was responsible for the early August massacre of Michaud's troops. Kérillis produced a July 23 report written by Major Aujac and addressed to Sarrail stating that the Malagasy troops were militarily unfit for combat and therefore should not be used in Michaud's attempt to relieve Suwayda. Despite the report Sarrail believed that the Malagasy were capable of participating in the campaign.[91] Kérillis neglected to state that Sarrail, as well as Michaud, who had been informed of Aujac's report, attempted to minimize Malagasy military incompetence by utilizing them to guard the supply column in the rear.[92] This maneuver, of course, ended in disaster when the Druzes succeeded in separating Aujac's supply column from Michaud's main fighting units.

The response of the Radicals and Republican Socialists to the initial stage of the Druze and Syrian revolt was as sterile as that of the conservatives and the ultra Right. Failing to grasp fully the serious difficulties facing the French empire and hoping to spare Sarrail and the Painlevé government undue embarassment, the Left, for the most part, was reticent. When the Radical and Republican Socialist press did comment on the Syrian question in the summer of 1925, it was to defend Sarrail from the Right's incessant attacks. At a time when the French empire was showing its first signs of disintegration, it behooved the left-wing press to ask why should the Right demand Sarrail's recall and not that of General Louis-Hubert Lyautey, the beleaguered resident general of Morocco. The answer was obvious. Lyautey was a royalist whereas Sarrail, "the republican general and a man of the Left," had attempted to undermine the Catholic church's influence in Lebanon.[93] Furthermore, by a specious process of reasoning, Lyautey was held responsible for Sarrail's difficulties in Syria. *L'Ere nouvelle* declared that "it is common knowledge that the events in Syria are connected with those in the Riff and may even be considered as the logical sequence of the latter . . . ; since the prime cause of the Riffian success is the failure of Marshal Lyautey, Lyautey is therefore responsible for the failure of Sarrail."[94] Emphasizing that Sarrail was being attacked because of his longtime affiliation with the Left, L'Ere nouvelle stoutly proclaimed in mid-August that "no republican will allow Sarrail to be sacrificed to the spite of the National Bloc!"[95] However, six weeks later, as the revolt entered its third month, it became increasingly difficult for the Left to defend Sarrail, and, as a result, Kérillis's documented charges that Sarrail had poorly handled the Druze situation remained unchallenged.

Meanwhile in Syria Sarrail's difficulties were intensifying. In early October nationalists, assisted by troops in the Syrian Legion, seized Hama. French troops from Aleppo, as well as recently arrived tanks and airplanes, were rushed to the city and quickly quashed the uprising. Left defenseless, Aleppo was besieged by marauding Bedouin tribes. Some one thousand French troops and two hundred Syrian gendarmes rushed to the scene and successfully prevented the dissident townspeople, whether nationalists, the poor, or criminals, from joining forces with the tribal warriors.[96]

But the French encountered even greater difficulties at Damascus, where the imminence of danger was not anticipated.[97] Desperately needing about ten thousand additional troops and with all available manpower dispersed throughout the mandate, French authorities believed that they could not afford the luxury of grouping a large concentration of manpower in the Syrian capital.[98] In the early dawn of October 18 a band of about three hundred Druze rebels entered the southern, southeastern, and eastern parts of the city. As sporadic fighting broke out between the rebels and isolated French detachments, a small minority of the population joined the rebels. During the evening of October 18 General François Soule received permission from Sarrail and Gamelin to shoot blank artillery shells over the southern sector of the town. But the attempt to intimidate the insurgents failed. On October 19 the rebels stormed, looted, and burned the Azm Palace, which served as the high commissioner's Syrian residence. The rebels then pressed into the center of Damascus, pillaging the bazaars. Soule and Gamelin immediately responded by ordering a selective artillery shelling of the southern and central portions of the town.[99] The shelling, which took the lives of several hundred people, was halted at noon the next day when all resistance within the city ended.[100]

Was the sporadic and selective firing upon Damascus, which was denounced worldwide as a barbaric act, a military necessity? It is difficult, if not impossible, to answer that question. British Consul W. A. Smart believed that there was no justification for the French action. According to Smart, the French badly overestimated the seriousness of the situation. Damascus was not prepared to revolt if only because the Damascenes were not foolish enough to take senseless risks by cooperating with the totally inadequate number of invaders. However, if a few thousand Druzes had quickly followed in the wake of the original three hundred invaders, a general uprising would have occurred.[101] On the other hand, Major A. G. Salisbury-Jones, British liaison officer to the French Army of the Levant, maintained that the shelling, although too hastily undertaken, was "probably the only solution open to the French. . . . The failure to take desperate steps to meet a desperate situation might have easily led to the fall of Damascus and a general rising throughout the country."[102]

Sarrail and Gamelin maintained that on October 18 they faced a painful predicament. They did not have the manpower to clear the insurgents from the impenetrable southern area of the city. Even if they had possessed the necessary troops, military action would have entailed house-to-house fighting, resulting in incalculable human and material loss.[103] Although French colonial bureaucrats wanted the destruction of Damascus to serve as a "quick, crushing lesson to the rebels,"[104] Sarrail and Gamelin adopted sporadic shelling as the easiest means to convince the Moslem majority of Damascus not to support the invaders and to dissuade the Moslems from attempting to massacre the European population.[105] There is little question that as a short-term measure, the shooting achieved its purpose. The townspeople were intimidated, for when Zayd Atrash approached Damascus on October 26 with one thousand Druze warriors, a group of Damascene notables requested that he not attempt to enter the city for fear that the French artillery barrage would be resumed. Atrash complied and moved westward into southern Lebanon.

The shelling of Damascus intensified the demand in France that Sarrail be recalled. Kérillis asked who was responsible for the Damascus insurrection. "Nothing is easier than to answer: 1. Sarrail, 2. Sarrail, 3. Sarrail."[106] The high commissioner, "a criminal" and "bloody tyrant," had provoked the Damascus uprising by parading on camels the corpses of twenty-four Arab bandits through the city on October 14. Instead of intimidating the population as Sarrail hoped to do, the display of the corpses, Kérillis falsely asserted, roused the Damascenes to fury.[107] *Le Temps* also criticized Sarrail for the events in

Syria and warned that unless peace were restored there, France would lose her mandate. But *Le Temps* believed that ultimate blame for the rebellion must rest upon the cartel, for it was "the men on the Left, who, incapable of rising to the notion of the national interest, subordinated everything to partisan feelings." Partisan political considerations, *Le Temps* lamented, had been responsible for Sarrail's appointment.[108]

However, it was Minister of Foreign Affairs Briand, not the conservative and nationalist press, who played the decisive role in forcing Painlevé to recall Sarrail. Briand had requested Sarrail's recall immediately following Michaud's defeat in early August. Although receptive to Briand's August suggestion, Painlevé did not remove Sarrail then because Herriot had warned that the Radicals would not sanction Sarrail's recall unless Lyautey, who was intensely disliked by the Left, was dismissed as resident general of Morocco.[109] If Painlevé had not heeded Herriot's advice, the government risked the loss of sizable Radical support. Radical desertion over the question of Sarrail's recall, coupled with the loss of Socialist support as the result of the government's failure to introduce a steep income tax, would have forced Painlevé either to resign or to move sharply rightward and form a cabinet based upon a moderate-conservative coalition.[110] Cherishing neither alternative, the premier moved quickly but carefully. First, on August 18 Lyautey, while allowed to maintain total control of the civil functions in Morocco, was deprived of his military command. Then on September 3, without consulting Sarrail, Painlevé recalled Michaud and appointed General Gamelin as general officer commanding the French troops in Syria. Although Sarrail still maintained control of the civil and administrative duties of his office, his days in Syria were numbered. Philippe Berthelot, Briand's chief adviser at the Quai d'Orsay, told the British ambassador that Sarrail would be recalled "once General Gamelin had got properly into the saddle."[111] But it was only in late September when Lyautey had been forced to resign that Painlevé had a free hand to recall Sarrail if the circumstances warranted such action. Following the shelling of Damascus, Briand insisted that Sarrail be recalled. If Sarrail were not replaced, Briand refused to participate in Painlevé's newly organized Cabinet that assumed office on October 29.[112]

Briand's latest insistence that Sarrail be recalled can be appreciated. On October 16, only a few days before the shelling of the Syrian capital, the Locarno Treaty had been signed. The spirit of good will that characterized the proceedings at Locarno had been expressed by

Briand when he declared that war must be replaced by peace, concili-
ation, and international arbitration. The incident at Damascus a few
days later had obviously done nothing to enhance France's prestige or
the spirit of Locarno. Consequently, when faced with the late October
ultimatum of the minister of foreign affairs, Painlevé considered Sarrail more expendable than Briand, the person who symbolized France's
desire to pursue a policy of peace and international reconciliation.
Thus on October 30 the Painlevé government recalled Sarrail as high
commissioner of the Levant.

Sarrail's recall was well received in nationalist and conservative circles. While *Le Figaro* gloated that Sarrail "will have much spare time
to prepare his answer to the 'calumnies' hurled against him and to
meditate about the difficulties of Middle Eastern politics,"[113] *L'Echo de
Paris* jubilantly claimed most of the credit for Sarrail's recall; after all,
Kérillis's publication of classified materials four weeks earlier had
made Sarrail's position as high commissioner untenable. Indeed, it
had taken twenty-five years, but Sarrail had finally been "tracked
down."[114]

The attacks continued. On November 20, five days following his
return to Paris, several ultranationalist associations organized a
demonstration of ten thousand persons at the Salle Wagram. Pierre
Taittinger, president of the fascist-leaning Patriotic Youth, journalists
such as Kérillis and Camille Aymard, and right-wing deputies such as
Désiré Ferry, Charles Desjardins, and André François-Poncet recited
"the errors and mistakes committed" by Sarrail as high commissioner.
Then the cheering audience adopted a resolution denouncing Sarrail's
"criminal blunders" and the government's failure to punish him.[115]
Thereupon a crowd of one thousand left the hall and marched to the
general's apartment on the boulevard Perière. After chanting "Down
with Sarrail" and singing "La Marseillaise," the demonstrators were
persuaded to disperse.[116]

After several delays, the question of Sarrail's tenure as high commissioner reached the Chamber of Deputies on December 18.[117] Désiré
Ferry once again led the attack against Sarrail. The deputy first re-
viewed Sarrail's initial Lebanese policy and found it to be incongruous. Sarrail had encouraged the Moslems at the expense of the
loyal Christians; yet, it was the Moslems who had revolted. Sarrail
wanted the Lebanese Representative Council to elect a Lebanese native
to be governor; yet, when the Representative Council wanted to discuss the qualifications of the various candidates, Sarrail dissolved the
council and appointed a French administrator as governor. Ferry next

put forth a favorite right-wing theme. While emphasizing the mandate's tranquility during Weygand's term as high commissioner, Ferry
placed sole responsibility for the Druze rebellion on Sarrail. Citing
official documents that had appeared in *L'Echo de Paris* eleven weeks
earlier, Ferry demonstrated that despite frequent warning from French
military authorities that Druze discontent with Carbillet could lead to
an insurrection, Sarrail refused to satisfy the Druzes' grievances.

Continuing his accusations, Ferry read Sarrail's July letter in which
the high commissioner had invited several of the Atrashes to Damascus so that he could arrest them. Ferry insisted that this action revealed that Sarrail lacked "honor" because "for the first time in history
a representative of France set a . . . trap for men whom he lured under
the pretext of hearing their complaints." Immediately Republican
Union Deputy Gaston About shouted: "Do not confuse France with
Sarrail." And Joseph Brom reiterated what had been a right-wing cry
for the past twenty-five years: "General Sarrail is not France."[118]

Ferry concluded his blistering personal attack by insisting that Sarrail's recall was not adequate punishment. He wanted sanctions taken
against the former high commissioner. Taunting the cartel, Ferry
asked: "Are there two kinds of justice, one for the soldiers, the other
for the leaders? And for the leaders, is there a different justice according to their membership in certain political cliques?" Then Ferry
attacked the Radicals, Republican Socialists, and Socialists: "I know
that, because of party considerations, you have spared those responsible, [and] avoided sanctions. You will try to hide the truth." If
Sarrail were not punished, the French electorate, Ferry told the car-
tellists, "will judge you severely, it will tell you that it is not enough to
make declarations of peace to the world, and it will shout at you, as it
already is whispering, 'the cartel is war.' "[119]

The debate ended abruptly. The noncommunist Left refused to
allow Ferry to continue his tirade. Responding to demands from the
Left, Chamber President Herriot suspended the session. No sooner
had Herriot announced the suspension than Sarrail, who had been in
the public gallery watching the proceedings, stood up to leave. The
general was immediately recognized by the deputies. The result was
pandemonium. The Right hooted and jeered while the Left cheered,
"Long live Sarrail." The impassioned cheers and denunciations "reminded one of the fierce days of the Dreyfus case."[120]

When the debate resumed two days later, the Communists entered
the discussion. Jacques Doriot, deputy from the Seine, correctly observed that the Chamber was not debating the basic question at hand,

namely, France's colonial policy in Syria. Instead, the deputies had been mesmermized by the question of Sarrail. In fact, what was taking place in the Chamber, stated Doriot, was a struggle between two sects, clericals and laics, Jesuits and Freemasons. If the politicians would devote their energies to a close analysis of France's colonial policies instead of to Sarrail, they would discover, Doriot claimed, that France was only in Syria to protect the interests of French capitalists. The only solution to the Moroccan and Syrian rebellions was complete evacuation of these territories.

Little heed was paid to Doriot's suggestions. The question of Sarrail still overshadowed the debate. But now it was the noncommunist Left that assumed the offensive. Supported by the Socialists, Painlevé attempted to demolish each of the criticisms expounded by Sarrail's detractors. To the argument that Sarrail alone was responsible for the insurrection, Painlevé noted that it was Weygand who had appointed Carbillet. But Weygand's responsibility for the Druze rebellion did not end there. Painlevé emphasized that all was not peaceful in the mandate before Sarrail's arrival. Certainly large-scale military action was not needed there after 1920, but the peace that reigned in the mandate during Gouraud's and Weygand's tenures was an extremely tenuous one, brigandage and assassinations were frequent, and the Druzes, never accepting French rule, were prepared to revolt at a propitious moment. To substantiate his argument, Painlevé read a July, 1924, report submitted by Carbillet to Weygand in which the former warned that Druze discontent was such that a single incident "can be the spark that will create a big uproar."

Next, Painlevé emphasized that one of the immediate causes of the Druze rebellion was the Moroccan revolt that had erupted in May, 1925. The sudden and unexpected success of Abd-el-Krim encouraged the Atrashes to attempt a similar uprising. Regarding Sarrail's July invitation to the Atrashes to come to Damascus, Painlevé insisted that the Atrashes had never been promised safe conduct and knew that they had a chance of being arrested should they come to Damascus. Turning to Sarrail's use of Malagasy troops, Painlevé stated that no one expected them to collapse so disastrously, since they were commanded by French officers. In fact, Painlevé minimized Michaud's defeat, asserting that while the defeat was unfortunate, "we have in our colonial history a great number of distressing incidents." As for the shelling of Damascus, Painlevé correctly noted that immediately following the shelling, the world press had emphasized that Damascus had been destroyed. However, such was not true. The city had only been slightly damaged. Actually, most of the damage to the city was done by the Bedouins and desert thieves who took advantage of the uprising to plunder sections of the Syrian capital. The war minister concluded his defense of Sarrail by sending the Chamber into a frenzy. As left-wing deputies applauded and conservatives and nationalists called for a suspension of the session, Painlevé claimed that Sarrail was responsible for the relative ease with which Damascus had been subdued. Sarrail's pro-Moslem policies, which were evident from the first day of his arrival at Beirut, convinced the more than three hundred thousand Damascenes not to join the insurgents.[121]

When the December 20 debate concluded, several motions were presented for consideration. The Communist motion calling for the immediate cessation of hostilities, French evacuation, and recognition of Syrian independence found no support beyond the handful of Communist deputies. The motion of Ferry and Desjardins requesting the government to punish Sarrail was also overwhelmingly rejected. The Socialist-sponsored motion requesting that the League of Nations assume control of the mandate was also solidly defeated. Radicals, Republican Socialists, conservative republicans, and a sprinkling of Socialists overwhelmingly supported Briand's solution to the Syrian problem. The premier renounced any policy of abandoning the mandate. France, not Sultan al-Atrash, had a grand and glorious mission to fulfill: France, ruling the mandate in the spirit expected by the League of Nations, would lead the Syrians to eventual peace and freedom. But in the meantime, while decrying the horrors of war, Briand emphasized that Syria must be pacified.[122]

Sarrail's experience in the Levant revealed several disturbing aspects of interwar France. First, the controversy surrounding Sarrail demonstrated that beneath the veneer of economic prosperity and political stability of the mid-1920s, France's political divisions ran dangerously deep. From any rational point of view the Right's persistent claims that Sarrail alone had been responsible for the Druze and Syrian rebellion makes little sense. Certainly Sarrail's miscalculations had been the most significant immediate cause of the Druze uprising. But his shortcomings neither fully explain the Druze rebellion nor explain why the rebellion successfully spilled over into Syria. The Syrian uprising, as the conservative *L'Asie française* remarked, had "more remote and more profound causes" than Sarrail's errors and miscalculations.[123] The Arabs resented France's financial, judicial, political, and bureaucratic practices. The native population, whether feudal

Druze chieftains or middle-class Damascene nationalists, wanted greater self-rule.

If Sarrail had played a relatively insignificant role in the Syrian uprising, why then was he so viciously condemned? The right-wing attacks against Sarrail and the Left's response to these attacks were inspired not by what had occurred in Syria, but by what Sarrail had come to represent by 1925. The name "Sarrail" symbolized laicism, André's attempt to establish civilian control over the army, the politicians' wartime efforts to control the High Command, a repudiation of Clemenceau's nationalist wartime political tactics, and last but not least, the army's devotion to the Republic. By insisting that it was Sarrail alone who had been responsible for the Syrian and Druze rebellion, the Right was not only repudiating many of these ideals, but was attempting to discredit much of the Left's military and political program of the past twenty-five years.[124] The Left, on the other hand, had no choice. Although obviously embarrassed by Sarrail's performance as high commissioner,[125] the Left had to defend Sarrail. What was at stake was an entire set of values. It is for this reason that at the conclusion of the Chamber debate of December 20 Republican Socialist Deputy René Chavagnes turned to the nationalists and stated that despite the Syrian rebellion and the voluminous attacks leveled against Sarrail, "he remains . . . one of the greatest military and republican figures of this country. . . . Your insults do not touch him."[126]

Although the 1925 Sarrail affair dramatized the wide gulf between the Left and Right, the Syrian experience also revealed that irreconcilable cleavages existed within the cartel. In fact, the Chamber debates of December 18 and 20 served as a reminder that the Socialist-Radical coalition forged in May, 1924, was now moribund. While the Radicals, Republican Socialists, and Socialists, could agree on the question of Sarrail, they could not agree on the question of France's colonial policy. The Socialists, who refused to support the Briand government's motion of December 20, wanted the League of Nations to administer the mandate whereas the Radicals and Republican Socialists, supported by the moderate and conservative republicans, first wanted to pacify a rebellious Syria and then in due time slowly grant independence to the Arabs. The colonial question, like the financial question, would continue to exacerbate relations between the Radicals and Socialists[127] until by mid-1926 all pretense at cooperation between the two largest left-wing parties was abandoned as the Radicals and Republican Socialists moved to the right and joined the moderate and conservative republicans in Poincaré's government of National Union.

Last, the 1925 Syrian problem was important because it revealed a glaring weakness in the liberals' approach to the colonial question. The liberals, that is, the Republican Socialists, Radicals, and the moderate republicans, failed to understand that the realities of colonial government were not consonant with the democratic principles they espoused at home. Certainly Sarrail's initial policy of encouraging greater Moslem political participation was laudable. But even in their embryonic form, these reforms were rejected by Herriot, Painlevé, and Briand. Sarrail's policies were considered inappropriate because they offended French and Lebanese Catholics. Although replacing Weygand with Sarrail, the liberals were not prepared to change the fundamental structure of the National Bloc's mandate policy and, as a result, French policy in the Middle East would continue to alienate the Arabs.

The Syrian rebellion demonstrated that not only was Sarrail's truncated program much too conservative for the Syrian nationalists, but that France's six-year policy in the mandate was bankrupt. Greater independence for the native population was needed. But even after the rebellion began, this prescription was rejected by the liberals. Briand and Painlevé, failing to sense that the French empire was in its initial stage of disintegration, believed that the only adequate response to colonial insurrection was one of repression. Although successfully breaking the Syrian rebellion by June, 1927, a colonial policy predicated upon the maintenance of French domination was not, as later events in Syria, North Africa, and Southeast Asia would demonstrate, an adequate response to the native population's desire for greater political autonomy.[128]

Failure to grant immediate independence to the Moslem population was simply another manifestation that French liberalism had great difficulty coping with the newly emerging problems of the twentieth century. Traditional responses to new situations, whether it be the colonial upheavals, the financial crisis of the 1930s, or Hitler's dynamic military and diplomatic initiatives, were no longer appropriate in the postwar period. The world was changing rapidly, but as the Chamber's overwhelming support for the Briand government's Syrian policy on December 20 revealed, France hardly noticed.

XI. Conclusion

If General Sarrail was not named a maréchal, you know the real reason for this injustice . . . it was because of the ardor of his republican convictions.

—ALPHONSE AULARD to Painlevé,
October 6, 1928

Recalled in October, 1925, as high commissioner to the Levant, Sarrail spent the last years of his life quietly retired at his Parisian home on the boulevard Perière. He died on March 23, 1929. In a simple civil ceremony, with Painlevé delivering the eulogy and Alfred Dreyfus in attendance, Sarrail was buried five days later at Les Invalides.

Upon the general's death, Georges Lemarchand, president of the Paris Municipal Council, commented that Sarrail had been a warrior both as a professional soldier and as a champion of the Republic.[1] The relationship between these two concepts—Republic and army— supplied the inner dynamics to much of the controversy surrounding Sarrail's career.

The Dreyfus affair had revealed that the army was a potential threat to the country's democratic political institutions; therefore the Radicals and Socialists who assumed power in the aftermath of the affair wanted to change the political composition of the officer corps. Sarrail and André were to be the means by which the victorious Dreyfusards were to republicanize the officer corps. By 1914, however, attempts to change the political coloration of the officer corps, as André and Sarrail readily admitted, had not succeeded. To have altered appreciably the officer corps by utilizing educational means and promotions from within the established bureaucracy, as Sarrail did at Saint-Maixent and as director of the infantry, would have taken decades. On the other hand, the sharpening domestic labor strife and Germany's adventurism as revealed in the two Moroccan crises made any

[215]

attempts at a widespread purge of the officer corps unrealistic.

Although Sarrail's attempts to alter the officer corps had not succeeded, his efforts were well rewarded. His prewar political patron,
Henri Brisson, one of the most powerful and esteemed Radicals of the
Third Republic, was responsible for Sarrail's rapid rise within the conservative military hierarchy. Sarrail had been colonel in 1905, general
in 1908, and director of infantry from 1907 to 1911. It was only in
1911 with the emergence of the nationalist revival that Sarrail's political support waned—but only temporarily, for on the eve of the war,
with the Left's resurgence in the spring, 1914, elections, Sarrail's political supporters, such as Pédoya and Noulens, had the necessary
leverage to impose their will upon the Viviani government. Had
World War I not broken out in 1914, Sarrail in all probability would
have replaced Joffre as chief of the General Staff.

Sarrail's prewar affiliation with the Left explains why he was
France's most politically powerful general during the first three years
of the war. The importance of Sarrail's wartime political support cannot be minimized, for his political supporters played a key role in
asserting civilian primacy over the High Command and in committing
the Allies to a Balkan campaign. Beginning in July, 1915, when Sarrail
was removed as commander of the Third Army, Painlevé, Renaudel,
Pédoya, Chaumet, Accambray, Margaine, and Franklin-Bouillon
dictated their demands to the G.Q.G. These politicians were responsible for Sarrail's appointments as commander of the French Eastern
Army and commander in chief of the Allied Eastern Army. Furthermore, they successfully thwarted all of the attempts by Joffre, Briand,
and the Allies to recall Sarrail from the Balkans, forced the Viviani
government to undertake a Balkan campaign against the advice of
Joffre and the British government, pressured Joffre to send French
reinforcements to the Balkans, forced Briand and Joffre to insist that
London and Rome increase their troop strength in the Balkans, and
demanded that the December 2, 1915, decree be abolished, thus
breaking the G.Q.G.'s control of the Eastern Army.

In retrospect, it is clear that until mid-1917 the salient feature of
France's wartime domestic political scene was that if the *union sacrée*
were to be maintained, Sarrail had to have a prominent command and
his Eastern Army had to be adequately supplied so as to assure that a
defeat would not be forthcoming. This meant that if Sarrail's political
supporters were to be appeased, political considerations had to
override diplomatic and military concerns. Viviani, Joffre, and Briand
had discovered this to be a political fact of life.

Although several left-wing politicians had succeeded in protecting Sarrail from the G.Q.G.—and in the process had not only done much to reassert civilian control over the High Command but had significantly undermined the Briand and Viviani governments—effective civilian control of the High Command, which was an accomplished fact by late 1917, did not assure Sarrail's position as commander of the Allied Eastern Army. When in late 1917 the *union sacrée* collapsed and the political pendulum swung to the Right as a result of the mutinies, the espionage cases, and the fear of the Red peril, Sarrail's power simply evaporated. While several of his former supporters went along with the nationalist tide, many found it expedient not to defend a general who had been tainted by the *Bonnet rouge* scandal. Encountering no political opposition, Clemenceau was able to recall Sarrail as commander of the Allied Eastern Army.

Any assessment of Sarrail's wartime career as military commander must conclude that although successful during the Battle of the Marne, he was much less successful in the Balkans. As commander of the Allied Eastern Army, Sarrail faced serious problems. First and foremost, Kitchener, Robertson, Cadorna, and Joffre failed to appreciate the strategic possibilities of a Balkan campaign and thus did not support the Eastern Army with the necessary manpower needed to achieve a decisive breakthrough. Joffre must assume much of the responsibity for this failure. In the autumn of 1915 Joffre impressed upon London that neither a Dardanelles nor a Balkan campaign would be of any military value, that Sarrail did not possess the capabilities to lead such a campaign, and that the Viviani government's decision to commit French divisions to the Dardanelles or to the Balkans was simply a means to satisfy Sarrail's left-wing political friends. Furthermore, Joffre's attempt in December, 1915, to have a French general other that Sarrail appointed commander of the Allied Eastern Army and the generalissimo's repeated attempts in 1916 to have Sarrail removed demonstrated to the British and Italians that Joffre had little confidence in a Balkan campaign if it were led by Sarrail. Joffre's hostility toward both Sarrail and a Balkan campaign reinforced the British High Command's fundamental belief that the Western front alone held the key to victory. Thus it was not surprising that from November, 1915, to October, 1916, London rejected all of Joffre's and Briand's frequent requests that Britain commit additional divisions to the Balkans. Kitchener, Robertson, and even the Easterner Lloyd George recognized that Joffre's requests were predicated upon French domestic political exigencies, and not strategical considerations.

If not successful in convincing London to reinforce the Allied Eastern Army, Joffre and Briand were nevertheless instrumental in persuading the British and the Italians to remain at Salonika and to undertake an offensive. Although sanctioning an offensive in August, 1916, Robertson, Joffre, and Cadorna were extremely pessimistic concerning the outcome of the offensive. Joffre and Robertson believed that, with 325,000 troops, Sarrail could do nothing more than hold the Bulgarians in the southern Balkans, thus allowing the Rumanians to mobilize. Sarrail and the Serbs, on the other hand, were the only ones who believed that the offensive could achieve decisive results. The capture of Monastir in November, 1916, accomplished without the moral and material support of the Allied High Command, demonstrated that although spawned by French domestic political considerations, a Balkan campaign did have vast strategic possibilities.

The second major problem Sarrail encountered in the Balkans was the Greek question. Until the spring of 1917 the Allies had no common Greek policy. Italy, Russia, and Great Britain supported Constantine's policy of neutrality. Russia and Italy feared that if the pro-Entente Venizelos were to assume power, his plans for an enlarged Greece would impinge upon their postwar territorial aspirations. London was concerned that if Venizelos led Greece into the war, Britain would have to lend military support to the Entente's new partner and thus the Allies would be irrevocably committed to what appeared to be a fruitless and debilitating Balkan campaign.

Until mid-1916 Briand also supported Constantine while hoping that the Greek king would eventually join the Allies. But beginning in June, 1916, Briand slowly became disillusioned with Constantine's anti-Allied maneuvers. Thus the French premier was prepared to support Venizelos's June plans to proclaim a provisional government at Salonika. In August Briand was prepared to land troops at Piraeus; in December, following the royalist shooting of French troops in Athens, the premier proposed Constantine's removal; and from December, 1916, until March, 1917, in an attempt to assure that the royalist army would not strike the Eastern Army, Briand suggested that Sarrail's army occupy Thessaly. However, opposition from London, Rome, and Czarist Russia prevented Briand from implementing his policies.

The Allies' vacillation placed Sarrail in an awkward position. This was particularly true in August, 1916, when a Balkan campaign had been agreed upon. The security of the Eastern Army dictated that hostile royalist troops no longer be permitted to move freely through Macedonia and Salonika while Allied troops were fighting on the Serbian and Bulgarian borders. Thus, Sarrail assisted the August, 1916, Venizelist revolution at Salonika. Military considerations also explain Sarrail's late 1916 and early 1917 requests that the Allies occupy Thessaly and that royalist troops and paramilitary organizations be removed from Thessaly.

Sarrail's support of the Venizelists and his advocacy of a harsh policy toward Constantine alienated Italy, Russia, and Great Britain. Sarrail's role in the Albanian question also antagonized Italy, Serbia, and Venizelos. Particularly galling to Italy and the Balkan Allies was the dramatic emergence of the independent Albanian state of Koritza and the public reception accorded Essad Pasha by Sarrail at Salonika. Fears of French intentions in Albania reached such proportions that as a result of intense Allied diplomatic pressure, Paris ordered Sarrail's successful 1917 autumn offensive in the Lake Ohrid area terminated. Italy, Serbia, and Venizelos feared that their postwar territorial aspirations might be jeopardized by the continued penetration of French troops into central and eastern Albania. It is not surprising that when Clemenceau decided to relieve Sarrail in December, 1917, the French premier had the enthusiastic support of all the Allies.

Sarrail's close association with the political Left continued beyond 1918. In the immediate postwar years he assumed an active role in the League of the Rights of Man and in 1924, when the Radicals and Socialists captured control of the Chamber of Deputies, Sarrail was appointed French high commissioner to the Levant. Almost immediately he would become entangled in an unfamiliar and ultimately fatal situation—Levantine politics.

Lacking the diplomatic, cultural, and political preparation for this new assignment, Sarrail found himself in the midst of a cauldron boiling with religious hatred, intense dislike for the French, and a desire on the part of both the feudal Druze and Syrian nationalists for greater political autonomy. Although the long-range and more fundamental causes of the 1925 Druze and Syrian rebellion were to be found in the native population's deep-seated discontent with France's administrative, political, financial, and educational policies, Sarrail's failure to understand the Druze political situation was the basic immediate cause of the revolt.

The 1925 rebellion might have been averted had Sarrail demonstrated a good deal of flexibility, tact, and a willingness to compromise. However, these were qualities that, for the most part, Sarrail lacked. Throughout his life, Sarrail revealed a consistent streak of intransigence, if not recalcitrance. As a young officer he first became a freethinker and then married a Protestant, despite his family's strong objections; during the Battle of the Marne he refused to retreat, despite Germany's unrelenting pressure, and he refused to sever connections with Verdun, despite Joffre's suggestions that he do so; in July, 1915, he refused to acquiesce to Joffre's decision that he no longer have a command; in early 1916 he refused to accept Joffre's decision that only three French divisions be committed to the Balkans; in mid-1916 he refused to tolerate Cordonnier's pleas that the offensive against the Bulgarians proceed more slowly; in early 1917 at the Rome Conference he successfully resisted Britain's attempts to evacuate Monastir; in mid-1917 he rejected Italy's request that its division at Salonika be shifted to southern Albania; from early 1916 to June, 1917, Sarrail persistently urged the overthrow of Constantine, despite the Allies' desire that the Greek king be maintained in power; and in 1916 and 1917 Sarrail rejected the British, Russian, Italian, and French High Command's contention that a Balkan offensive was useless. Sarrail's inflexibility, which in the past had often been a virtue, became a liability in 1925. The Druzes rebelled when Sarrail categorically refused their frequent requests that Carbillet's program be rescinded.

The public debate that ensued in France concerning the Druze and Syrian rebellion revealed two ominous aspects of France's interwar history. First, French politicians, with the exception of the Communists and a large segment of the Socialists, revealed themselves to be terribly short-sighted. Most of the politicians considered the 1925 rebellion as if it were a prewar tribal rebellion in Timbuktu and not as a significant step in the breakdown of France's overseas empire. Consequently, there was no serious attempt by the Radicals, moderate republicans, or the Right to ask basic questions concerning the deeper causes of the rebellion and the nature of realignments needed in French colonial policy. By maintaining the basic policies of the past, French liberals, supported by the Right, were committing France to a bleak colonial future.

Second, the entire question of the 1925 rebellion was consumed by the figure of General Sarrail. By 1925 Sarrail had become synonymous with certain values: the army's loyalty to the Republic, anticlericalism, and civilian control of the army. Revealing a deep chasm within the French body politic, the Right's vitriolic attacks against Sarrail in 1925 were nothing less than a total repudiation of the religious, political, and military ideas of those who had emerged victorious in the aftermath of the Dreyfus affair.

Sarrail was not intimidated by the 1925 attacks, nor had he been by those during the prewar years. And for good reason. He fully recognized the symbolic significance of the twenty-five years of intermittent but savage right-wing attacks against him. Shortly before his death Sarrail commented, "From the moment I entered André's Cabinet, I have been constantly attacked—and I am proud of it."[2]

Abbreviations

Notes

Bibliography

Index

Abbreviations

AAE   Archives du Ministère des Affaires Etrangères, Paris

A.F.   *Les Armées françaises dans la grande
guerre*

AMG   Archives du Ministère de la Guerre, Vincennes

Archives Marine   Archives Centrales de la Marine, Paris

B.N. Sarrail   Papiers du général Sarrail, Bibliothèque
Nationale, Paris

Cab.   Cabinet Office Papers, Public Record Office, London

Comités secrets   *Chambre des Députés, Journal officiel,
Les Comités secrets,* 1916-17

Commission de l'armée   Chambres des Députés, Procès-verbaux
de la Commission de l'armée

Der Weltkrieg   *Der Weltkrieg 1914 bis 1918*

F.O.   Foreign Office Papers, Public Record Office, London

J.O.C.   *Journal officiel, Chambre des Députés,
Débats parlementaires*

Mandates Commission   League of Nations, Permanent Mandates
Commission

P.P.S.   Personal Papers of General Sarrail

W.O.   War Office Papers, Public Record Office,
London

CHAPTER I

1. Raoul Girardet, *La Société militaire dans la France contemporaine, 1815-1939* (Paris, 1953), pp. 9-20, 26-33.
2. Richard D. Challener, *The French Theory of the Nation in Arms, 1866-1939*, Columbia Studies in the Social Sciences, no. 579 (New York, 1955), pp. 10-45; Joseph Monteilhet, *Les Institutions militaires de la France, 1814-1932: De la paix armée à la paix désarmée*, 2d ed. (Paris, 1932), pp. 132-39. See also the report on recruitment presented by the monarchist deputy Justin de Chasseloup-Laubet (France, Assemblée Nationale, *Journal officiel, Chambre des Députés, Débats parlementaires* [hereafter cited as *J.O.C.*], Apr. 6, 1872, no. 975, pp. 2380-2400.
3. Jules Simon, *La Politique radicale*, 3d ed. (Paris, 1869), pp. 179-247.
4. Joseph Reinach, *La Vie politique de Léon Gambetta, suivie d'autres essais sur Gambetta* (Paris, 1918), p. 26. See also Monteilhet, *Les Institutions militaires de la France*, p. 112; Paul Bert, *L'Instruction civique à l'école*, 6th ed. (Paris, 1882), p. 30.
5. Charles de Freycinet, *Souvenirs, 1878-1893*, 5th ed. (Paris, 1913), pp. 53, 398, 403-20, 471-72, 475; Reinach, *La Vie politique de Léon Gambetta*, p. 106.
6. François Du Barail, *Mes souvenirs*, 10th ed. (Paris, 1896-97), 1:332. 340-41, 437-40. For the typical officer's distaste for civilian politicians, see Henri Choppin, *L'Armée française, 1870-1890* (Paris, 1890), pp. 69-99.
7. Girardet, *La Société militaire*, pp. 198-99. Girardet states that approximately 30 percent of each graduating class at Saint-Cyr from 1868 to 1883 was drawn from the aristocracy (ibid., p. 186).
8. Théodore Iung, *La République et l'armée* (Paris, 1892), p. 204.
9. Girardet, *La Société militaire*, pp. 197-98. It is estimated that for this period 70 percent of the 234 generals holding field commands, 45 percent of the War Ministry staff, 32 percent of the General Staff, and 31 percent of the faculty at Saint-Cyr, including the commandant, were antirepublicans (François Bédarida, "L'Armée et la république: Les Opinions politiques des officiers français en 1876-78," *Revue historique* 232 [1964]: 119-64).
10. Iung, *La République et l'armée*, pp. 39-40.
11. For a detailed account of the would-be coup, see Deputy Henri Brisson's "Rapport fait au nom de la commission chargée de faire une enquête parlementaire sur les élections des 14 et 28 octobre 1877," *J.O.C.*, Mar. 27, 1879, no. 1216, pp. 2556, 2562. Correspondence of the war minister and several field commanders exchanged during the crisis is also presented in the report.
12. Adrien Dansette, *Le Boulangisme* (Paris, 1946), pp. 246-47.
13. Joseph Reinach, *Histoire de l'affaire Dreyfus* (Paris, 1901-11), vols. 3-5; Emile Legrand-Girarde, *Un Quart de siècle au service de la France: Carnets 1894-1918* (Paris, 1954), p. 133.
14. Reinach, *Histoire de l'affaire Dreyfus*, 4:575-92, 5:136-40; Guy Chapman,

The Dreyfus Case: A Reassessment (London, 1955), pp. 254-56; Joseph Paul-Boncour, *Entre deux guerres: Souvenirs sur la troisième république* (Paris, 1945-46), 1:110-11.

15. Joseph Caillaux, *Mes mémoires* (Paris, 1942-47), 1:137-42.

16. Quoted in Reinach, *Histoire de l'affaire Dreyfus*, 4:249.

17. Galliffet to Waldeck-Rousseau, July 19, 1899, Papiers de Waldeck-Rousseau, Bibliothèque de l'Institut de France, Paris, MS 4567. See also Pierre Sorlin, *Waldeck-Rousseau* (Paris, 1966), p. 407.

18. Galliffet to Waldeck-Rousseau, Aug., 1899 [concerning Guérin], Papiers de Waldeck-Rousseau, MS 4567.

19. Sorlin, *Waldeck-Rousseau*, p. 418, n. 119; Chapman, *Dreyfus Case*, p. 284.

20. Galliffet to Waldeck-Rousseau, Aug., 1899 [concerning Dreyfus's pardon], Papiers de Waldeck-Rousseau. MS 4567.

21. Galliffet to Waldeck-Rousseau, Sept. 8, 1899, quoted in Reinach, *Histoire de l'affaire Dreyfus*, 5:580. See also Galliffet's letter of May 1, 1900, to Princess Radziwill in Marie Dorothea Elisabeth Radziwill, *Lettres de la princesse Radziwill au général de Robilant, 1889-1914* (Bologna, 1933-34), 2:344.

22. Abel Combarieu, *Sept ans à l'Elysée avec le président Emile Loubet: De l'affaire Dreyfus à la Conférence d'Algésiras, 1899-1906* (Paris, 1932), p. 66; Charles Seignobos, *L'Evolution de la troisième république, 1875-1914* (Paris, 1921), p. 218.

23. Jean-José Frappa, *Makédonia: Souvenirs d'un officier de liaison en Orient* (Paris, 1921), pp. 25-26; Emile Mayer, *Nos chefs de 1914: Souvenirs personnels et essais de psychologie militaire* (Paris, 1930), pp. 263-64; Jérôme Carcopino, *Souvenirs de la guerre, 1915-1917* (Paris, 1970), p. 135.

24. Maurice Sarrail, Personal Papers of General Sarrail (hereafter cited as P.P.S.), in possession of the Sarrail family. Among these papers is a manuscript on the Teisseire family that Sarrail wrote for his son in the 1920s and a study on the Dejean family written by Sarrail during the same period.

25. Maurice Sarrail, "Souvenirs," in possession of the family. This is a three-hundred page manuscript, written in 1927 or 1928, which is devoted almost exclusively to the pre-1914 period. The "Souvenirs," pp. 1-111, constitute the only source for the remainder of this chapter except where indicated.

26. Although the general and his younger brother were both named "Maurice," there was apparently no confusion. Friends and family called the general "Paul," and his letters to his brother and parents are signed "Paul."

27. Maurice Sarrail, "Lettres à ses parents, 1877-1883," Papiers du général Sarrail, Bibliothèque Nationale, Paris (hereafter cited as B.N. Sarrail), n.a.f. 15002. This collection of 143 letters, written by Sarrail while in Algeria and Tunisia in the first years after his graduation from Saint-Cyr, presents his impressions and experiences of North Africa. Practically devoid of introspection, these letters contain little religious or political comment. When religious issues are raised, they are quickly skirted (see, e.g., Sarrail to his mother, Aug. 26, 1881, ibid., fol. 97).

28. Sarrail, "Souvenirs," p. 17.

29. France, Archives du Ministère de la Guerre, Service Historique, Château de Vincennes, Vincennes, "Etat des services du général Sarrail." About 25 percent of Sarrail's class was drawn from the aristocracy. Eighty-six cadets possessed the nobiliary particle before their name (Sarrail, "Souvenirs," pp. 24-38).

30. "Etat des services du général Sarrail."

31. Sarrail, "Souvenirs," p. 84.

32. See, e.g., in B.N. Sarrail, n.a.f. 15002, Sarrail to his mother, n.d. [1877-early 1878], fols. 18-19; Sarrail to his mother, Apr. 19, 1878, fols. 25-28; Sarrail to his father, June 16, 1881, fol. 72; Sarrail to his mother, Feb. 25, 1883, fols. 195-96.

33. Sarrail, "Souvenirs," p. 50.
34. Sarrail to his mother, Sept. 13, 1883, B.N. Sarrail, n.a.f. 15002, fol. 218. See also Sarrail to his mother, July 20, 1881, ibid., fol. 86.
35. Sarrail, "Souvenirs," p. 96.
36. Ibid. Despite the rejection of his application for the General Staff, Sarrail was promoted to major in 1898.
37. Ibid., p. 106.
38. Dreyfus to Sarrail, Nov. 30, 1914, P.P.S.
39. Sarrail, "Souvenirs," pp. 109-11.

CHAPTER II

1. Louis André, *Cinq ans de ministère* (Paris, 1907), p. 9.
2. Ibid., pp. 10-17.
3. Ibid., pp. 41, 25-56; Combarieu, *Sept ans à l'Elysée*, p. 75.
4. André, *Cinq ans de ministère*, chap. 2; Emile Coste, *L'Officier dans la nation* (Paris, 1903), pp. 7-15; Georges Duruy, *L'Officier éducateur: Leçons faites à l'Ecole Polytechnique* (Paris, 1904), pp. 1-34, 80-103, 229-37.
5. André, *Cinq ans de ministère*, pp. 304, 229-300, 306.
6. Ibid., pp. 42, 316-20. Those most disappointed with André's conservative program were his staff officers. See Jules Mollin to Vadecard, Mar. 11, 1902, quoted in *J.O.C.*, Oct. 28, 1904, p. 2233; Jules-Henri Mollin, *La Vérité sur l'affaire des fiches* (Paris, 1905), p. 54; Antoine Louis Targe to Louis Havet, Aug. 23, 1902, Correspondance de Louis Havet, Bibliothèque Nationale, Paris, n.a.f. 24506, fols. 154-55.
7. René Rémond, *La Droite en France en 1815 à nos jours* (Paris, 1954), pp. 148-68.
8. See Henri Rochefort's daily editorials for 1901 in *L'Intransigeant*, e.g., those of Jan. 2 and Feb. 18; *Le Gaulois*, Mar. 15, Dec. 29, 1901, by Jules Delafosse; July 17, 1902, by L. Desmoulins; June 1, 1904, by Rousset.
9. Sarrail, "Souvenirs," p. 112.
10. Targe to Havet, Aug. 10, 1900, Correspondance de Louis Havet, n.a.f. 24506, fols. 141-42.
11. Sarrail, "Souvenirs," pp. 117-21.
12. André, *Cinq ans de ministère*, p. 17.
13. Sarrail, "Souvenirs," pp. 122-24.
14. Speech by Sarrail at Saint-Maixent quoted in *La Dépêche de Toulouse*, Sept. 30, 1902.
15. *L'Aurore*, Jan. 8, 1904. Reflecting the anticlericalism prevalent in the years immediately following the Dreyfus affair, General André forbade all Catholic-educated professors from teaching at Saint-Cyr and denied military scholarships to candidates who had been graduated from Catholic secondary schools.
16. *La Lanterne*, Jan. 9, 1904. Sarrail's action drew favorable comment from *L'Aurore*, Jan. 8, 1904; *L'Action*, Feb. 8, 1904.
17. *La Libre Parole*, Jan. 10, 13, 1904.
18. Captain d'Arbeux, *L'Officier contemporain: La Démocratisation de l'armée, 1899-1910* (Paris, 1911), pp. 99-100.
19. Maurice Sarrail, "Notes sur les conditions d'admission à imposer aux élèves de l'école militaire d'infanterie," n.d. [1904], "Notes diverses et lettres reçues," B.N. Sarrail, n.a.f. 15007, fols. 62-62v.
20. Arbeux, *L'Officier contemporain*, p. 113.
21. Sarrail, "Notes sur les conditions d'admission," B.N. Sarrail, n.a.f. 15007, fol. 66v.
22. Maurice Sarrail, "Dossier des notes données par Sarrail aux élèves de l'Ecole de Saint-Maixent, 1901-1904," ibid., fols. 1-60. This collection contains Sarrail's

private comments on the students at Saint-Maixent. The comments for the 1901-2 and 1902-3 classes only concern the students' military aptitude and achievement. However, those notes referring to the class of 1903-4 are political comments. For example, Cadet Davet (fol. 45): "Average student, republican sentiments, trained well but has never done anything"; Cadet Pujol (fol. 51): "Noted by his colonel as being of pleasant but firm disposition, argumentative, a reactionary, must be watched, black as the Great Inquisition"; Cadet Sepetti (fol. 52): "Has worked, is a reactionary, has succeeded, capable of becoming a good officer."

23. Sarrail, "Notes sur les conditions d'admission," ibid., fols. 62v-68v.

24. *J.O.C.*, Oct. 28, 1904, pp. 2223-26. The entire attack is found on pp. 2221-26. Similar charges were made by Charles Laurent in *Le Matin*, Sept. 10, 18, 25, 1904.

25. *J.O.C.*, Oct. 28, 1904, p. 2226.

26. Ibid., pp. 2232-39. The complete account of how the system operated is presented by Mollin in *La Vérité sur l'affaire des fiches*. Vadecard's assistant at the Grand Orient, Jean Bidegain, sold a large collection of the *fiches* to Gabriel Syveton, nationalist deputy from the Seine.

27. André, *Cinq ans de ministère*, pp. 314-21.

28. *Le Figaro*, Nov. 2, 1904.

29. See *Le Figaro's* series, "Les Délateurs de l'armée," which ran from Oct. 27, 1904, to Jan. 27, 1905. For additional documents consult the issues of Feb. 11, 15, 16, 17, 18, 19, 28, and Mar. 1, 6, 1905.

30. *Le Figaro*, Mar. 18, 1905.

31. Sarrail, "Souvenirs," p. 137.

32. Emilien Cordonnier, *Ai-je trahi Sarrail?* (Paris, 1930), p. 38.

33. *J.O.C.*, Nov. 15, 1904, pp. 2462-63.

34. Henri Brisson, *Souvenirs: Affaire Dreyfus avec documents* (Paris, 1908), pp. 59-63, 126, 222-23. For a fine character sketch of Brisson, see Freycinet, *Souvenirs*, pp. 290-91. Brisson represented the Bouches du Rhône department.

35. *Le Temps*, editorial, Mar. 13, 1908.

36. The P.P.S. contains thirty-eight letters from Brisson to Sarrail covering the years 1904-11.

37. Brisson to Sarrail, Feb. 1, 1905, P.P.S. Sarrail confirms that Brisson was responsible for this promotion (Sarrail, "Souvenirs," pp. 138-39).

38. Picquart to Brisson, Jan. 14, 1907, P.P.S.

39. Picquart to Brisson, Mar. 18, 1908, ibid.

40. Right-wing comment on Sarrail for the years 1904-7 includes the following newspapers: *Le Gaulois* (Paul Roche on Jan. 29, Ch. Demailly on Feb. 7, 1904; "Echos de Partout" on Jan. 11, Mar. 1, 3, 7, 9, 17, L. Desmoulins on Mar. 23, 1905); *L'Eclair* (Nov. 3, 1904; Ernest Judet on Mar. 17, 22, 28, 29, 1905; Mar. 10, May 11, 1907); *Nouvelliste de Rouen* (Jacques Dyssord on Mar. 6, 7; F. Champanhet on Mar. 18, 1905); *L'Intransigeant* (Henri Rochefort on Mar. 26, 1905); *L'Autorité* (Paul de Cassagnac on Apr. 9, 1904).

41. *La Lanterne*, Mar. 20, 1905. Berteaux represented the Seine-et-Oise. See also *L'Aurore*, Mar. 31, 1905.

42. Monteilhet, *Les Institutions militaires de la France*, pp. 193-251; Challener, *French Theory of the Nation in Arms*, pp. 60-67.

43. *J.O.C.*, Mar. 16, 1905, p. 925. The speaker was Alfred Gérault-Richard from Guadeloupe.

44. Sarrail, "Souvenirs," pp. 152-53.

45. France, Ministère de la Guerre, État-Major de l'Armée, Service Historique, *Les Armées françaises dans la grande guerre* (Paris, 1923-39), (hereafter cited as *A.F.*), tome 1, vol. 1, no. 3, p. 9. General Michel's entire report is reprinted on pp. 7-11.

46. Joseph Joffre, *Mémoires du maréchal Joffre, 1910-1917* (Paris, 1932), 1:10-11.

47. Georges Michon, *La Préparation à la guerre: La Loi de trois ans, 1910-1914* (Paris, 1935), pp. 93-111, 137-44; Challener, *French Theory of the Nation in Arms,* pp. 84-88; Monteilhet, *Les Institutions militaires de las France,* pp. 267-302; Pierre Varillon, *Joffre* (Paris, 1956), pp. 135-45.

48. It should be noted that by 1913 Sarrail was in no position to determine French military strategy. His prewar strategy has been culled for the most part from testimony he gave immediately following the war. See France, Assemblée Nationale, Chambre des Députés, Session de 1919, *Procès-verbaux de la Commission d'Enquête sur le rôle et la situation de la métallurgie en France: Défense du Bassin de Briey* (Paris, 1919), pt. 1, pp. 349, 354. See also Sarrail's testimony in *Le Procès de l'assassin de Jaurès, 24-29 mars 1919* (Paris, 1920), pp. 200-205; Mayer, *Nos chefs de 1914,* p. 253.

49. Michon, *La Préparation de la guerre,* pp. 144-68.

50. Coblentz maintains that Sarrail foresaw the German sweep through Belgium; however, there is no evidence to substantiate this statement (Paul Coblentz, *The Silence of Sarrail,* trans. Arthur Chambers [London, 1930], p. 42).

51. Sarrail, "Souvenirs," p. 149.

52. André to Sarrail, Mar. 26, 1907, P.P.S.

53. Sarrail, "Souvenirs," pp. 150-51.

54. Dubois to Reinach, May 29, 1914, Correspondance de Joseph Reinach, Bibliothèque Nationale, Paris, n.a.f. 13537, fols. 95-96. Dubois complained that he had drawn Sarrail's wrath because while he was a member of Eugène Etienne's War Ministry in 1913, he helped to suppress *le système des fiches.* Dubois is evidently referring to the prefectural reports, since by 1914 any system of gathering information concerning an officer's political inclinations was called *le système des fiches.*

55. Jaurès to Sarrail, Oct. 5 [1907-9], P.P.S. See also in P.P.S. the letters of Brisson to Sarrail, Mar. 20, June 12, 1908; Aug. 21, 1909; Nov. 2, 1910.

56. *J.O.C.,* Mar. 21, 1911, 1st sess. p. 1326. Pédoya's statements can be found in *J.O.C.,* Mar. 14, 1911, 1st sess., p. 1180, and 2d sess., pp. 1185-88. For Driant's comments, see ibid., 1st sess., pp. 1174-80, and 2d sess., p. 1187.

57. *L'Eclair,* Mar. 20, 1911. See also Judet's comments on Sarrail in *L'Eclair,* Mar. 7, 9, 11, 15, 16, 21, 23, 1911.

58. *Le Gaulois,* Mar. 20, 1911, article by Desmoulins; *La Gazette de France,* Mar. 20, 23, 24, 1911; *L'Autorité,* Mar. 21, and G. B. on Mar. 22, 28, 1911; *L'Eclair,* Apr. 1, and Driant on June 13, 1911; *L'Action française,* articles by Robert de Boisfleury on Mar. 19, 20, 23, July 4, 1911. Boisfleury's 1911 criticism of Sarrail was simply the continuation of a systematic attempt to discredit Sarrail (see, e.g., Boisfleury's articles in ibid., Apr. 30, May 14, 28, July 26, Dec. 9, 1909, and Feb. 7, 1910).

59. *L'Aurore,* Mar. 17, 1911. See also Marcel Brossé's article in *L'Aurore,* Mar. 23, 1911; *La Lanterne,* Mar. 23, 1911.

60. *Le Temps,* Mar. 16, 1911.

61. Seignobos, *L'Evolution de la troisième république,* pp. 252-67.

62. Eugen Weber, *The Nationalist Revival in France, 1905-1914,* University of California Publications in History, vol. 60 (Berkeley, 1959), pp. 93-119.

63. Adolphe Messimy, *Mes souvenirs . . .* (Paris, 1937), pp. 71-78, 80-82; Joffre, *Mémoires,* 1:11-14; Varillon, *Joffre,* pp. 116-20.

64. Alexandre Millerand, *Pour la défense nationale: Une Année au ministère de la guerre . . .* (Paris, 1913), pp. 106, 253-55, 318-22.

65. *L'Eclair,* Oct. 31, 1913.

66. Sarrail, "Souvenirs," p. 166.

67. Ibid., p. 163.

68. Sarrail to his brother, Maurice, May 15, 1912, P.P.S.

69. Sarrail, "Souvenirs," p. 164.

70. Percin to Sarrail, Oct. 31, 1913, P.P.S.

71. Thomas to Sarrail, Sept. 2, 1913, ibid.
72. Sarrail, "Souvenirs," p. 179.
73. La Lanterne, June 21, 1914; Le Bonnet rouge, June 14, 18 (article by Miguel Almereyda), 20, 1914.
74. J.O.C., July 15, 1914, pp. 3080-83.
75. Sarrail to his brother, Maurice, July 18, 1914, P.P.S. Concerning Messimy's promise, Sarrail told his brother: "Keep it under your hat; for if it were known, you know the press campaign which would be organized. I was flabbergasted. Will he [Messimy] do it? I don't know. But what is clear is that he said it resolutely."
76. Guillaumat to Sarrail, Jan. 28, 1913, B.N. Sarrail, n.a.f. 15007, fol. 265. See also Pétain to Sarrail, Oct. 7, 1907, ibid., fol. 337.

CHAPTER III

1. Joffre, Mémoires, 1:207-19.
2. Emile E. Herbillon, Le Général Alfred Micheler, 1914-1918, d'après ses notes, sa correspondance et les souvenirs personnels (Paris, 1934), pp. 11-12; Maurice Sarrail, "Souvenirs de 1914-1915: I," Revue politique et parlementaire 107 (1921): 161-65, 168.
3. For the role of the VI Corps on Aug. 20-24, see A.F., tome 1, vol. 1, chap. 11, esp. pp. 367-68, 376-89; Germany, Reichsarchiv, Der Weltkrieg 1914 bis 1918 (Berlin, 1925-39), (hereafter cited as Der Weltkrieg), 1:320-25, 339-45; Joffre, Mémoires, vol. 1, chap. 3 passim; Pierre Lehautcourt Palat, La Grande Guerre sur le front occidental (Paris, 1917-29), vol. 3, chap. 7, esp. pp. 175-79, 227-31; Sarrail, "Souvenirs de 1914-1915: I," pp. 169-73; Albert Tanant, La Troisième Armée dans la bataille: Souvenirs d'un chef d'état-major (Paris, 1922), pp. 48-63.
4. For VI Corps operations on Aug. 25-27, see A.F., tome 1, vol 2, pp. 254-58, 268-72.
5. For the role of the VI Corps on Aug. 27-29, see ibid., pp. 282, 285, 288; Palat, La Grande Guerre, 5:58-66.
6. Joffre, Mémoires, 1:350.
7. Ruffey to Sarrail, Apr. 24, 1914, B.N. Sarrail, n.a.f. 15007, fol. 338.
8. Sarrail, "Souvenirs de 1914-1915: I," pp. 173-74.
9. A.F., tome 1, vol. 2, pp. 294-96; Palat, La Grande Guerre, 5:68-70.
10. A.F., tome 1, vol. 2, p. 301. For Third Army operations on Aug. 31, see ibid., pp. 296-301; Palat, La Grande Guerre, 5:304-13; Sarrail, "Souvenirs de 1914-1915: I," pp. 176-78.
11. Coblentz, Silence of Sarrail, pp. 64-70; Sarrail, "Souvenirs," pp. 187-88; Sarrail, "Souvenirs de 1914-1915: I," pp. 178-80; A.F., tome 1, vol. 2, pp. 727-58.
12. Gabriel Hanotaux, La Bataille de la Marne, 2d. ed. (Paris, 1922), 1:309-11, 316-17; Der Weltkrieg, 4:3-5, 104-5.
13. Hanotaux, La Bataille de la Marne, 1:308, 318-19; Palat, La Grande Guerre, 6:172-74. The Third Army had been greatly weakened since the Battle of the Frontiers. The IV Corps became part of Maunoury's newly created Sixth Army. The VI Corps's 42nd Division became part of Foch's newly created Ninth Army.
14. For the role of the Third Army on Sept. 6, see A.F., tome 1, vol. 3, pp. 550-76; Sarrail, "Souvenirs de 1914-1915: II," Revue politique et parlementaire 107 (1921): 399-400; Der Weltkrieg, 4:109-14.
15. Hanotaux, La Bataille de la Marne, 1:336, 2:227-35; Sarrail, "Souvenirs de 1914-1915: II," pp. 401-2; A.F., tome 1, vol. 3, pp. 648-54.
16. A.F., tome 1, vol. 3, pp. 593, 577-84; Palat, La Grande Guerre, 6:275.
17. Hanotaux, La Bataille de la Marne, 1:329.
18. A.F., tome 1, vol. 3, p. 618.
19. Ibid., pp. 601-4, 623-26, 639-45; Hanotaux, La Bataille de la Marne, 2:220-

24; *Der Weltkrieg,* 4:159-61, 302-3.
  20. *A.F.,* tome 1, vol. 3, pp. 654-56.
  21. Hanotaux, *La Bataille de la Marne,* 2:216-20, 236-37; Sarrail, "Souvenirs de 1914-1915: II," pp. 401-2; *Der Weltkrieg,* 4:301-2, 304-5.
  22. Herbillon, *Le Général Alfred Micheler,* p. 25.
  23. For the Third Army's advance for the period Sept. 11-15, see *A.F.,* tome 1, vol. 3, pp. 1089-1145.
  24. Ibid., vol. 4, pp. 418-19, 430-31, 436.
  25. For the Battle of Saint-Mihiel and the Third Army's Argonne encounter, see ibid., chap. 16; Palat, *La Grande Guerre,* 7:96-141; Sarrail, "Souvenirs de 1914-1915: II," pp. 399-417.
  26. For the Third Army's 1915 role in the Argonne, see *A.F.,* tome 3, pp. 196-207; Sarrail, "Souvenirs de 1914-1915: IV," *Revue politique et parlementaire* 108 (1921): 221-47; Tanant, *La Troisième Armée,* pp. 172-96.
  27. Joffre, *Mémoires,* 2:109-20.
  28. Sarrail, "Souvenirs," p. 185.
  29. Sarrail, "Souvenirs de 1914-1915: IV," p. 221; Sarrail, "Souvenirs," p. 197.
  30. Sarrail, "Souvenirs," p. 192.
  31. Cordonnier to Sarrail, May 12, 1915, B.N. Sarrail, n.a.f. 15007, fol. 246.
  32. Sarrail, "Souvenirs," p. 193.
  33. Sarrail, "Souvenirs de 1914-1915: III," *Revue politique et parlementaire* 108 (1921): 86-87.
  34. Sarrail, "Souvenirs," p. 199.
  35. Mayer, *Nos chefs de 1914,* pp. 278-79; Sarrail, "Souvenirs," p. 185.
  36. Gabriel Terrail, *Joffre: Première crise du commandement* (Paris, 1919), pp. 48-59. See also Raymond Poincaré, *Au service de la France: Neuf années de souvenirs* (Paris, 1926-33), 6:254.
  37. Joffre, *Mémoires,* 2:104-5.
  38. Ibid., 1:425, 433, 2:106. Presenting a different analysis of Sarrail's activities in the Argonne, Franchet d'Esperey believed that the Third Army was doing well (Esperey to Sarrail, May 4, 1915, B.N. Sarrail, n.a.f. 15007, fol. 254).
  39. Joffre, *Mémoires,* 2:107-9, 121.

CHAPTER IV

  1. Poincaré, *Au service de la France,* 4:546. Viviani's second ministry, formed on Aug. 26, 1914, reflected the spirit of the *union sacrée.* War Minister Millerand and Finance Minister Alexandre Ribot, both members of the Republican Union party, represented the conservative republicans while Minister without Portfolio Jules Guesde and Minister of Public Works Marcel Sembat were the Socialist representatives.
  2. In his pioneering and indispensable work, *Generals and Politicians: Conflict between France's High Command, Parliament and Government, 1914-1918* (Berkeley, 1951), Jere Clemens King analyzes the relationship between the military and civilian authorities (chaps. 2-3). See also Joffre, *Mémoires,* 1:209, 221; Poincaré, *Au service de la France,* 5:105, 122-23, 137, 143, 145, 169-70, 328, 340-41; Emile E. Herbillon, *Souvenirs d'un officier de liaison pendant la guerre mondiale: Du général en chef au gouvernement* (Paris, 1930), 1:136, 162; Abel Ferry, *Les Carnets secrets, 1914-1918* (Paris, 1957), pp. 37, 67.
  3. Poincaré, *Au service de la France,* 5:38, 42, 52, 174, 6:24; Ferry, *Les Carnets secrets,* pp. 38, 42, 50, 57, 79; Herbillon, *Souvenirs d'un officier de liaison,* 1:92, 139.
  4. King, *Generals and Politicians,* chap. 3 *passim.*
  5. Jean Pédoya, *La Commission de l'armée pendant la grande guerre: Documents inédits et secrets* (Paris, 1921), pp. 11, 15-16; Ferry, *Les Carnets secrets,* pp.

81-84, 86; Herbillon, *Souvenirs d'un officier de liaison*, 1:161; Poincaré, *Au service de la France*, 6:229, 232, 277-78, 292-99.
6. Poincaré, *Au service de la France*, 6:335-36; Ferry, *Les Carnets secrets*, pp. 98, 101. Ferry, a member of the Radical Left party, represented the Vosges.
7. Ferry, *Les Carnets secrets*, pp. 100, 98, 101; Poincaré, *Au service de la France*, 6: 336; Michel Corday, *The Paris Front: An Unpublished Diary, 1914-1918* (New York, 1934), p. 95.
8. There are conflicting accounts of the events that took place on July 20 and 22. According to Joffre and Ferry, the Cabinet, without consulting Joffre, decided to appoint Sarrail commander of the Eastern Expeditionary Corps on July 20 (Ferry, *Les Carnets secrets*, p. 98; Joffre, *Mémoires*, 2:121). According to Poincaré, however, Sarrail was not mentioned during the Cabinet meeting of July 20. Poincaré claims that the Cabinet gave Sarrail the Eastern command on July 22 because it was understood that "Joffre would like Sarrail to go to the Dardanelles where his qualities of vigor and energy would find good use" (Poincaré, *Au service de la France*, 6:332, 337).
9. Maurice Sarrail, *Mon commandement en Orient, 1916-1918* (Paris, 1920), pp. vii-viii.
10. Sarrail, "Souvenirs," p. 204. Painlevé was a deputy from the Seine, Ceccaldi from the Aisne, Noulens from the Gers, Malvy from the Lot.
11. Ibid., pp. 204-5.
12. Viollette was a Republican Socialist deputy from the Eure-et-Loir.
13. Poincaré, *Au service de la France*, 6:340-41. See also Léopold Marcellin, *Politique et politiciens pendant la guerre* (Paris, 1923?), 1:97.
14. Poincaré, *Au service de la France*, 6:342. See also Sarrail, "Souvenirs," p. 204.
15. Francis Bertie, British ambassador to France, to Edward Grey, British foreign secretary, Aug. 6, 1915, Grey Papers, Public Record Office, London, F.O. 800/58.
16. Ibid. See also Sarrail, "Souvenirs," p. 205. Renaudel represented the Var and Franklin-Bouillon the Seine-et-Oise.
17. See Briand's testimony in France, Chambre des Députés, Procès-verbaux de la Commission de l'armée, Apr. 8, 1916, Service des Archives, Assemblée Nationale, Paris (hereafter cited as Commission de l'armée), 5:103. Because of the censorship of the press and the great hesitancy to raise delicate issues in public parliamentary debate, uninhibited and unrestricted political discussions took place only in the various senatorial and Chamber commissions. The twenty-four volumes of unpublished minutes of the Chamber Army Commission, spanning the period from Jan. 9, 1915, to Oct. 19, 1919, thereby afford an abundance of insights into the period. See also Sarrail, "Souvenirs," p. 205.
18. Sarrail, *Mon commandement*, p. viii.
19. *La Guerre sociale*, July 25, 1915. See also Hervé's articles in ibid., Aug. 6, 14, 1915.
20. Poincaré, *Au service de la France*, 6:344-46, 7:14, 16, 25, 28-29, 31-32, 42.
21. *J.O.C.*, Aug. 20, 1915, pp. 1383-84.
22. Poincaré, *Au service de la France*, 7:46.
23. *J.O.C.*, Aug. 26, 1915, p. 1399.
24. Sarrail, *Mon commandement*, pp. viii, xi.
25. For an introduction to the Dardanelles campaign, see Alan Moorehead, *Gallipoli* (New York, 1956). For the account of French participation in the Dardanelles, see *A.F.*, tome 8, vol. 1, pp. 3-126; George H. Cassar, *The French and the Dardanelles: A Study in Failure in the Conduct of War* (London, 1971).
26. Sarrail, *Mon commandement*, p. ix.
27. Joffre to Millerand, Aug. 3, 1915, Archives du Ministère de la Guerre, Service Historique, Château de Vincennes, Vincennes (hereafter cited as AMG),

20N/87, dossier 13, no. 8.

28. Ferry, *Les Carnets secrets*, p. 108; Cassar, *French and the Dardanelles*, pp. 162-63.

29. Poincaré, *Au service de la France*, 7:37.

30. Charles Paix-Séailles to Sarrail, Aug. 11, 1915, P.P.S. In this letter Paix-Séailles voiced opinions which he stated had the approval of Joseph Caillaux and Léon Accambray, Radical-Socialist deputies from the Sarthe and the Aisne respectively.

31. Georges Meyer to Sarrail's brother, Maurice, July 26, 1915, P.P.S. Meyer was a journalist with *La Gazette de l'armée* and in close touch with the politicians (Gabriel Terrail, *Sarrail et les armées d'Orient* [Paris, 1920], pp. 12-13).

32. Poincaré, *Au service de la France*, 7:30, 36-38.

33. Pédoya, *La Commission de l'armée*, pp. 355-56, 359.

34. Poincaré, *Au service de la France*, 7:68-69, 73-74, 76-79; Joffre, *Mémoires*, 2:122-23.

35. "Note of a Conference . . . at Calais," Sept. 11, 1915, Cabinet Office Papers, Public Record Office, London, Anglo-French and Allied Conferences: I.C. Series (hereafter cited as Cab. 28)/1/I.C.-1.

36. Lord Maurice Hankey, *The Supreme Command, 1914-1918* (London, 1961), 1:411.

37. Reginald Esher to Kitchener, Aug. 11, 1915, Kitchener Papers, Public Record Office, London, folder 59/W1/62. At this time Lord Esher, a prominent Liberal M.P. in the decades preceding the war, was ostensibly representing the Red Cross in France. But in reality Esher performed political intelligence work for Asquith and Kitchener.

38. Hankey, *Supreme Command*, 1:410-11. See also Asquith's summary report of the Cabinet meeting of Sept. 3, 1915, sent to King George V, Cabinet Office Papers, Public Record Office, London, Cabinet Papers: Confidential Prints, 1915-16 (hereafter cited as Cab. 37)/134/1, p. 1; Winston S. Churchill, *The World Crisis, 1911-1918* (New York, 1923-29), 2:492; Frederick Maurice, *Lessons of Allied Co-operation: Naval, Military and Air, 1914-1918* (London, 1942), p. 51.

39. Poincaré, *Au service de la France*, 7:111.

40. For Bulgaria, Greece, and the Allies' Balkan policy, see Maurice Larcher, *La Grande Guerre dans les Balkans: Direction de la guerre* (Paris, 1929), chaps. 1-2 passim, pp. 69-74; Doros Alastros, *Venizelos: Patriot, Statesman, Revolutionary* (London, 1942), pp. 140-60; Erich von Falkenhayn, *General Headquarters, 1914-1916 and Its Crucial Decisions* (London, 1919), pp. 159-62; *A.F.*, tome 8, vol. 1, pp. 144-46; A. F. Frangulis, *La Grèce et la crise mondiale* (Paris, 1926), 1:1 ff.; Albert Pingaud, *Histoire diplomatique de la France pendant la grande guerre* (Paris, 1938), 1:163-72, 191-209, 224-32, 234-40, 2:32-75; Edouard Driault and Michel Lhéritier, *Histoire diplomatique de la Grèce de 1821 à nos jours*, vol. 5, *La Grèce et la grande guerre de la révolution turque au Traité de Lausanne, 1908-1923* (Paris, 1926), pp. 185-97; Gerard E. Silberstein, *The Troubled Alliance: German-Austrian Relations 1914 to 1917* (Lexington, Ky., 1970), chaps. 6-7.

41. Memo by Millerand, "Note au sujet d'une intervention en Serbie," Sept. 24, 1915, AMG, 20N/62, dossier O bis, no. 5487. The two French divisions dispatched from Gallipoli and the four divisions sent from France would have given Sarrail six divisions. Despite Joffre's repeated statements, the latest being on Sept. 21, that he would not release four divisions from France, the Viviani government was preparing to utilize these divisions in the Balkans.

42. *A.F.*, tome 8, vol. 1, p. 148; Frangulis, *La Grèce et la crise mondiale*, 1:263-64, 270-71.

43. Millerand to Sarrail, Sept. 29, 1915, AMG, 20N/62, dossier O bis, no. 3B/148. Sarrail's detailed report on what his army might have done in the Dardanelles may be found in his *Mon commandement*, no. 1, pp. 297-301.

44. A.F., tome 8, vol. 1–annexes, vol. 2, no. 96, pp. 129-34.
45. Ibid., no. 101, pp. 140-42.
46. Ibid., tome 8, vol. 1, p. 151.
47. Ibid., tome 8, vol. 1–annexes, vol. 2, no. 100, p. 136. See the testimonies of Viviani and Millerand in France, Sénat, Procès-verbaux de la Commission des affaires étrangères, Oct. 15, 1915, Archives du Sénat, Palais du Luxembourg, Paris (hereafter cited as Commission des affaires étrangères du Sénat), pp. 12, 22-23, 26, 29.
48. A.F., tome 8, vol. 1–annexes, vol. 2, no. 108, pp. 149-50.
49. Pingaud, Histoire diplomatique, 2:86, 91-92.
50. Poincaré, Au service de la France, 7:135-40; Sarrail, Mon commandement, pp. xiv-xv.
51. Sarrail, Mon commandement, p. xv. See also Sarrail, "Souvenirs," p. 206.
52. The Oct. 6 conference was related in Commission de l'armée, Oct. 11, 1915, morning session, 2:34-35.
53. Paul Cambon, French ambassador to England, to Delcassé, Oct. 6, 1915, Papiers de Théophile Delcassé, Archives du Ministère des Affaires Etrangères, Quai d'Orsay, Paris, vol. 24, fol. 272, no. 2301.
54. Minutes of Dardanelles Committee meeting, Oct. 6, 1915, Cabinet Office Papers, Public Record Office, London, Minutes of Meetings of War Council, Dardanelles Committee, and War Committee (hereafter cited as Cab. 22)/2/17, pp. 1-3, 6-7. The Dardanelles Committee consisted of the prominent members of the Cabinet as well as the chief of staff and various experts in other fields who were called in as the situation required; the purpose of the Dardanelles Committee was to deal with the day-to-day problems of the war. Churchill was at this time chancellor of the Duchy of Lancaster, which allowed him to attend the Cabinet and Dardanelles Committee sessions.
55. Hankey, Supreme Command, 1:428.
56. English Note, Oct. 7, 1915, Papiers de Théophile Delcassé, vol. 24, fol. 273; Cambon to Delcassé, Oct. 7, 1915, ibid., fol. 274, no. 2309.
57. Hankey, Supreme Command, 1:429; A.F., tome 8, vol. 1, pp. 154-56; Charles à Court Repington, The First World War, 1914-1918 (Boston, 1920), 1:49. Repington was military correspondent for the London Times.
58. A.F., tome 8, vol. 1, p. 156.
59. Minutes of Dardanelles Committee meeting, Oct. 11, 1915, Cab. 22/2/19, pp. 11-15; A.F., tome 8, vol. 1-annexes, vol. 2, no. 166, p. 194.
60. Poincaré, Au service de la France, 7:179.
61. J.O.C., Oct. 12, 1915, pp. 1587-88. The previous day Cambon had informed London of Viviani's forthcoming statement. Grey immediately commented that Viviani's statement was not truthful (Grey to Cambon, Oct. 11, 1915, Cab. 37/136/3).
62. J.O.C., Oct. 13, 1915, pp. 1596-97, 1602-3.
63. Ibid., p. 1609.
64. Poincaré, Au service de la France, 7:117.
65. France, Chambre des Députés, Procès-verbaux de la Commission des affaires extérieures, Oct. 19, 1915, Service des Archives, Assemblée Nationale, Paris (hereafter cited as Commission des affaires extérieures de la Chambre), pp. 7-9, 17, 22-23, 49-50. Throughout October Hervé called for the sending of more troops to Salonika. See his articles in La Guerre sociale, Oct. 5, 6, 7, 11, 13, 23, 24, 25, 26, 29, 1915.
66. Margaine to Sarrail, Oct. 20, 1915, P.P.S. The pressure for a Balkan campaign came almost exclusively from the Chamber, not from the Senate. In October, 1915, the Senate Foreign Affairs Commission, led by Charles de Freycinet, Georges Clemenceau, and Paul Doumer, did not want French and British troops removed from the Western front (Commission des affaires étran-

gères du Sénat, Oct. 15, 1915, 1:38-39, 47, 59-60, 82, 97). The highlights of the Senate Foreign Affairs Commission sessions of Oct. 12, 18, and 21, 1915, were sketched by Stephen Pichon, senator from the Jura and a member of the commission (see Correspondance de Stephen Pichon, Bibliothèque de l'Institut de France, Paris, vol. 4398, fols. 279-82; and "Résolution adoptée par la Commission des affaires étrangères du Sénat," Oct. 21, 1915, fol. 283).

67. Poincaré, *Au service de la France,* 7:188.

68. Pingaud, *Histoire diplomatique,* 2: 106.

69. Minutes of Dardanelles Committee meeting, Oct. 25, 1915, Cab. 22/2/22, pp. 2-7.

70. At the Army Commission session of Oct. 26, 1915, the Left, spearheaded by Painlevé, Edouard Vaillant, Socialist from the Seine, Jules Cels, Radical Left deputy from the Lot-et-Garonne, and Maurice Bernard, Radical Left deputy from the Doubs, continued its attack upon the government's military and diplomatic Balkan policy. The left-wing deputies again voiced fears that as a result of the Viviani government's delays and indecisions, Sarrail's campaign would be a disaster (Commission de l'armée, Oct. 26, 1915, vol. 2, esp. pp. 5-6, 22-27, 36-37, 46-47, 168).

71. Poincaré, *Au service de la France,* 7:198-99.

72. Ibid., pp. 193, 205-8.

73. *A.F.,* tome 8, vol. 1, p. 163; Poincaré, *Au service de la France,* 7:201-2, 207.

74. "Notes of a Conference Held at 10 Downing Street," Oct. 29, 1915, Cab. 28/1/I.C.-2, pp. 1-2; memos by Joffre and Kitchener, Oct. 29, 30, 1915, Cab. 28/1/I.C.-2a, pp. 1-2; Hankey, *Supreme Command,* 1:433; William Robertson, *Soldiers and Statesmen, 1914-1918* (London, 1926), 2:94-98; Maurice, *Lessons of Allied Co-operation,* p. 54; Churchill, *World Crisis,* 2:504-5.

75. Alphonse Aulard and George H. Cassar link the resignation of the Viviani Cabinet with its failure to solve an irreconcilable conflict. French left-wing politicians demanded that Sarrail's campaign be adequately supplied. Joffre, on the other hand, was not prepared to commit more than three French divisions to the Dardanelles or to the Balkans. Likewise, until Oct. 30 Kitchener would not send more than one British division to the Balkans (Alphonse Aulard, Emile Bouvier, and André Ganem, *1914-1918: Histoire politique de la grande guerre* [Paris, 1924], pp. 161-63; Cassar, *French and the Dardanelles,* p. 183). The most common explanation for the resignation of the Viviani government is that it was not supplying the strong leadership needed in wartime. Many deputies believed that the Viviani government had been greatly stymied in the energetic prosecution of the war by allowing the High Command too much independence. It was felt that a new government would govern forcefully, thereby bringing the High Command under civilian control. See Pierre Renouvin, *La Crise européenne et la première guerre mondiale,* 4th ed. rev. (Paris, 1962), pp. 325-26; François Goguel, *La Politique des partis sous la troisième république,* 3d ed. (Paris, 1958), p. 159; Georges Bonnefous, *Histoire politique de la troisième république,* vol. 2, *La Grande Guerre, 1914-1918* (Paris, 1957), p. 95. Jere King and Jacques Chastenet assert that the disaster of the Serbian collapse and the failure of Joffre's September, 1915, offensive were the basic factors that forced a discredited Viviani to resign (King, *Generals and Politicians,* p. 82; Jacques Chastenet, *Histoire de la troisième république,* vol. 4, *Jours inquiets et jours sanglants, 1906-1918* [Paris, 1955], p. 242).

76. Pingaud notes that Briand's strong advocacy of a Balkan campaign was a decisive factor in explaining his political success in October, 1915 (*Histoire diplomatique,* 2:105).

CHAPTER V

1. *A.F.*, tome 8, vol. 1, pp. 170-73; Great Britain, Committee of Imperial Defence, *History of the Great War Based on Official Documents: Military Operations*, Cyril Falls, *Macedonia* (hereafter cited as Falls, *History of the Great War*), 4 vols. (London, 1933-35), 1:43.
2. Sarrail, *Mon commandement*, p. 19.
3. *A.F.*, tome 8, vol. 1, pp. 180-94, 204-6, 208-12; Sarrail, *Mon commandement*, pp. 24-25, 30-32.
4. *A.F.*, tome 8, vol. 1–annexes, vol. 2, no. 373, p. 385.
5. The 22nd Division landed at Salonika on Nov. 6, the 26th Division on Nov. 23, the 28th Division in early December, and the 27th Division only arrived in January, 1916 (Falls, *History of the Great War*, 1:85-86).
6. *A.F.*, tome 8, vol. 1, pp. 234-54.
7. Ibid., tome 8, vol. 1–annexes, vol. 2, nos. 466, 477, 503, pp. 465, 477, 497; Georges Suarez, *Briand: Sa vie—son oeuvre avec son journal et de nombreux documents inédits* (Paris, 1938-41), 3:190.
8. *A.F.*, tome 8, vol. 1–annexes, vol. 2, no. 496, p. 492.
9. Sarrail to Painlevé, Nov. 12, 1915, Fonds Painlevé, Archives Nationales, Paris, box 26, file 4.
10. *A.F.*, tome 8, vol. 1–annexes, vol. 2, no. 515, p. 507.
11. Sarrail, *Mon commandement*, p. 42.
12. *A.F.*, tome 8, vol. 1–annexes, vol. 2, nos. 557, 559, 568, pp. 557, 559, 569.
13. Sarrail, *Mon commandement*, p. 44. Also Kitchener to Asquith, Nov. 17, 1915, Foreign Office Papers, Public Record Office, London (hereafter cited as F.O.), 371, vol. 2278, file 164598, paper 173938. War Minister Galliéni officially notified Sarrail on Nov. 19 that no reinforcements would be forthcoming (*A.F.*, tome 8, vol. 1–annexes, vol. 2, nos. 579, 618, pp. 574, 608).
14. Sarrail to Painlevé, Nov. 21, 1915, Fonds Painlevé, box 26, file 4.
15. Painlevé to Sarrail, Nov. 22, 1915, B.N. Sarrail, n.a.f. 15007, fol. 278.
16. *A.F.*, tome 8, vol. 1, pp. 306-33, 335-75; ibid., tome 8, vol. 1–annexes, vol. 2, nos. 672, 693, pp. 664, 685.
17. *A.F.*, tome 8, vol. 1–annexes, vol. 2, no. 693, p. 684.
18. Robertson, *Soldiers and Statesmen*, 2:83.
19. *J.O.C.*, Nov. 3, 1915, p. 1682. In the spirit of the *union sacrée*, the Briand government included representatives from the entire political spectrum. Jules Guesde (Socialist), Denys Cochin (Right), Painlevé (Republican Socialist), Joseph Thierry (conservative Republican Union Party), Charles de Freycinet (Independent), and Louis-Jean Malvy (Radical-Socialist).
20. Commission de l'armée, Nov. 27, 1915, 3:23-24, 60-65, 73-75, 77, 111-18, 125, 150, 161, 163-64.
21. Ibid., pp. 101-2, 105-10, 117, 156-58, 165-66. Radical Left deputy Bernard represented the Doubs and Socialist Cachin represented the Seine department.
22. Ibid., pp. 122-23.
23. "Conférence tenue au Ministère des Affaires Etrangères à Paris . . . ," Nov. 17, 1915, Cab. 28/1/I.C.-3, pp. 2-5. See also Grey to Bertie, Nov. 17, 1915, War Office Papers, Public Record Office, London (hereafter cited as W.O.), 106/1337.
24. Robertson, *Soldiers and Statesmen*, 2:99.
25. "Conseil franco-anglais tenu à Calais," Dec. 5, 1915, Cab. 28/1/I.C.-4, pp. 2-7.
26. Commission de l'armée, Dec. 18, 1915, 3:60-61, 69-70.
27. *A.F.*, tome 8, vol. 1–annexes, vol. 3, no. 780, pp. 33-35; Falls, *History of the Great War*, 1:49.
28. *A.F.*, tome 8, vol. 1–annexes, vol. 3, no. 850, p. 94. See also "Conference between Sir E. Grey and Lord Kitchener and M. Briand and General Galliéni at

Paris," Dec. 9, 1915, Cab. 37/139/24.

29. Note personnelle de Painlevé, Nov., 1916, Fonds Painlevé, box 26, file 5, p. 1.

30. Margaine to Sarrail, Dec. 10, 1915, P.P.S.

31. Commission de l'armée, Dec. 18, 1915, 3:36-37, 40, 73-74, 76-81. For Accambray's suggestion that Sarrail replace Joffre, see Accambray to Briand, Nov. 18, 1915, quoted in Terrail, *Sarrail et les armées d'Orient,* pp. 196-227.

32. *A.F.,* tome 8, vol. 1–annexes, vol. 3, nos. 929, 955, pp. 170, 190.

33. Ibid., no. 1027, pp. 265-70.

34. Sarrail, *Mon commandement,* p. 71.

35. Sarrail to Painlevé, Dec. 26, 1915, Fonds Painlevé, box 26, file 4. On the same day Sarrail also wrote similar letters to Briand (quoted in Suarez, *Briand,* 3:224-25) and Galliéni (quoted in Sarrail, *Mon commandement,* p. 72).

36. *A.F.,* tome 8, vol. 1–annexes, vol. 3, no. 1017, pp. 260-61.

37. Minutes of War Committee meetings, Dec. 8, 13, 1915, Cab. 22/3/17, pp. 4-5, and Cab. 22/3/18, p. 3; Poincaré, *Au service de la France,* 7:362; *A.F.,* tome 8, vol. 1–annexes, vol. 3, nos. 1038, 1039, pp. 278-79.

38. Poincaré, *Au service de la France,* 7:362. Bourgeois was a Democratic Left senator from the Marne. See also Corday, *Paris Front,* p. 137.

39. Bourgeois to Sarrail's brother Maurice, Jan. 3, 1916, P.P.S.

40. *A.F.,* tome 8, vol. 1–annexes, vol. 3, no. 1054, p. 291.

41. Galliéni to Kitchener, Jan. 10, 1916, Kitchener Papers, fol. 57/WH/32.

42. *A.F.,* tome 8, vol. 1–annexes, vol. 3, no. 1068, p. 304. By Jan. 10, in what appeared at the time to be an insignificant move, London decided to circumscribe Sarrail's newly granted authority: Mahon was ordered by the War Office to follow only those orders of Sarrail that pertained to the defense of Salonika; therefore, technically speaking, Sarrail was the supreme commander of the Allied Eastern Army only for the defense of Salonika (Falls, *History of the Great War,* 1:103).

43. Painlevé to Sarrail, Jan. 8, 1916, B.N. Sarrail, n.a.f. 15007, fols. 284-87.

44. *A.F.,* tome 8, vol. 1–annexes, vol. 3, no. 1023, p. 264.

45. Sarrail, "Souvenirs," p. 218.

46. Painlevé to Sarrail, Jan. 8, 1916, B.N. Sarrail, n.a.f. 15007, fols. 284-87. Leblois received his *grand officier* of the Legion of Honor the following spring.

47. *A.F.,* tome 8, vol. 1–annexes, vol. 3, nos. 1123, 1125, pp. 349-51. Mahon supported Sarrail's appraisal, believing that with two additional divisions Salonika would be an impregnable fortress (Balfour to Hankey, Jan. 17, 1916, Cab. 22/80).

48. A copy of this letter can be found in Fonds Painlevé, box 30. This letter has no date, addressee, or signature. However, the letter is in Painlevé's handwriting. Bouët was in Paris at this time (Poincaré, *Au service de la France,* 8:34). There is some difficulty determining the addressee. Poincaré, Galliéni, Bourgeois, or Briand, all Easterners, would be logical choices.

49. *A.F.,* tome 8, vol. 1–annexes, vol. 3, no. 1126, p. 352.

50. Painlevé to Sarrail, Feb. 18, 1916, B.N. Sarrail, n.a.f. 15007, fol. 292.

CHAPTER VI

1. Falkenhayn, *General Headquarters, 1914-1916,* pp. 188-90; Sarrail, *Mon commandement,* pp. 69-71.

2. The clearest statement of Briand's Eastern policy during the first months of 1916 can be found in Commission de l'armée, Apr. 8, 1916, 5:15-17.

3. For Robertson's and Joffre's views, see *A.F.,* tome 8, vol. 1–annexes, vol. 3, no. 1187, pp. 427-30; minutes of War Committee meeting, Feb. 22, 1916, Cab. 22/8, pp. 14-17.

4. *A.F.,* tome 8, vol. 1–annexes, vol. 3, nos. 1211, 1219, pp. 464, 470-71; Sarrail, *Mon commandement,* pp. 83-84.

5. *A.F.,* tome 8, vol. 1–annexes, vol. 3, no. 1226, p. 486. See also ibid., no. 1213, p. 465.

6. Ibid., nos. 1225, 1245, pp. 485, 513.

7. "Résumé of a Discussion at the Foreign Office, Paris, on March 27, 1916, Regarding the Withdrawal of Troops from Salonica," Cab. 28/1/I.C.-7b, pp. 1-2. See also memo by Robertson, Mar, 22, 1916, presented to a meeting of the War Committee on Mar. 23, 1916, Cab. 22/14, app. 79/A; Conclusions of Mar. 23 War Committee meeting, Cab. 22/14. Joffre's recommendation that the Allies remain at Salonika was done to appease Briand. Joffre and the G.Q.G. agreed with Robertson that the Allies' best policy was to withdraw from the Balkans completely. See G.Q.G. memo, "Note au sujet des forces alliées de Salonique," Spring, 1916, Papiers du général Maurice Pellé, Bibliothèque de l'Institut de France, Paris, MS 4425.

8. Robertson to Mahon, Mar. 31, 1916, W.O. 106/1339, no. 14979.

9. *A.F.,* tome 8, vol. 1–annexes, vol. 3, no. 1270, pp. 566-67.

10. Ibid., no. 1274, pp. 576-77.

11. Ibid., no. 1282, p. 590. Of particular interest was Joffre's warning to Sarrail not to inform Mahon of the impending offensive (Joffre to Sarrail, Apr. 30, 1916, in Sarrail, *Mon commandement,* no. 28, p. 350). Joffre's warning is not printed in the official *A.F.*

12. *A.F.,* tome 8, vol. 1–annexes, vol. 3, nos. 1291, 1295, 1296, pp. 600-601, 606.

13. David Lloyd George, *War Memoirs of David Lloyd George* (Boston, 1933-37), 2:5-6.

14. Sarrail, "Souvenirs," p. 220.

15. Lloyd George, *War Memoirs,* 3:335.

16. *A.F.,* tome 8, vol. 1–annexes, vol. 3, no. 1280, pp. 586-87.

17. Ibid., no. 1302, pp. 618-21; Cambon to Grey, May 13, 1916, F.O. 371, vol. 2619, file 91420, paper 91420. The War Committee, which consisted of a small handful of Britain's leading military and political figures, had replaced the Dardanelles Committee in November, 1915, as the leader of England's military, economic, and political wartime effort.

18. Memo by Robertson, "Offensive Operations in the Balkans," May 16, 1916, submitted to the War Committee on May 17, Cab. 22/23, app. 88/A, pp. 1,3. See also the comments of F. B. Maurice, director of British Military Operations, minutes of War Committee meeting, May 17, 1916, Cab. 22/23, p. 3.

19. This statement was attributed to Lloyd George in Painlevé, "Notes d'un entretien de Painlevé avec David Lloyd George," Nov. 6, 1916, Fonds Painlevé, box 26, file 5. These are personal notes of a private two-hour conversation that he had with Lloyd George.

20. Ferry, *Les Carnets secrets,* p. 153. For an example of Pellé's derogatory comments concerning Sarrail, see Charles E. Callwell, *Field-Marshal Sir Henry Wilson: His Life and Diaries* (London, 1927), 1:248.

21. Terrail, *Joffre,* pp. 220-21.

22. Briand to Cambon, May 21, 1916, Archives du Ministère des Affaires Etrangères, Quai d'Orsay, Paris (hereafter cited as AAE), série: Guerre 1914-18, vol. 1037, fols. 20-21, nos. 1682-84.

23. Painlevé to Sarrail, Dec. 10, 17, 1915, Feb. 9, 1916, B.N. Sarrail, n.a.f. 15007, fols. 280-83, 288-90. See also Viollette's comments in Commission de l'armée, June 29, 1916, 3:3; Hervé's articles in *La Victoire,* Jan. 9, 13, May 13, July 9, 1916; Comments by Georges Leygues, chairman of the Chamber Foreign Affairs Commission, in Commission des affaires extérieures de la Chambre, July 26, 1916, p. 5.

24. Commission de l'armée, Apr. 8, 1916, 5:7. The speaker is Margaine. See also ibid., pp. 8, 10. For similar comments by Accambray, Renaudel, and Jean-Pierre Raffin-Dugens, Socialist from the Isère, see ibid., pp. 70-71, 101-2, 115-16.
25. Ibid., pp. 7, 22-23, 63, 74, 79-80, 102, 104-7.
26. *L'Action française*, Jan. 24, 5, 1916.
27. *La Libre Parole*, May 31, June 3, 1916. See also *L'Echo de Paris*, May 2, June 2, July 5, 1916.
28. Germain Bapst, "Journal de guerre," July 5, 1916, Bibliothèque Nationale, Paris, n.a.f. 11704, fol. 383. Bapst's eight-volume "Journal," a daily account of Parisian events for the years 1914-18, is a potpourri of gossip, half-truths, and occasional truths. Bapst, a conservative scion, had close prewar and wartime political and social ties with the High Command and War Ministry. See his *Le Maréchal Canrobet: Souvenirs d'un siècle* (Paris, 1910-14). See also Bertie to Grey, Nov. 7, 1916, Lloyd George Papers, Beaverbrook Library, London, E/3/14/25. The right-wing explanation for Sarrail's immobility has been perpetuated by several influential works (see, e.g., Gordon Wright, *Raymond Poincaré and the French Presidency* [Stanford, 1942], p. 197; Suarez, *Briand*, 3:274; S. P. Cosmin, *Dossiers secrets de la Triple Entente: Grèce, 1914-1922* [Paris, 1969]), pp. 118-19, 191).
29. English memo presented to Cambon, May 26, 1916, Cab. 22/26, app. 91/A. See also the minutes of War Committee meeting, May 26, 1916, Cab. 22/26, pp. 1-3. Lord Bertie in Paris correctly informed Grey on June 8 that there was no great domestic political pressure in France for an immediate Balkan offensive (Bertie to Grey, June 8, 1916, Grey Papers, F.O. 800/59).
30. Robertson to Mahon, Apr. 26, 1916, W.O. 106/1340, no. 15781; Robertson to Mahon, Mar. 7, 1916, W.O. 106/1339, no. 14144.
31. W. E. Fairholme, British military attaché at Athens, to Robertson, May 12, 1916, Cab. 22/27, app. 92/A4, p. 2. For similar views, see Philip Howell, Mahon's chief of staff, to his wife, Rosalind, Jan. 2, 1916, Howell Papers, Centre for Military Archives, King's College, University of London, IV/C/3; Charles Hardinge, at the time viceroy of India, to Arthur Nicolson, permanent undersecretary of state for foreign affairs, Nov. 12, 1915, Arthur Nicolson Papers, Public Record Office, London, F.O. 800/380, p. 3; Admiral Roger Keyes, at the time chief of staff to the vice-admiral of the Mediterranean Fleet, to his wife, Eva, Jan. 16, 1916, Keyes Papers, Churchill College Library, Cambridge University, 2/20.
32. Sarrail to Painlevé, May 9, 1916, Fonds Painlevé, box 26, file 4.
33. Painlevé, "Notes d'un entretien de Painlevé avec David Lloyd George," Nov. 6, 1916, ibid., file 5. The judgments expressed here are those of Lloyd George.
34. Robertson to Milne, June 3, 1916, F.O. 371, vol. 2619, file 91420, paper 106998.
35. Francis Elliot, British ambassador to Athens, to Grey, June 3, 1916, ibid., paper 107146; Grey to Bertie, June 3, 1916, ibid., paper 106998.
36. Milne to Robertson, June 6, 1916, W.O. 106/1340, G.C. 149.
37. *A.F.*, tome 8, vol. 1-annexes, vol. 3, no. 1323, p. 658.
38. Sir George Buchanan, British ambassador to Russia, to Grey, June 1, 1916, F.O. 371, vol. 2619, file 91420, paper 105704; Maurice Paléologue, French ambassador to Russia, to Briand, May 29, 1916, AAE, série: Guerre 1914-18, vol. 1037, fol. 56, no. 517; Paléologue to Briand, June 1, 1916, ibid., fol. 74, no. 532.
39. Bertie to Grey, June 8, 1916, F.O. 371, vol. 2619, file 91420, paper 110911. Robertson was hoping that Lord Kitchener, who had departed for Russia in early June, would persuade Russia to forego a Balkan offensive (Robertson to John Hanbury-Williams, chief of the British mission in Russia, June 3, 1916, W.O. 106/1340, no. 17478). Kitchener, of course, never reached Russia. On June 5 the *Hampshire*, with the war minister on board, struck a mine and Kitchener and

much of the crew perished.

40. "Proceedings of a Conference held at . . . London," June 9, 1916, Cab. 28/1/I.C.-8; for the French position, see pp. 3, 5, 7, 9, 19, 21, 23, 29, 31; the British rebuttal can be found on pp. 15, 17, 19, 25, 27, 29.

41. Lloyd George, War Memoirs, 2:7.

42. "Proceedings of a Conference held at . . . London," June 9, 1916, Cab. 28/1/I.C.-8, p. 35.

43. A translation of Joffre's June 17 orders can be found in Cab. 22/31, app. 96/C1.

44. A.F., tome 8, vol. 1-annexes, vol. 3, nos. 1345, 1346, pp. 689, 691. See also minutes of War Committee meeting, June 21, 1916, Cab. 22/31, pp. 8-10.

45. A.F., tome 8, vol. 1-annexes, vol. 3, nos. 1350, 1351, pp. 696-98.

46. Falls, History of the Great War, 1:46-48.

47. Foreign Office memo, Apr. 19, 1916, F.O. 371, vol. 2613, file 12522, paper 75901. As late as April, 1916, Elliot was asking the Foreign Office whether "it is desired to obtain eventual cooperation of Greece or not" (Elliot to Grey, Apr. 20, 1916, ibid., file 12522, paper 76006).

48. Briand to Guillemin, Jan. 25, 1916, AAE, série: Guerre 1914-18, vol. 250, dossier 8, fol. 130, no. 127.

49. See above, chapter VI, pp. 89, 93, 97.

50. Sarrail, Mon commandement, pp. 55-65. See also ibid., no. 15, pp. 322-30. A detailed account of the vexations that the Eastern Army encountered in January and February, 1916, can be found in the reports filed by the Eastern Army's Second Bureau. The daily reports, which contain an extremely detailed account of Greek domestic politics, are entitled "Revue de la Presse" (AMG, 20N/77, dossiers 1, 2).

51. Although presented with a fait accompli, Briand considered Sarrail's actions justified (Jean Guillemin, French ambassador at Athens, to Briand, Feb. 2, 1916, AAE, série: Guerre 1914-18, vol. 251, dossier 9, fol. 21, no. 235).

52. A.F., tome 8, vol. 1–annexes, vol. 3, nos. 1069, 1168, pp. 304, 387-88; Sarrail, Mon commandement, pp. 73-75, 93-100; Suarez, Briand, 3:276-80. Sarrail's recommendations had the full support of Guillemin, Paul Braquet, the military attaché at Athens, and Henri de Roquefeuil, naval attaché and chief of French intelligence in Greece. Braquet and Roquefeuil suggested that only Constantine's departure could assure the Eastern Army's security (Roquefeuil to Marie-Jean-Lucien Lacaze, French naval minister, Jan. 11, 1916, Archives Centrales de la Marine, Paris [hereafter cited as Archives Marine], série Xf, carton 4, book 1, no. 39; Roquefeuil to Lacaze, Feb. 3, 1916, ibid., book 2, no. 75; Briand to Guillemin, Jan. 25, 1916, AAE, série: Guerre 1914-18, vol. 250, dossier 8, fol. 129, no. 127; Guillemin to Briand, Jan. 31, 1916, ibid., fol. 228, no. 243; Braquet to Galliéni, Jan. 1, 23, 1916, AMG, série: Attachés militaires: Grèce, carton 5, dossier: 1er Semestre 1916, nos. 1, 27; Braquet to Roques, May.6, 1916, ibid., carton 7, dossier: Série P:1916, no. 22/P).

53. Briand to Guillemin, Feb. 15, 1916, AAE, série: Guerre 1914-18, vol. 252, dossier 10, fol. 6, no. 234. Convinced that Constantine would join the Entente, Joffre advised Briand that it would be folly to have the Greek army demobilize or depart from Salonika, for if such were to occur, not only would Greece be of no potential military value to the Allies, but the move would be interpreted to mean that Greece intended to remain neutral; consequently, with no fear of an armed Greece, Germany and Bulgaria would declare war against Rumania (Joffre to Briand, Jan. 25, 1916, ibid., vol. 250, dossier 8, fol. 135, no. 15844; G.Q.G. memo, "Note au sujet de la démobilisation de l'armée grecque," Jan. 28, 1916, ibid., fol. 158).

54. A.F., tome 8, vol. 1–annexes, vol. 3, no. 1171, pp. 402-3; Briand to Guillemin, Jan. 24, 1916, AAE, série: Guerre 1914-18, vol. 250, dossier 8, fol. 99,

no. 123; Frangulis, *La Grèce et la crise mondiale*, 1:350.
55. Falls, *History of the Great War*, 1:124.
56. Sarrail, *Mon commandement*, no. 32, p. 354; Pingaud, *Histoire diplomatique*, 2:299-301.
57. Elliot to Grey, May 30, 1916, F.O. 371, vol. 2621, file 103982, paper 103982; Guillemin to Briand, May 30, 1916, AAE, serie: Guerre 1914-18, vol. 255, dossier 14, fols. 241-42, no. 1128.
58. Briand to Guillemin, May 30, 1916, AAE, série: Guerre 1914-18, vol. 255, dossier 14, fols. 244-45, no. 1118; Briand to Guillemin, June 1, 1916, ibid., vol. 256, dossier 15, fol. 5, no. 637.
59. Sarrail, *Mon commandement*, no. 33, p. 355; Braquet to Sarrail, May 29, 1916, AMG, série: Attachés militaires: Grèce, carton 7, dossier: Série P: 1916, no. 26/P.
60. Sarrail, *Mon commandement*, pp. 110-12; Maurice Sarrail, "La Grèce venizéliste," *La Revue de Paris* 16 (1919): 685-86.
61. Sarrail, "La Grèce venizéliste," pp. 687, 690; Sarrail, *Mon commandement*, p. 100; Sarrail, "Souvenirs," pp. 228-32.
62. A. C. Wratislaw, British consul-general at Salonika, to Elliot, May 30, 1916, F.O. 371, vol. 2620, file 10191, paper 118820. See also Sarrail, "La Grèce venizéliste," p. 687.
63. Sarrail, *Mon commandement*, nos. 32, 35, pp. 354, 357.
64. Cambon to Briand, June 2, 1916, AAE, série: Guerre 1914-18, vol. 256, dossier 15, fol. 29, no. 680. On the same day that England rejected Briand's suggestion, Guillemin impatiently wrote to Briand asking whether or not Venizelos should receive French military support (Guillemin to Briand, June 2, 1916, ibid., fol. 25, no. 1158).
65. See the comments of Robert Cecil, British minister of blockade and parliamentary undersecretary to the Foreign Office, Foreign Office memo, May 31, 1916, F.O. 371, vol. 2621, file 103982, paper 103982.
66. Had the Venizelists attempted a revolution at Salonika without the Allies' formal support, Sarrail would have supported it (Sarrail to Guillemin, June 6, 1916, AMG, 20N/77, dossier 4, no. A1).
67. Briand to Cambon, June 13, 1916, AAE, série: Guerre 1914-18, vol. 1037, fol. 188, no. 1947.
68. Sarrail, *Mon commandement*, chap. 7; Lieutenant de Vaisseau Guiot, "L'Affaire grecque: Guerre 1914-18," Service Historique de l'Etat-Major Général de la Marine MS, n.d., Bibliothèque Historique des Archives Centrales de la Marine, 1:277-318.
69. Sarrail, *Mon commandement*, p. 126.
70. Sarrail to Noulens, June 15, 1916, Fonds Painlevé, box 26, file 14.
71. Painlevé to Sarrail, July 6, 1916, B.N. Sarrail, n.a.f. 15007, fol. 300.
72. Falls, *History of the Great War*, 1:135, 145-46; *A.F.*, tome 8, vol. 1–annexes, vol. 3, nos. 1370, 1377, 1387, 1392, pp. 727-28, 738, 752-53, 759-60; ibid., tome 8, vol. 1, pp. 527-28.
73. Italian Minister of Foreign Affairs Sidney Sonnino rebuffed all of Briand's initial overtures to send Italian troops to Salonika. Only Briand's July, 1916, warning to Rome that if Italy expected to have a postwar role in the Balkans, she would have to support the forthcoming offensive convinced Sonnino to send an Italian division to Salonika (François Charles-Roux, *Souvenirs diplomatiques: Rome-Quirinal, février 1916-février 1919* [Paris, 1958], pp. 107-11).
74. *A.F.*, tome 8, vol. 1–annexes, vol. 3, nos. 1406, 1413, pp. 772, 780-81.
75. Cordonnier, *Ai-je trahi Sarrail?*, p. 102.
76. *A.F.*, tome 8, vol. 1–annexes, vol. 3, no. 1462, p. 841.
77. "Protocole du 11 août, 1916," AAE, série: Guerre 1914-18, vol. 989, dossier 2, fol. 60; Robertson to Milne, Aug. 15, 19, 1916, quoted in Falls, *History of the*

Great War, 1:170-71.
78. Painlevé to Sarrail, Aug. 19, 1916, B.N. Sarrail, n.a.f. 15007, fols. 303-4.
79. Joffre, *Mémoires*, 2:330.

CHAPTER VII

1. *A.F.*, tome 8, vol. 2, pp. 8-63; Sarrail, *Mon commandement*, pp. 158-62.
2. *A.F.*, tome 8, vol. 2, pp. 63-64.
3. Abrami to Sarrail, June 24, 1916, P.P.S. Abrami, Republican Left deputy from the Pas-de-Calais, had served on Sarrail's staff until June, 1916. Upon his return to Paris his lengthy letters kept Sarrail informed of the political situation. See also Marcellin, *Politique et politiciens pendant la guerre*, 1:309.
4. Abrami to Sarrail, June 24, 1916, P.P.S.
5. Ibid.
6. Bertie to Grey, Feb. 14, 1916, Grey Papers, F.O. 800/59.
7. Abrami to Sarrail, Sept. 18, 1916, P.P.S.
8. Esher to Robertson, Aug. 21, 1916, Robertson Papers, Centre for Military Archives, King's College, University of London, I/21/40.
9. Bertie to Hardinge, at the time permanent undersecretary of state for foreign affairs, Sept. 3, 1916, Bertie Papers, Public Record Office, London, F.O. 800/168.
10. Abrami to Sarrail, Sept 18, 1916, P.P.S. See also Poincaré, *Au service de la France*, 8:325-26; Terrail, *Joffre*, p. 207.
11. Quoted in Terrail, *Joffre*, p. 207. See also Herman Leroy Lewis, British assistant military attaché at Paris, to War Minister Lloyd George, Sept. 12, 1916, Lloyd George Papers, E/3/14/10.
12. Joffre, *Mémoires*, 2:331; Poincaré, *Au service de la France*, 8:325.
13. Abrami to Sarrail, Sept. 18, 1916, P.P.S.
14. Note by Florand, Sept. 25, 1916, Fonds Painlevé, box 26, file 5. The note is incorrectly dated; it must have been written on Aug. 25, 1916. Matté, who worked in the censor's office, notified Florand of Briand's order; Florand, in turn, notified Painlevé. See also Marcellin, *Politique et politiciens pendant la guerre*, 1:309.
15. Abrami to Sarrail, Sept. 18, 1916, P.P.S.
16. *La Libre Parole*, Sept. 2, 1916.
17. *L'Echo de Paris*, Aug. 31, Sept. 3, 4, 1916; *La Libre Parole*, Sept. 1, 1916; *L'Intransigeant*, Sept. 6, 1916; *Le Petit Parisien*, Sept. 6, 1916; *Le Matin*, Aug. 31, Sept. 6, 1916; *Le Temps*, Sept. 4, 1916. Germain Bapst noted some of the stories circulating in conservative society that explained Sarrail's failure to launch his Aug. 20 offensive: Sarrail "has lost his mental faculties" as a result of the blistering summer heat, and he did not want to advance for fear that a failure would damage his opportunity to replace Joffre (Bapst, "Journal de guerre," Sept. 2, 6, 1916, n.a.f. 11704, fols. 492-93, 499).
18. Abrami to Sarrail, Sept. 18, 1916, P.P.S. See also the Sept. 11, 1916, memo, drawn up by the Rumanian ambassador to France, which refers to Rumania's request a few days earlier that Sarrail be recalled (memo by Rumanian ambassador to France, Sept. 11, 1916, AAE, série: Guerre 1914-18, vol. 342, dossier 7, fol. 78).
19. Auguste de Saint-Aulaire, French ambassador to Rumania, to Briand, Sept. 4, 1916, AAE, série: Guerre 1914-18, vol. 342, dossier 7, fol. 30. At the Cabinet meeting of Sept. 7 Briand undoubtedly had no intention of mentioning another aspect of the Rumanian question, namely, that there was an obvious misunderstanding between Rumania and the Allies concerning the exact purpose of Sarrail's offensive. The military convention that the Entente signed with Rumania on Aug. 17, 1916, stated that the Eastern Army would undertake a "significant offensive (*offensive affirmée*) in order to facilitate the mobilization and concentration of all Rumanian military forces" (*A.F.*, tome 8, vol. 1–annexes, vol. 3, no. 1457, pp.

835-36). France and England interpreted this to mean that first and foremost Sarrail should attack in the southern Balkans in order to prevent the Bulgarian troops there from moving northward against Rumania. This order had been sent to Sarrail while negotiations were taking place with Rumania as well as immediately following the signing of the Aug. 17 convention (see above, chapter VI, pp. 103, 104, 105). Rumania, however, believed that the scope of Sarrail's offensive was going to be considerably more extensive. "Significant offensive" to Prime Minister Bratiano meant a military action that would at least force the Bulgarians to send all of their Danubian troops to the southern Balkans if it did not break "the Bulgarian front immediately" (Saint-Aulaire to Briand, Sept. 4, 1916, AAE, série: Guerre 1914-18, vol. 342, dossier 7, fol. 30, no. 378). See also Auguste de Saint-Aulaire, *Confession d'un vieux diplomate* (Paris, 1953), p. 341.

20. Abrami to Sarrail, Sept. 18, 1916, P.P.S.

21. Ibid.

22. Joffre, *Mémoires*, 2:331.

23. Abrami to Sarrail, Sept. 18, 1916, P.P.S. See also Corday, *Paris Front*, p. 196.

24. Painlevé, "Les Opérations du général Sarrail," Fonds Painlevé, box 26, file 5, pp. 3-6. This memo is dated Sept. 8, 1916, that is, the day following the Cabinet meeting. There is no guarantee, of course, that all the details found in the memo were used by Painlevé at the previous day's Cabinet session. We do know, however, that at the Sept. 7 Cabinet meeting, Painlevé revealed "the odious character of the planned coup" against Sarrail (Abrami to Sarrail, Sept. 18, 1916, P.P.S.) and he rebuked the premier for instigating the press campaign against Sarrail (Poincaré, *Au service de la France*, 9:335). Painlevé's basic assertion that from Aug. 18 to Sept. 7 Sarrail had successfully fulfilled his basic assignment by preventing the Bulgarian and German troops in Macedonia from moving northward to the Danube was not initially accepted by the G.Q.G. The French High Command incorrectly stated on Sept. 8, 1916, that Rumania's early September military setbacks were the result of the Eastern Army's not having fulfilled its primary assignment (G.Q.G., "Note," Sept. 8, 1916, AAE, série: Guerre 1914-18, vol. 1038, fol. 291). Three months later the G.Q.G. correctly wrote that the Eastern Army had gone "beyond the assignment which had been assigned it by the Convention with Rumania. Not only were no Bulgarian troops standing opposite it able to be directed toward the Danube, but the enemy even had to reinforce its Macedonian front with three divisions" (memo by G.Q.G., "Note sur la question roumaine," Nov. 26, 1916, Papiers du général Maurice Pellé, MS 4429, p. 9).

25. Commission de l'armée, Sept. 8, 1916, 8:30. The speaker is Camille Picard, Radical Left deputy from the Vosges. See also Pierre Renaudel's articles in *L'Humanité*, Sept. 4, 7, 1916.

26. *La Victoire*, Sept. 6, 1916, editorial by Hervé. See also *Le Radical*, Sept. 17, 1916.

27. *J.O.C.*, Sept. 22, 1916, pp. 1908-9.

28. *A.F.*, tome 8, vol. 2, pp. 73, 89.

29. Ibid., tome 8, vol. 1, nos. 412,420, 424, 426, 427, 436, 437, 441, 452, pp. 382, 391, 399-402, 408, 410, 412, 423.

30. Ibid., tome 8, vol. 2, pp. 110-11.

31. Cordonnier, *Ai-je trahi Sarrail?*, pp. 314, 306, 312-15.

32. Ibid., pp. 316-17; *A.F.*, tome 8, vol. 3, pp. 113-18, 120-26.

33. Sarrail, "Souvenirs," p. 250.

34. Cordonnier, *Ai-je trahi Sarrail?*, pp. 328-29.

35. Sarrail to Joffre, Oct. 14, 1916, AAE, série: Guerre 1914-18, vol. 1039, fols. 159-60, no. 495/3. While critical of Cordonnier's "inertia," Sarrail praised Cordonnier's intellectual and military abilities and suggested that he be appointed a corps commander.

36. In addition to Abrami's letters, Painlevé sent messengers to inform Sarrail of the political machinations taking place in Paris. Painlevé wrote a letter of introduction for M. Fleurot, a lawyer working in the Paris municipal government, who arrived in Salonika in mid-September. Fleurot was instructed to tell Sarrail of "the full-fledged plot which we had to cope with" (Painlevé to Sarrail, Sept. 16, 1916, B.N. Sarrail, n.a.f. 15007, fols. 305-6).

37. It will be recalled that Cordonnier assisted Sarrail at Saint-Maixent. In early August, 1916, Joffre asked Sarrail whether Cordonnier, as commander of the French troops in the Balkans, should have the rank of commander of a French detachment or commander of the French Eastern Army. Sarrail recommended the latter position (Sarrail to Joffre, Aug. 8, 1916, AMG, 20N/61, dossier 3, no. 2).

38. Sarrail, "Souvenirs," pp. 249-50.

39. Ibid., p. 249. See also Sarrail, *Mon commandement*, pp. 167-68.

40. Milne to Robertson, Oct. 27, 1916, Cab. 22/61, app. 126/B. The Serbs also thought Cordonnier was moving too slowly ("Rapport du commandant Requin, officier de liaison du Général Commandant en Chef, envoyé en mission auprès du Général Commandant en Chef de l'Armée d'Orient," Nov. 2, 1916, Papiers du général Maurice Pellé, MS 4429, p. 4).

41. Memo by Lt. Col. C. C. M. Maynard, "Notes ȯn Second Visit to Salonika," Oct. 16, 1916, W.O. 106/1347, pp. 4, 8, 5. Maynard, who observed Cordonnier's performance at first hand, was the liaison officer between the War Office and the British army at Salonika as well as the British liaison officer between Chantilly and the British troops at Salonika. He states that his views were shared by General Milne (ibid., p. 1).

42. Ibid., p. 6. This is Maynard's judgment.

43. Cordonnier's pessimism concerning the outcome of Sarrail's offensive was evident even before the offensive was unleashed. On Aug. 25, 1916, Cordonnier wrote Bapst: "If, right now, I had three French divisions fall from heaven in addition to those I already command, the result would be tremendous and immediate. But I do not have them. Therefore do not count on obtaining decisive results when the Allied effort is inferior to that of the enemy" (Correspondance de Germain Bapst, Bibliothèque Nationale, Paris, n.a.f. 24528, fols. 458-59).

44. Milne to Robertson, Oct. 28, 1916, Cab. 22/65, app. 130/A1, pp. 4-5. See also Milne to Robertson, Oct. 11, 1916, ibid., app. 121/B3.

45. Sarrail, completely confident in the Serbs, had pinned the outcome of his offensive on them as well as on the French divisions further to the west. Milne's judgment of the Serbs, which undoubtedly colored much of his attitude concerning the outcome of the offensive, was quite different. He considered the Serbs useless (Milne to Robertson, June 30, 1916, Cab. 22/34, app. 99/B2; Milne to Robertson, Oct. 11, 1916, Cab. 22/56, app. 121/B3; Milne to Robertson, Oct. 8, 1916, Cab. 22/55, app. 120/D, p. 1).

46. Milne to Robertson, Oct. 8, 1916, Cab. 22/55, app. 120/D, p. 1. Milne's October reports only confirmed Robertson's basic belief that a Balkan campaign would be a failure. On Sept. 12, the day on which Sarrail launched his counterattack, Robertson reminded the War Committee that the Balkan offensive would fail (minutes of War Committee meeting, Sept. 12, 1916, Cab. 22/48, p. 8).

47. Milne to Robertson, Oct. 30, 1916, Cab. 22/65, app. 130/A1, p. 4. See also Milne to Robertson, Oct. 27, 1916, Cab. 22/61, app. 126/B. The evidence would suggest that Falls is incorrect when he writes that Milne "had never . . . been a pessimist as to the possibility of beating the Bulgarians" (Falls, *History of the Great War*, 1:318).

48. Quoted by Lloyd George, who succeeded Kitchener as war minister in July, 1916, in minutes of War Committee meeting, Oct. 17, 1916, Cab. 22/57, p. 2. Admiral Palmer headed the British Naval Mission in Greece.

49. Joffre, *Mémoires*, 2:332-33; Joffre to Roques, Oct. 16, 1916, AAE, série:

Guerre 1914-18, vol. 1039, fols. 171-73, no. 13605.

50. Roques to Joffre, Oct. 17, 1916, AAE, série: Guerre 1914-18, vol. 1039, fols. 169-70, no. 20D/S.

51. Joffre, *Mémoires*, 2:335, 386n, 402. See also Marcellin, *Politique et politiciens pendant la guerre*, 1:311.

52. Suarez, *Briand*, 3:466-71; Buchanan to Grey, Oct. 13, 18, 1916, F.O. 371, vol. 2628, file 207054, papers 207054, 210921; James Rennell Rodd, British ambassador to Rome, to Grey, Oct. 2, 1916, ibid., vol. 2627, file 196241, paper 196241; Sonnino to Tommasco Tittoni, Italian ambassador to France, Sept. 19, 20, 1916, Sidney Sonnino Papers (Ann Arbor, Mich.: University Microfilms, 1970), reel 38, nos. 1390, 1395.

53. Falls, *History of the Great War*, 1:211-14; Pingaud, *Histoire diplomatique*, 2:307-8; memo by Harold Nicolson, a junior official in the Foreign Office, Jan. 27, 1917, F.O. 371, vol. 2880, file 26310, paper 26310, esp. pp. 2-3; Cecil to Bertie, May, 1917, Cabinet Office Papers, Public Record Office, London, Cabinet Memoranda (hereafter cited as Cab. 24)/12, pp. 5-6.

54. George Ward Price, *The Story of the Salonica Army* (New York, 1918), p. 121. Price was the war correspondent in Salonika for the *Daily Telegraph*. For the events of Aug. 30-31, see Sarrail, "La Grèce venizéliste," pp. 691-93; E. P. Stebbing, *At the Serbian Front in Macedonia* (London, 1917), pp. 54-55; Wratislaw to Elliot, Sept. 3, 1916, F.O. 371, vol. 2624, file 172623, paper 189912. See also John E. Kehl, American consul at Salonika, to Robert Lansing, secretary of state, Sept. 6, 1916, in U.S. National Archives, National Archives and Records Service, "Records of the Department of State Relating to Internal Affairs of Greece, 1910-1929" (Washington, D.C.: National Archives Microfilm Publications, 1965), microcopy 443, roll 4, 868.00/81, no. 281; Michel-Auguste Graillet, French consul at Salonika, to Briand, Aug. 31, 1916, AAE, série: Guerre 1914-18, vol. 286, dossier 1, fols. 11-12, no. 154; Graillet to Briand, Sept. 1, 1916, ibid., fols. 22-24, no. 112.

55. Wratislaw to Elliot, Sept. 3, 1916, F.O. 371, vol. 2624, file 172623, paper 189912.

56. Sarrail, "Souvenirs," p. 213.

57. Frappa, *Makédonia*, pp. 191-92. Mathieu was an aide to Sarrail. British observers support Frappa's judgments (Wratislaw to Elliot, Sept. 24, 1916, F.O. 371, vol. 2625, file 181510, paper 203978).

58. Sarrail, "La Grèce venizéliste," pp. 689-93.

59. Roquefeuil to Lacaze, June 25, 1916, Archives Marine, série Xf, carton 4, book 6, no. 283; Roquefeuil to Lacaze, July 17, 29, 31, 1916, ibid., carton 5, book 7, nos. 315, 337, 342; Roquefeuil to Lacaze, Aug. 20, 26, 27, 1916, ibid., book 8, nos. 378, 389, 393.

60. Briand to Guillemin, Aug. 22, 1916, AAE, série: Guerre 1914-18, vol. 259, dossier 19, fol. 66, no. 890.

61. Roquefeuil to Lacaze, Aug. 23, 1916, Archives Marines, série Xf, carton 1, book: Télégrammes, départ (janvier 1916 au 31 août 1916), no. 1115.

62. Roquefeuil to Lacaze, Aug. 25, 1916, ibid., no. 1135.

63. Roquefeuil to Sarrail (for Captain Mathieu), Aug. 26, 1916, ibid., no. 125 SR.

64. Guillemin to Briand, Sept. 1, 1916, AAE, série: Guerre 1914-18, vol. 260, dossier 20, fol. 3, no. 1640. This is the only documented account of Roquefeuil's role in the August, 1916, Salonika revolution. It should be noted that Roquefeuil's role as chief of French intelligence in Greece has created a good deal of controversy. Roquefeuil's critics charge that because he wanted to overthrow Constantine he not only took an active role in Greek domestic politics, but his official reports to Paris deliberately exaggerated the danger that the Greek king posed for the Entente (see, e.g., Louis Dartige du Fournet, *Souvenirs de guerre d'un amiral,*

1914-1916 [Paris, 1920], pp. 112-18, 286-87; Basil Thomson, *The Allied Secret Service in Greece* [London, 1931]; Frangulis, *La Grèce et la crise mondiale,* 1:396-404, 406). A laudatory appraisal is presented in Emmanuel Clergeau, *Le Commandant de Roquefeuil en Grèce* (Paris, 1934).

65. Bertie to Grey, Aug. 31, 1916, F.O. 371, vol. 2621, file 103982, paper 172817; memo by H. Nicolson, Jan. 27, 1917, ibid., vol. 2880, file 26310, paper 26310, p. 7.

66. Joffre to Sarrail, Sept. 1, 1916, AAE, série: Guerre 1914-18, vol. 286, dossier 1, fol. 20, no. 9.138-39; Briand to Guillemin, Sept. 24, 1916, quoted in Frangulis, *La Grèce et la crise mondiale,* 1:404-5.

67. Bertie to Grey, Sept. 5, 1916, F.O. 371, vol. 2624, file 172629, paper 176361.

68. Roquefeuil to Lacaze, Sept. 28, 1916, Archives Marines, série Xf, carton 5, book 9, no. 437.

69. Roquefeuil to Lacaze, Oct. 1, 1916, quoted in Guiot, "L'Affaire grecque," 2:551.

70. See Nicholas II's comments as quoted by King George V in King George V to Asquith, Sept. 4, 1916, Asquith Papers, Bodleian Library, Oxford University, Oxford, vol. 4, fols. 224-25.

71. A. P. Izvolsky, Russian ambassador to Paris, to B. Stürmer, Russian minister of foreign affairs, Oct. 6/19, 1916, Russia, Ministry of Foreign Affairs, *Die Europäischen Mächte und Griechenland während des Weltkrieges . . . ,* ed. E. Adamow (hereafter cited as Adamow, *Die Europäischen Mächte und Griechenland*) (Dresden, 1932), no. 274, p. 188; Stürmer to Briand, "Note russe," Oct. 18, 1916, AAE, série: Guerre 1914-18, vol. 262, dossier 23, fols. 33-34.

72. Izvolsky to P. N. Miliukov, Russian minister of foreign affairs, Apr. 23/May 6, 1917, Adamow, *Die Europäischen Mächte und Griechenland,* no. 360, p. 251.

73. Paléologue to Briand, Sept. 28, 1916, AAE, série: Guerre 1914-18, vol. 261, dossier 21, fol. 173, no. 990.

74. As early as June, 1916, Rome warned that it would not tolerate Venizelos's return to political power (Camille Barrère, French ambassador to Italy, to Briand, June 8, 1916, ibid., vol. 256, dossier 15, fols. 120-21, no. 383; Elliot to Grey, June 7, 1916, F.O. 371, vol. 2620, file 101961, paper 110254).

75. Barrère to Briand, Oct. 15, 1916, AAE, série: Guerre 1914-18, vol. 286, dossier 1, fol. 187, no. 88; Barrère to Briand, Oct. 17, 1916, ibid., vol. 1039, fol. 164, no. 692; Barrère to Briand, Jan. 1, 1917, ibid., vol. 1041, fol. 1, no. 28; Sonnino to Tittoni, Oct. 28, 1916, Sonnino Papers, reel 38, no. 1673.

76. Memo by Pierre de Margerie, director of political and commercial affairs in the Ministry of Foreign Affairs, "Note pour le Ministre," June 30, 1916, AAE, série: Guerre 1914-18, vol. 229, dossier 8, fols. 58-60; Briand to Barrère, July 11, 1916, ibid., fols. 89-91, no. 848; Barrère to Briand, July 14, 1916, ibid., fol. 95, no. 589.

77. Memo by Margerie, "Note au sujet d'Essad Pacha et de l'offensive des alliés à Salonique," Aug. 1, 1916, ibid., fols. 109-10; Briand to Barrère, Aug. 11, 1916, ibid., fol. 136, no. 1151; Barrère to Briand, Aug. 13, 1916, ibid., fol. 144, no. 687; Briand to Barrère, Aug. 14, 1916, ibid., fol. 150, no. 1169.

78. Joffre to Sarrail, Aug. 18, 1916, ibid., fol. 5, no. 7665/M.

79. Sarrail to Joffre, Aug. 21, 1916, ibid., vol. 1038, fol. 233, no. 38/3.

80. Barrère to Briand, Sept. 27, 1916, ibid., vol. 230, dossier 9, fol. 82, no. 804. Italian hostility to the French presence in the Balkans was manifested as early as January, 1916, when the remnants of the Serbian army which reached Durazzo and Valona in December, 1915, and January, 1916, were transported to the Greek island of Corfu, where the French assumed responsibility for reorganizing and re-equipping the Serbs. With a careful eye on the postwar settlement, the Italians

believed that France, under a guise of assisting the Serbs, was planning a permanent occupation of the island as a first step to driving Italy out of the Balkans (Rodd to Grey, Jan. 5, 1916, F.O. 371, vol. 2609, file 1580, paper 5634).

81. There is no concrete evidence that France had any intention of invalidating the Allied promises made to Italy concerning Albania. However, the French government did instruct Louis de Fontenay, the French ambassador to Essad's government, that he was to attempt to "guide" and "control" the Albanian chief's actions. Such instructions were not unreasonable considering that Essad had previously negotiated with the Central Powers (memo by Margerie, "Note pour le Ministre," Aug. 11, 1916, AAE, série: Guerre 1914-18, vol. 229, dossier 8, fol. 137).

82. Tittoni to Briand, Sept. 3, 1916, ibid., vol. 230, dossier 9, fol. 5.

83. Barrère to Briand, Sept. 27, 1916, ibid., fol. 83, no. 805.

84. Henri de Gondrecourt, chief of the French military mission in Italy, to Joffre, Sept. 29, 1916, ibid., fols. 91-92, no. 686.

85. Sonnino to Luigi Cadorna, commander in chief of the Italian army, Sept. 24, 1916, Sonnino Papers, reel 38, no. 1430.

86. Barrère to Briand, Aug. 24, 1916, AAE, série: Guerre 1914-18, vol. 229, dossier 8, fols. 161-62, no. 586.

87. Briand to Fontenay, Oct. 23, 1916, ibid., vol. 230, dossier 9, fols. 190-91, no. 7; Briand to Guillemin, Nov. 3, 1916, ibid., fol. 223, no. 1126; Margerie, "Note," Oct. 9, 1916, ibid., fol. 135.

88. Barrère to Briand, Nov. 6, 1916, ibid., fol. 235, no. 965.

89. See M. P. Aubrey Herbert's January, 1917, report, which was circulated to the War Cabinet. Returning from a recent trip to the Balkans, Herbert claimed that the Italians found it "galling to be commanded by a Freemason" (Cabinet Office Papers, Public Record Office, London, Cabinet Registered Files [hereafter cited as Cab. 21]/47, p. 5).

90. Gondrecourt to Joffre, Sept. 28, 1916, AAE, série: Guerre 1914-18, vol. 1039, fol. 48, no. 676. See also Rodd to Grey, Oct. 2, 1916, F.O. 371, vol. 2627, file 196241, paper 196241; Terrail, *Sarrail et les armées d'Orient*, pp. 117-18; Charles-Roux, *Souvenirs diplomatiques*, p. 121.

91. Rodd to Grey, Oct. 5, 1916, F.O. 371, vol. 2627, file 196241, paper 198884. See also E. P. Demidov, Russian ambassador to Greece, to Stürmer, Sept. 23/Oct. 6, 1916, Adamow, *Die Europäischen Mächte und Griechenland*, no. 243, p. 167.

92. See Robertson's comments at the Oct. 31, 1916, meeting of the War Committee (minutes of War Committee meeting, Oct. 31, 1916, Cab. 22/61, p. 8). See also Robert Blake, ed., *The Private Papers of Douglas Haig, 1914-1918* (London, 1952), p. 173.

93. Grey to Briand, "Note anglaise," Oct. 18, 1916, AAE, série: Guerre 1914-18, vol. 287, dossier 2, fol. 22.

94. See Asquith's comments in minutes of War Committee meeting, Oct. 24, 1916, Cab. 22/59, p. 2.

95. Milne to Robertson, July 20, 1916, Robertson Papers, I/14/27a, no. M.6. Although Milne and Robertson had little confidence in Sarrail, General Mahon, his chief of staff, General Howell, Admirals de Roebeck and Palmer, and several of Robertson's staff officers sent on a mission to Salonika admired Sarrail (see Lloyd George's comments in Painlevé, "Notes d'un entretien de Painlevé avec Lloyd George," Nov. 6, 1916, Fonds Painlevé, box 26, file 5; Howell to his wife, Rosalind, Jan. 2, 1916, Howell Papers, IV/C/3).

96. Minutes of War Committee meeting, Oct. 31, 1916, Cab. 22/61, p. 8. This is Asquith's statement.

97. See Lloyd George's comment in minutes of War Committee meeting, Oct. 24, 1916, Cab. 22/59, p. 3; Terrail, *Sarrail et les armées d'Orient*, p. 119; Harry Burnham to Lloyd George, Oct. 5, 1916, Lloyd George Papers, E/2/6/2. Viscount

Burnham was a Liberal MP as well as managing proprietor of the *Daily Telegraph*.
98. Minutes of War Committee meeting, July 20, 1916, Cab. 22/37, p. 2.
99. Note personnelle de Painlevé, November, 1916, Fonds Painlevé, box 26, file 5, p. 4.
100. Bertie to Grey, Nov. 3, 1916, F.O. 371, vol. 2624, file 161747, paper 221152.
101. The War Committee believed that there would be no serious political repercussions within France if Sarrail were dismissed (see Arthur Balfour's remarks in minutes of War Committee meeting, Oct. 24, 1916, Cab. 22/59, p. 10; Robertson to Milne, Nov. 4, 1916, Robertson Papers, I/14/50, no. 566).
102. Painlevé to Sarrail, Oct. 28, 1916, B.N. Sarrail, n.a.f. 15007, fol. 308.
103. Painlevé to Sarrail, Oct. 30, Nov. 4, 1916, ibid., fols. 311, 315-16.
104. Sarrail to Painlevé, Nov. 5, 1916, Fonds Painlevé, box 26, file 4.
105. Joffre, *Mémoires*, 2:338-40, 403; *A.F.*, tome 8, vol. 2–annexes, vol. 2, no. 801, p. 12.
106. Suarez, *Briand*, 4:13. See also Joffre, *Mémoires*, 2:402-3.
107. Bokanowski to Sarrail, Nov. 21, 1916, P.P.S. Bokanowski represented the Seine department.
108. For the military operations from Oct. 16 to Nov. 19, 1916, see *A.F.*, tome 8, vol. 3, pp. 129-31, 147-61, 163-68, 188-213.
109. Milne to Sarrail, Nov. 19, 1916, P.P.S.
110. Sarrail to Joffre, Dec. 2, 1916, AMG, 20N/225, dossier 1, no. 9.
111. Sarrail, *Mon commandement*, p. 182.
112. *A.F.*, tome 8, vol. 3, pp. 223-48, 257-68, 284-87; Falls, *History of the Great War*, 1:239-41; Germany, Reichsarchiv, *Schlachten des Weltkrieges*, vol. 5, *Herbstschlacht in Macedonien-Cernabogen 1916*, by Georg Struss, (Berlin, 1925), pp. 32-33, 42-44, 49-51, 55-56.
113. Joffre to Briand, Oct. 2, 1916, AAE, série: Guerre 1914-18, vol. 1039, fol. 72, no. 1073.
114. *A.F.*, tome 8, vol. 2–annexes, vol. 1, nos. 484, 502, 503, 517, pp. 448, 458-60, 473; Charles-Roux, *Souvenirs diplomatiques*, pp. 120-21.
115. Minutes of War Committee meeting, Oct. 9, 1916, Cab. 22/55, pp. 1-13, 15, 17.
116. *A.F.*, tome 8, vol. 2–annexes, vol. 1, no. 522, p. 478.
117. Minutes of War Committee meeting, Oct. 12, 1916, Cab. 22/56, pp. 2-3.
118. The British reinforcements were composed of four battalions and a cavalry brigade from Egypt and two battalions from England. Most of these reinforcements were attached to the British Tenth and 27th divisions already at Salonika (Falls, *History of the Great War*, 1:202).
119. Conclusions of meeting of War Committee, Oct. 12, 1916, Cab. 22/56, pp. 2-3. The British High Command possessed no evidence whatsoever that Bulgarian and German troops were being withdrawn from Macedonia to be used against Rumania.
120. Commission de l'armée, Oct. 17, 1916, 10:240. The speaker is Socialist deputy Jean-Pierre Raffin-Dugens. See also the comments by Renaudel, ibid., pp. 253-55, and Radical-Socialist from the Pyrénées-Orientales, Victor Dalbiez, p. 146.
121. Ibid., pp. 315-19.
122. Conference of Allied ministers at Boulogne, Oct. 20, 1916, Cab. 28/1/I.C.-11, pp. 3, 5, 9-10. See also *A.F.*, tome 8, vol. 2–annexes, vol. 1, no. 662, pp. 612-13. Lloyd George, who was in attendance at Boulogne, said that Joffre had insisted that France could not spare two divisions (minutes of War Committee meeting, Oct. 24, 1916, Cab. 22/59, p. 3).
123. Conference of Allied ministers at Boulogne, Oct. 20, 1916, Cab. 28/1/I.C.-11, pp. 4, 10.

124. Minutes of War Committee meeting, Oct. 24, 1916, Cab. 22/59, pp. 1-2, 6.

125. Conclusions of War Committee meeting, Oct. 24, 1916, ibid., pp. 2-3.

126. *A.F.*, tome 8, vol. 2–annexes, vol. 1, no. 741, p. 677.

127. Milne to Robertson, Oct. 30, 1916, Cab. 22/65, app. 130/A1, p. 6. Milne did not elaborate upon this casual, off-handed statement, which was literally buried in an eighteen-page report. Despite this ring of optimism, Milne claimed that Sarrail would not take Monastir and that the Allies would need twenty-four, preferably twenty-nine, divisions if the Bulgarians were to be pushed back. Much of the report neglects the campaign then underway, which is surprising since he mentioned that the Bulgarian army was on the verge of breaking. Instead, he dwelled upon the strategic possibilities of a spring, 1917, offensive.

128. Minutes of War Committee meeting, Nov. 7, 1916, Cab. 22/64, p. 3; *A.F.*, tome 8, vol. 2–annexes, vol. 1, no. 769, p. 718.

129. *A.F.*, tome 8, vol. 2–annexes, vol. 1, no. 687, p. 637. See also ibid., nos. 704, 777, pp. 646-47, 732-33; Charles-Roux, *Souvenirs diplomatiques*, pp. 122-24.

130. *A.F.*, tome 8, vol. 2, pp. 186, 279-87.

131. Bokanowski to Sarrail, Nov. 21, 1916, P.P.S.

132. *J.O.C.*, Nov. 21, 23, 1916, pp. 3447, 3465.

133. Joffre, *Mémoires*, 2:403-4.

134. Favre to Sarrail, Nov. 27, 1916, P.P.S.

135. France, Assemblée Nationale, *Chambre des Députés, Journal officiel, Les Comités secrets* (hereafter cited as *Comités secrets*), Nov. 28, 1916, pp. 118, 115-17. The minutes of the secret sessions, held in 1916-17, have been collected in a separate volume at the Service des Archives, Assemblée Nationale, Paris.

136. Abrami to Sarrail, Nov. 30, 1916, P.P.S. Meunier-Surcouf, member of the Liberal Action party, represented the Côtes-du-Nord.

137. A copy of the report can be found in Fonds Painlevé, box 26, file 5.

138. *Comités secrets*, Nov. 28, 1916, pp. 121, 122.

139. Ibid., pp. 122-28.

140. Abrami to Sarrail, Nov. 30, 1916, P.P.S.

141. *Comités secrets*, Nov. 28, 1916, pp. 132-39.

142. Abrami to Sarrail, Nov. 30, 1916, P.P.S. The *J.O.C.* simply records that the session was suspended at 4:20 p.m. and resumed at 4:50 p.m. Gaston Thomson was a member of the Democratic Left party from Constantine department, Algeria.

143. *Comités secrets*, Nov. 28, 1916, pp. 141-45, 147.

144. Ibid., Nov. 30, 1916, pp. 148-50.

145. Ibid., pp. 156-61.

146. Favre to Sarrail, Nov. 30, 1916, P.P.S.

147. Abrami to Sarrail, Nov. 30, 1916, ibid.

148. Favre to Sarrail, Nov. 30, 1916, ibid.

149. Abrami to Sarrail, Nov. 30, 1916, ibid.

150. All these themes are thoroughly discussed in *Comités secrets*, Dec. 1-3, 1916, pp. 170-216.

151. Joffre, *Mémoires*, 2:406-7.

152. *Comités secrets*, Dec. 4, 1916, p. 233.

153. Ibid., pp. 238, 235-40.

154. Ibid., pp. 243-44, 242.

155. Ibid., pp. 246, 245. Masse represented the Hérault.

156. *J.O.C.*, Dec. 7, 1916, pp. 3564-65.

157. Abrami to Sarrail, Dec. 27, 1916, P.P.S.

158. Joffre, *Mémoires*, 2:415.

159. *J.O.C.*, Dec. 13, 1916, pp. 3646-47. Tardieu's comments can be found in ibid., pp. 3642-44; Lairolle's on pp. 3644-45.

160. Ibid., pp. 3656-57.

161. Joffre, *Mémoires*, 2:434, 422, 425, 427.
162. Favre to Sarrail, Nov. 27, 1916, P.P.S.
163. Repington, *First World War*, 2:2.
164. Mathiez to Sarrail, Feb. 14, 1916, P.P.S.
165. Painlevé to Sarrail, Jan. 22, 1917, B.N. Sarrail, n.a.f. 15007, fols. 319-20.
166. Sarrail to his brother, Maurice, Dec. 20, 1916, P.P.S. Montauban was Sarrail's home.

CHAPTER VIII

1. Falls, *History of the Great War*, 1:217-24; *A.F.*, tome 8, vol. 2, pp. 333-34; Dartige du Fournet, *Souvenirs de guerre*, pp. 149-50, 168-69, 187-94, 197 ff; Frangulis, *La Grèce et la crise mondiale*, 1:468-89; Guiot, "L'Affaire grecque," 1:364-84, 2:491-505; Lieutenant de Vaisseau Missoffe, "Le Guet-apens d'Athènes et le commandement de l'amiral Dartige du Fournet," Ecole de Guerre Navale MS, 1925, Bibliothèque Historique des Archives Centrales de la Marine, Paris, pp. 41-52, 68-71.
2. *A.F.*, tome 8, vol. 2–annexes, vol. 2, no. 1115, p. 297.
3. Grey to Bertie, Dec. 4, 1916, F.O. 371, vol. 2630, file 222074, paper 245571; Izvolsky to A. P. Neratov, provisional Russian minister of foreign affairs, Nov. 21/Dec. 4, 1916, Adamow, *Die Europäischen Mächte und Griechenland*, no. 292, p. 202; Pingaud, *Histoire diplomatique*, 2:324.
4. Joffre to Sarrail, Dec. 5, 1916, AAE, série: Guerre 1914-18, vol. 1040, fol. 201.
5. *A.F.*, tome 8, vol. 2–annexes, vol. 2, no. 1203, p. 399; Briand to Sarrail, Dec. 7, 1917, AMG, 20N/190, dossier 4, no. 12.
6. Neratov to A. Benckendorff, Russian ambassador to England, Nov. 21/Dec. 4, 1916, Adamow, *Die Europäischen Mächte und Griechenland*, no. 290, p. 200; Neratov to Izvolsky, Nov. 22/Dec. 5, 1916, ibid., no. 293, p. 203; M. Giers, Russian ambassador to Italy, to Neratov, Nov. 22/Dec. 5, 1916, ibid., no. 294, p. 204; Izvolsky to Neratov, Nov. 23/Dec. 6, 1916, ibid., no. 295, p. 205; memo by Cecil, "Memorandum by the Foreign Office on Future Policy in Greece, December 11, 1916," in app. 2 of the minutes of War Cabinet meeting, Dec. 13, 1916, Cab. 21/1, p. 5. The War Cabinet was basically the same as the Dardanelles and War Committees but smaller in composition.
7. *A.F.*, tome 8, vol. 2–annexes, vol. 2, nos. 1203, 1246, pp. 399, 433-36.
8. Ibid., nos. 1205, 1277, pp. 401, 460-61.
9. Minutes of War Cabinet meeting, Dec. 9, 1916, Cabinet Office Papers, Public Record Office, London, Minutes of Meetings of War Cabinet (hereafter cited as Cab. 23)/1, p. 5.
10. Falls, *History of the Great War*, 1:224; Frangulis, *La Grèce et la crise mondiale*, 1:500.
11. Briand to Cambon, Dec. 12, 1916, AAE, série: Guerre 1914-18, vol. 265, dossier 26, fol. 52, no. 4177.
12. *A.F.*, tome 8, vol. 2–annexes, vol. 2, no. 1367, p. 561.
13. Briand to Cambon, Dec. 19, 1916, AAE, série: Guerre 1914-18, vol. 265, dossier 26, fol. 180; Briand to Guillemin, Dec. 20, 1916, ibid., dossier 27, fol. 8, no. 2271.
14. Joffre to Sarrail, n.d. [Dec. 19-20, 1916], ibid., dossier 26, fol. 182. See also *A.F.*, tome 8, vol. 2–annexes, vol. 2, nos. 1366, 1367, 1393, pp. 559-60, 561, 593.
15. Memo by H. Nicolson, Jan. 27, 1917, F.O. 371, vol. 2880, file 26310, paper 26310.
16. Minutes of Anglo-French Conferences, Dec. 26-27, 1916, Cab. 28/2/I.C.-13a, b, c, pp. 4-6, 3-5, 1-4.
17. Minutes of Anglo-French Conferences, Dec. 27, 1916, Cab. 28/2/I.C.-13c,

p. 4. See also Pingaud, *Histoire diplomatique*, 2:326.

18. Conclusions of Anglo-French Conferences, Dec. 26-28, 1916, Cab. 28/2/I.C.-13, p. 1.

19. Memo by H. Nicolson, Jan. 27, 1917, F.O. 371, vol. 2880, file 26310, paper 26310; memo from Lyautey to Briand, "Note pour les Affaires Etrangères," Jan. 1, 1917, AAE, série: Guerre 1914-18, vol. 267, dossier 28, fol. 4.

20. *A.F.*, tome 8, vol. 2–annexes, vol. 3, no. 1424, p. 1.

21. Sarrail to Painlevé, Jan. 21, 1917, Fonds Painlevé, box 26, file 4. For an account of the Rome Conference, see Sarrail, *Mon commandement*, chap. 22; Lloyd George, *War Memoirs*, vol. 3, chap. 10; Hankey, *Supreme Command*, 2:608-12; *A.F.*, tome 8, vol. 2, pp. 377-84; Charles-Roux, *Souvenirs diplomatiques*, chap. 10; Conclusions of Allied Conference, Rome, Jan. 5-7, 1917, Cab. 28/2/I.C.-15; Conference of Allies at Rome, Jan. 5-7, 1917, Cab. 28/2/I.C.-15a: Minutes of Allied Conferences, Rome, Jan. 5-7, 1917, Cab. 28/2/I.C.-15b.

22. *A.F.*, tome 8, vol. 2–annexes, vol. 3, no. 1486, p. 106.

23. Ibid., tome 8, vol. 2, pp. 391-92, 396-97; ibid., tome 8, vol. 2–annexes, vol. 3, nos. 1518, 1520, pp. 162-63, 166.

24. Ibid., tome 8, vol. 2–annexes, vol. 3, no. 1538, p. 202.

25. Ibid., no. 1550, p. 225.

26. Ibid., no. 1601, p. 326. See also notes of Anglo-French Conference, Calais, Feb. 27, 1917, Cab. 28/2/I.C.-17b, pp. 5-6. The reason for England's change of policy from one advocating a defensive position at the Rome Conference to enthusiastic acceptance of Sarrail's offensive, only became clear in April; Turkish troops were being transferred from the eastern Balkans and Constantinople into the Middle East; England was hoping that Sarrail's offensive would force the Turks to concentrate their resources in the Balkans, thus preventing them from moving into Palestine (*A.F.*, tome 8, vol. 2–annexes, vol. 3, no. 1745, p. 529; Falls, *History of the Great War*, 1:301).

27. Sarrail to Painlevé, May 2, 1917, quoted in Sarrail, *Mon commandement*, no. 91, p. 404.

28. Milne to Robertson, Apr. 30, 1917, Cab. 24/12, G.T. 610, p. 2; Sarrail to Painlevé, May 2, 1917, quoted in Sarrail, *Mon commandement*, no. 91, p. 405; ibid., p. 245.

29. For the English attack of Apr. 24-26, see Falls, *History of the Great War*, 1:302-16. The May offensive is described in ibid., chap. 14; *A.F.*, tome 8, vol. 2, pp. 454-76; Luigi Villari, *The Macedonian Campaign* (London, 1922), pp. 129-36.

30. "Report by Lieut.-Colonel E. A. Plunkett, liaison officer, after Third Visit to Salonica, April 23rd-May 22nd," June 1, 1917, Cab. 24/15, G.T. 923, p. 1. Plunkett was the War Office's liaison officer at Salonika.

31. Falls, *History of the Great War*, 1:323.

32. Dieterich and Painlevé agreed (Rodd to Balfour, July 12, 1917, F.O. 371, vol. 2887, file 112749, paper 142512; Painlevé to Sarrail, Apr. 29, 1917, B.N. Sarrail, n.a.f. 15007, fol. 321).

33. Sarrail to Lyautey, Mar. 20, 1917, quoted in Sarrail, *Mon commandement*, no. 90, pp. 403-4; *A.F.*, tome 8, vol. 2–annexes, vol. 2, no. 1025, pp. 209-10; ibid., tome 8, vol. 2–annexes, vol. 3, nos. 1458, 1484, 1607, pp. 59, 104, 334.

34. *A.F.*, tome 8, vol. 2–annexes, vol. 3, no. 1933, p. 818.

35. For the Serbian politico-military conflict and its repercussions upon the army, see ibid., nos. 1458, 1484, 1607, 1982, pp. 59, 104, 334, 874. For the details of the conspiracy, see Milos Boghitchevitch, *Le Procès de Salonique* (Paris, 1927).

36. Cambon to Balfour, Feb. 21, 1917, F.O. 371, vol. 2876, file 19522, paper 40538. See also Sarrail, *Mon commandement*, pp. 231-32; *A.F.*, tome 8, vol. 2–annexes, vol. 3, nos. 1455, 1467, 1476, 1494, 1497, pp. 55, 82, 93-95, 118, 123; Briand to Guillemin, Feb. 15, 1917, AAE, série: Guerre 1914-18, vol. 269, dossier 30, fol. 189; Briand to Guillemin, Feb. 16, 1917, ibid., vol. 270, dossier 31, fol. 8, no. 151.

37. Minutes of War Cabinet meeting, Feb. 16, 1917, Cab. 23/1, p. 2. See also Milne to Robertson, Feb. 15, 1917, included in minutes of War Cabinet meeting, Feb. 16, 1917, ibid., pp. 3-4; Cambon to Briand, Feb. 4, 1917, AAE, série: Guerre 1914-18, vol. 269, dossier 30, fol. 38.

38. Elliot to Balfour, Mar. 9, 1917, F.O. 371, vol. 2876, file 19580, paper 51525.

39. Cecil to Bertie, May ?, 1917, Cab. 24/12, G.T. 620, p. 24. Cecil served as foreign secretary while Balfour was in the United States.

40. Balfour to Lord Stamfordham, George V's secretary, Feb. 27, 1917, Cab. 24/6, G.T. 84.

41. "Joint Note by the Admiralty War Staff and General Staff on the use of Volo as an Additional Base for the Allied Forces in Macedonia," Jan. 29, 1917, F.O. 371, vol. 2876, file 19522, paper 27694, p. 2.

42. Elliot to Balfour, Jan. 25, 1917, ibid., paper 20796. See also Elliot to Balfour, Jan. 18, 1917, ibid., vol. 2868, file 1196, paper 14665.

43. Elliot to Balfour, Jan. 27, Feb. 5, 1917, ibid., papers 21969, 21971, 29225; Milne to Robertson, Jan. 27, 1917, ibid., vol. 2876, file 19522, paper 27694, p. 3.

44. Memo from Mackenzie to Elliot, "A Confidential Note on French Policy," Mar. 4, 1917, reprinted in Compton Mackenzie, *Aegean Memories* (London, 1940), p. 116. See also ibid., p. 85; Compton Mackenzie, *Greek Memories* (London, 1939), p. 75. Mackenzie was chief of British counterintelligence in Greece.

45. For example, see the memorandum by War Minister Lyautey, "Note," Feb. 15, 1917, AAE, série: Guerre 1914-18, vol. 1041, fols. 179-81. See also his statements in *A.F.*, tome 8, vol. 2–annexes, vol. 3, nos. 1466, 1467, 1476, pp. 81-2, 95; Briand to Guillemin, Jan. 30, 1917, AAE, série: Guerre 1914-18, vol. 268, dossier 29, fol. 231, no. 97; Briand to Guillemin, Feb. 17, 1917, ibid., vol. 270, dossier 31, fol. 23, no. 152; Guillemin to Briand, Mar. 3, 1917, ibid., vol. 271, dossier 32, fols. 35-37, no. 513; Briand to Barrère, Mar. 13, 1917, ibid., fol. 153; memo by Briand, "Question de Larissa-Volo," January, 1917, ibid., vol. 1041, fol. 56; memo by Lacaze, "Note," Feb. 13, 1917, ibid., fols. 168-69; Emmanuel Clergeau, Roquefeuil's successor in February as naval attaché in Greece, to Lacaze, Feb. 10, 1917, Archives Marine, série Xf, carton 1, book 2, no. 2086; Sarrail to Lyautey, Feb. 7, 1917, AMG, 20N/189, dossier 1, file 1, no. 15; memo by the Eastern Army's Second Bureau, "Quelle peut être à l'heure actuelle la nature et l'importance du danger grec," Feb. 18, 1917, ibid., 20N/194, dossier 1, no. 3; memo by the G.Q.G's Second Bureau, "La Situation actuelle en Grèce," Mar. 3, 1917, ibid., série: Attachés militaires: Grèce, carton 7, dossier 1b, no. 10676; Guillemin to Briand, Mar. 14, 1917, ibid., dossier: A.E., janvier–novembre 1917, no. 2B/4993; Sarrail, "Souvenirs," p. 256.

46. Roquefeuil to Lacaze, Dec. 9, 1916, Archives Marine, série Xf, carton 5, book 11, no. 533; Roquefeuil to Lacaze, Dec. 27, 1916, ibid., book 12, no. 552.

47. Roquefeuil to Lacaze, Dec. 19, 20, 1916, Jan. 18, 1917, AMG, 20N/189, dossier 1, file 5, nos. 6, 8, 24; Roquefeuil to Lacaze, Jan. 3, 1917, Archives Marine, série Xf, carton 5, book 12, no. 564.

48. For the intelligence reports submitted by Roquefeuil and Clergeau to Sarrail for the period December, 1916 to April, 1917, see AMG, 20N/190, dossier 1, nos. 1-96; for intelligence information gathered by French consuls, field commanders, and military intelligence agents for the period December, 1916, to Feb. 16, 1917, see ibid., dossier 3; Roquefeuil to Lacaze, Jan. 10, 1917, Archives Marine, série Xf, carton 5, book 12, no. 576; Clergeau to Lacaze, Feb. 15, 21, 1917, ibid., carton 1, book 2, nos. 2098, 2130.

49. Roquefeuil to Lacaze, Jan. 3, 1917, Archives Marine, série Xf, carton 5, book 12, no. 564.

50. Clergeau to Lacaze, Feb. 26, Mar. 4, 14, 1917, ibid., carton 1, book 2, nos. 2155, 2195, 2256.

51. Clergeau to Lacaze, Mar. 24, 1917, ibid., no. 2316.

52. Clergeau to Lacaze, Mar. 16, Apr. 4, 1917, ibid., nos. 2270, 2411; Clergeau to Sarrail, Mar. 19, 1917, ibid., no. 2284.

53. The only detailed discussion of the Allied Commission of Military Control is presented in Guiot, "L'Affaire grecque," 2:841-87.

54. Elliot to Balfour, Jan. 18, 27, 1917, F.O. 371, vol. 2868, file 1196, papers 14665, 21969; memo by Ribot, Apr. 9, 1917, AAE, série: Guerre 1914-18, vol. 272, dossier 34, fols. 80-81; Demidov to Miliukov, Mar. 23/Apr. 5, 1917, Adamow, *Die Europäischen Mächte und Griechenland*, no. 347, p. 241.

55. Roquefeuil to Lacaze, Jan. 18, 1917, AMG, 20N/189, dossier 1, file 5, no. 24.

56. Sarrail to Cauboue, Jan. 18, 1917, contained in a memo by the Eastern Army's Second Bureau, "Les Evénements de Grèce," Feb. 10, 1917, ibid., 20N/194, dossier 1, no. 4, p. 4; Lyautey to Sarrail, Jan. 30, 1917, ibid., 20N/189, dossier 2, no. 42.

57. Sarrail to Cauboue, Jan. 24, 1917, ibid., dossier 1, file 1, no. 1. See also Sarrail to Cauboue, Jan. 26, 1917, contained in a memo by the Eastern Army's Second Bureau, "Les Evénements de Grèce," Feb. 10, 1917, ibid., 20N/194, dossier 1, no. 4, p. 6.

58. Cauboue to Sarrail, Feb. 5, 1917, Archives Marine, série Xf, carton 23, book: Lettres du général Cauboue, no. 23.

59. For a summary of Cauboue's relations with royalist Greece, see Cauboue's forty-nine page report, "Mission du contrôle militaire interallié en Grèce (janvier à juillet 1917)," July 13, 1917, AMG, 20N/193, dossier 2. For Cauboue's daily reports to Sarrail, see ibid., 20N/189, dossier 4; Archives Marine, série Xf, carton 23, book: Lettres du général Cauboue; ibid., carton 22, book: Télégrammes: départ du 24 janvier 1917 au 29 juillet 1917. For Cauboue's letters to the royalist political authorities listing the infractions committed by them, see AMG, 20N/191, dossiers 1, 2. Almost all of Cauboue's reports were of a military nature. However, when he suggested that the Allied blockade of Greece not be lifted, Briand reminded him not to meddle in questions that did not involve the Commission of Military Control (Briand to Guillemin, Jan. 30, 1917, AAE, série: Guerre 1914-18, vol. 268, dossier 29, fol. 231, no. 97). Nevertheless, Cauboue immediately wrote to Sarrail, urging that the latter write Lyautey recommending that the blockade not be lifted (Cauboue to Sarrail, Feb. 6, 1917, AMG, 20N/189, dossier 4, no. 20).

60. Sarrail to Cauboue, Apr. 30, 1917, Archives Marine, série Xf, carton 3, book: Contrôle militaire, no. 406.

61. Briand to Guillemin, Feb. 3, 1917, AAE, série: Guerre 1914-18, vol. 269, dossier 30, fol. 26, no. 108.

62. Sarrail to Lyautey, Feb. 7, 1917, AMG, 20N/189, dossier 1, file 1, no. 15.

63. Bousquier to Lyautey, Jan. 14, 1917, AAE, série: Guerre 1914-18, vol. 267, dossier 28, fols. 168-70, no. 18; Bousquier to Lyautey, Jan. 27, Feb. 1, 1917, AMG, série: Attachés militaires: Grèce, carton 7, dossier 5, nos. 49, 56. For Bousquier's optimistic reports concerning Constantine's intentions for the period December, 1916, to January, 1917, see ibid., 20N/190, dossier 2.

64. Lyautey to Sarrail, Dec. 30, 1916, AMG, 20N/189, dossier 2, no. 29; Sarrail to Cauboue, Jan. 24, 1917, ibid., dossier 1, file 1, no. 1; Guillemin to Sarrail, Feb. 20, 1917, ibid., dossier 3, no. 126.

65. Memo by E. A. Plunkett, "French Attitude towards Greece and towards British Political Considerations," Feb. 6, 1917, W.O. 106/1347.

66. Memo by Fairholme, "Note on a Conversation with General Sarrail, 23 March 1917," Mar. 25, 1917, Cab. 24/10, G.T. 449, pp. 2-3.

67. Guillemin to Briand, Feb. 8, 1917, AAE, série: Guerre 1914-18, vol. 269, dossier 30, fol. 92, no. 314; Guillemin to Briand, Mar. 3, 1917, ibid., vol. 271, dossier 32, fols. 35-37, no. 513.

68. See above, pp. 146, 147.
69. Bertie to Balfour, Mar. 30, 1917, F.O. 371, vol. 2865, file 34, paper 67185.
70. Memo by H. Nicolson, Mar. 30, 1917, and Cecil's comments, ibid. See also Elliot to Balfour, Mar. 31, 1917, ibid., vol. 2883, file 47742, paper 68052.
71. A.F., tome 8, vol. 2–annexes, vol. 3, nos. 1734, 1738, 1781, 1791, pp. 514, 521, 608, 620.
72. Painlevé to Sarrail, May 7, 1917, B.N. Sarrail, n.a.f. 15007, fols. 323-24. See also Guiot, "L'Affaire grecque," 2:927-1006.
73. A.F., tome 8, vol. 2–annexes, vol. 3, nos. 1957, 1993, pp. 840, 885. French intelligence reports for the period May-June, 1917, suggest that the royalist paramilitary organizations in northern Greece could wage effective guerilla warfare against the Eastern Army. For a wealth of information concerning the activities, strength, organization, and potential of the various royalist military organizations, see AMG, 20N/193, dossiers 3, 6, 7.
74. A.F., tome 8, vol. 2–annexes, vol. 3, no. 1993, p. 885.
75. Falls, History of the Great War, 1:352-62; Sarrail, Mon commandement, pp. 238-44; A.F., tome 8, vol. 2, pp. 486-90; Frangulis, La Grèce et la crise mondiale, 1:533-38; Charles Regnault, La Conquête d'Athènes, juin-juillet 1917 (Paris, 1920).
76. Falls, History of the Great War, 1:351.
77. Alexandre Ribot, Journal d'Alexandre Ribot et correspondances inédites, 1914-1922 (Paris, 1936), pp. 67-72; "Memorandum on the Anglo-French-Italian Conference, April 19, 1917," St. Jean de Maurienne, Cab. 28/2/I.C.-20.
78. Ribot to Cambon, Apr. 14, 1917, AAE, série: Guerre 1914-18, vol. 27, dossier 34, fol. 126, no. 173.
79. Fairholme to Elliot, May 10, 1917, F.O. 371, vol. 2878, file 23980, paper 105230, pp. 1-2. Also memo by Cecil, Mar. 31, 1917, ibid., vol. 2865, file 34, paper 67185.
80. Memo by H. Nicolson, July 18, 1917, ibid., vol. 2887, file 112749, paper 141104. See also memo by Cecil submitted to the French government, "Memorandum britannique sur la politique en Grèce," May 28, 1917, AAE, série: Guerre 1914-18, vol. 273, dossier 35, fol. 38. Jonnart was a member of the Chamber of Deputies, 1889-1914, and of the Senate, 1914-28; he served as minister of public works in 1893-94 and as governor general of Algeria in 1903-11. He would return to Algeria as governor general in 1918 and would be the French ambassador to the Vatican in 1921-24.
81. "Summary of the Proceedings of the Anglo-French Conference," May 4-5, 1917, Cab. 28/2/I.C.-21, pp. 8, 4-7.
82. Lloyd George's belief that Sarrail's May offensive could force the Bulgarians to seek peace was predicated upon a report filed by E. A. Plunkett (memo by Plunkett, "Military Situation on Salonica Front—March 1917," Mar. 31, 1917, Cab. 24/9, G.T. 337, pp. 2-3, 5). Robertson believed that any chance of forcing Bulgaria to change sides was extremely remote (memo by Robertson, "Situation at Salonica," Apr. 2, 1917, ibid., G.T. 347; memo by Robertson, "Note on a Proposal to Occupy Larissa," Apr. 13, 1917, Cab. 24/10, G.T. 430).
83. Lloyd George, War Memoirs, 3:334, 328.
84. Robertson, Soldiers and Statesmen, 2:143. See also memo by Robertson, "Situation at Salonica," Apr. 2, 1917, Cab. 24/9, G.T. 347, p. 2.
85. "Summary of the Proceedings of the Anglo-French Conference held at Paris on May 4 and 5, 1917," Cab. 28/2/I.C.-21, pp. 2, 5, 8, 1. All reports reaching London in the spring of 1917 indicated that Constantine had complied with the Jan. 8 ultimatum and that the royalist army posed no danger to the Eastern Army (Milne to Robertson, Apr. 28, 1917, Cab. 24/12, G.T. 607; Fairholme to Director of Military Intelligence, War Office, Apr. 16, 1917, Cab. 24/11, G.T. 586).
86. "Note of an Anglo-French Conference held at London, May 28, 1917," Cab.

28/2/I.C.-23, p. 6. As early as May 1, Lloyd George recognized that if British troops were to be withdrawn from Salonika, France would have to be given a free hand to deal with Constantine. He had a good deal of difficulty persuading the War Cabinet to follow his policy (minutes of War Cabinet meeting, May 1, 1917, Cab. 23/13, pp. 7-8). The Foreign and War Offices opposed military operations against Greece. It was feared that if Venizelos assumed power, the Entente would have to defend Greece against a German attack (memo by Cecil, May 24, 1917, Cab. 21/52, p. 1; see also Cecil to Bertie, May ?, 1917, Cab. 24/12, G.T. 620, p. 20). Furthermore, both Robertson and Cecil feared that the sending of Allied troops to Larissa or Athens would lead to a long war with royalist Greece, making it extremely difficult if not impossible to withdraw British troops from the Balkans (memo by Robertson, "Note on a Proposal to Occupy Larissa," Apr. 13, 1917, Cab. 24/10, G.T. 430; memo by Robertson, "Withdrawal of the British from Salonica," May 1, 1917, Cab. 24/12, G.T. 606; memo by Robertson, "French Proposal for the Occupation of Greece," May 25, 1917, Cab. 24/14, G.T. 840; Hankey to Robertson, May 24, 1917, Cab. 21/49).

87. Ribot to Barrère, May 6, 1917, AAE, série: Guerre 1914-18, vol. 994, dossier 8, fol. 80, no. 1107; Barrère to Ribot, May 1, 1917, ibid., fol. 75, no. 563.

88. Cambon to Ribot, May 19, 1917, ibid., fol. 85, no. 814; Ribot to Barrère, May 6, 1917, ibid., fol. 80, no. 1107.

89. Barrère to Ribot, May 1, 1917, ibid., fol. 75, no. 563.

90. Barrère to Ribot, May 1, 1917, ibid.; Ribot to Barrère, May 6, 1917, ibid., fol. 80, no. 1107; Pingaud, *Histoire diplomatique*, 2:331; Pietro Pastorelli, *L'Albania nella politica estera italiana, 1914-1920* (Naples, 1970), p. 60.

91. Barrère to Ribot, Apr. 9, 1917, AAE, série: Guerre 1914-18, vol. 272, dossier 34, fol. 75, no. 452; Frangulis, *La Grèce et la crise mondiale*, 1:529; Giers to M. I. Tereshchenko, Russian minister of foreign affairs, May 16/29, 1917, Adamow, *Die Europäischen Mächte und Griechenland*, no. 363, p. 253; Alessandro de Bosdari, *Delle guerre balcaniche della grande guerra e di alcuni fatti precedenti ad esse*, 2d ed. (Milan, 1931), p. 182.

92. Barrère to Ribot, June 11, 1917, AAE, série: Guerre 1914-18, vol. 232, dossier 11, fol. 98, no. 77; Pastorelli, *L'Albania nella politica estera italiana*, p. 60.

93. Ribot to Painlevé, June 8, 1917, AAE, série: Guerre 1914-18, vol. 232, dossier 11, fol. 64, no. 2092.

94. Briand to Sarrail, Dec. 13, 1916, ibid., vol. 230, dossier 9, fol. 303, no. 46.

95. Sarrail to Briand, Dec. 15, 1916, ibid., dossier 9, no. 1871.

96. Briand to Barrère, Jan. 15, 1917, ibid., vol. 231, dossier 10, fol. 17, no. 40.

97. Barrère to Briand, Feb. 6, 1917, ibid., fol. 56, no. 70.

98. Briand to Lyautey, Mar. 3, 1917, ibid., fol. 109, no. 817.

99. Briand to Barrère, Mar. 12, 1917, ibid., fol. 134, no. 616.

100. Sarrail to Lyautey, Mar. 21, 1917, quoted in Sarrail, *Mon commandement*, p. 222.

101. Briand to Jean Jusserand, French ambassador to the United States, Mar. 20, 1917, AAE, série: Guerre 1914-18, vol. 231, dossier 10, fol. 165, no. 398.

102. Henri Descoins, "Six mois d'histoire de l'Albanie (novembre 1916-mai 1917)," *Revue d'histoire de la guerre mondiale* 7-8 (1929-30): 333-34.

103. Descoins to Sarrail, Dec. 9, 1916, AMG, 20N/190, dossier 3, no. 18. See also Descoins, "Six mois d'histoire de l'Albanie," pp. 334-35.

104. Tubert to Sarrail, Dec. 21, 1916, AMG, 20N/131, dossier 6, no. 364/0, p. 3. Tubert was an aide to Colonel Descoins.

105. Joseph Swire, *Albania: The Rise of a Kingdom* (London, 1929), p. 268; Guillemin to Briand, Oct. 31, 1916, AAE, série: Guerre 1914-18, vol. 230, dossier 9, fol. 210, no. 2016; Sarrail, "La Grèce venizéliste," p. 700; Descoins, "Six mois d'histoire de l'Albanie," p. 320; Jacques Bourcart, *L'Albanie et les Albanais* (Paris, 1921), pp. 154-55. Serving in the French army, Bourcart spent the war years in Albania.

106. Tubert to Sarrail, Dec. 21, 1916, AMG, 20N/131, dossier 6, no. 364/0, p. 3; Roquefeuil to Sarrail, Sept. 26, 1916, ibid., 20N/151, dossier 3, no. 139; Bourcart, *L'Albanie et les Albanais*, p. 154; Edith Pierpont Stickney, *Southern Albania or Northern Epirus in European International Affairs, 1912-1923* (Stanford, 1926), p. 68; Descoins, "Six mois d'histoire de l'Albanie," pp. 323, 332.

107. Paul Leblois, at the time commander of the French Eastern Army, to Joseph Bardi de Fourtou, member of Sarrail's staff in Salonika, Nov. 25, 1916, AMG, 20N/501, dossier 1, no. 197; Descoins, "Six mois d'histoire de l'Albanie," pp. 327-28, 42-43.

108. Swire, *Albania*, p. 269.

109. Tubert to Sarrail, Dec. 21, 1916, AMG, 20N/131, dossier 6, no. 364/0, p. 3.

110. For criticism of Descoins, see Sarrail to his brother, Maurice, Feb. 4, 1917, P.P.S.; Sarrail, "Souvenirs," p. 262; the February, 1917, report, "Situation politique," written by a member of the Eastern Army's Second Bureau, AMG, 20N/131, dossier 6, p. 5bis. Descoins, for his part, noted that sometimes he was without "written and explicit instructions" (Descoins, "Six mois d'histoire de l'Albanie," p. 323). This may explain his far-reaching and unexpected initiatives of Dec. 10, 1916.

111. Ribot to Painlevé, Apr. 30, 1917, AAE, série: Guerre 1914-18, vol. 231, dossier 10, fol. 256, no. 1537.

112. Painlevé to Ribot, May 9, 1917, ibid., fol. 269, no. 3578.

113. Ribot to Painlevé, May 12, 1917, ibid., fol. 276, no. 1722.

114. Ribot to Barrère, June 5, 1917, ibid., vol. 232, dossier 11, fol. 21; Ribot to Painlevé, June 8, 1917, ibid., fol. 64, no. 2092.

115. Ribot to Barrère, June 5, 1917, ibid., fols. 20-22; Ribot to Barrère, June 7, 1917, ibid., fol. 54, no. 1329.

116. Ribot to Painlevé, June 8, 1917, ibid., fols. 64-65, no. 2092.

117. Painlevé to Sarrail, June 10, 1917, ibid., fol. 88.

118. Painlevé to Ribot, June 26, 1917, ibid., fol. 246, no. 3190.

119. Ribot to Painlevé, July 17, 1917, ibid., vol. 233, dossier 12, fol. 103.

120. Sarrail to Painlevé, July 20, 1917, ibid., fols. 119-20.

121. Barrère to Ribot, June 27, 1917, ibid., vol. 232, dossier 11, fol. 253, no. 861.

122. Barrère to Ribot, June 21, 1917, ibid., fol. 176, no. 829; Ribot to Jonnart, June 22, 1917, ibid., fol. 190, no. 61; Sarrail to Painlevé, June 24, 1917, ibid., fol. 221, no. 5397/2; Jonnart to Ribot, June 25, 1917, ibid., fol. 225, no. 95; Painlevé to Sarrail, June 25, 1917, ibid., fol. 238, no. 3008; Painlevé to Sarrail, June 29, 1917, ibid., fol. 264, no. 83; Painlevé to Ribot, June 30, 1917, ibid., fol. 285, no. 3374.

123. Sarrail to Painlevé, Aug. 20, 1917, ibid., vol. 233, dossier 12, fol. 53, no. 2365; Barrère to Ribot, Aug. 28, 1917, ibid., fol. 82, no. 1164. At the Paris conference of July 25-26, 1917, Sonnino had agreed that Italy would withdraw from northern Greece as Sarrail's troops in Athens and Thessaly returned to Salonika. The simultaneous withdrawal took about five weeks (Inter-Ally Conference, Paris, July 25, 1917, 2d sess., Cab. 28/2/I.C.-24b, pp. 23-31).

124. Inter-Ally Conference, Paris, July 25, 1917, 2d sess., Cab. 28/2/I.C.-24b, pp. 5, 7, 9, 11, 13, 15, 17.

125. Notes of Inter-Ally Conference, London, Aug. 7, 1917, ibid., I.C.-25a, pp. 4, 2-3; notes of Inter-Ally Conferences, London, Aug. 7, 1917, 2d sess.; Aug. 8, 1917, ibid., I.C.-25, pp. 3-5; I.C.-25b, pp. 2-4.

126. *A.F.*, tome 8, vol. 2–annexes, vol. 4, no. 2091, p. 137. See also ibid., nos. 2052, 2111, pp. 56, 161; Milne to Robertson, Aug. 25, 1917, Cab. 24/26, G.T. 2040, p. 3.

127. Sarrail, *Mon commandement*, pp. 264-65.

128. Sarrail to Painlevé, July 15, 1917, quoted in Sarrail, *Mon commandement*, no. 95, p. 408.

129. *A.F.*, tome 8, vol. 2–annexes, vol. 4, no. 2178, pp. 250-51.

130. Ibid., no. 2103, p. 154.

131. Ibid., no. 2105, p. 155.

132. Ibid., nos. 2085, 2178, pp. 130-31, 252.

133. Ibid., tome 8, vol. 2, pp. 510-22; Sarrail, *Mon commandement*, pp. 272-73, 281.

134. Ribot to Painlevé, Sept. 25, 1917, AAE, série: Guerre 1914-18, vol. 234, dossier 13, fol. 185, no. 3536.

135. Ribot to Barrère, Sept. 28, 1917, ibid., fol. 201, no. 2376.

136. Jean Decrais to Sarrail, Sept. 27, 1917, Fonds Clemenceau, Archives du Ministère de la Guerre, Château de Vincennes, Vincennes, carton 144, file: Expédiés, dossier 2, no. 413. Decrais served in the War Ministry under Lyautey and later under Painlevé and as an intermediary between Sarrail and Painlevé. See also *A.F.*, tome 8, vol. 2, p. 540.

137. Sarrail to Painlevé, Sept. 21, 1917, AAE, série: Guerre 1914-18, vol. 1043, fols. 74-75, no. 2826; Ribot to Barrère, Oct. 1, 1917, ibid., fol. 96, no. 2398; Sarrail to Decrais, Sept. 29, 1917, Fonds Clemenceau, carton 144, file: Reçus, dossier 2, no. 171; *A.F.*, tome 8, vol. 2–annexes, vol. 4, no. 2200, pp. 275-76.

138. Sarrail to Painlevé, Sept. 30, 1917, quoted in Sarrail, *Mon commandement*, p. 276.

139. Greek government to Ribot, "Note du gouvernement grec," Oct. 11, 1917, AAE, série: Guerre 1914-18, vol. 234, dossier 14, fol. 37, no. 3528.

140. Sarrail to Painlevé, Sept. 27, 1917, ibid., dossier 13, fol. 207, no. 2891; Ribot to Barrère, Oct. 6, 1917, ibid., dossier 14, fol. 23, no. 1381.

141. Sarrail to Painlevé, Oct. 6, 1917, quoted in Sarrail, *Mon commandement*, pp. 281, 280.

142. *A.F.*, tome 8, vol. 2, pp. 523-28; Sarrail, *Mon commandement*, pp. 281-82.

143. *A.F.*, tome 8, vol. 2–annexes, vol. 4, no. 2240, p. 338. See also ibid., no. 2239, p. 337.

144. Sarrail to Painlevé, Nov. 13, 1917, AAE, série: Guerre 1914-18, vol. 234, dossier 14, fol. 105, no. 7464/2.

145. *A.F.*, tome 8, vol. 2, p. 533.

CHAPTER IX

1. Margaine to Sarrail, Sept. 27, 1917, P.P.S.

2. Lloyd George to Ribot, June 6, 1917, quoted in Lloyd George, *War Memoirs*, 6:187-88.

3. Milne to Robertson, May 26, 1917, Cab. 24/15, G.T. 940, p. 3; minutes of War Cabinet meeting, June 5, 1917, Cab. 23/3, pp. 2-3.

4. Memo signed "D.D.," May 31, 1917, Cab. 21/49, p. 3. Captain Stead was aide-de-camp to Admiral Ernest Troubridge at Salonika.

5. Poincaré, *Au service de la France*, 9:158-59.

6. Painlevé is quoted in Henry Norman to Lloyd George, June 7, 1917, Lloyd George Papers, F/41/6/2. Norman, a pioneer in the field of electronic communications, traveled to France as a representative of the minister of munitions. See also Lady Algernon Gordon [Blanche] Lennox, ed., *The Diary of Lord Bertie of Thame, 1914-1918* (London, 1924), 2:134-35.

7. Minutes of War Cabinet meeting, Aug. 7, 1917, Cab. 23/3, p. 3; minutes of War Cabinet meeting, Aug. 3, 1917, ibid., p. 4.

8. Robertson to Milne, Sept. 15, 1917, Robertson Papers, I/34/32. See also Bertie to Balfour, June 24, 1917, Lloyd George Papers, F/51/4/25. War Minister

Painlevé wrote Sarrail in March, June, and August, 1917, that "you have the full confidence of the government" (Painlevé to Sarrail, Mar. 23, June 8, 1917, AMG, 20N/189, dossier 2, nos. 59, 66; Painlevé to Sarrail, Aug. 18, 1917, quoted in Sarrail, *Mon commandement*, p. 268).

9. Margaine to Sarrail, Sept. 27, 1917, P.P.S.

10. Sarrail to Decrais, Jan. 20, 1917, Fonds Painlevé, box 26, file 4. See also Sarrail, "Souvenirs," p. 210.

11. Decrais to Sarrail, Apr. 18,1917, Fonds Clemenceau, carton 144, dossier 2, file: Expédiés, no. 180. See also Sarrail, "Souvenirs," p. 211.

12. Sarrail to Decrais, Apr. 21, 1917, Fonds Clemenceau, carton 144, dossier 2, file: Reçus, no. 79. See also Sarrail, "Souvenirs," p. 211.

13. Repington, *First World War*, 2:59.

14. Sarrail, "Souvenirs," p. 211.

15. Paul Painlevé, *Comment j'ai nommé Foch et Pétain* (Paris, 1923), 75-83, 103, 113-23, 144, 153, 205-9, 215-16; Guy Pedroncini, *Les Mutineries de 1917* (Paris, 1967).

16. For a sampling of political opinion concerning the question of home-front defeatists in 1917, see *L'Action française* for May, June, and July; Clemenceau's articles in *L'Homme enchaîné*, particularly those for early June and mid-July; Poincaré, *Au service de la France*, 9:148-49, 154, 171-72, 175.

17. Painlevé, *Comment j'ai nommé Foch et Pétain*, p. 153; Malvy's comments in *J.O.C.*, July 7, 1917, pp. 1706-12.

18. Richard M. Watt, *Dare Call It Treason* (New York, 1963), pp. 42-43, 135-37, 254-59, 262; Poincaré, *Au service de la France*, 9:230-32; *La Victoire*, Nov. 13, 1917, editorial by Hervé.

19. Mathieu to Paix-Séailles, May 3, 1916, Fonds Painlevé, box 26, file 14. The five letters, ranging in content from several sentences to two thousand words, are dated Mar. 8, Apr. 5, May 3, May 10, 1916, and the last letter has three different entries—June 9, 14, and 17, 1916.

20. Mathieu to Paix-Séailles, Apr. 5, 1916, ibid.

21. Mathieu to Paix-Séailles, May 10, 1916, ibid.

22. Mathieu to Paix-Séailles, Mar. 8, 1916, ibid.

23. A copy of Sarrail's letter to Noulens, dated June 15, 1916, can be found in Fonds Painlevé, box 26, file 4. A portion of the letter is quoted in chap. VI, p. 103, of the present study.

24. A copy of the letter can be found in Fonds Painlevé, box 26, file 4.

25. The complete document can be found in *A.F.*, tome 8, vol. 1—annexes, vol. 3, no. 1330, p. 666.

26. A copy of Guillemin's telegram can be found in Fonds Painlevé, box 26, file 4.

27. Mathieu to Sarrail, Sept. 9, 1917, P.P.S. Jérôme Carcopino, chief of the Eastern Army's Second Bureau, confirmed that Sarrail knew nothing of Mathieu's actions (*Souvenirs de la guerre en Orient*, p. 151).

28. Sarrail to Decrais, Sept. 9, 1917, Fonds Clemenceau, carton 144, dossier 3, file: Reçus, no. 183.

29. Painlevé to Sarrail, Aug. 18, 1917, quoted in Sarrail, *Mon commandement*, p. 268.

30. Decrais to Sarrail, Aug. 10, 1917, Fonds Clemenceau, carton 144, dossier 5, file: Expédiés, no. 347.

31. Decrais to Sarrail, Aug. 22, 1917, ibid., dossier 3, file: Expédiés, no. 3632; Bapst, "Journal de guerre," n.a.f. 11705, fols. 315v-16 (Aug. 30, 1917), fol. 320 (Sept. 2, 1917), fol. 328 (Sept. 7, 1917), fol. 339 (Sept. 9, 1917).

32. Poincaré, *Au service de la France*, 9:257.

33. King, *Generals and Politicians*, p. 183.

34. All of the above themes put forth by the nationalist coalition can be found

Notes to Pages 179–85 / [261]

in the September, October, and November, 1917, issues of *L'Homme enchaîné* and *L'Action française*; Poincaré, *Au service de la France*, 9:282, 322-23, 335, 359, 366.

35. King, *Generals and Politicians*, pp. 183-84, 190-91; Eugen Weber, *Action Française: Royalism and Reaction in Twentieth-Century France* (Stanford, 1962), pp. 104-6; Robert Wohl, *French Communism in the Making, 1914-1924* (Stanford, 1966), pp. 89-94.

36. *J.O.C.*, Nov. 20, 1917, p. 2963.

37. Sarrail to Painlevé, Nov. 15, 1917, Fonds Painlevé, box 26, file 4.

38. Poincaré, *Au service de la France*, 9:402, 388-89; King, *Generals and Politicians*, p. 203.

39. Sarrail, *Mon commandement*, pp. 293-94.

40. Memo by Robertson, "Situation in Macedonia," Nov. 14, 1917, Cab. 24/32, G.T. 2615, p. 3.

41. Minutes of War Cabinet meeting, Nov. 19, 1917, Cab. 23/4, p. 3; minutes of War Cabinet meeting, Nov. 21, 1917, ibid., p. 3; Bertie to Balfour, Nov. 28, 1917, F.O. 371, vol. 2895, file 232631, paper 234840; "Proces-Verbal of the Second Session of the Supreme War Council Held at . . . Versailles," Dec. 1, 1917, Cab. 28/3/I.C.-36, p. 4.

42. "Extraits d'une conversation entre Pachitch, Président du Conseil des Ministres de Serbie et son excellence Clemenceau," Nov. 22, 1917, AAE, série: Guerre 1914-18, vol. 388, dossier 22, fol. 42; Venizelos to Clemenceau, Dec. 7, 1917, ibid., vol. 234, dossier 14, fols. 130-31.

43. Stephen Pichon, minister of foreign affairs in the Clemenceau government, to Clemenceau, Dec. 13, 1917, ibid., fols. 156-57, no. 4669; Clemenceau to Guillaumat, Sarrail's successor in Salonika, Dec. 22, 1917, ibid., fol. 158, no. 13353.

44. Sarrail to his brother, Maurice, Dec. 11, 1917, P.P.S.

45. Herbillon, *Souvenirs d'un officier de liaison*, 2:186.

46. In April, 1918, the Seine Federation of the Republican Socialist party and the Executive Committee of the Radical and Radical-Socialist parties voted resolutions praising Sarrail for the eminent service that he rendered the country. Both citations, dated Apr. 28, 1918, can be found in P.P.S.

47. For Caillaux's wartime activities, see Alfred Fabre-Luce, *Caillaux* (Paris, 1933), pp. 121-59; Paul Vergnet, *L'Affaire Caillaux* (Paris, 1918); Rudolph Binion, *Defeated Leaders: The Political Fate of Caillaux, Jouvenel, and Tardieu* (New York, 1960), chaps. 5-6.

48. Most of the "Rubicon" is reprinted in Vergnet, *L'Affaire Caillaux*, pp. 82-91. See also Georges Bonnefous, *Histoire politique*, 2:370-71.

49. Paix-Séailles to Sarrail, Feb. 18, 1917, P.P.S.

50. Coblentz, *Silence of Sarrail*, pp. 180-81; Corday, *Paris Front*, p. 337. Although Caillaux was arrested and jailed on Jan. 14, 1918, his trial did not begin until February, 1920. The High Court (Senate) found Caillaux innocent of treason; however, he was found guilty of having written letters to the enemy, thereby damaging the military and political security of the state. Having spent more than two years in prison already, he was immediately released.

51. Cordonnier's deposition, dated Dec. 12, 1917, can be found in Fonds Painlevé, box 26, file 14. See also Cordonnier, *Ai-je trahi Sarrail?*, pp. 156-64.

52. Sarrail to Decrais, Sept. 23, 1917, Fonds Clemenceau, carton 144, dossier 3, file: Reçus.

53. Sarrail's deposition, dated Jan. 18, 1918, can be found in Fonds Painlevé, box 26, file 14. See also Sarrail, "Souvenirs," p. 213.

CHAPTER X

1. Coblentz, *Silence of Sarrail*, p. 181.

2. The second electoral district was composed of these *arrondissements* in Paris: 1, 2, 3, 4, 11, 12, 20.
3. *L'Oeuvre*, Nov. 5, 1919.
4. The basic purpose of the League of the Rights of Man, born during the Dreyfus affair, was to guarantee the protection of the individual's civil liberties. The League also advocated greater social and economic reforms for the lower classes and an international order based upon the League of Nations. See the remarks of the League's president, Ferdinand Buisson, "Notre programme," *Les Cahiers des droits de l'homme*, Jan. 5, 1920, pp. 3-4.
5. See Sarrail's articles in *La République sociale*, Nov. 4, 11, 1922; *L'Ere nouvelle*, Nov. 16, 1922; *L'Ancien Combattant*, Nov. 4, 16, Dec. 16, 1923. See also his articles "Le Problème des réparations: L'Occupation de la Ruhr," *Les Cahiers des droits de l'homme*, Jan. 10, 1923, pp. 3-5; "Deux nouveaux tracts pour la réforme militaire," ibid., May 10, 1924, pp. 219-20, and the reprint of his speech at the Nov. 14, 1920, meeting of the League of the Rights of Man, "Discours du général Sarrail," ibid., Dec. 5, 1920, p. 11.
6. See Sarrail's articles, "L'Armée démocratique," *Les Cahiers des droits de l'homme*, Apr. 10, 1921, p. 152; "L'Armée et le droit de vote," ibid., June 10, 1922, p. 278, and his articles in *L'Ancien Combattant*, Nov. 16, 1922; *La Nouvelle République*, Dec. 3, 1920; *L'Ere nouvelle*, Oct. 22, 1921; Jan. 24, Mar. 29, Sept. 5, Nov. 16, 1922; Jan. 22, Aug. 25, 1923; Apr. 24, 1924.
7. Article by Sarrail, *L'Ancien Combattant*, Nov. 16, 1922.
8. Article by Sarrail, *La Nouvelle République*, Dec. 3, 1920.
9. See Sarrail's articles, "L'Armée démocratique," *Les Cahiers des droits de l'homme*, Apr. 10, 1921, pp. 152-57; "Deux nouveaux tracts pour la réforme militaire," ibid., May 10, 1924, pp. 219-20. See also the reprint of Sarrail's speech at the Nov. 14, 1920, meeting of the League of the Rights of Man, "Discours du général Sarrail," ibid., Dec. 5, 1920, pp. 10-12, and his articles in *L'Ere nouvelle*, June 29, 1920; Mar. 18, 1922; Mar. 3, 1923; Apr. 9, 1924; *Le Provençal*, Jan. 5, 1920.
10. See Sarrail's articles in *L'Ere nouvelle*, July 30, Dec. 26, 1922; July 27, Sept. 22, 1923; Jan. 4, 1924.
11. See Sarrail's article, "L'Armée de la Société des nations," *Les Cahiers des droits de l'homme*, May 25, 1923, pp. 219-22, and the reprint of his speech to the Nov. 14, 1920, meeting of the League of the Rights of Man, "Discours du général Sarrail," ibid., Dec. 5, 1920, p. 11. See also Sarrail's articles in *L'Ere nouvelle*, Dec. 20, 1921; Jan. 22, Nov. 15, 1923.
12. See Sarrail's article, "L'Armée démocratique," *Les Cahiers des droits de l'homme*, Apr. 10, 1921, p. 153, and his articles in *L'Ere nouvelle*, Mar. 30, 1921; July 29, Dec. 26, 1922; June 20, 1923; *Le Provençal*, Jan. 5, 1920.
13. For a cogent discussion of France's interwar military organization and strategy, see Challener, *French Theory of the Nation in Arms*, chaps. 4-7; Judith M. Hughes, *To the Maginot Line: The Politics of French Military Preparation in the 1920's* (Cambridge, Mass., 1971).
14. Edouard Bonnefous, *Histoire politique de la troisième république*, vol. 4, *Cartel des gauches et union nationale, 1924-1929* (Paris, 1960), pp. 19-20, 26-40; Coblentz, *Silence of Sarrail*, pp. 187-88. Sarrail was officially placed on the active list on Aug. 2, 1924. The cartel also voted amnesties to Malvy and Caillaux.
15. Coblentz, *Silence of Sarrail*, p. 189. Even before Sarrail was formally placed on the active list, some Radical politicians wanted him to be a member of the Superior War Council or war minister in a cartel government (Accambray to Sarrail, May 25, 1924, P.P.S.).
16. Maxime Weygand, *Mémoires: Mirages et réalité* (Paris, 1950-57), 2:286-87. Upon dismissing Weygand, Herriot named him director of the Centre des Hautes Etudes Militaires and awarded him the Grand Cross of the Legion of Honor.

17. Sarrail was officially named high commissioner on Nov. 29, 1924.

18. Accambray to Sarrail, May 25, 1924, P.P.S.

19. Barabant to Sarrail, Dec. 3, 1924, ibid. Barabant represented the Côte d'Or. See also Messimy to Sarrail, Dec. 18, 1924, ibid., in which Messimy called Sarrail's appointment "a stunning setback" for the Right.

20. George Antonius, *The Arab Awakening: The Story of the Arab National Movement* (New York, 1965), chaps. 7-14; Roger de Gontaut-Biron, *Comment la France s'est installée en Syrie, 1918-1919* (Paris, 1922); Stephen Hemsley Longrigg, *Syria and Lebanon under the French Mandate* (London, 1958), chap. 3; Jukka Nevakivi, *Britain, France and the Arab Middle East, 1914-1920* (London, 1969); A. L. Tibawi, *A Modern History of Syria Including Lebanon and Palestine* (London, 1969), chaps. 8-10; Zeine N. Zeine, *The Struggle for Arab Independence: Western Diplomacy and the Rise and Fall of Feisal's Kingdom in Syria* (Beirut, 1960).

21. There is no adequate study of France's administration in Lebanon and Syria for the period 1920-24. However, see Antonius, *Arab Awakening*, pp. 368-76; France, Ministère des Affaires Etrangères, *Rapport à la Société des nations sur la situation de la Syrie et du Liban, 1922-23* (Paris, 1923); *Rapport à la Société des nations sur la situation de la Syrie et du Liban, 1924* (Geneva, 1925); League of Nations, Permanent Mandates Commission (hereafter cited as Mandates Commission), *Minutes of the Fourth Session*, Geneva, June 24-July 8, 1924, pp. 26-34; *Minutes of the Fifth Session (Extraordinary)*, Geneva, Oct. 23-Nov. 6, 1924, pp. 99-116; *Minutes of the Eighth Session (Extraordinary) Including the Report of the Commission to the Council*, Rome, Feb. 16-Mar. 6, 1926, pp. 14-22, 75-78, 80-88, 94-95, 107-18; Longrigg, *Syria and Lebanon under the French Mandate*, chap. 4; Elizabeth P. MacCallum, *The Nationalist Crusade in Syria* (New York, 1928), chaps. 2-4; Tibawi, *Modern History of Syria*, pp. 338-45; Arnold J. Toynbee, *Survey of International Affairs, 1925* (London, 1927), 1:388-91, 397-406; Weygand, *Mémoires*, 2:252-53; Edmond Rabbath, *L'Evolution politique de la Syrie sous mandat de 1920 à 1925* (Paris, 1928), pp. 162-233.

22. Mandates Commission, *Minutes of the Eighth Session (Extraordinary)*, pp. 53, 59; *Report to the Council of the League of Nations on the Work of the Eighth (Extraordinary) Session of the Permanent Mandates Commission*, annex 4, attached to the Minutes of the Eighth Session, pp. 202-3, 206; *Comments Submitted . . . on the Situation in Syria and the Lebanon in 1924 . . .* , attached to the Minutes of the Eighth Session, p. 1; Toynbee, *Survey of International Affairs*, 1:405; Alice Poulleau, *A Damas sous les bombes: Journal d'une Française pendant la révolte syrienne, 1924-1926* (Paris, 1930), pp. 12-13; Rabbath, *L'Evolution politique de la Syrie*, pp. 257-66, 273-76.

23. Harold Satow, British consul-general at Beirut, to Austen Chamberlain, British foreign secretary, Dec. 8, 1924, F.O. 371, vol. 10165, file E11423.

24. Coblentz, *Silence of Sarrail*, pp. 194-95.

25. Satow to Chamberlain, Dec. 1, 1924, F.O. 371, vol. 10165, file E11158; Satow to Chamberlain, Jan. 5, 1925, ibid., vol. 10850, file E273; Poulleau, *A Damas sous les bombes*, p. 17.

26. Coblentz, *Silence of Sarrail*, p. 191; *Le Temps*, Dec. 26, 1924.

27. France, Ministère des Affaires Etrangères, *Rapport à la Société des nations sur la situation de la Syrie et du Liban, 1925* (Paris, 1926), p. 7; Longrigg, *Syria and Lebanon under the French Mandate*, p. 149; Toynbee, *Survey of International Affairs*, 1:419.

28. Satow to Chamberlain, Jan. 16, 1925, F.O. 371, vol. 10850, file E494.

29. Coblentz, *Silence of Sarrail*, pp. 203-5; Ministère des Affaires Etrangères, *Rapport à la Société des nations . . . Syrie et du Liban, 1925*, pp. 7-8; Longrigg, *Syria and Lebanon under the French Mandate*, p. 149; Toynbee, *Survey of International Affairs*, 1:419-20.

30. Coblentz, *Silence of Sarrail*, pp. 195-98; Longrigg, *Syria and Lebanon under the French Mandate*, pp. 149-50; Toynbee, *Survey of International Affairs*, 1:417-18.

31. Coblentz, *Silence of Sarrail*, pp. 191-92. However, the Quai d'Orsay emphasized to Sarrail before his departure that France's position in the Middle East rested upon maintaining close ties with the Catholics; thus the high commissioner should continue to favor Catholic interests in the Middle East (Jules Laroche, *Au Quai d'Orsay avec Briand et Poincaré, 1913-1926* [Paris, 1957], p. 217).

32. Coblentz, *Silence of Sarrail*, p. 192.

33. *L'Echo de Paris*, Jan. 23, 1925.

34. Harry W. Paul, *The Second Ralliement: The Rapprochement between Church and State in France in the Twentieth Century* (Washington, D.C., 1967), chaps. 3-5.

35. Adrien Dansette, *Religious History of Modern France*, trans. John Dingle (New York, 1961), 2:346.

36. Edouard Bonnefous, *Histoire politique*, 4:40-43; Paul, *Second Ralliement*, pp. 108-25. For a detailed daily report of organized Catholic resistance to the cartel's laic policy, see *La Croix*, June-Dec., 1924.

37. Charles Maurras in *L'Action française*, July 2, 3, 1924; *Le Gaulois*, July 2, 1924; *Le Figaro*, July 2, 1924.

38. *Le Gaulois*, Dec. 1, 1924; *L'Echo de Paris*, Dec. 1, 1924; *La Croix*, Dec. 1, 4, 20, 1924; *L'Action française*, Dec. 3, 1924.

39. *La Croix*, Jan. 27, 1925; *L'Action française*, Jan. 24, 25, 27, 1925.

40. *J.O.C.*, Jan. 23, 1925, pp. 259-60. Biré represented the Vendeé, Fould, the Hautes-Pyrénées, and Poitou-Duplessy, the Charente.

41. Ibid., Jan. 31, 1925, pp. 462-68. Greek Catholic Patriarch Cadi agreed that the Maronite and Catholic clergy's resistance to Sarrail in Lebanon was the result of orders received from France (discussion between Monsignor Cadi and one of Sarrail's aides, Apr. 29, 1925, P.P.S., p. 6).

42. Michel Soulié, *La Vie politique d'Edouard Herriot* (Paris, 1962), p. 218. For a detailed daily report of Catholic resistance to the cartel's religious policies, see *La Croix*, Jan.-Mar., 1925.

43. Quoted in Toynbee, *Survey of International Affairs*, 1:418-19.

44. Soulié, *La Vie politique d'Edouard Herriot*, p. 191; Toynbee, *Survey of International Affairs*, 1:419.

45. Briand to Sarrail, May 18, 1925, P.P.S.

46. Coblentz, *Silence of Sarrail*, pp. 207-8; Ministère des Affaires Etrangères, *Rapport à la Société des nations . . . Syrie et du Liban, 1925*, p. 8; Longrigg, *Syria and Lebanon under the French Mandate*, p. 150; Satow to Chamberlain, Mar. 2, Apr. 9, 1925, F.O. 371, vol. 10850, files E1463, E2486; Toynbee, *Survey of International Affairs*, 1:420.

47. Goguel, *La Politique des partis sous la troisième république*, pp. 231-32; Edouard Bonnefous, *Histoire politique*, 4:82. See also Painlevé's speech to the Chamber of Deputies in *J.O.C.*, Apr. 21, 1925, pp. 2214-15.

48. Toynbee, *Survey of International Affairs*, 1:421.

49. Briand to Sarrail, May 18, 1925, P.P.S.

50. A. G. Salisbury-Jones, British liaison officer to the French Army of the Levant, to Samuel Hoare, British secretary for air, May 6, 1925, F.O. 371, vol. 10835, file 6458, p. 4.

51. W. A. Smart, British consul at Damascus, to Chamberlain, Feb. 12, 1925, ibid., vol. 10850, file E1101.

52. Ministère des Affaires Etrangères, *Rapport à la Société des nations . . . Syrie et du Liban, 1925*, p. 8.

53. Smart to Chamberlain, Feb. 12, 1925, F.O. 371, vol. 10850, file E1101.

54. Smart to Chamberlain, Jan. 30, 1925, ibid., file E849.

55. Coblentz, *Silence of Sarrail*, pp. 213-14; Ministère des Affaires Etrangères, *Rapport à la Société des nations . . . Syrie et du Liban, 1925*, pp. 9-10; Mandates Commission, *Minutes of the Eighth Session (Extraordinary)*, p. 161.

56. Mandates Commission, *Minutes of the Eighth Session (Extraordinary)*, p. 54; Ministère des Affaires Etrangères, *Rapport à la Société des nations . . . Syrie et du Liban, 1925*, pp. 11-12; Charles Joseph Andréa, *La Révolte druze et l'insurrection de Damas, 1925-1926* (Paris, 1937), chap. 2; Toynbee, *Survey of International Affairs*, 1:402-9. For a fascinating account of the *moeurs*, attitudes, and social structure of the Druzes, see Gabriel Carbillet, *Au Djebel Druse: Choses vues et vécues* (Paris, 1929).

57. Toynbee, *Survey of International Affairs*, 1:409-10.

58. Smart to Chamberlain, July 15, 1925, F.O. 371, vol. 10850, file E4413.

59. For Carbillet's policies, see Ministère des Affaires Etrangères, *Rapport à la Société des nations . . . Syrie et du Liban, 1925*, pp. 16-19; Toynbee, *Survey of International Affairs*, 1:412-16; Mandates Commission, *Minutes of the Eighth Session (Extraordinary)*, pp. 54-55, 101-3, 122-23, 136; "Les Affaires de Syrie," n.d., Fonds Painlevé, box 42, file: Syrie (notes Carbillet), pp. 9-16.

60. C. E. S. Palmer, British consul at Damascus, to George Nathaniel Curzon, British foreign secretary, Dec. 24, 1923, F.O. 371, vol. 10162, file E330.

61. "Les Affaires de Syrie," Fonds Painlevé, box 42, file: Syrie (notes Carbillet), pp. 2-9; Ministère des Affaires Etrangères, *Rapport à la Société des nations . . . Syrie et du Liban, 1925*, p. 20.

62. Coblentz, *Silence of Sarrail*, pp. 222-24, 226; Toynbee, *Survey of International Affairs*, 1:422-23.

63. Mandates Commission, *Minutes of the Eighth Session (Extraordinary)*, pp. 128-29.

64. Coblentz, *Silence of Sarrail*, p. 224.

65. Mandates Commission, *Minutes of the Eighth Session (Extraordinary)*, p. 129.

66. Smart to Chamberlain, June 23, 1925, F.O. 371, vol. 10850, file E4005.

67. Satow to Chamberlain, Feb. 21, 1925, ibid., file E1764. Also Robert Crewe, British ambassador to France, to Eyre Crowe, British permanent undersecretary of state for foreign affairs, Dec. 12, 1924, ibid., vol. 10165, file E11320.

68. Toynbee, *Survey of International Affairs*, 1:422-24; Mandates Commission, *Minutes of the Eighth Session (Extraordinary)*, pp. 144-45; Ministère des Affaires Etrangères, *Rapport à la Société des nations . . . Syrie et du Liban, 1925*, pp. 22-23; Sarrail's report to Painlevé, "Rapport sur les opérations du Djebel Druze," Aug. 6, 1925, Fonds Painlevé, box 42, file 2; Henri de Kérillis's article in *L'Echo de Paris*, Oct. 2, 1925.

69. "Les Affaires de Syrie," Fonds Painlevé, box 42, file: Syrie (notes Carbillet), pp. 34-35.

70. Mandates Commission, *Minutes of the Eighth Session (Extraordinary)*, pp. 130-33; "Report to the Council . . . on the Work of the Eighth (Extraordinary) Session . . .," ibid., annex 4, pp. 205-6; Antonius, *Arab Awakening*, p. 377; Salisbury-Jones to Hoare, Oct. 7, 1925, F.O. 371, vol. 10835, file E6624; Poulleau, *A Damas sous les bombes*, p. 128.

71. Smart to Chamberlain, June 23, July 10, 1925, F.O. 371, vol. 10850, files E4005, E4310.

72. While critical of Sarrail, Smart attacked the incompetence of French colonial officialdom (Smart to Chamberlain, July 15, 1925, ibid., file E4413.).

73. Sarrail to Painlevé, July 14, 18, 1925, Fonds Painlevé, box 42, file 1, nos. 120, 122; Sarrail to Painlevé, Aug. 6, 1925, ibid., file 2, no. 1/CM.

74. Sarrail to Painlevé, July 27, 1925, ibid., file 1; Salisbury-Jones to Hoare, July 30, 1925, F.O. 371, vol. 10835, file E4810.

75. Sarrail to Painlevé, July 30, 1925, Fonds Painlevé, box 42, file 1, no. 134;

Salisbury-Jones to Hoare, July 30, 1925, F.O. 371, vol. 10835, file E4810.
76. Sarrail to Painlevé, Oct. 17, 1925, quoted in Coblentz, *Silence of Sarrail*, pp. 253-54; Sarrail to Painlevé, Aug. 9, 1925, Fonds Painlevé, box 42, file 1, no. 314/6. Sarrail's analysis of the causes of the Druze rebellion can be found in a personal memorandum written at the end of August, 1925 (Sarrail, Exposé d'ensemble . . . , B.N. Sarrail, n.a.f. 15007, fols. 235-36).
77. French intelligence report to Sarrail, "Quelques dessous de la révolte druze," Sept. 20, 1925, P.P.S., pp. 2-3. See also Smart to Chamberlain, July 15, 1925, F.O. 371, vol. 10850, file E4413; Salisbury-Jones to Hoare, July 30, 1925, ibid., vol. 10835, file E4810.
78. Coblentz, *Silence of Sarrail*, pp. 225-27; Ministère des Affaires Etrangères, *Rapport à la Société des nations . . . Syrie et du Liban, 1925*, pp. 20-23; Mandates Commission, *Minutes of the Eighth Session (Extraordinary)*, p. 156.
79. Salisbury-Jones to Hoare, Aug. 6, 1925, F.O. 371, vol. 10835, file E4996.
80. Coblentz, *Silence of Sarrail*, pp. 231-36; Longrigg, *Syria and Lebanon under the French Mandate*, p. 154; Toynbee, *Survey of International Affairs*, 1:425; Sarrail's report to Painlevé, "Rapport sur les opérations du Djebel Druze," Aug. 6, 1925, Fonds Painlevé, box 42, file 2; Sarrail to Painlevé, Aug. 10, 1925, ibid., no. 162; *Times* (London), Aug. 10, 1925.
81. Sarrail to Painlevé, Aug. 4, 1925, Fonds Painlevé, box 42, file 1, no. 145.
82. For Sarrail's failure to appreciate fully the immediate implications of Sultan al-Atrash's early August victory, see Sarrail to Painlevé, Aug. 7, 1925, ibid., file 1; Sarrail to Painlevé, Aug. 9, 1925, ibid., no. 160.
83. Longrigg, *Syria and Lebanon under the French Mandate*, pp. 154-55; Mandates Commission, *Minutes of the Eighth Session (Extraordinary)*, pp. 56-57; Toynbee, *Survey of International Affairs*, 1:425-26; Ministère des Affaires Etrangères, *Rapport à la Société des nations . . . Syrie et du Liban, 1925*, pp. 25-27. The extent of the rebellion is a disputed question. Antonius claims that it "developed into a national rising" (Antonius, *Arab Awakening*, p. 377). Longrigg states that the rebellion "was no national uprising. A small minority of Syrians participated, the majority played the role of victims or spectators. Wide areas were undisturbed" (Longrigg, *Syria and Lebanon under the French Mandate*, p. 156).
84. Longrigg, *Syria and Lebanon under the French Mandate*, p. 157.
85. Salisbury-Jones to Hoare, Oct. 7, 1925, F.O. 371, vol. 10835, file E6624.
86. Longrigg, *Syria and Lebanon under the French Mandate*, p. 157; Toynbee, *Survey of International Affairs*, 1:427; Sarrail to Painlevé, Sept. 17, 18, 1925, Fonds Painlevé, box 42, file 4, nos. 256/257, 260.
87. Crewe to Chamberlain, Sept. 15, 1925, F.O. 371, vol. 10851, file E5576.
88. *L'Echo de Paris*, Aug. 2, 8, 11, 13, Sept. 12, 18, 1925; *L'Action française*, Aug. 9, 10, 14, Sept. 21, 1925; *La Croix*, Aug. 12, 22, 29, 1925. Sarrail's daily messages to War Minister Painlevé were laconic, but it cannot be said that he concealed important information from the government. See Sarrail's messages in Fonds Painlevé, box 42; Albert Londres's article in *Le Petit Parisien*, Nov. 10, 1925.
89. *L'Echo de Paris*, Aug. 22, 23, Sept. 1, 3, 11, 12, 23, 1925; *L'Action française*, Aug. 9, 31, 1925; *La Croix*, Sept. 4, 25, 1925; *L'Eclair*, Aug. 8, 1925.
90. *L'Echo de Paris*, Sept. 29, 30, Oct. 1, 2, 4, 6, 1925.
91. Ibid., Oct. 5, 1925.
92. Coblentz, *Silence of Sarrail*, pp. 235-36.
93. *L'Ere nouvelle*, Aug. 10, 1925. See also *L'Oeuvre*, Aug. 9, 13, 1925. The Socialist bimonthly, *Le Populaire de Paris*, contained no comments in 1925 on the Syrian rebellion. *Le Quotidien* was almost as reticent.
94. *L'Ere nouvelle*, Aug. 13, 1925. The Riff is the area where Abd-el-Krim was leading his revolt in Morocco.
95. Ibid. See also ibid., Aug. 14. 1925.
96. For the French military action in early October, see Longrigg, *Syria and*

Lebanon under the French Mandate, pp. 157-58; Ministère des Affaires Etrangères, *Rapport à la Société des nations . . . Syrie et du Liban, 1925*, pp. 28-29; Toynbee, *Survey of International Affairs*, 1:427-28.
97. Mandates Commission, *Minutes of the Eighth Session (Extraordinary)*, p. 155.
98. Smart to Chamberlain, Oct. 5, 15, 1925, F.O. 371, vol. 10851, files E6391, E6607; Sarrail to Painlevé, Oct. 19, 1925, Fonds Painlevé, box 42, file 5, no. 350.
99. Sarrail to Painlevé, Nov. 2, 1925, Fonds Painlevé, box 42, file 5, no. 385; Toynbee, *Survey of International Affairs*, 1:428-31.
100. Exactly how many Damascenes died as a result of the shelling is disputed. The French authorities estimated that about two hundred were killed while Arab sources claim fourteen hundred people died (MacCallum, *Nationalist Crusade in Syria*, p. 136).
101. Smart to Chamberlain, Oct. 25, 1925, F.O. 371, vol. 10851, file E6884; Smart to Chamberlain, Nov. 10, 1925, ibid., vol. 10852, file E7250.
102. Salisbury-Jones to Hoare, Oct. 28, 1925, ibid., vol. 10835, file E6947.
103. Ministère des Affaires Etrangères, *Rapport à la Société des nations . . . Syrie et du Liban, 1925*, p. 31; Gamelin, "Summary Report of Events which Occurred at Damascus on 18th, 19th, and 20th October, 1925," Oct. 30, 1925, reprinted in Coblentz, *Silence of Sarrail*, p. 246.
104. Norman Mayers, acting British consul at Beirut, to Chamberlain, Oct. 30, 1925, F.O. 371, vol. 10852, file E6953.
105. Ministère des Affaires Etrangères, *Rapport à la Société des nations . . . Syrie et du Liban, 1925*, p. 32; Gamelin, "Summary Report of Events which Occurred at Damascus . . . ," in Coblentz, *Silence of Sarrail*, pp. 245, 249.
106. *L'Echo de Paris*, Oct. 22, 21, 1925; *Le Figaro*, Oct. 21, 1925; *La Croix*, Oct. 23, 1925.
107. *L'Echo de Paris*, Oct. 29, 1925. Actually the camel parade of corpses "passed almost unnoticed" in Damascus (Smart to Chamberlain, Nov. 9, 1925, F.O. 371, vol. 10852, file E7290).
108. *Le Temps*, Oct. 29, 1925.
109. Edouard Bonnefous, *Histoire politique*, 4:87; Eric Phipps, British chargé d'affaires in Paris, to Chamberlain, Aug. 9, 1925, F.O. 371, vol. 10850, file E4692.
110. Crewe to Chamberlain, Sept. 15, 1925, F.O. 371, vol. 10851, file E5576.
111. Crewe to Chamberlain, Sept. 2?, 1925, ibid., file E5871. See also Satow to Chamberlain, Sept. 8, 1925, ibid., file E5709; Salisbury-Jones to Hoare, Sept. 10, 1925, ibid., vol. 10835, file E5814.
112. Edouard Bonnefous, *Histoire politique*, 4:88.
113. *Le Figaro*, Oct. 31, 1925.
114. *L'Echo de Paris*, Oct. 31, Nov. 1, 1925; *La Croix*, Oct. 31, Nov. 3, 4, 1925; *L'Action française*, Nov. 2, 6, 1925; *Le Temps*, Nov. 1, 1925.
115. *L'Echo de Paris*, Nov. 21, 1925.
116. *Le Temps*, Nov. 22, 1925; interview with Sarrail's daughter, Nov. 10, 1965.
117. In the Chamber the Painlevé government faced right-wing demands for interpellation on Nov. 5, 1925. However, Painlevé successfully staved off debate by arguing that any discussion on the Syrian question should await Sarrail's return to Paris so that he could testify before the Foreign Affairs Commission. Further delay was caused by the defeat of the Painlevé government on Nov. 22 when Painlevé attempted to adopt the Socialist proposal to postpone payments on the national debt. On Nov. 28 Briand became the premier and Painlevé the war minister.
118. *J.O.C.*, Dec. 18, 1925, pp. 4437-45. About represented the Haute-Saône.
119. Ibid., pp. 4448, 4445-47.
120. *New York Times*, Dec. 19, 1925; *Le Quotidien*, Dec. 19, 1925.
121. *J.O.C.*, Dec. 20, 1925, pp. 4519-32, 4540-44.

122. Ibid., pp. 4536-38, 4550, 4555-56, 4560-61.
123. Henri Froidevaux, "Quelques causes du malaise syrien," *L'Asie française* 26, no. 237 (1926): 6. *L'Asie française* was the organ of the Comité de l'Asie française, a group of prominent geographers, industrialists, and colonial administrators.
124. Jacques Nobécourt, *Une Histoire politique de l'armée: De Pétain à Pétain, 1919-1942* (Paris, 1967), p. 129 emphasizes that it was Sarrail's symbolic importance which explains why those defeated in the Dreyfus affair so viciously took out "their vengeance against him."
125. See, e.g., article by Pierre Bertrand in *Le Quotidien*, Oct. 30, 1925.
126. *J.O.C.*, Dec. 20, 1925, p. 4550. Chavagnes represented the Loir-et-Cher.
127. Herriot's position on the key motions presented to the Chamber on December 20 clearly revealed both the impotency and brittleness of the cartel. On the Socialist motion to allow the League to administer the mandate, the Radical leader abstained. He also abstained on the motion calling for Briand to pacify the mandate and then to administer it in accordance with the original spirit and intentions of the League (ibid., pp. 4559-61).
128. In 1936, with the advent of Socialist Léon Blum's Popular Front government, French control of Syria apparently ended. But the 1936 Franco-Syrian treaty, which declared Syria a republic, was not ratified by the Blum government or by the succeeding French governments. Consequently, at the outbreak of World War II Syria was still ruled as completely as she had been in 1920 by French colonial officialdom. During the war frequent general strikes and anti-French riots eventually forced Charles de Gaulle to remove all French control of Syria. In 1944 the United States and Soviet Russia formally recognized Syria's independence.

CONCLUSION

1. *Le Temps*, Mar. 27, 1929. See also *L'Ere nouvelle*, Mar. 24 (articles by Gabriel Cudenet and Henri Bézies), Mar. 25, 1929 (article by Charles-Henry); *La Dépêche de Toulouse*, Mar. 24, 1929; *L'Oeuvre*, Mar. 24 (article by Jean Piot), Mar. 28, 1929.
2. Sarrail, "Souvenirs," p. 112.

Bibliography

MANUSCRIPT SOURCES

France

Paris
Archives du Ministère des Affaires Etrangères, Quai d'Orsay.
  Cambon, Paul. Papiers.
  Delcassé, Théophile. Papiers.
Archives Nationales.
  Painlevé, Paul. Fonds Painlevé.
    The Fonds Painlevé consists of ninety-five boxes of Painlevé's correspondence, reports, articles, and memorabilia. As of 1972 this collection had not yet been completely catalogued.
Bibliothèque Historique des Archives Centrales de la Marine.
  Guiot, Lieutenant de Vaisseau. "L'Affaire grecque: Guerre 1914-18." n.d.
  Marloy, Lieutenant de Vaisseau. "Expédition des Dardanelles: Transfert des opérations des Dardanelles à Salonique: Les Opérations de Sulva et du Cap Helles." 1921.
  Missoffe, Lieutenant de Vaisseau. "Le Guet-apens d'Athènes et le commandement de l'amiral Dartige du Fournet." 1925.
Bibliothèque de l'Institut de France.
  Pellé, Maurice. Papiers.
  Pichon, Stephen. Correspondance.
  Waldeck-Rousseau, René. Papiers.
Bibliothèque Nationale.
  Bapst, Germain. Correspondance.
  ———. "Journal de guerre."
  Havet, Louis. Correspondance.
  Reinach, Joseph. Correspondance.
  Sarrail, Maurice. Papiers.
Sarrail Family.
  Personal Papers of Maurice Sarrail.
  "Souvenirs" of Maurice Sarrail.

[270] / Bibliography

Vincennes
Archives du Ministère de la Guerre, Château de Vincennes.
Clemenceau, Georges. Fonds Clemenceau.

Great Britain

Cambridge
Cambridge University Library.
 Crewe, Robert, Marquess of Crewe. Papers.
 Hardinge, Charles. Papers.
Churchill College Library, Cambridge University.
 Keyes, Roger. Papers.
 McKenna, Reginald. Papers.
 Robeck, John de. Papers.

London
Beaverbrook Library.
 ⁃ Lloyd George, David. Papers.
British Museum.
 Balfour, Arthur James. Papers.
Centre for Military Archives, King's College, University of London.
 Howell, Philip. Papers.
 Robertson, William. Papers.
Public Record Office.
 Balfour, Arthur James. Papers.
 Bertie, Francis. Papers.
 Cecil, Robert. Papers.
 Chamberlain, Austen. Papers.
 Grey, Edward. Papers.
 Kitchener, Horatio. Papers.
 Nicolson, Arthur. Papers.

Oxford
Bodleian Library, Oxford University.
 Asquith, Herbert Henry. Papers.

Italy

Sidney Sonnino Papers. Ann Arbor, Mich.: University Microfilms, 1970.

OFFICIAL ARCHIVES

France

Paris
Archives Centrales du Ministère de la Marine.
 Série Xf.

Archives du Ministère des Affaires Etrangères, Quai d'Orsay.
Série: Guerre 1914-18.
Archives du Sénat, Palais du Luxembourg.
Procès-verbaux des séances de la Commission de l'armée, December, 1914-December, 1919.
    The twenty-three volumes contain the summary of the sessions.
Procès-verbaux des séances de la Commission de l'armée (auditions), December, 1914-December, 1919, cartons 158-59.
    These procès-verbaux are incomplete. Thus the summaries of the sessions mentioned above take on significance.
Procès-verbaux de la Commission des affaires étrangères, 1915-18.
    The four volumes of the Foreign Affairs Commission are not complete.
Chambre des Députés, Service des Archives, Assemblée Nationale.
Procès-verbaux de la Commission des affaires extérieures, 1915-19.
    The unpublished minutes of the Chamber Foreign Affairs Commission are not bound; they are filed according to session and cover the period 1915-19.
Procès-verbaux de la Commission de l'armée, January 9, 1915-October 19, 1919. 24 vols.

Vincennes
Archives du Ministère de la Guerre, Service Historique, Château de Vincennes.
"Etat des services du général Sarrail."
Série: Attachés militaires: Grèce.
Série 20N (L'Armée d'Orient).

Great Britain

London
Public Record Office.
    Admiralty Papers.
        Admiralty Papers 137.
    Cabinet Office Papers.
        Cab. 21: Cabinet Registered Files.
        Cab. 22: Minutes of Meetings of War Council, Dardanelles Committee, and War Committee.
        Cab. 23: Minutes of Meetings of War Cabinet.
        Cab. 24: Cabinet Memoranda, "G" War Series, vols. 1-5.
        Cab. 24: Cabinet Memoranda, "G.T." Series, vols. 6-91.
        Cab. 25: Supreme War Council, 1917-19.
        Cab. 28: Anglo-French and Allied Conferences: I.C. Series.
        Cab. 37: Cabinet Papers: Confidential Prints, 1915-16.
    Foreign Office Papers.
        F.O. 371.
    War Office Papers.
        W.O. 106: Military Operations and Intelligence.

W.O. 157: General Staff Intelligence Reports.
W.O. 158: Correspondence and Papers of Military Headquarters.

United States

"Records of the Department of State Relating to Internal Affairs of Greece, 1910-1929." Washington, D.C.: National Archives Microfilm Publications, 1965.

GOVERNMENT DOCUMENTS AND OFFICIAL HISTORIES

France

Assemblée Nationale. *Chambre des Députés, Journal officiel, Les Comités secrets, 1916-17.* The minutes of the secret sessions were published at intervals from 1919 to 1933. They have been collected in a separate volume at the Service des Archives, Assemblée Nationale, Paris.
———. *Journal officiel, Chambre des Députés, Débats parlementaires* (1871-1925).
———. *Journal officiel. Sénat, Débats parlementaires* (1900-1925).
———, Chambre des Députés, Session de 1919. *Procès-verbaux de la Commission d'Enquête sur la rôle et la situation de la métallurgie en France: Défense du Bassin de Briey,* 2 vols. Paris: Imprimerie Nationale, 1919.
Haut-Commissariat en Syrie et au Liban. *Recueil des actes administratifs du Haut-Commissariat de la République Française en Syrie et au Liban, 1919-1924.* Beirut, 1925.
———. *La Syrie et le Liban sous l'occupation et le mandat français, 1919-1927.* Paris: Berger-Levrault, 1927.
Ministère des Affaires Etrangères. *Rapport à la Société des nations sur la situation de la Syrie et du Liban, 1922-1923.* Paris: Imprimerie Nationale, 1923.
———. *Rapport à la Société des nations sur la situation de la Syrie et du Liban, 1924.* Geneva: League of Nations, 1925.
———. *Rapport à la Société des nations sur la situation de la Syrie et du Liban, 1925.* Paris: Imprimerie Nationale, 1926.
Ministère de la Guerre, Etat-Major de l'Armée, Service Historique. *Les Armées françaises dans la grande guerre.* 68 vols. Paris: Imprimerie Nationale, 1923-39.

Germany

Reichsarchiv. *Schlachten des Weltkrieges.* 37 vols. Berlin: Gerhard

Stalling, 1921-30. Vol. 5, *Herbstschlacht in Macedonien-Cerna-bogen 1916*, by Georg Struss, 1925; Vol. 11, *Weltkriegsende an der macedonischen Front*, by Alfred D. Dieterich, 1925.
———. *Der Weltkrieg 1914 bis 1918.* 14 vols. Berlin: Mittler, 1925-39.

Great Britain

Committee of Imperial Defence. *History of the Great War Based on Official Documents: Military Operations.* Cyril Falls, *Macedonia*, 4 vols. London: H. M. Stationery Office, 1933-35.
———. *History of the Great War Based on Official Documents: Naval Operations.* 9 vols. London: Longmans, Green & Co., 1920-31. Vol. 4, *Naval Operations*, by Henry Newbolt, 1928.

League of Nations

Permanent Mandates Commission. *Minutes.* Second to eleventh sessions, inclusive.
———. *Comments Submitted by the Accredited Representative of France on the Commission's Observations with Regard to the Report on the Situation in Syria and the Lebanon in 1924 and the Provisional Report on the Situation in These Territories in 1925.* Attached to *Minutes of the Eighth Session.*
———. *Report to the Council of the League of Nations on the Work of the Eighth (Extraordinary) Session of the Permanent Mandates Commission.* Annex 4 attached to *Minutes of the Eighth Session.*

Russia

Laloy, Emile, ed. *Les Documents secrets des Archives du Ministère des Affaires Etrangères de Russie publiés par les Bolcheviks.* 4th ed. Paris: Bossard, 1919.
Ministry of Foreign Affairs. *Documents diplomatiques secrets russes, 1914-1917: D'après les Archives du Ministère des Affaires Etrangères à Petrograd.* Translated by J. Polonsky. Paris: Payot, 1928.
———. *Die Europäischen Mächte und Griechenland während des Weltkrieges: Nach den Geheimdokumenten des ehem. Ministeriums für Auswartige Angelegenheiten.* Edited by E. Adamow. Dresden: Carl Reissner, 1932.

NEWSPAPERS

Dates following certain newspapers indicate issues in which an article by General Sarrail appears.

L'Action
L'Action française
L'Ancien Combattant (Ardèche)
   September 28, November 16, 1922; January 25, June 7, July 15,
   September 30, November 4, December 16, 1923.
L'Aurore
L'Autorité
Le Bonnet rouge
Bonsoir
   December 7, 13, 22, 1919; January 6, 31, February 23, March 4, 15,
   1920.
La Croix
La Dépêche de Toulouse
L'Echo de Paris
L'Eclair
L'Ere nouvelle
   January 28, February 1, 14, 21, March 8, 22, 31, April 4, 8, 20, June
   11, 20, 22, 23, 29, July 11, 25, September 11, October 22, Novem-
   ber 15, 23, December 9, 22, 1920.

   March 30, April 23, May 18, July 24, August 19, September 25,
   October 22, December 8, 20, 1921.

   January 24, March 18, 29, May 25, June 14, 24, July 12, 29, 30,
   August 15, September 5, 15, 26, October 17, 31, November 16, 25,
   December 11, 26, 1922.

   January 9, 22, February 17, March 3, 14, 27, April 11, 22, May 14,
   24, June 6, 20, July 11, 27, August 12, 25, September 8, 22, October
   16, 29, November 15, 30, December 23, 1923.

   January 4, 23, February 17, 26, March 19, April 9, 24, May 8, 26,
   June 8, 1924.
Le Figaro
La France (Bordeaux)
   October 20, 23, 1920.
Le Gaulois
La Gazette de France
La Guerre sociale
L'Homme enchaîné
L'Humanité
L'Intransigeant
Le Journal
La Lanterne
La Libre Parole
Le Matin
New York Times
La Nouvelle République
   December 3, 1920.
Nouvelliste de Rouen
L'Oeuvre

Pas de Calais libéré
   April 13, May 7, August 12, September 17, October 1, 1922.
Le Petit Parisien
La Petite République
Le Populaire de Paris
Le Provençal
   January 5, 1920.
Le Quotidien
Le Radical
Le Rappel
La République sociale
   November 4, 11, 1922.
Le Temps
Times (London)
Tribune de la Nièvre
   April 7, 1921.
La Victoire

BOOKS AND ARTICLES

Addison, Christopher. *Four and a Half Years: A Personal Diary from June 1914 to January 1919.* 2 vols. London: Hutchinson, 1934.
————. *Politics from Within, 1911-1918.* 2 vols. London: Herbert Jenkins, 1924.
Alastros, Doros. *Venizelos: Patriot, Statesman, Revolutionary.* London: Percy Lund Humphries, 1942.
Albrecht-Carré, René. *Italy at the Paris Peace Conference.* New York: Columbia University Press, 1938.
Alexandre, René. *Avec Joffre d'Agadir à Verdun: Souvenirs, 1911-1916.* Paris: Berger-Levrault, 1932.
Allier, Raoul. "La Séparation des églises et de l'état: L'Enquête du Siècle." *Cahiers de la quinzaine,* 6th ser. 14 (1905).
Amery, Leopold S. *My Political Life.* 2 vols. London: Hutchinson, 1953.
André, Louis. *Cinq ans de ministère.* Paris: Louis Michaud, 1907.
Andréa, Charles Joseph. *La Révolte druze et l'insurrection de Damas, 1925-1926.* Paris: Payot, 1937.
Antonius, George. *The Arab Awakening: The Story of the Arab National Movement.* New York: Capricorn, 1965.
Arbeux, Captain d'. *L'Officier contemporain: La Démocratisation de l'armée, 1899-1910.* Paris: Bernard Grasset, 1911.
Arthur, George. *Life of Lord Kitchener.* 3 vols. New York: Macmillan Co., 1920.
Asquith, Herbert Henry. *Memories and Reflections, 1852-1927.* 2 vols. Boston: Little, Brown & Co., 1928.
Aulard, Alphonse, Bouvier, Emile, and Ganem, André. *1914-1918:*

Histoire politique de la grande guerre. Paris: Aristide Quillet, 1924.
Bankwitz, Philip. *Maxime Weygand and Civil-Military Relations in Modern France.* Cambridge, Mass.: Harvard University Press, 1967.
Bapst, Germain. *Le Maréchal Canrobert: Souvenirs d'un siècle.* 6 vols. Paris: Plon-Nourrit, 1910-14.
Bariéty, Jacques. "L'Appareil de presse de Joseph Caillaux et l'argent allemand (1920-1932)." *Revue historique* 247 (1972): 375-406.
Baumont, Maurice. *La Faillite de la paix, 1918-1939.* Paris: Presses Universitaires de France, 1945.
Baumont, Michel. "Abel Ferry et les étapes du contrôle aux armées, 1914-1918." *Revue d'histoire moderne et contemporaine* 15 (1968): 162-208.
Beaverbrook, William. *Politicians and the War, 1914-1916.* Garden City, N.Y.: Doubleday & Co., 1928.
Bédarida, François. "L'Armée et la république: Les Opinions politiques des officiers français en 1876-78." *Revue historique* 232 (1964): 119-64.
Bert, Paul. *L'Instruction civique à l'école.* 6th ed. Paris: Picard-Bernheim, 1882.
Bidegain, Jean. *Le Grand Orient de France.* Paris: Librairie Anti-Sémite, 1905.
Binion, Rudolph. *Defeated Leaders: The Political Fate of Caillaux, Jouvenel, and Tardieu.* New York: Columbia University Press, 1960.
Blake, Robert, ed. *The Private Papers of Douglas Haig, 1914-1918.* London: Eyre and Spottiswoode, 1952.
Boghitchevitch, Milos. *Le Procès de Salonique.* Paris: André Delpeuch, 1927.
Bonham-Carter, Victor. *The Strategy of Victory, 1914-1918: The Life and Times of the Master Strategist of World War I: Field-Marshal Sir William Robertson.* New York: Holt, Rinehart & Winston, 1964.
Bonnefous, Georges, and Bonnefous, Edouard. *Histoire politique de la troisième république.* 7 vols. Paris: Presses Universitaires de France, 1956-67.
Bosdari, Alessandro de. *Delle guerre balcaniche della grande guerra e di alcuni fatti precedenti ad esse.* 2d ed. Milan: A. Mondadori, 1931.
Boucher, Arthur. *Les Doctrines dans la préparation de la grande guerre.* Paris: Berger-Levrault, 1925.
Bourcart, Jacques. *L'Albanie et les Albanais.* Paris: Bossard, 1921.
Bourget, Jean Marie. *Gouvernement et commandement: Les Leçons de la guerre mondiale.* Paris: Payot, 1930.
Bourget, Paul. *L'Emigré.* Paris, 1907.
Bréal, Auguste. *Philippe Berthelot.* 2d ed. Paris: Gallimard, 1937.
Brett, Maurice V., and Esher, Oliver Viscount, eds. *Journals and Letters of Reginald, Viscount Esher.* 4 vols. London: Ivor Nicholson and Watson, 1934-38.

Brisson, Henri. *Souvenirs: Affaire Dreyfus avec documents.* Paris: E. Cornély, 1908.
Brogan, David W. *The Development of Modern France, 1870-1939.* London: Hamish Hamilton, 1940.
Buchanan, George. *My Mission to Russia and Other Diplomatic Memories.* 2 vols. Boston: Little, Brown & Co., 1923.
Buisson, Ferdinand. "Notre programme." *Les Cahiers des droits de l'homme.* January 5, 1920, pp. 3-4.
Byrnes, Robert F. *Antisemitism in Modern France.* New Brunswick: Rutgers University Press, 1950.
Cadorna, Luigi. *Altre pagine sulla grande guerra.* Milan: A. Mondadori, 1925.
Caillaux, Joseph. *Devant l'histoire: Mes prisons.* Paris: Editions de la Sirène, 1922.
――――. *Mes mémoires.* 3 vols. Paris: Plon, 1942-47.
Callwell, Charles E. *Field-Marshal Sir Henry Wilson: His Life and Diaries.* 2 vols. New York: Charles Scribner's Sons, 1927.
Carbillet, Gabriel. *Au Djebel Druse: Choses vues et vécues.* Paris: Argo, 1929.
Carcopino, Jérôme. *Souvenirs de la guerre, 1915-1917.* Paris: Hachette, 1970.
Carrias, Eugène. *La Pensée militaire française.* Paris: Presses Universitaires de France, 1960.
Cassar, George H. *The French and the Dardanelles: A Study in Failure in the Conduct of War.* London: George Allen & Unwin, 1971.
Castex, Henri, and de La Far, A. André. *Les Dessous de la guerre 14-18.* Paris: Bernard Grasset, 1967.
Challener, Richard D. "The French Foreign Office: The Era of Philippe Berthelot." In *The Diplomats, 1919-1939,* edited by Gordon A. Craig and Felix Gilbert, pp. 49-86. Princeton: Princeton University Press, 1953.
――――. *The French Theory of the Nation in Arms, 1866-1939.* Columbia Studies in the Social Sciences, no. 579. New York: Columbia University Press, 1955.
Chalmin, Pierre. *L'Officier français de 1815 à 1870.* Paris: Marcel Rivière, 1957.
Chambers, Frank P. *The War Behind the War, 1914-1918: History of the Political and Civilian Fronts.* New York: Harcourt, Brace & Co., 1939.
Chapman, Guy. *The Dreyfus Case: A Reassessment.* London: Rupert Hart-Davis, 1955.
――――. "France: The French Army and Politics." In *Soldiers and Governments: Nine Studies in Civil–Military Relations,* edited by Michael Howard, pp. 53-72. Bloomington: Indiana University Press, 1959.
Charles-Roux, François. *Souvenirs diplomatiques: Rome-Quirinal, février 1916-février 1919.* Paris: Arthème Fayard, 1958.
Charnay, Jean-Paul. *Société militaire et suffrage politique en France depuis 1789.* Paris: Ecole Pratique des Hautes Etudes, 1964.

Chastenet, Jacques. *Histoire de la troisième république.* 7 vols. Paris: Hachette, 1952-63.
Choppin, Henri. *L'Armée française, 1870-1890.* Paris: Albert Savine, 1890.
Churchill, Randolph S. *Lord Derby "King of Lancashire": The Official Life of Edward, Seventeenth Earl of Derby, 1865-1948.* London: Heinemann, 1959.
Churchill, Winston S. *The World Crisis, 1911-1918.* 4 vols. New York: Charles Scribner's Sons, 1923-29.
Clemenceau, Georges. *Grandeurs et misères d'une victoire.* Paris: Plon, 1930.
Clergeau, Emmanuel. *Le Commandant de Roquefeuil en Grèce.* Paris: Les Editions de France, 1934.
Coblentz, Paul. *The Silence of Sarrail.* Translated by Arthur Chambers. London: Hutchinson, 1930.
Colrat, Raymond. "Partant pour la Syrie." *L'Opinion républicaine,* December 25, 1925, pp. 19-20.
Combarieu, Abel. *Sept ans à l'Elysée avec le président Emile Loubet: De l'affaire Dreyfus à la Conférence d'Algésiras, 1899-1906.* Paris: Hachette, 1932.
Combes, Emile. *Mon ministère: Mémoires, 1902-1905.* Paris: Plon, 1956.
Contamine, Henry. *La Revanche, 1871-1914.* Paris: Berger-Levrault, 1957.
Corcos, Fernand. *Catéchisme des partis politiques.* Paris: Editions Montaigne, 1927.
Corday, Michel. *The Paris Front: An Unpublished Diary, 1914-1918.* New York: E. P. Dutton, 1934.
Cordonnier, Emilien. *Ai-je trahi Sarrail?* Paris: Les Etincelles, 1930.
Cosmin, S. P. *Dossiers secrets de la Triple Entente: Grèce 1914-1922.* Paris: Nouvelles Editions Latines, 1969.
――――. *L'Entente et la Grèce pendant la grande guerre, 1914-1917.* 2 vols. Paris: Société Mutuelle d'Edition, 1926.
Coste, Emile. *L'Officier dans la nation.* Paris: Henri Charles-Lavauzelle, 1903.
Dansette, Adrien. *Le Boulangisme.* Paris: Arthème Fayard, 1946.
――――. *Destin du catholicisme français, 1926-1956.* Paris: Flammarion, 1957.
――――. *Religious History of Modern France.* Translated by John Dingle. 2 vols. New York: Herder and Herder, 1961.
Dartige du Fournet, Louis. *Souvenirs de guerre d'un amiral, 1914-1916.* Paris: Plon, 1920.
Daudet Ernest. "Quelques scènes du drame hellénique (juin-décembre 1916): I: Les Journées de juin." *Revue des deux mondes* 60 (1920): 267-94.
――――. "Quelques scènes du drame hellénique (juin-décembre 1916): II: De juin à octobre." *Revue des deux mondes* 60 (1920): 521-50.
David, Robert. *Le Drame ignoré de l'Armée d'Orient: Dardanelles-Serbie-Salonique-Athènes.* Paris: Plon, 1927.

Deschanel, Paul. *Gambetta*. New York: Dodd, Mead & Co., 1920.
Descoins, Henri. "Six mois d'histoire de l'Albanie (novembre 1916-mai 1917)." *Revue d'histoire de la guerre mondiale* 7-8 (1929, 1930): 318-42, 17-43.
Desmazes, René. *Joffre: La Victoire du caractère*. Paris: Nouvelles Editions Latines, 1955.
Driault, Edouard. *Le Roi Constantin*. Versailles: By the author, 1930.
Driault, Edouard, and Lhéritier, Michel. *Histoire diplomatique de la Grèce de 1821 à nos jours*. 5 vols. Paris: Presses Universitaires de France, 1925-26.
Du Barail, François Charles. *Mes souvenirs*. 10th ed. 3 vols. Paris: Plon, 1896-97.
Ducasse, André. *Balkans 14-18 ou le chaudron du diable*. Paris: Robert Laffont, 1964.
Duruy, Georges. *L'Officier éducateur: Leçons faites à L'Ecole Polytechnique*. Paris: R. Chapelot, 1904.
Earles, Edward Mead, ed. *Makers of Modern Strategy: Military Thought from Machiavelli to Hitler*. Princeton: Princeton University Press, 1941.
Epée, Jean d'. *L'Officier français, sa situation sociale dans la nation et dans l'armée, ce qu'il réclame*. Paris: Henri Charles-Lavauzelle, 1908.
Ernest-Charles, Jean. *Painlevé*. Paris: Rasmussen, 1925.
Esher, Reginald Viscount. *The Tragedy of Lord Kitchener*. London: John Murray, 1921.
Fabre-Luce, Alfred. *Caillaux*. 5th ed. Paris: Gallimard, 1933.
Falkenhayn, Erich von. *General Headquarters, 1914-1916, and Its Crucial Decisions*. London: Hutchinson, 1919.
Ferdinand-Lop, S. *Une Fédération des peuples . . . ?* Paris: A. Delpech, n.d. [1924]. Preface by Maurice Sarrail.
Feriet, René de. *L'Application d'un mandat: La France, puissance mandataire en Syrie et au Liban: Comment elle a compris son rôle*. Paris: Jouve, 1926.
Ferry, Abel. *Les Carnets secrets, 1914-1918*. Paris: Bernard Grasset, 1957.
———. *La Guerre vue d'en bas et d'en haut*. Paris: Bernard Grasset, 1920.
Fix, Nathanaël Théodore. *Souvenirs d'un officier d'état-major, 1846-1894*. 2 vols. Paris: F. Juven, 1898.
Forster, Edward S. *A Short History of Modern Greece, 1821-1956*. 3d ed. New York: Frederick A. Praeger, 1958.
Franck, Paul. "La France protectrice de l'enseignement jésuite." *L'Opinion républicaine*, December 12, 1925, p. 11.
Frangulis, A. F. *La Grèce et la crise mondiale*. 2 vols. Paris: Félix Alcan, 1926.
Frappa, Jean-José. *Makédonia: Souvenirs d'un officier de liaison en Orient*. Paris: Flammarion, 1921.
———. "Sarrail." *L'Opinion républicaine*, December 12, 1925, p. 18.

Freycinet, Charles de Saulses de. *Souvenirs, 1878-1893.* 5th ed. Paris: Charles Delagrave, 1913.

Froidevaux, Henri. "Quelques causes du malaise syrien." *L'Asie française* 26, no. 237 (1926): 6-9.

Galliéni, Joseph. *Les Carnets de Galliéni.* Paris: Albin Michel, 1932.

Gambiez, F., and Suire, M. *Histoire de la première guerre mondiale.* 2 vols. Paris: Fayard, 1968.

Gilbert, Martin. *Winston S. Churchill: Vol. 3, 1914-1916.* London: Heinemann, 1971.

Girardet, Raoul. *La Société militaire dans la France contemporaine, 1815-1939.* Paris: Plon, 1953.

Goguel, François. *La Politique des partis sous la troisième république.* 3d ed. Paris: Editions du Seuil, 1958.

Gontaut-Biron, Roger de. *Comment la France s'est installée en Syrie, 1918-1919.* Paris: Plon, 1922.

Gorce, Paul-Marie de la. *The French Army: A Military-Political History.* Translated by Kenneth Douglas. New York: George Braziller, 1963.

Gottlieb, W. W. *Studies in Secret Diplomacy during the First World War.* London: George Allen & Unwin, 1957.

Grey, Edward. *Twenty-Five Years, 1892-1916.* 2 vols. New York: Frederick A. Stokes, 1925.

Guinn, Paul. *British Strategy and Politics, 1914 to 1918.* London: Oxford University Press, 1965.

Haddah, George. *Fifty Years of Modern Syria and Lebanon.* Beirut: Dar-al-Hayat, 1950.

Halasz, Nicholas. *Captain Dreyfus: The Story of a Mass Hysteria.* New York: Simon and Schuster, 1955.

Hankey, Maurice. *The Supreme Command, 1914-1918.* 2 vols. London: George Allen & Unwin, 1961.

Hanotaux, Gabriel. *La Bataille de la Marne.* 2 vols. 2d ed. Paris: Plon, 1922.

Hazlehurst, Cameron. *Politicans at War, July 1914 to May 1915.* London: Jonathan Cape, 1971.

Helsey, Edouard. "Le Guet-apens d'Athènes (1er décembre 1916)." *Revue des deux mondes* (1955), pt. 2. pp. 487-500.

Herbillon, Emile E. *Le Général Alfred Micheler, 1914-1918, d'après ses notes, sa correspondance et les souvenirs personnels.* Paris: Plon, 1934.

————. *Souvenirs d'un officier de liaison pendant la guerre mondiale: Du général en chef au gouvernement.* 2 vols. Paris: Editions Jules Tallandier, 1930.

Herriot, Edouard. *Jadis: D'une guerre à l'autre, 1914-1936.* 2 vols. Paris: Flammarion, 1952.

Hitti, Philip K. *A Short History of Lebanon.* London: Macmillan & Co., 1965.

————. *Syria: A Short History; Being a Condensation of the Author's History of Syria, Including Lebanon and Palestine.* London: Macmillan & Co., 1959.

Hittle, J. D. *The Military Staff: Its History and Development*. Harrisburg: Military Service Publishing Co., 1944.

Howard, Harry N. *An American Inquiry in the Middle East: The King-Crane Commission*. Beirut: Khayats, 1963.

Howard, Michael, ed. *Soldiers and Governments*. London: Eyre and Spottiswoode, 1957.

Howell, Rosalind. *Philip Howell: A Memoir by His Wife*. London: George Allen & Unwin, 1942.

Hughes, Judith M. *To the Maginot Line: The Politics of French Military Preparation in the 1920's*. Cambridge, Mass.: Harvard University Press, 1971.

Huntington, Samuel P. *The Soldier and the State: The Theory and Politics of Civil-Military Relations*. Cambridge, Mass.: Harvard University Press, 1957.

Isorni, Jacques, and Cadars, Louis. *Histoire véridique de la grande guerre*. 2 vols. Paris: Flammarion, 1968.

Iung, Théodore. *La République et l'armée*. Paris: G. Charpentier et E. Fasquelle, 1892.

Jenkins, Roy. *Asquith: Portrait of a Man and an Era*. New York: Chilmark, 1964.

Joffre, Joseph Jacques Césaire. *Mémoires du maréchal Joffre, 1910-1917*. 2 vols. Paris: Plon, 1932.

Jolly, Jean. *Dictionnaire des parlementaires français, 1899-1940*. 2 vols. Paris: Presses Universitaires de France, 1960–.

Katzenbach, Edward. "Charles Louis de Saulces de Freycinet and the Army of Metropolitan France." Ph.D. dissertation, Princeton University, 1953.

Kayser, Jacques. "Opposons la vérité aux calomnies." *L'Opinion républicaine*, December 12, 1925, pp. 7-9.

————. "Réponse à M. de Kérillis." *L'Opinion républicaine*, December 12, 1925, pp. 12-16.

King, Jere Clemens. *Generals and Politicians: Conflict between France's High Command, Parliament and Government, 1914-1918*. Berkeley: University of California Press, 1951.

Koeltz, Louis. *La Guerre de 1914-1918*. 2 vols. Paris: Editions Sirey, 1966.

Kovacs, Arpad. "French Military Institutions before the Franco-Prussian War." *American Historical Review* 51 (1946):217-35.

————. "French Military Legislation in the Third Republic, 1871-1940." *Military Affairs* 13 (1949):1-13.

Kupperman, Alfred. "Les Débuts de l'offensive morale allemande contre la France (décembre 1914-décembre 1915)." *Revue historique* 249 (1973):91-114.

Larcher, Maurice M. *La Grande Guerre dans les Balkans: Direction de la guerre*. Paris: Payot, 1929.

Laroche, Jules. *Au Quai d'Orsay avec Briand et Poincaré, 1913-1926*. Paris: Hachette, 1957.

Laurent, R. *Le Parti démocrate populaire, 1924-1944*. Le Mans, France: Imprimerie Commerciale, 1965.

Lawson, J. C. *Tales of Aegean Intrigue*. London: Chatto and Windus, 1920.

Legrand-Girarde, Emile Edmond. *Un Quart de siècle au service de la France: Carnets 1894-1918*. Paris: Presses Littéraires de France, 1954.

Lennox, Lady Algernon Gordon [Blanche], ed. *The Diary of Lord Bertie of Thame, 1914-1918*. 2 vols. London: Hodder & Stoughton, 1924.

Leuquet, R. "Sarrail a envoyé à Paris 141 télégrammes." *L'Opinion républicaine*, December 12, 1925, pp. 9-10.

Liddell Hart, Basil H. "French Military Ideas before the First World War." In *A Century of Conflict, 1850-1950: Essays for A. J. P. Taylor*, edited by Martin Gilbert. New York: Atheneum, 1967.

———. *Reputations Ten Years After*. Boston: Little, Brown & Co., 1928.

Lloyd George, David. *War Memoirs of David Lloyd George*. 6 vols. Boston: Little, Brown & Co., 1933-37.

Longrigg, Stephen Hemsley. *Syria and Lebanon under the French Mandate*. London: Oxford University Press, 1958.

MacCallum, Elizabeth P. *The Nationalist Crusade in Syria*. New York: Foreign Policy Association, 1928.

Mackenzie, Compton. *Aegean Memories*. London: Chatto and Windus, 1940.

———. *First Athenian Memories*. London: Cassell, 1931.

———. *Greek Memories*. London: Chatto and Windus, 1939.

Magnus, Philip. *Kitchener: Portrait of an Imperialist*. New York: E. P. Dutton, 1959.

Marcellin, Léopold. *Politique et politiciens pendant la guerre*. 2 vols. Paris: La Renaisssance du Livre, 1923?.

Marder, Arthur J. *From the Dreadnought to Scapa Flow: The Royal Navy in the Fisher Era, 1904-1919*. 5 vols. London: Oxford University Press, 1961-70.

Maurice, Frederick. *Lessons of Allied Co-operation: Naval, Military and Air, 1914-1918*. London: Oxford University Press, 1942.

Mayer, Arno J. *Political Origins of the New Diplomacy, 1917-1918*. New Haven: Yale University Press, 1959.

Mayer, Emile. *Nos chefs de 1914: Souvenirs personnels et essais de psychologie militaire*. Paris: Stock, Delamain et Boutelleau, 1930.

Messimy, Adolphe Marie. *Mes souvenirs: Jeunesse et entrée au Parlement, Ministre des Colonies et de la Guerre en 1911 et 1912: Agadir: Ministre de la Guerre du 16 juin au 26 août 1914: La Guerre*. Paris: Plon, 1937.

Michel, Paul-Henri. *La Question de l'Adriatique, 1914-1918*. Paris: Alfred Costes, 1938.

Michon, Georges. *La Préparation à la guerre: La Loi de trois ans, 1910-1914*. Paris: Marcel Rivière, 1935.

Millerand, Alexandre. *Pour la défense nationale: Une Année au ministère de la guerre, 14 janvier 1912-12 janvier 1913*. Paris: Bibliothèque Charpentier, 1913.

Mollin, Jules-Henri. *La Vérité sur l'affaire des fiches*. Paris: Librairie Universelle, 1905.

Monroe, Elizabeth. *Britain's Moment in the Middle East, 1914-1956*. London: Chatto and Windus, 1963.

Monteilhet, Joseph. *Les Institutions militaires de la France, 1814-1932: De la paix armée à la paix désarmée*. 2d ed. Paris: Félix Alcan, 1932.

Montgomery-Cuninghame, Thomas. *Dusty Measure: A Record of Troubled Times*. London: John Murray, 1939.

Moorehead, Alan. *Gallipoli*. New York: Harper & Brothers, 1956.

Mordacq, Henri Jean Jules. *Les Légendes de la grande guerre*. Paris: Flammarion, 1935.

———. *Le Ministère Clemenceau: Journal d'un témoin*. 4 vols. Paris: Plon, 1930-31.

———. *L'Officier dans l'armée nouvelle*. Paris: Henri Charles-Lavauzelle, 1906.

Nedeff, N. *Les Opérations en Macédoine: L'Epopée de Doïran, 1915-1918*. Translated by Le Commandant Goetzmann. Sofia, Bulgaria: Armeyski Voeno-Isdatelski Fond, 1927.

Néré, Jacques. *La Troisième République, 1914-1940*. Paris: Armand Colin, 1965.

Nevakivi, Jukka. *Britain, France and the Arab Middle East, 1914-1920*. London: Athlone Press, 1969.

Nicholas of Greece, Prince. *Political Memoirs, 1914-1917: Pages from My Diary*. London: Hutchinson, 1928.

Nicolson, Harold. *King George the Fifth: His Life and Reign*. London: Constable, 1952.

Nobécourt, Jacques. *Une Histoire politique de l'armée: De Pétain à Pétain, 1919-1942*. Paris: Editions du Seuil, 1967.

Nolte, Ernst. *Three Faces of Fascism: Action française, Italian Fascism, National Socialism*. Translated by Leila Vennewitz. New York: Holt, Rinehart & Winston, 1966.

Ollé-Laprune, Jacques. *La Stabilité des ministres sous la troisième république, 1879-1940*. Paris: R. Pichon et R. Durand-Auzias, 1962.

Ormesson, Wladimir d'. *Auprès de Lyautey*. Paris: Flammarion, 1963.

Owen, Frank. *Tempestuous Journey; Lloyd George, His Life and Times*. London: Hutchinson, 1954.

Packer, Charles. *Return to Salonika*. London: Cassell, 1964.

Page, Thomas Nelson. *Italy and the World War*. New York: Charles Scribner's Sons, 1920.

Painlevé, Paul. *Comment j'ai nommé Foch et Pétain*. Paris: Félix Alcan, 1923.

Palat, Pierre Lehautcourt. *La Grande Guerre sur le front occidental*. 14 vols. Paris: Librairie Chapelot, 1917-29.

Paléologue, Maurice. *An Ambassador's Memoirs*. Translated by F. A. Holt. 4th ed. 3 vols. New York: George H. Doran, 1923-25.

Palmer, Alan. *The Gardeners of Salonika*. New York: Simon and Schuster, 1965.

Parti Socialiste. *La Guerre et la paix*. Paris: Librairie de l'Humanité, 1918.
Pastorelli, Pietro. *L'Albania nella politica estera italiana, 1914-1920*. Naples: Editore Jovene, 1970.
Patterson, A. Temple, ed. *The Jellicoe Papers: Selections from the Private and Official Correspondence of Admiral of the Fleet Earl Jellicoe of Scapa*. 2 vols. London: Navy Records Society, 1966-68.
Paul, Harry W. *The Second Ralliement: The Rapprochement between Church and State in France in the Twentieth Century*. Washington, D.C.: Catholic University of America Press, 1967.
Paul-Boncour, Joseph. *Entre deux guerres: Souvenirs sur la troisième république*. 3 vols. Paris: Plon, 1945-46.
Paxton, Robert O. *Parades and Politics at Vichy*. Princeton: Princeton University Press, 1966.
Pédoya, Jean Marie Gustave. *L'Armée évolue*. 3 vols. Paris: R. Chapelot, 1908.
―――. *La Commission de l'armée pendant la grande guerre: Documents inédits et secrets*. Paris: Flammarion, 1921.
Pedroncini, Guy. *Les Mutineries de 1917*. Paris: Presses Universitaires de France, 1967.
―――. *Les Négociations secrètes pendant la grande guerre*. Paris: Flammarion, 1969.
Pichot-Duclos, René. *Au G.Q.G. de Joffre*. Paris: Arthaud, 1947.
Pierrefeu, Jean de. *G.Q.G. Secteur I: Trois ans au Grand Quartier Général par le rédacteur du communiqué*. 2 vols. Paris: L'Edition Française Illustrée, 1920.
Pingaud, Albert. *Histoire diplomatique de la France pendant la grande guerre*. 3 vols. Paris: Editions Alsatia, 1938.
Poincaré, Raymond. *Au service de la France: Neuf années de souvenirs*. 10 vols. Paris: Plon, 1926-33.
Porch, Douglas. *Army and Revolution: France 1815-1848*. Boston: Routledge and Kegan Paul, 1974.
Porter, Charles W. *The Career of Théophile Delcassé*. Philadelphia: University of Pennsylvania Press, 1936.
Poulleau, Alice. *A Damas sous les bombes: Journal d'une Française pendant la révolte syrienne, 1924-1926*. Paris: Bretteville Frères, 1930.
Price, George Ward. *The Story of the Salonica Army*. New York: E. J. Clode, 1918.
Priestley, Herbert I. *France Overseas: A Study of Modern Imperialism*. New York: Appleton-Century, 1938.
Le Procès de l'assassin de Jaurès, 24-29 mars 1919. Paris: Editions de l'Humanité, 1920.
Rabbath, Edmond. *L'Evolution politique de la Syrie sous mandat de 1920 à 1925*. Paris: Les Presses Modernes, 1928.
Radziwill, Marie Dorothea Elisabeth. *Lettres de la princesse Radziwill au général de Robilant, 1889-1914*. 4 vols. Bologna: Nicola Zanichelli, 1933-34.
Ralston, David B. *The Army of the Republic: The Place of the Mili-*

tary in the Political Evolution of France, 1871-1914. Cambridge, Mass.: Massachusetts Institute of Technology Press, 1967.

Recouly, Raymond. "La Mission de M. Jonnart en Grèce: I: L'Abdication du Roi Constantin." *Revue des deux mondes* 42 (1917): 803-32.

————. "La Mission de M. Jonnart en Grèce: II: Le Retour de M. Venizélos." *Revue des deux mondes* 43 (1918): 400-20.

Regnault, Charles. *La Conquête d'Athènes, juin-juillet 1917.* Paris: L. Fournier, 1920.

Reinach, Joseph. *Histoire de l'affaire Dreyfus.* 7 vols. Paris: E. Fasquelle, 1901-11.

————. *La Vie politique de Léon Gambetta, suivie d'autres essais sur Gambetta.* Paris: Félix Alcan, 1918.

Rémond, René. *La Droite en France en 1815 à nos jours.* Paris: Aubier, 1954.

Renouvin, Pierre. *La Crise européenne et la première guerre mondiale.* 4th rev. ed. Paris: Presses Universitaires de France, 1962.

————. *War and Aftermath, 1914-1929.* Translated by Rémy Inglis Hall. New York: Harper & Row, 1968.

Repington, Charles à Court. *The First World War, 1914-1918.* 2 vols. Boston: Houghton Mifflin Co., 1920.

Revol, Joseph Fortuné. *Histoire de l'armée française.* Paris: Larousse, 1929.

Ribot, Alexandre. *Journal d'Alexandre Ribot et correspondances inédites, 1914-1922.* Paris: Plon, 1936.

Roberts, Stephen H. *History of French Colonial Policy, 1870-1925.* London: P. S. King, 1929.

Robertson, William. *Soldiers and Statesmen, 1914-1918.* 2 vols. London: Cassell, 1926.

Rodd, James Rennell. *Social and Diplomatic Memories, 1902-1919.* London: Edward Arnold, 1925.

Rolland, Henri de. *Galliffet.* Paris: Editions de la Nouvelle France, 1945.

Roskill, Stephen. *Hankey, Man of Secrets.* London: Collins, 1970.

Rothwell, V. H. *British War Aims and Peace Diplomacy, 1914-18.* London: Oxford University Press, 1971.

Saint-Aulaire, Auguste de. *Confession d'un vieux diplomate.* Paris: Flammarion, 1953.

Salandra, Antonio. *Italy and the Great War: From Neutrality to Intervention.* London: Edward Arnold, 1932.

Sarrail, Maurice. "L'Armée démocratique." *Les Cahiers des droits de l'homme,* April 10, 1921, pp. 152-57.

————. "L'Armée et le droit de vote." *Les Cahiers des droits de l'homme,* June 10, 1922, pp. 276-78.

————. "L'Armée de la Société des nations." *Les Cahiers des droits de l'homme,* May 25, 1923, pp. 219-22.

————. "Constantin Roi." *Revue politique et parlementaire* 104-5 (1920): 321-31.

———. "Contre les deux ans." *Les Cahiers des droits de l'homme,* December 5, 1920, pp. 10-12.

———. "Deux nouveaux tracts pour la réforme militaire." *Les Cahiers des droits de l'homme,* May 10, 1924, pp. 219-21.

———. "La Grèce venizéliste." *Revue de Paris* 16 (1919): 685-706.

———. *Mon commandement en Orient, 1916-1918.* Paris: Flammarion, 1920.

———. "Les Plans de campagne allemand et français d'avant-guerre." *La Grande Revue* 115 (1924): 3-38.

———. "Le Problème des réparations: L'Occupation de la Ruhr." *Les Cahiers des droits de l'homme,* January 10, 1923, pp. 3-5.

———. "Un projet gouvernemental sur la réforme de la justice militaire." *Les Cahiers des droits de l'homme,* January 25, 1924, pp. 27-31.

———. "La Réforme de la justice militaire." *Les Cahiers des droits de l'homme,* December 25, 1921, pp. 555-57.

———. "La Réforme de la justice militaire." *Les Cahiers des droits de l'homme,* February 20, 1922, pp. 75-77.

———. "Souvenirs de 1914-1915." *Revue politique et parlementaire* 107 (1921): 161-80, 399-417; 108 (1921): 81-104, 221-47.

———. "Les Têtes de pont du Rhin." *Revue politique et parlementaire* 104 (1920): 40-49.

Schaper, B. W. *Albert Thomas: Trente ans de réformisme social.* Assen, Netherlands: Van Gorcum, 1959.

Seager, Frederic H. *The Boulanger Affair: Political Crossroads of France, 1886-1889.* Ithaca: Cornell University Press, 1969.

Seicaru, Pamfil. *La Roumanie dans la grande guerre.* Paris: Minard, 1968.

Seignobos, Charles. *L'Evolution de la troisième république, 1875-1914.* Paris: Hachette, 1921.

Shapiro, David, ed. *The Right in France, 1890-1919.* London: Chatto and Windus, 1962.

Silberstein, Gerard E. *The Troubled Alliance: German-Austrian Relations 1914 to 1917.* Lexington: University Press of Kentucky, 1970.

Silvestre de Sacy, Jacques. *Le Maréchal de Mac Mahon, Duc de Magenta, 1808-1893.* Paris: Les Editions Inter-Nationales, 1960.

Simon, Jules. *La Politique radicale.* 3d ed. Paris: Librairie Internationale, 1869.

Smith, C. Jay, Jr. *The Russian Struggle for Power, 1914-1917: A Study of Russian Foreign Policy during the First World War.* New York: Philosophical Library, 1956.

Sorlin, Pierre. *Waldeck-Rousseau.* Paris: Armand Colin, 1966.

Soulié, Michel. *La Vie politique d'Edouard Herriot.* Paris: Armand Colin, 1962.

Spector, Sherman David. *Rumania at the Paris Peace Conference.* New York: Bookman Press, 1962.

Stebbing, E. P. *At the Serbian Front in Macedonia.* London: John Lane, 1917.

Steed, Henry Wickham. *Through Thirty Years, 1892-1922: A Personal Narrative.* 2 vols. New York: Doubleday & Co., 1924.

Stein, Leonard. *Syria.* London: Ernest Benn, 1926.

Stickney, Edith Pierpont. *Southern Albania or Northern Epirus in European International Affairs, 1912-1923.* Stanford: Stanford University Press, 1926.

Suarez, Georges. *Briand: Sa vie—son oeuvre avec son journal et de nombreux documents inédits.* 6 vols. Paris: Plon, 1938-41.

Swire, Joseph. *Albania: The Rise of a Kingdom.* London: Williams and Northgate, 1929.

Tanant, Albert. *La Troisième Armée dans la bataille: Souvenirs d'un chef d'état-major.* Paris: La Renaissance du Livre, 1922.

Temperley, H. W. V., ed. *History of the Peace Conference.* 6 vols. London: Frowde, Hodder & Stoughton, 1920-24.

Terrail, Gabriel. *Joffre: Première crise du commandement.* Paris: Ollendorff, 1919.

——. *Sarrail et les armées d'Orient.* Paris: Ollendorff, 1920.

Thibaudet, Albert. *La République des professeurs.* Paris: Bernard Grasset, 1927.

Thomas, Marcel. *L'Affaire sans Dreyfus.* Paris: Arthème Fayard, 1961.

Thomazi, Auguste. *La Marine française dans la grande guerre (1914-1918).* 4 vols. Paris: Payot, 1924-29.

Thomson, Basil. *The Allied Secret Service in Greece.* London: Hutchinson, 1931.

Thomson, David. *Democracy in France since 1870.* 5th ed. London: Oxford University Press, 1969.

Tibawi, A. L. *A Modern History of Syria Including Lebanon and Palestine.* London: Macmillan & Co., 1969.

Toynbee, Arnold J. *Survey of International Affairs, 1925.* 2 vols. London: Oxford University Press, 1927.

Tuchman, Barbara W. *The Guns of August.* New York: Macmillan Co., 1962.

Uhry, Jules. "Avec Gouraud et Weygand triomphe la politique du père Chanteur et du père Rémy." *L'Opinion républicaine,* December 12, 1925, pp. 4-6.

Usborne, C. V. *Blast and Counterblast: A Naval Impression of the War.* London: John Murray, 1935.

Vagts, Alfred. *A History of Militarism.* Rev. ed. New York: Meridian Books, 1959.

Varillon, Pierre. *Joffre.* Paris: Arthème Fayard, 1956.

Vergnet, Paul. *L'Affaire Caillaux.* Paris: La Renaissance du Livre, 1918.

Villari, Luigi. *The Macedonian Campaign.* London: T. F. Unwin, 1922.

Watt, Richard M. *Dare Call It Treason.* New York: Simon and Schuster, 1963.

Weber, Eugen. *Action Française: Royalism and Reaction in Twentieth-Century France.* Stanford: Stanford University Press, 1962.

———. The Nationalist Revival in France, 1905-1914. University of California Publications in History, vol. 60. Berkeley: University of California Press, 1959.

Weber, Frank G. Eagles on the Crescent: Germany, Austria, and the Diplomacy of the Turkish Alliance, 1914-1918. Ithaca: Cornell University Press, 1970.

Wetterlé, Abbé E. En Syrie avec le général Gouraud. Paris: Flammarion, 1924.

Weygand, Maxime. Mémoires: Mirages et réalité. 3 vols. Paris: Flammarion, 1950-57.

Williamson, Samuel R., Jr. The Politics of Grand Strategy: Britain and France Prepare for War, 1904-1914. Cambridge, Mass.: Harvard University Press, 1969.

Wohl, Robert. French Communism in the Making, 1914-1924. Stanford: Stanford University Press, 1966.

Wormser, Georges. La République de Clemenceau. Paris: Presses Universitaires de France, 1961.

Wright, Gordon. Raymond Poincaré and the French Presidency. Stanford: Stanford University Press, 1942.

Zeine N. Zeine. The Struggle for Arab Independence: Western Diplomacy and the Rise and Fall of Feisal's Kingdom in Syria. Beirut: Khayat's, 1960.

Zeman, Z. A. B. A Diplomatic History of the First World War. London, Wiedenfeld and Nicolson, 1971.

Živojinović, Dragan. America, Italy, and the Birth of Yugoslavia, 1917-1919. Boulder: East European Quarterly, 1972.

Index

Lardemelle, Charles, 76, 78
Larissa: Sarrail wants to occupy, 146, 148; Briand wants to occupy, 147, 148, 154; Great Britain fears French intentions concerning, 155; France prepares to occupy, 159
League of Patriots, 7, 194
League of the Rights of Man, 177; Sarrail belongs to, 185, 219
Lebanese Representative Council, 191, 196
Lebanon, 186, 188, 189, 190, 191, 195, 196; and Sarrail's policies, 191-92, 196
Leblois, Antoine, 86
Leblois, Paul, 12, 76, 78, 107, 126, 136, 170; Sarrail saves his position, 86
Lebouc, Georges, 41
Le Four de Paris, 51
Le Foyer, Lucien, 19, 22
Left, the: and 1870 defeat, 4-5; reasons for supporting Sarrail, 24, 32, 34, 141-42, 194, 213, 220; and 1905 recruitment law, 26; and 1913 recruitment law, 27; and repercussions of 1914 election, 33-34; splits over the Syrian revolt, 213-14. *See also* André, Louis; Brisson, Henri; Herriot, Edouard; Joffre, Joseph, Left critical of; Painlevé, Paul, undermines Joffre's authority, demands reinforcements for Eastern Army, and Syrian rebellion; Sarrail, Maurice Paul Emmanuel, and the Left, and Painlevé; *Union sacrée*; Viviani, René
Lejaille, Claude, 12, 18, 23
Lemarchand, Georges: comments upon the significance of Sarrail, 215
Lemerle, Paul, 23
Leygues, Georges: demands reinforcements for Eastern Army, 63; warns Viviani, 71-72; impact upon wartime civilian-military relationship, 141; and Clemenceau, 181
Libre Parole, La, 8; critical of Sarrail, 95, 110-11
Lloyd George, David, 69, 72, 130, 148, 149, 150, 154, 163, 217; not convinced of Joffre's arguments, 97; and reinforcements to Balkans, 128-29, 132; and political aspects of Balkan campaign, 131; de-

nounces Westerners, 132; agrees that Constantine be deposed, 160; assigns new mission to Eastern Army, 161; gives up on Balkan campaign, 161-62, 167-68; requests Sarrail's recall, 173, 174, 180
Longwy, 39
Loubet, Emile, 8, 9
Lyautey, Louis-Hubert, 16, 143, 150, 157; and French domestic politics, 205-6, 208

M
Macedonia. *See* Balkan campaign; Cordonnier, Emilien; Sarrail, Maurice Paul Emmanuel; Serbia
McMahon, Henry, 188
Mac-Mahon, Patrice de, 6
Macukovo, 103, 152
Maginot, André, 142
Mahon, Bryan, 66, 70, 75, 76, 85, 90, 91, 93; and Sarrail, 96
Malvy, Louis-Jean, 178, 179, 181; visited by Sarrail, 58; stops Castelnau's trip to Salonika, 110
Margaine, Alfred: and Sarrail, 72, 83, 142, 173, 174, 181; and changing military-civilian relationship, 216
Marne, Battle of the, 35, 41, 42, 53, 54; and Sarrail's Third Army, 44-47, 217, 220
Martin, Tommy, 200, 201, 204
Masse, Pierre, 139
Mata Hari, 179
Mataxos, Colonel, 99
Mathieu, Captain: and Saint-Maixent, 22, 23; and Salonika revolution, 119, 120; and *Bonnet rouge* scandal, 176-78; and trial, 183-84
Mathiez, Albert: admires Sarrail, 142
Matin, Le: Sarrail and *fiches* scandal, 21
Maud'huy, Louis, 12, 53
Maunoury, Joseph, 42, 46
Mazarakis, Colonel, 118
Medjidli, 114, 126
Mercy-le-Haut, 39
Messimy, Adolphe-Marie, 27, 32, 35, 53; reorganizes High Command, 31; promises that Sarrail would replace Joffre, 34
Metz, 36, 38, 48
Meunier-Surcouf, Charles, 134-35